EYEWITNESS COMPANIONS

Astrology

JULIA & DEREK PARKER

DK

LONDON, NEW YORK,
MELBOURNE, MUNICH AND DELHI

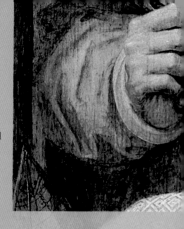

To Irena Zoe Drew, with affection

Editors:	Tom Broder, Laura Nickoll
Senior Art Editors:	Nicola Rodway,
	Helen Spencer
Executive	
Managing Editor:	Adèle Hayward
DTP Designer:	Traci Salter
Production Controller:	Rebecca Short
Art Director:	Peter Luff
Publisher:	Stephanie Jackson

Produced for Dorling Kindersley by
Blue Island Publishing and DK Delhi

Blue Island Publishing

Editorial Director:	Rosalyn Thiro
Art Director:	Stephen Bere
Managing Editor:	Michael Ellis

DK Delhi

Editorial Manager:	Dipali Singh
Senior Editor:	Rohan Sinha
Editors:	Ankush Saikia,
	Pankhoori Sinha
Design Managers:	Arunesh Talapatra,
	Romi Chakraborty
Designer:	Neha Ahuja
DTP Designers:	Tarun Sharma,
	Pushpak Tyagi

First published in 2007 by Dorling Kindersley Limited
80 Strand, London WC2R ORL

A Penguin Company

2 4 6 8 10 9 7 5 3

A CIP catalogue record for this book is
available from the British Library

ISBN 13: 978-1-4053-2198-3

Colour reproduction by Media Development and Printing, UK

Printed and bound in China by L-Rex Printing Company

See our complete catalogue at

www.dk.com

CONTENTS

INTRODUCTION

Astrology's place in the world is not entirely clear: is it a form of scientific study, or a belief system more akin to a religion or philosophy? It is certainly not regarded as a science in the sense that most scientists would use the term today, but if we look back to the original meaning of science – *scientia* (knowledge) – we do perhaps find a definition more sympathetic to the realm of astrology. Any thinking man or woman with a thirst for knowledge must surely make some attempt to connect their experience of life with the wider universe – to relate their actions, reactions, emotions, and thought processes to the universe outside them. And this is essentially what astrology does – it provides a way of relating the pattern made by the Sun, Moon, planets and other heavenly bodies to life on Earth, and specifically to our own lives.

Perhaps this does make astrology sound rather like a religion – which is not surprising, considering religion is often seen as a rival to science in attempting to make sense of the nature of life. However, unlike religion, astrology has as its base observable and quantifiable facts. Further, if we accept as a definition of science that it is "a branch of knowledge involving systematized observation and experiment", the term is accurately descriptive of astrology. No statement a modern astrologer makes will have been invented by him or her: it is the result of considered observation and experiment, whether it was first formulated 1,400 years ago by the Babylonian scholar Akkullanu or by English astrologer John Addey in the 1970s. And if a modern astrologer attempts to enlarge knowledge of the subject by making a statement which seems new, that statement will certainly be the result of observation and analysis.

This has been seen during the last 30 years in the work which has examined the astrological effect of Chiron (*see p239*), which has come to be known as "the wounded healer". Chiron has been observed to have a special effect on those who have suffered and whose experience may be used to help other wounded people. But how convincing are these observations?

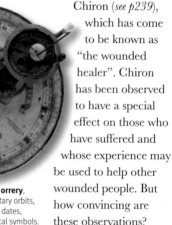

On this 18th-century orrery, which shows the planetary orbits, the disc is marked with dates, months, and the zodiacal symbols.

EVIDENCE, FACTS, OPINIONS

Any astrologer who has practised for half a century or so can produce case-book records that show, again and again, that when one planet in a birth chart is in a certain relationship to another, a particular personality

Ptolemy was one of the great minds of astrology and astronomy, and his works are still used today.

and it is interesting to note that three major reference books give different figures for the area of Nicaragua, with differences of up to 1,000 square kilometres. We must conclude that a dusty answer awaits anyone who cries for certainties in this our world.

POPULAR ASTROLOGY

It is unfortunately still necessary, when writing seriously about astrology, to point out that anyone who still believes that it has anything to do with the popular columns found in newspapers and magazines should disabuse themselves of that idea immediately. There is some fun to be obtained from reading these columns, and a shrewd astrologer who is also (and maybe more importantly) a first-class journalist can hit a sufficient number of buttons in the average column to suggest that something curious is going on. Tell a reader with an Aries Sun sign that they are likely to bruise their head, and you have a reasonable chance of being right.

trait appears in the individual whose horoscope is in question. Clearly, this is to some extent unverifiable, just as in psychology it is impossible to prove that, say, a certain incident in childhood has had a certain effect on an adult. But examined in sufficient detail, the evidence is persuasive. It is such verification of astrological theory that, over the years, convinces many people that the subject is worth taking seriously – that a horoscope or birth chart can indeed reveal a great deal about the nature of a person born on a particular day, at a particular moment, in a particular place.

However, it must be said that those who demand positive, measurable proof – as one might demand proof that the area of Nicaragua is 130,700 square kilometres, for example – are unlikely to find it. That is not as great a drawback as one might suppose,

Although there are generalizations which can be made, and successfully made, in the area of Sun-sign astrology, this is not the astrology we want to introduce to the readers of this book. Nor do we deal here with the aspect which, understandably, the general reader finds most interesting: the possibility of predicting the future.

HOPES OF PREDICTION

Most astrologers will agree that it is impossible to predict a future event reliably. Astrology is a remarkable tool with which to consider the subject, however. The famous psychiatrist C. G. Jung developed from it his theory of synchronicity. That is, of meaningful events occurring at the same time: if life has a pattern, then time is an essential aspect of that pattern, and anything that happens is related to everything else that happens through the time at which an event occurs.

History is studded with failed predictions, however, and the few that have turned out to be accurate – fascinating though they are – have usually demonstrated that they cannot be particular enough to be useful. For example, one British astrologer predicted serious danger to shipping on 6 March 1987 – the day on which the car ferry *Herald of Free Enterprise* sank off Zeebrugge with the loss of 187 lives. But such a prediction could not have been of use to save those lives unless it were possible to particularize – the longitude and latitude of the disaster, for example, or the time of sailing, or… But there are too many intangibles.

The form of prediction that seems reliable can best be compared to a weather forecast or an economic report: "there is a chance of rain tomorrow morning", or "in spring the recession may ease". As to, "on Monday 11 August 2007, you will meet your soul mate," forget it. No, the fascination of astrology, and its strength, is in "the nature of the beast" – how and why one man or

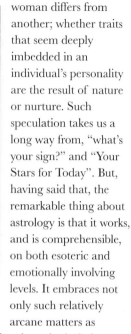

GEMINI, with Twins held aloft, as depicted in the late 19th century by Edward Burne-Jones.

woman differs from another; whether traits that seem deeply imbedded in an individual's personality are the result of nature or nurture. Such speculation takes us a long way from, "what's your sign?" and "Your Stars for Today". But, having said that, the remarkable thing about astrology is that it works, and is comprehensible, on both esoteric and emotionally involving levels. It embraces not only such relatively arcane matters as retrogradation, hypothetical planets, heliocentric planetary nodes, and midpoints, but also the interpretation of human characteristics, which is so much part of the popular appeal of Sun sign astrology.

THE AIMS OF THIS BOOK

With the aid of this book and by using the ephemerides (or tables of planets' positions) provided, it will be possible for a reader to draw up his or her horoscope – an exciting and fascinating process. By "reading" the chart and correlating the information it contains with the interpretations of the planets' positions, it will be possible to decide whether astrology holds an allure and is sufficiently intriguing for further study. If so, the next step will be to produce a fully calculated birth chart, which contains far more detail. This gets closer to the work of professional astrologers, who look, not only at the position of each planet vis-à-vis its companions in the solar system, but also at the angles they make to one another. Those angles must be accurate to within a matter of a very few degrees, which means using extremely detailed tables of planetary movements. In this book, we provide a simplified but good approximation, which is sufficient for the purpose of an all-round introduction to the subject.

Any thinking man or woman must make some attempt to connect their experience of life with the wider universe

One way of thinking about this is to compare the roughly drawn map of a country provided in a local guide book with the full ordnance survey map of the same area. The former will show you the major towns, the main roads which connect them; show you the quickest way from A to B; the major topographical features; and give a broad understanding of the terrain. The ordnance survey map will show the minor roads too, and give you map references – in it, you can "read" the detail.

Anyone who finds this book sufficiently interesting and wants to take the subject at least one large step

further could simply feed the words "birth chart" into their Web search engine. Of approximately 750,000 sites currently listed, a very large number offer a fully calculated chart drawn up for the time, date, and place of your birth. This will lend an extra dimension to the statements and interpretations in this book. This is especially useful if the Sun (an "honorary planet" to astrologers), is moving from one sign into another on the day of your birth. A fully calculated birth chart will give you the exact time when Mars moves from Taurus into Gemini, say, or Venus from Capricorn into Aquarius. This can make all the difference between a broadly sketched out character portrait and a fully fleshed out depiction of the person.

As an introduction to the practice of astrology, this book aims to present the facts simply but in enough detail to enable the reader to decide whether the road it indicates is sufficiently interesting for further, more detailed travel.

We hope that we show that it is.

An illustration of "Twelve Heathen Philosophers" from a Bohemian astrological manuscript of the 14th century.

The
HISTORY OF
ASTROLOGY

Pre-history

It is impossible to say when mankind first had the notion that the movements of the planets might have an effect on us all. However, we do know that by 1500BCE tables existed setting out the times when planets rose and set, and by 1000BCE astrologers were versed in the notion that the heavens was a great circle around which these beings revolved.

Star Maps and Mythical Beasts

The effect of the Sun on the Earth is very evident in the light and warmth it provides, and the Moon's effect is nearly as apparent. It creates the seas' tides, for example, and affects basic plants and animals, and the menstrual cycle. While no-one can say for sure, we can reasonably presume that such effects were observed long before the advent of writing, and that gradually the subtler effects of other planets were then noticed and studied.

An astrological tablet from the ancient city of Uruk in Iraq.

Writing in the 1st century BCE, Cicero had an interesting explanation for the development of astrology. He said that: "The Egyptians and Babylonians reside in vast plains where no mountains obstruct their view of the entire hemisphere, and so they have applied themselves mainly to that kind of divination called astrology."

Not only in the Middle East but also in the Far East, and in the Incan, Mayan, and Mexican civilizations, the planets that could be seen by the naked eye – Mercury, Venus, Mars, Jupiter, and Saturn – were identified as influential gods.

EARLY ASTROLOGERS

Astronomer/astrologers (and for centuries one name described them both) observed the strange ways in which the planets behaved – sometimes hesitating, sometimes appearing to move backwards, sometimes meeting each other then parting – and began to elaborate a theory based on these movements, as well as the mysterious and frightening eclipses of the Sun and Moon.

The earliest astrologers whose names we know lived in the 7th century BCE in the reigns of Sarandon of Babylonia (681–668BCE) and his successor Ashurbanipal. Astrologers such as Akkullanu, Balasi, and Nabua-heriba worked in rooms attached to the Temple of Ea (the god of oracles), and advised the kings on the great events of their reigns. It is impossible to overestimate their influence: the king would quite simply have made no important move without the advice of his astrologers.

THE ZODIAC

At some time between the 7th and 5th centuries BCE the path of the Sun about the Earth was divided into 12 sections, each measuring 30° within the 360° of the zodiac circle. Each section was marked by a particular constellation of stars and corresponded to a particular month of the year.

In the 5th century BCE, astronomers began to rationalize ways of measuring the movements of the heavenly bodies so that it was possible to develop the whole system of astrology and elaborate it. From Babylonia the study of the heavens spread to Greece, where mathematicians developed it still further. By the 1st century CE it had taken a form that we recognize today – astrologers in the 21st century still use more or less the same rules to plot and interpret a horoscope as their ancient predecessors did.

> ### EARLY HOROSCOPES
>
> Individual horoscopes were very basic at first. A horoscope of 225BCE, for example, records that "in year 77, the fourth day, in the last part of the night, Aristokrates was born. That day: Moon in Leo, Sun in 12° of Gemini, Jupiter in 18° Sagittarius. The place of Jupiter means his life will be regular, he will become rich, he will grow old, his days will be numerous. Venus in 4° Taurus. The place of Venus means wherever he may go it will be favourable to him..."

How the mythical creatures of the zodiac were born – the Virgin, the Fish, the Ram, and the rest – is unknown. Astrologers claim that associations between the signs and planets and certain human characteristics were empirically made, and there is much evidence to suggest that the elaboration of astrological techniques came about, not through psychic guesswork, or even via the symbolic unconscious, but (as in science) through observation and careful record-keeping.

The growth of astrology outside Babylonia and Assyria took very different paths. Persian interest in the planets was quite separate from Western astrology, for example, and Islamic astrology even more dissimilar, being derived from Greek, Indian, and Persian sources. Muslims were strongly interested in the subject and encouraged by the Koran: "He it is Who hath set for you the stars that ye may guide your course by them amid the darkness of the land and the sea." Simultaneously, the Chinese were developing their own version of a zodiac, with 12 consecutive years represented by 12 animals. Indeed, few civilizations grew without the aid of those who claimed to be able to see the shape of the present and the future in the behaviour of the stars.

Egyptian gods in an astrological scene from the Tomb of Seti I, created in around 1200–1085BCE.

ANCIENT EGYPT & CLASSICAL GREECE

Ancient Egypt is sometimes credited with being the mother of astrology. While the culture did look obsessively to the heavens, and so opened the door to the study of the planets, it is the texts of Ptolemy and Valens of Antioch that hold the keys to astrology, and continue to provide inspiration and source material for astrologers today.

This ceramic calendar from Egypt has Greek symbols of the zodiac around its edge.

Egyptian Star Gazers, Greek Teachers

When the Greek historian Herodotus visited Egypt in about 450BCE, he noted that Egyptian astrologers "can tell what fortune and what end and what disposition a man shall have according to the day of his birth … when an ominous thing happens they take note of the outcome and write it down, and if something of a like kind happens again, they think it will have a like result."

A carved sphinx sits at the Tomb of Ramses II; when the tomb was excavated, gold discs were found with symbols marking the rising and setting points of stars.

From this account, it is clear that the Egyptians were engaging in a rational and carefully researched examination of the relationship between the planets and events on Earth. However, the idea that ancient Egypt was a major source of knowledge and made a great contribution to the development of astrology is misleading. The claim that the first horoscope was cast in Egypt in 2767BCE is equally suspect, though at a very early date Egyptian astronomers were certainly thoroughly familiar with the positions of the stars. When the tomb of Rameses II (1292–1225BCE) was excavated, for example, it was found to contain two circles of gold marked in 360° and bearing symbols which show the rising and setting of stars. This seems to suggest that the Pharaoh was interested in ascending degrees – the degree of the ecliptic rising over the eastern horizon at any particular time – an important matter in astrology. The tomb of Rameses V (1150–1145BCE) contained similar evidence of scholarship of the planets; papyri offering astrological hints for every hour of every month of the year were found there.

The sole major contribution to the early history of astrology made by the Egyptians, however, was the invention of the *decans*. They divided the circle of the ecliptic into 36 sections, with three *decans*, or divisions of 10°, to each section. The first sight we have of these is on a coffin lid of the Middle Kingdom, on which the sky is shown with the names of the *decans* in columns. Since the zodiac did not exist at that time, the *decans* were geared to the constellations. Later, though, they were linked to the zodiac, and so became of true astrological significance. This is especially the case with medical astrology, in which each *decan* is specific to a particular ailment (stomach trouble being attributable to the first *decanate* of Virgo, for example).

An engraving depicting Hermes Trismegistus, who collected the texts of Egyptian astrological knowledge.

HERMETIC TEXTS

The most famous collection of Egyptian astrological knowledge was brought together in the *Four Astrological Books of Hermes*. These were reputedly collected by the Egyptian god Thoth, later known to the Greeks as Hermes Trismegistus, and later still to the Romans as Mercury. The texts were sacred, and only the highest of Egyptian priests were allowed to touch them. A complete set is said to have

been buried in the tomb of Alexander the Great – alas, still undiscovered. Hermes was said to have devised an astrological system of his own, and among the Hermetic texts were a book on medical astrology, another on the *decans*, one on zodiacal plants, and one on the astrological degrees.

ASTROLOGICAL MAN

It is difficult to say how much, if anything at all, of the Hermetic books have survived. In the 5th century CE, *Liber Hermetis*, a Latin text translated from the Greek, claimed to reproduce some of the text. However, it is mainly notable for the first known appearance of the "astrological man", in which the zodiac signs are placed onto a figure of a body, with Aries at the head and Pisces at the feet (*see pp30 and 50*).

Most educated Greeks of classical times were familiar with the idea that whatever happened in the heavens was reflected in events on Earth. If the heavens were carefully observed, it was possible to predict events in the skies. Therefore, they reasoned, terrestrial events could be predicted by correlating them with heavenly events. Neither religious nor scientific philosophers objected to the theory, which was regarded as proceeding from common sense.

This was the first age when astrological books began to be widely available. Chaldean astrologers from Babylonia flocked into Greece through Daphnae and the ports of Egypt, and debates on the subject began to warm up. Of the Greek intellectuals and philosophers, Cato and Ennius were hostile, but Sulla, Posidonius, and Varro were "believers", as were Vitruvius, Propertius, and Ovid. From the 1st century CE virtually everyone, whether Christian, pagan, or Jew, believed in astrology and to some extent followed it.

The Greeks adopted the zodiac as early as the 6th century BCE, and it is thought to have been Democritus (460–c357BCE) who was first to give the signs their Greek names, such as Aphrodite (Venus), Hermes (Mercury), Ares (Mars), and so on. Previously, they had been known by their Chaldean names or simply by descriptions, such as "the Fiery Star" (Mars) and "the Twinkling Star" (Mercury).

It was a Chaldean called Berosus, a priest of the Sun god Marduk in Babylon, who in about 260BCE set up the first recorded school of astrology on the island of Kos, where there was a famous school of medicine. Through books that are now lost he spread knowledge of astrological techniques throughout the Greek world. He was famous in his own time, and it is said that Athens raised a statue of him with a golden tongue, marking his skill as an orator. He passed on his school to Antipatrus and Achinapolus, who taught medicine, and experimented in drawing birth charts for the moment of conception rather than the moment of birth. Their theory was that the sign the Moon was in at the moment of conception would be in the Ascendant at the time of birth. The theory was said to have originated in Hermetic literature. There was also work on astrological weather forecasting and medical astrology.

PTOLEMY'S TETRABIBLOS

As we turn from Greece towards Rome, it is in Alexandria that one man drew together all the skeins of astrological theory and did his best to rationalize them in a single book. Claudius Ptolemæus (c100–c178CE) – known simply as Ptolemy – arrived there to teach at the university that had been founded 400 years earlier. Ptolemy is famous as a mathematician, astronomer, and geographer, and his *Almagest* became the acknowledged textbook of astronomy for several centuries after his death.

His *Tetrabiblos* is the first really substantial textbook of astrology to come down to us complete. Spread over four books, it begins with the rational argument that, since it is clear that the Sun and Moon have an effect upon terrestrial life – through the seasons, the movements of the tides, and so on – it is surely worth considering the effects the other heavenly bodies may have as well.

"Since it is clearly practicable to make predictions concerning the proper quality of the seasons, there also seems no impediment to the formation of similar prognostications concerning the destiny and disposition of every human being, for even at the time of any individual's primary conformation, the general quality of that individual's temperament may be perceived; and the corporeal shape and mental

ALEXANDER THE GREAT

Alexander the Great was born at a particularly propitious moment – partly because his mother, Olympias, was advised by the astrologer Nektanebos to hold back until the precise moment when a great man would be born. Then he announced, "Queen, you will now give birth to a ruler of the world," and as Alexander was born thunder and lightning welcomed him. Later, when he was 11, as Nektanebos was showing him the stars, it is said that the child pushed the astrologer down a pit, pointing out that there was something to be said for keeping your eyes on the earth.

The Ptolemaic System postulated a view of the universe in which the Earth was at its centre. It was proposed by Ptolemy in the 2nd century and widely accepted for at least 1,000 years.

capacity with which the person will be endowed at birth may be pronounced; as well as the favourable and unfavourable events indicated …"

Ptolemy's book covers an enormous and diverse range, as his chapter headings show: "Of Masculine and Feminine Planets", "Of Places and Degrees", "Of the Power of the Aspects to the Sun", "Of the Time of Predicted Events", "Of the Investigation of the Weather", "Of Parents", "Of Length of Life", "Of Marriage", "Of Foreign Travel".

After 2,000 years, the *Tetrabiblos* remains an astonishing book, with well over 400 pages of closely written text in its most modern translation. It still has its value today, and no one with a serious interest in astrology should neglect to read it.

Ptolemy provides us with the major Classical texts of both astronomy and astrology.

THE ROLE OF ASTROLOGY

It is not easy to tell how much astrology was used on a day-to-day basis in Classical Greece, but several Greek writers warn their readers not to get too involved in the predictions made by travelling Chaldeans – which suggests that, as always, there were plenty of credulous people ready to be gulled by fake astrologers. By 188CE Vettius Valens of Antioch, the first known professional consultant astrologer, had amassed a fine library of horoscopes and set out over 100 of them in his *Anthologiae*, showing how he interpreted them and advised his clients.

If in Greece astrology remained low-key, in Imperial Rome it moved right into the sunlight, soon to become a major factor in the government of the state.

IMPERIAL ROME

Towards the end of the 3rd century BCE, the Romans began to take a serious interest in Greek literature and drama. Inevitably, the Greek preoccupation with astrology began to intrigue Roman writers and philosophers, and it was taken up by many emperors as a way to bolster their greatness and to pre-empt any plots against them.

Julius Caesar famously ignored the astrological advice to beware of grave danger until the "Ides of March" was past.

Emperors and Plotting Astrologers

By the 1st century BCE, the statesman Cicero (106–64BCE) was reporting in his *De divinatione* (published just after the assassination of Emperor Julius Caesar) the Greek belief that: "It is not merely probable, but certain, that just as the temperature of the air is regulated by celestial force, so also children at their birth are influenced in mind and body, and by this force their minds, manner, disposition, physical condition, career in life, and destinies are determined."

There was, however, also some suspicion of astrologers – in some cases, justified. A sizable slave revolt in Sicily around 133BCE was led by an astrologer

The Roman senator Cicero was convinced of astrology's validity, reasoning that the "celestial force" affected man's destiny just as it affected the Earth's temperature.

called Eunus, and less than 30 years later the astrologer Athenio led another slave revolt, insisting that the planets had revealed that he was the true King of Sicily. If so, he did not live to take up his throne. No wonder the Roman emperors were suspicious of the subject: clearly what men saw in "the stars" could spur them on to extraordinary and dangerous actions.

FIGULUS, THE POTTER

Gradually, men in public office began to express their belief in, and enthusiasm for, the subject. P. Nigidius Figulus, a Roman senator and *praetor* (a magistrate) was the first Roman astrologer whose name we know – he was called Figulus (Potter) because he argued that the Earth spun as fast as a potter's wheel. It was claimed that he "was not matched

even by [the astrologers of] Egyptian Memphis [the ancient capital of Egypt] in observations of the sky and calculations keeping pace with the stars", and he is said to have foretold the greatness of the Roman Emperor Octavius on the day of his birth. Later, the scholar Varro (116–27BCE), one of the most learned of Roman scholars, commissioned a horoscope of Rome itself and of its founder, Romulus. It is the first example of the use of astrology to reveal the past by examining a horoscope drawn up for the moment of a city's foundation. It is also the first horoscope of a historical figure. The historian Plutarch (c46–120CE) fell upon the result with great interest, and reported it enthusiastically.

The Roman Emperor Augustus proclaimed himself a Capricorn, though he was actually a Libran.

THE TURNING TIDE

The sceptics began to be outnumbered by the believers – and though some of the former had great influence, astrology often came off best. Julius Caesar (100–44BCE), for instance, famously scorned the astrological advice of one Spurinna that (as Plutarch reports) he should "beware a danger which would not threaten him beyond the Ides of March". But he paid the price when he was assassinated right on cue.

The next emperor, Augustus (63BCE–4CE), was introduced to astrology when he was in exile and seemed unlikely ever to return to Rome. He was persuaded to consult an astrologer, Theogenes, about his future. The historian Suetonius describes how when Theogenes had drawn up Augustus's chart, "he rose and threw himself at his feet; and this gave Augustus so implicit a

faith in his destiny that he even ventured to publish his horoscope, and struck a silver coin stamped with Capricorn, the sign under which he had been born." Actually, Augustus was a Libran; he put it about that he was a Capricornian because that sign more markedly signalled a strong and dominant ruler.

TIBERIUS AND THRASYLLUS

The successor to Augustus was Tiberius (42BCE–37CE), a man who became besotted with astrology. His personal astrologer, Thrasyllus, was one of the most influential who ever lived.

Thrasyllus was an Alexandrian, an editor of Plato and Democritus, who happened to be on the island of Rhodes – just at the time when Tiberius found it expedient to remove himself from Rome, where he had been involved in a quarrel with his father-in-law, the Emperor. Rhodes was a relatively uncivilized and barren island, and the two men began to pass a lot of time together, the astrologer reputedly teaching Tiberius how to set up and interpret charts. He also predicted that his pupil would shortly be recalled to Rome and a bright future. When Augustus sent for Tiberius in 4CE and officially proclaimed him his heir, Thrasyllus travelled with his patron, and received the valuable gift of Roman citizenship.

During Tiberius's nine-year reign as emperor, Thrasyllus was constantly at his side, advising him on personal matters and affairs of state. Life under Tiberius was never comfortable, and if Thrasyllus was more or less safe, other astrologers had to watch their step. Two of them, Pituanius and P. Marcius, were unwise enough to attach themselves to Scribonius Libo, a slightly dim *praetor* who attempted to organize a coup against the Emperor – their heads ended up on pikes. There were other plots and counterplots, and it was Thrasyllus who advised the Emperor to leave Rome in 26CE, while he himself remained in the city and supported the *praetor* Sejanus in his plan to succeed Tiberius. No doubt with the aid of his charts he sailed through the rocky waters of the next few years, and managed to stay alive when hundreds were tortured and executed. He is said to have foretold his own death, to the hour.

THE ASTROLOGER'S SON

Thrasyllus died shortly before Tiberius, and the new emperor, Caius – known as Caligula – knew the astrologer's family rather well. In fact, Thrasyllus had been distinctly worried to hear that his grand-daughter Ennia was having an affair with Caligula.

Emperor Nero presided over a reign of terror, but the astrologer Balbillus prospered during it and was made Prefect of Egypt.

Thrasyllus was right to be concerned: though Caligula had promised to marry Ennia on ascending the throne, he failed to do so, and when she married someone else he had her husband executed. In despair, Ennia then killed herself.

Thrasyllus's son, Tiberius Claudius Balbillus, emerged in Roman society after Caligula's death. The new emperor, Claudius, had been a childhood friend, and Balbillus became familiar at court, accompanying Claudius to England as both astrologer and chief engineer. On their return, the Emperor presented Balbillus with a golden crown of honour. Later he was made high priest of the Temple of Hermes in Alexandria, and head of the state university with its superb library. Balbillus then happily split his time between Alexandria and Rome.

Balbillus, however, was unable to stay away from politics, and when Claudius died, he set up his charts and told Agrippina the

Younger of the precise moment when her son Britannicus should leave the house if he was to be a future Roman emperor. She detained the boy until the given time, when he went out and was proclaimed Emperor Nero (37–68CE). Years before, Balbillus had told Agrippina that this would happen – her son would become an emperor just as she had wished – but that also he would murder his mother. Both the predictions proved true.

For his role in Nero's glory, Balbillus was rewarded by being appointed the Prefect of Egypt. Unlike many others, he survived the fearful carnage during the Emperor's reign. Another astrologer who drew up Nero's chart at the time of his birth is said to have taken one look at it before fainting with horror.

A DEATH FORETOLD

Succeeding Roman emperors were not so greatly preoccupied with astrology, although Vespasian (9–79CE) not only consulted Balbillus but also allowed games to be held at Ephesus in his honour – the Great Balbillean Games were held until well into the 3rd century. Hadrian and Septimus Severus were adherents; the latter covered the ceilings of his palace with astrological paintings – including one of his own horoscope.

Belief in astrology was bolstered by the apparent ease with which astrologers could foretell events in the lives of the emperors. What the public did not know was that many of the emperors went out of their way to deliberately fulfil the predictions, in order to show how favoured they were by the heavens.

During successive reigns, life for astrologers alternated between the placid and the exhilarating. Exciting times were far more common, as most emperors were continually apprehensive about plots against them. Anyone who possessed a copy of an emperor's chart was naturally suspected of advising one or more plotters.

> ### THE HOROSCOPE OF TIBERIUS
>
> When exiled to Rhodes, Tiberius is said to have consulted many astrologers about his future, killing them the moment they had interpreted his horoscope. When the astrologer Thrasyllus examined his charts and suggested that Tiberius had a brilliantly successful life ahead of him, the future Emperor manoeuvered him to the edge of a perilous cliff and, preparing to throw him over, asked, "And what do you see for yourself?" Thrasyllus replied, "I am in terrible danger." Much impressed, Tiberius spared the astrologer, and when recalled as Emperor relied continually on him for advice, rarely making a move without it.
>
> **Tiberius**

There was still a great deal of belief in astrological forecasting. Vespasian's son Domitian (51–96CE), for instance, became distinctly nervous when several astrologers predicted his death. As the time announced for it came nearer and nearer, he grew even more edgy. He sent for an astrologer, Ascletarius-Asclation, and asked him if he could foretell his own death. The astrologer replied that he could: he would be torn to pieces by dogs. Domitian had him executed immediately to dispel the prediction. As the astrologer's body was awaiting cremation, however, a sudden rainstorm put out the fire and a pack of feral dogs destroyed the corpse.

The following day, as the time of his forecast death drew closer, Domitian grew increasingly nervous. Finally, to placate him, his courtiers assured him that the fatal hour was past. Much relieved, he decided to take a bath. As he was doing so, an assassin broke in and stabbed him to death.

THE EARLY CHRISTIANS

Christianity and astrology have been odd bedfellows. Initially, there was little disharmony, but as time went on the divisions grew more polar. However, at times and in places when one might expect hostility to be at its most fervent, Christianity has shown little desire for acrimony and has instead displayed a decided curiosity about the subject.

Tertullian was a sceptic of astrology.

Following the Stars

The early Christians did not shrink from the idea that a star (probably a triple conjunction of Jupiter, Saturn, and Uranus, in fact) guided the three wise men to the cradle of the new-born Jesus in Bethlehem. Indeed, it would almost certainly have seemed highly probable to early Christians that the birth of the son of God should be signalled in the heavens.

For the following three centuries, astrology and the new religion co-existed peacefully, though there were some critics. St Clement of Rome – a friend and confidant of St Peter and his

This 6th-century mosaic from Italy depicts the importance of the "star", which led the kings to the birthplace of Christ.

third successor as pope – reportedly asserted that the planets and stars had been fixed in heaven by God in order "that they might be for an indication of things past, present, and future." He referred to the 12 apostles as the 12 Months of Christ, who himself was the Year of Our Lord.

CONFLICT ARISES

Clement admitted that "the stars" could have an evil effect, but asserted that man could resist this, for it was unthinkable that God should make man sin through an evil disposition of the planets and then punish him for it. On the other hand, Tertullian, born in

about 160CE and perhaps the most influential of early Christian theologians, argued that it was the fallen angels who had taught man astrology. But the most prominent of early Christian antagonists of astrology was St Augustine (345–430), who argued against it in his books *Christian Doctrine* and *The City of God*.

Like many churchmen, Augustine did not study the subject, but simply regurgitated old arguments from pre-Christian eras. His objections were founded on a misconception of the nature of astrological theory, even as practised in his own time. When, for instance, he argued that astrology is ridiculous because a cow and a human baby born at the same instant do not have precisely the

St Augustine fervently argued against astrology.

same life, he simply displayed his own ignorance of what astrology claimed, proportionately weakening his stronger arguments.

ASTROLOGY'S DEFENDERS

Other early theologians took different positions. Julius Firmicus Maternus, a contemporary of St Augustine, was the author of a lengthy treatise on astrology. His *Matheseos* (c354) accepts the doctrine of free will but finds it strange that man should think of stars and planets as mere decorations of the heavens. Producing the chief anti-astrological arguments one by one, he demolishes them with ease, demonstrating clearly that the critics had for the most part simply not tried to understand the nature or technique of the theory they attacked. He admits freely that some astrologers are rogues and others fools, and certainly admits the difficulty of the subject. However, he claims that the human mind is as competent to cope with astrology as with the mapping of the heavens and the prediction of the planets' courses.

In a brilliantly presented and enormously complex argument, Firmicus scathingly demolishes superstition and its practitioners – "magicians" who only want to frighten people. He violently opposes secrecy, and demands that astrologers, rather than shrinking from public view as though ashamed, should place themselves under the protection of God, praying that He grant them "grace to attempt the explanation of the courses of the stars". The *Matheseos* is an important book, and was to be quoted again and again in following centuries by Christian astrologers and theologians who wanted to assuage the fears of laymen when the Church authorities condemned astrology.

A TIME OF PERSECUTION

It was in 358CE that major persecution of astrologers began. Emperor Constantine, a convert, began a campaign against the so-called "superstitious" practice of claiming that the heavenly bodies had something to do with affairs on Earth, and astrologers fell under the death penalty. This was in a sense part of the coming battle between Christianity and science. Ptolemy and others believed that astrology was based on scientific cause and effect and that its use in treating medical conditions, for example, was entirely rational. The Church, however, was more interested in faith. Many early Christian theologians asserted that in the past there had been room for astrology, but that – as Clement of Alexandria (c150–215) had written – the 12 apostles had now replaced the 12 zodiac signs as ultimate authorities on the conduct of human life.

The break away from astrology was neither abrupt nor complete. The fact that astrology grew somewhat faded during the first 1,000 years after the birth of Christ was not so much the result of the antagonism of the Christian Church as because of the decline of classical learning. New books from Greece concerned themselves more with astronomy than astrology (the two terms gradually acquired very different meanings), while some were simply not translated into Latin and therefore had no effect in Western Europe.

Those astrological books which were translated often lacked sections describing how to set up a horoscope. The *Astronomica* of Manilius (fl. 1st century), for instance, is an astonishing poem about astronomy and astrology. While it contains versified calculations showing how to draw a map of the sky for a particular moment, it does not explain how to interpret such a chart. Similarly, Boethius (c450–524) asserts

that "the celestial movements of the stars constrain human forces in an indissoluble chain of causes", but fails to show how this actually works.

ASTROLOGY BEYOND WESTERN EUROPE

At the same time, astrology was flourishing elsewhere. By 200CE textbooks in Sanskrit were circulating in India, explaining an astrology very different to that in the West. It had five elements instead of four, for instance, and great importance was given to "invisible" points of the zodiac, such as lunar nodes (points where the lunar orbit intersects the ecliptic). By the 8th century, accurate and complex horoscopes were being cast in India. In Persia too, there was a slightly different system, largely based on the importance of astronomical conjunctions.

But it was in the Islamic world that the subject became an almost all-consuming passion. Islamic philosophers found justification in the Koran for the study of astrology as an instrument of God's Will. The invention of the astrolabe (perhaps the oldest scientific instrument), which could reveal the degree of the ecliptic in the ascendant at any given moment, was enormously useful to astrologers. From the 7th century, a huge compendium of astronomical and astrological knowledge was built up, and Islamic astronomers became much more skilled and knowledgeable than their Western colleagues.

Astrologers whose names are still relatively unknown in the West increased the skill of Islamic astrologers. The first Jewish astrologer we know of, Masha'Allah (c762–816), advised the correct moment of the foundation of the city of Baghdad, and worked on world history as illuminated by conjunctions of the planets Jupiter and Saturn; al-Kindi (c801–866) was one of the first scholars to consider how astrology might work, and wrote a book, *De Radiis*, in which he argued that

---

FREE WILL

It was largely as a result of influence from Islamic sources that astrology returned to the West. This was reinforced by the gradually strengthening notion that the stars were stationed in space by God as an instrument for governing the world – that, as the theologian Bernard Sylvester put it, the stars and planets were "gods who serve God in person, who receive from God the secrets of the future, which they impose upon the lower species of the universe." The presence of free will was always asserted, however. As St Clement pointed out in the 1st century, "sometimes we resist our desires and sometimes yield to them." The stars could not force us to either course of action.

St Clement of Rome

stellar rays conveyed the influence of the planets into the realm of Earth. An astrologer whose name is familiar in the West – Albumasar (really, Abu-Mashar, 787–886), worked in Baghdad and wrote the enormously influential *Great Introduction to the Science of Astrology*, a complex and highly structured book which was studied and revered by subsequent generations.

A PERIOD OF AMBIVALENCE

Between the time of Constantine and the present day, the Christian Church has been ambivalent about astrology. Authorities that one might suppose to have condemned it, let it alone. The Inquisition, for instance, only burned one astrologer – Cecco d'Ascoli, whose death was in fact politically inspired, and the popes, who might have been expected to react most strongly against astrology, were often wholeheartedly supportive. Julius II, Leo X, and Paul III all consulted their personal astrologers – some on church matters, others on more personal affairs. Paul III (1468–1549) knighted astrologer Luca Gaurico, and made him a bishop. Gaurico would appear whenever a new building was proposed for Rome, and "cry out in a loud voice" when the propitious moment had arrived to lay a marble foundation stone. Paul was assured by another astrologer, Marius Alterius, that in his 83rd year he would

Luca Gaurico would work out the best moment to lay a building's foundation stone.

experience a year of success with women. In fact, he died when he was 81, but no doubt the prospect had been something to look forward to. Leo X (1513–21) claimed that his astrologer, Franciscus Pruilus, could foretell events to the very hour, while Adrian VI and Clement VII allowed almanacs to be dedicated to them.

Recent archbishops of Canterbury have more or less violently opposed astrology (sometimes to the extent of forbidding Church property to be used for meetings). So it is ironic that, at the sacred heart of Canterbury Cathedral, each archbishop who walks to his consecration does so by passing over a carpet that conceals a huge and beautiful zodiac inscribed on the floor.

THE MIDDLE AGES

Historians have claimed that the period that stretches roughly from the beginning of the 11th century to the end of the 13th was particularly dark for astrology. Indeed, it is claimed that its use more or less disappeared in the Western world. However, this is far from true – especially in the field of astrological medicine.

William the Conqueror instructed his astrologer to calculate the most auspicious time for his coronation in 1066.

The Black Death and Court Astrology

For many centuries, the study of medicine was inextricably linked with the study of astrology. Indeed as late as the 18th century, it was still impossible to qualify as a doctor unless one had passed an examination in astrology, and the use of planetary positions in diagnosis and treatment was commonplace.

The Black Death in the mid-14th century illustrates the connection. As it ravaged Eurasia, killing some 25 million people in Europe alone, astrologers soon began to publish their views on its cause. The medical faculty of the University of Paris was commanded by King Philip VI to give its opinion of the origin of the plague. While other astrologers blamed the total lunar eclipse of 18 March 1347 (eclipses were always considered baleful), the faculty opined that a triple conjunction of Mars, Jupiter, and Saturn in Aquarius in March 1345 was responsible for the "pernicious corruption of the surrounding air, as well as other signs of mortality, famine, and other catastrophes." It was a reasoned theory that greatly enhanced the reputation of astrology.

It should be noted that now and in later times of plague, astrologers did brave service to the public by using their medical knowledge. Both amateur and professional doctors often remained with the sick, rather than attempting to flee the contagion.

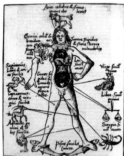

In this early 16th-century drawing of a "zodiac man," astrological signs are applied to areas of the body.

MEDICAL ASTROLOGY

The various theories of medical astrology had by this time been thoroughly explored. They were based not only on the familiar "zodiac man" but on the ancient theory of the "humours" – blood, phlegm, choler, and melancholy – which must be kept in balance if a subject were to remain healthy.

The position of the Moon was extremely important, especially when a surgeon was about to bleed a patient – and bleeding was considered the miracle cure for almost every ailment, for it helped to restore balance with the other humours. Bleeding was not supposed to take place when the Moon occupied the zodiac sign which ruled the part of the body that was injured or was causing illness – for instance if the Moon was in Scorpio, it would be madness to bleed the loins (Scorpio's body area). Otherwise, bleeding was easier when the Moon was full, but took an age if she was new (something recognized, incidentally, in 21st-century blood transfusion).

All this had been known for centuries, of course – as we know from the writings of those astrologers who, by the beginning of the 8th century, were beginning to appear out of the mist: for example Aldhelm (639–709), who wrote treatises on the subject, and Alcuin (c732–804), who became a friend and advisor of Emperor Charlemagne. The Church in England was particularly keen on the subject, and many churches had fine zodiacs – the Abbey of Croyland, for instance, had one with Jupiter represented in gold, Mars in iron, the Sun in lattern (a yellow metal similar to brass), and Mercury in amber.

COURT ASTROLOGY

William the Conqueror commissioned his own astrologer to set the time for his Coronation – midday on Christmas Day 1066 – which is used by many modern astrologers as the "birth time" of England. The death of King Harold had previously been predicted by the appearance of a comet – an event shown in the Bayeux tapestry, with a worried-looking astrologer announcing its presence to the ill-fated King.

Arguably the greatest of 11th-century English scholars was Adelard (or Æthelhard), who wrote books on astronomy and alchemy, and translated a number of Arabic astrological texts, which explained how a reader might set up a chart. He believed that the planets were "superior and divine animals" which were "the causes and principle of inferior natures", and that one who studied them could understand the present and past, and predict the future.

During the time of the Black Death in the mid-14th century, astrologers were turned to as a source of explanation for the plague that was then sweeping through Asia and Europe, killing millions.

Adelard was enthusiastic about the importance of astrology in the study of medicine, and was sure that this made for better doctors than "the narrow medical man who thinks of no effects except those of inferior nature merely."

Some authorities were less enthusiastic. William of Conches, for instance – who had travelled extensively before becoming associated with the court of Geoffrey Plantagenet, where he tutored the future King Henry II of England – was one of the earliest scholars to differentiate between astrology and astronomy. Astrologers, he said, treated celestial phenomena as they appeared to be, whether accurately or not, while astronomers dealt with things as they were, whether they seemed to be or not.

This illustration from an Arabic manuscript of the 13th century shows a woman giving birth, while, in the top right corner, an astrologer uses an instrument to chart the positions of the stars.

ASTROLOGY AND THE CHURCH

William of Conches' voice was a lonely one, however. During the 12th century, a vast number of Latin astrological texts flooded into northern Europe. The scholar Gerard of Cromona (1114–87) alone translated over 70 books, among them Ptolemy's *Almagest* and previously unknown works by Aristotle.

The Church did not curtail the spread of astrological knowledge: after all, many leading churchmen were convinced that the stars and planets had been placed in the sky by God for a reason, and were as eager as anyone else to theorize about that reason. The greatest scholars, such as Roger Bacon (1214–92), Albertus Magnus (c1200–80), and St Thomas Aquinas (1225–74), all took part in the debate, and found it impossible not to agree with the conclusion of

This section of the Bayeux tapestry depicts Halley's Comet, which was seen as a bad omen for King Harold.

Robert Grosseteste (c1175–1253): "nature below effects nothing unless celestial power moves it and directs it from potency into act." In the end, all they could do was compromise: Berthold of Regensburg (c1200), for instance, had no doubt that "as God gave powers to stones and to herbs and to words, so also he gave power to the stars, that they have power over all things except over one thing … Over that thing, no man has any power, nor any might, neither have stars nor herbs not words nor stones nor angel nor devil nor any man, but God alone; it is man's free will."

ASTROLOGY AND SOCIETY

In less unhappy times than those of the Great Plague, the common people probably heard little of astrology, though they were occasionally affected by astrological predictions. In 1186, for example, the English were thrown into panic by the coming conjunction of planets in Libra, and services were held in many churches to persuade God to overrule the planets and mitigate disaster. Presumably He heard the pleas, for no disaster occurred.

The royalty and nobility of Europe were another matter: they universally consulted astrologers. In the 12th century we have news of the first notable court astrologer since Roman times – Michael Scot, who when he died in the 1230s was astrologer to the Holy Roman Emperor Frederick II. Scot was much revered as "an augur, a soothsayer, a second Apollo," and did serious work on, for example, the Moon's effects on menstruation. He also studied how different positions (according to planetary rules) during copulation could produce different effects at conception. After the wedding of Frederick and Isabella, sister of King Henry III of England, the couple refused to consummate the marriage until "the fitting hour" had been calculated by Scot.

EARLIEST PUBLIC CLOCK

Before the invention of reliable timepieces, estimating the correct time was a major problem for astrologers, who needed to time births and events accurately. Midday was relatively easy to gauge, simply by observing the position of the Sun, but, beyond that, time was a pretty vague concept; it could only be measured by observing events in the sky, and to calculate these was a complex and difficult skill to attain. The earliest public clock in England dates from 1336, and is at Salisbury Cathedral; domestic clocks began to appear only some decades later.

The public clock at Salisbury Cathedral

But a greater court astrologer was to come – Guido Bonatti. This is the astrologer Dante describes as one of the sufferers in the fourth division of the eighth circle of the *Inferno* – that is among the spirits who during their life spent too much time trying to predict the future and are now condemned to pace about with their heads turned backwards. Bonatti, a professor at the University of Bologna, had a fine career advising the princes of Europe: among other things he would stand on the ramparts of a castle and at the auspicious moment strike a bell to announce the time to ride out to battle. He was scarcely modest in his claims:

"All things are known to the astrologer: all that has taken place in the past, all that will happen in the future – everything is revealed to him, since he knows the effects of the heavenly motions which have been, those which are, and those which will be, and since he knows at what time they will act, and what effects they ought to produce."

Few astrologers in later centuries would be prepared to claim so much.

NETARUM
PLECTEN
GRAPHIA.

LEO
℧

♌
CER

GEMENI

TAVRVS ♊

ÆQVINOCTIALIS

ARIES ♈

PISCES ♈

FIRMAMENTVM STEL;

80 70 60 50 40 30 20 10 20 30 40 50 60 70 80

LARV

Orbis Saturni.
Via ♃ Iovis
Orbita ♂ Martis
Venus et Mercurius circa Solem
♀ ☿
Sol
Terra
Luna

HYPOTHESIS BRAHEA,
in quâ centrum Lunæ et Fir-
mamenti est Terra, reliquorum
quinq; Planetarum Sol.

RENAISSANCE EUROPE

As science furthered its discoveries and developed its laws of the universe, astrology became increasingly contentious, and a schism eventually developed between the previously indistinguishable studies of astronomy and astrology. For most, however, astrology continued to be a compelling subject, and one that was readily turned to in times of need.

This 15th-century scientific manuscript contains articles relating to medicine, the computing of the calendar, the planets and stars, and human affairs.

Kings, Queens, and Mistresses

Astrologers have always been addicted to prophesying disaster, from famine to war, from the Black Death to the sinking of the Titanic. During February 1524, for instance, when there was a conjunction of all the planets in the water sign of Pisces, astrologers were agreed that nothing could be clearer than the fact that a second Great Flood was imminent – a flood that would drown the entire world.

More than 50 astrologers published over 100 books deliberating the implications of these worrying facts, while still being careful to cover their backs wherever possible. The philosopher Agostino Nifo (1473–c1538) suggested that, while there was likely to be more rain than usual, Jupiter's predominance over Saturn strongly suggested that this would be beneficial, not destructive. All the same, he concluded, it would be as well to watch out for floods.

When February passed with fair weather, the astrologers of Bologna University (an especially strong astrological faculty) were surprised – but were later convinced that their mistake was only in timing, for from March to December there was continuous rain, hail, and high winds.

The Pope even commanded prayers to mitigate the effects of the storms.

THE COURTS OF EUROPE

The Hapsburg Emperor Rudolph II (1552–1612) was the patron of several astrologers, while

Philip II of Spain heeded astrological advice not to visit Mary I in England because of a plot against him.

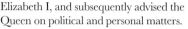

Philip II of Spain is documented as having taken specific astrological advice that warned against visiting Mary Tudor in England because of a plot against him. In England itself, the royal association with astrology – which had begun even before the arrival of William the Conqueror – continued to flourish. Henry VI (1421–71) consulted a Master Welch about the time of his coronation and later engaged Richard de Vinderose, an Englishman trained in France, as his court astrologer. Henry VIII (1491–1547) was advised by Nicholas Kratzer, a Bavarian mathematician and astrologer, and during his reign expressly instructed his clergy not to preach against astrology.

In Italy the philosopher Tomasso Campanella (1569–1639) argued the case for astrology before Pope Urban VIII, and later in France cast many horoscopes for the great and good. The philosopher and scientist Giordano Bruno (1548–1600) was another proponent of astrology, and firmly believed that "all things depend upon the upper world."

JOHN DEE

The most famous astrologer of the age in the whole of Europe, however, was John Dee (1527–1608), who was also an esteemed navigator, map-maker, and mathematician. He set the date and time for the coronation of

John Dee was greatly interested in the physical aspect of astrology.

Elizabeth I, and subsequently advised the Queen on political and personal matters.

Dee – a scientist who believed that the universe worked according to mathematical laws – was *the* major force in Renaissance astrology. He lectured in Paris to excited crowds of students, and worked in Prague and Krakow before his return to England. He was much interested in how astrology might actually work: probably, he concluded, by "rays" of some sort emanating from the planets – there was no reason why, just as magnetic forces could be measured, one should not in time discover the nature of these rays and how they are influential upon the human soul as well as the body. Dee pleaded for more detailed astronomical study, so that the true sizes and distances, and therefore influence, of the heavenly bodies could be established. Though incomplete, his *Propaedeumata* is probably the greatest English astrological work.

ASTROLOGY VERSUS ASTRONOMY

The 16th century was the age of the great astronomers; modern astronomers are reluctant to acknowledge the fact that they, too, once accepted astrology as part of the universal working of things. Tycho Brahe (1546–1601) spent a great deal of time on the subject, and defended it in lectures at the University of Copenhagen. Nicolaus Copernicus (1473–1543) had many well-thumbed astrological textbooks in his library, while Johannes Kepler (1571–1630) kept his own "horoscope book". When, in 1594, he took up the post of teacher of mathematics at Graz, Kepler produced annual almanacs which appear to have been very accurate. In the first one he prophesied very cold weather and an invasion by the Turks: on 1 January it was so cold, he later assured a correspondent, that when people blew their noses, those organs fell off; on the very same day, the Turks marched in and destroyed much of the country between Vienna and Neustat.

Astronomers today continue to deny that such a great scientist as Kepler could have believed in astrology, and are quick to quote his throwaway line about how astronomy – the sensible mother – benefits from the popularity of her foolish daughter, astrology. However, there is plenty of evidence to demonstrate that Kepler accepted the idea of astrological forecasting and horoscopes in general. In April 1599, he wrote to his friend and colleague Johann Herwart to ask,

Johannes Kepler is acknowledged as a great astronomer, but his astrological interests tend to be ignored by today's astronomers.

"How does the conformation of the heavens influence the character of a man at the moment of his birth?" He then went on to answer, "It influences a human being as long as he lives in the way in which a peasant haphazardly ties slings around pumpkins; these do not make the pumpkin grow, but they determine its shape. So do the heavens: they do not give a man morals, experiences, happiness, children, wealth, a wife, but they shape everything which a man has to do … In my case, Saturn and the Sun work together in the sextile aspect (I prefer to speak of what I know best). Therefore my body is dry and knotty, and not tall. My soul is faint-hearted and hides itself away in literary corners; it is distrustful and fearful …" He goes on to write a detailed interpretation of his birth chart. He repeated it at greater length in the fourth book of his *Harmonics*, which is dedicated to King James I.

ASTROLOGY IN LITERATURE

It was during the 17th century that astrology became more pervasive than ever before in England. Scarcely anyone spoke out against it except in its most superstitious aspects, and the country's greatest men argued persuasively in its favour – notably Sir Walter Ralegh in his *History of the World*:

"If we cannot deny but that God hath given virtue to spring and fountain to cold earth, to plants and stones, minerals, and to the excremental parts of the basest living creatures, why should we rob the beautiful stars of their working powers? For seeing that they are many in number and of eminent beauty and magnitude, we may not think that in the treasure of His wisdom which is infinite, there can

THE FRENCH COURT

The royal courts of France and England were no less enthusiastic about astrology than the Vatican. The widow of the French King Henry II, Catherine de'Medici, made sure that an astrologer was present at the birth of their son, the future Louis XIII (1601–43) who in turn ordered Jean-Baptiste Morin to attend at the birth of his son, the future Louis XIV (1638–1715). Later, Morin hid behind the curtains of the royal bedroom to observe the precise moment at which the young Louis XIV and his wife consummated their marriage, so that he could work out the conception chart of any future Dauphin who might be born as the result of the coupling.

Catherine de'Medici

During an outbreak of the plague in London in the late 16th century, the astrologer and physician Simon Forman remained in the city to tend the sick.

be wanting, even for every star, a peculiar value, virtue, and operation."

Shakespeare, whose plays were not written simply to delight the intelligentsia but to entertain the commoners too, knew that when he made an astrological joke everyone would understand it; and the plays are full of them. He also takes the modern view that, while the stars indicate a possible path, there is no compulsion on man to take it: "The fault, dear Brutus, is not in our stars But in ourselves, that we are underlings." Those who claim Shakespeare inveighs against astrology might note that in his plays the only people who speak against it are his villains.

SIMON FORMAN

Shakespeare very probably knew the most successful astrologer of his time, Simon Forman (1552–1611). The playwright's landlady in Silver Street, Mrs Mountjoy, was a client of Forman's, and the astrologer himself left accounts of attending Shakespeare's plays at the original Globe Theatre. Forman was a physician and astrologer, and had an enormous practice, advising clients from every stratum of society, including wealthy merchants, sea-captains, the gentry, and ordinary folk. Among his clients were the Countess of Essex and Emilia Lanier, who has been claimed as the Dark Lady of Shakespeare's sonnets.

Looking at his case books, one realizes that very little has changed since he practised from his house on the Strand in London: in his notebooks he jots down questions he was asked – enquiries about missing pets and stolen goods, about the faithfulness of wives and mistresses, whether a woman will become pregnant or her husband hanged for stealing.

William Shakespeare's plays contain many references to the interplay of astrology, fate, and free will.

Forman also used astrology for his own ends, notably, drawing up his clients' charts to discover when they might be susceptible to seduction. Either he had the charm of a Casanova (for his face was against him), or he was very accurate. He was a sensualist, and the female client who remained unseduced was a rare creature indeed.

THE 17TH TO 19TH CENTURIES

Despite the popularity of almanacs, which set out various charts and data relating to the movement of planets and other astronomical events, the scholarly reputation of astrology was low in the early 18th century. By the end of that century, however, it had reasserted its professional standing, as it developed among academic circles in Britain and the USA.

William Lilly's *The Starry Messenger* interprets the strange apparition of the three Suns which were seen in London in 1644.

War, Sex, and New Planets

Popular astrology received an enormous boost when, after the invention of moveable type, printed books began to circulate widely. Astrological almanacs were among the earliest books to be printed – the first was issued in Gutenberg, Germany, in 1448, eight years before the famous *Gutenberg Bible*.

By the beginning of the 18th century almanacs were affordable and extremely popular – almost everyone who could afford to had one, from King Charles I to mariners such as Lieutenant John Wheale (who took "a bottle of ink, a sheet almanac, and a pocket almanac" on his voyages).

The first man to flood England with his almanacs was William Lilly (1602–81), who wrote the first astrological textbook to be published in English, his lengthy *Christian Astrology* (1647).

This had an incalculable effect on the study of astrology in England. For well over a century, people taught themselves astrology from this book, which instructed them to be, in Lilly's words: "humane, courteous, familiar to all, easy of judgement; afflict not the miserable with terror of a harsh judgement; direct such to call on God, to divert his judgements impending over them … let no worldly wealth procure an erroneous judgement from thee, or such as may dishonour the art."

Isaac Newton argued with Edmund Halley about the merits of astrology, declaring that, whereas he had studied the subject, Halley had not.

A FIGHT FOR SURVIVAL

During the English Civil War (1642–51), astrologers took sides, producing almanacs in which victory was firmly predicted for each side as the troops went into battle. Private consultation thrived, as it has always done at times of trouble, with mothers enquiring about the prospects for survival of their conscripted sons and husbands.

The greatest of English scientists, Isaac Newton (1632–1727) clung, albeit reluctantly, to a belief in astrology until his death, and was allegedly very short with the astronomer Edmund Halley when the latter rebuked him for believing in such nonsense. Nevertheless, by the early 1700s astrology was at a low ebb – at least as far as serious speculation went.

In mainland Europe, meanwhile, the great age of the encyclopaedia began, and the classic *Encyclopédie*, edited by Diderot and D'Alembert and published in 1751, gave a great deal of not unsympathetic space to astrology. The first edition of *Encyclopaedia Brittanica*, which appeared 20 years later,

During the English Civil War astrologers drew sides like everyone else, with some finding auspicious signs for Cromwell's republicans, and some finding hopeful indications for the royalist cause.

frankly dismissed it as, "a conjectural science [which] has long ago become a just subject of contempt and ridicule." While this was not entirely true – scholars at some universities still insisted astrology was worth serious study – the French Revolution and the Napoleonic Wars did not attract much attention from astrologers – though, naturally enough, some studies were published of Napoleon Bonaparte's birth chart.

By the 1790s, England had enough professional astrologers – many self-taught, using Lilly's textbook – to publish *The Astrologer's Magazine*. This trade magazine was devoted to "a science which was studied by the patriarchs of the first ages, but which, by the craft and ignorance of pretenders, has been exposed to much calumny and error."

Virtually no serious research has been done into the history of astrology in Europe after the beginning of the Age of Enlightenment; but in England it is true to say that from about 1780 onwards the subject began slowly to climb back towards, if not respectability, then at least a firm place in society. This status was seriously rocked in 1824, however, when a Parliamentary Act was passed in Britain, condemning anyone "pretending or professing to tell fortunes … to deceive and impose on any of His Majesty's subjects". It was a net wide enough to catch a large number of not only charlatans but also respectable astrologers too.

ASTROLOGY IN THE USA

In America, the situation was similar. Charles Morton, Presbyterian minister at Charlestown, Massachusetts, had his *Compendium physicae* accepted at Harvard, where it formed the basis of the study of modern science. It shied away from popular fortune-telling, but insisted on a connection between the movements of the planets and human physical and mental health.

Other Harvard men declared an interest: Isaac Greenwood, the first Hollis Professor of Mathematics and Natural Philosophy, published a discourse in which he insisted that an "astrologer has a philosophical foundation, and we know not how many wonders and mysteries may be the genuine effects of this great alternative in nature." Yale was not far behind, and the American Reverend Doctor Samuel Johnson examined "the starry heavens and their power and influences." Meanwhile, it was asserted that every household in America except the poorest contained two books: the Holy Bible and the current astrological almanac. Farmers found the latter particularly useful – one argued that "for the better success in letting blood, taking physick, cutting of cattle, sheep and hogs, it is necessary to know where, or in what part of the body, the sign is." Another claimed that horses should be gelded "in the wain of the Moon, the signs being either Virgo or Aries."

A celestial globe of the late 18th century

ASTROLOGY IN EUROPE

Astrology in America was broadly imitative of astrology in Europe – though there were consultant astrologers throughout the 19th century, it was profit from the publication of almanacs that kept them solvent – and they continued to sell in enormous quantities. In mid-19th-century Britain, it was complained that practically no one in "the lower classes" was without an almanac, and most lived their lives by it, refusing to cut their grass if rain was predicted, and declining to dose their cattle if the day was inauspicious.

The two most popular publishers of almanacs in the 19th century were Robert Cross Smith and Richard James Morrison, both born in 1795. Smith worked under the pseudonym of Raphael, and made it famous by his predictions on love and marriage, finance, business, and travel. In his *The Straggling Astrologer*, he published the earliest weekly predictions to be made in a magazine.

Meanwhile Morrison, calling himself Zadkiel, took the high ground, advising his readers never to consult astrologers who charged only five shillings

ASTROLOGY FOR WOMEN

Apart from publishing lists of fortunate or unfortunate days, astrologers such as Sarah Jinner gave advice on a great range of human activities – including sex. Her fellow women astrologers offered their advice freely: "a lusty squab fat bedfellow very good physic in January" advised Dorothy Partridge, while it was generally agreed that the ideal time "to be as a husband to thy wife" was when the Moon was in Sagittarius. *The Ladies' Diary* (1704), an annual almanac, was especially popular – rather like one of today's women's magazines, it included recipes, essays on virtue and the nature of love, as well as astrological advice. By the 1750s it was selling 30,000 copies a year.

The discovery of Neptune and other "new planets" has not undermined astrology; instead these planets have been used to revise many horoscopes of the past.

for a consultation, when "no man of education would stoop to receive such beggarly remuneration." His magazine, *Zadkiel's Almanac*, received an enormous boost when in the issue for 1861 he suggested that anyone born on or near 26 August would fall under a very serious effect from Saturn. Later that year Prince Albert, the Prince Consort, died of typhoid. He had been born on 26 August.

MASS PRODUCTION

If any person can be singled out as being the one most responsible for the resurgence of astrology in the late 19th and early 20th century, it was W. F. Allen (1860–1917), who called himself Alan Leo. He joined Madame Blavatsky's Theosophical Society in London, became a professional astrologer, and set up a sort of factory in which he employed other astrologers to calculate charts, and clerks to write out his opinions on them; his Modern Astrology Publishing Company soon had branches in Paris and New York.

It was Leo's chief clerk who devised the simple system which made the firm's fortune: separate sheets of paper, each summarizing the effect of a particular aspect of a birth chart, were simply stapled together and sent out without the slightest attempt to synthesize the information. This method is still employed today by the less reputable and cheaper computer horoscope firms.

MODERN PLANETS

One of the problems facing Raphael, Zadkiel, and their contemporaries was the scientific reaction to the discovery of the so-called "modern" planets: Uranus (discovered in 1781) and Neptune (1846); Pluto was added later in 1930.

The anti-astrological camp latched onto this as proof that astrology was nonsense. Astrologers asserted that rather than creating new problems, the discoveries solved old ones. All over Europe astrologers reconsidered the birth charts of historical figures – Frederick the Great, Marie Antoinette, Catherine of Russia – and found that time and again the "new" planets, placed in the old charts, revealed elements of their subjects' personalities previously unaccounted for by the traditional planets. All that was necessary was a few years of empirical study to work out the particular influences of the "new" planets. It was determined, for example, that Uranus has a positive effect on originality and versatility, but also leads to a concern with sexual excess and possibly deviation. And it is agreed that Neptune concerns itself with the arts, particularly poetry and dancing, and encourages imagination and sensitivity. Many gaps in old birth charts, it was said, could now be filled. Astrology had no more been destroyed by the discovery of the "new" planets than Harvey's discovery of the circulation of the blood had devalued what had previously been known about the bodily processes; both discoveries had simply enlarged existing knowledge.

THE 20TH CENTURY

During the first half of the 20th century, astrology made its way from specialist magazines into the daily newspapers. The widespread consumption of horoscopes did not, however, diminish interest in the subject from various reputable philosophers, politicians, and scientists, and much influential research was carried out in the late 20th century.

Carl Gustav Jung
incorporated astrology
into the process of
his pioneering
psychoanalytical work.

The Age of Popular Astrology

The avidly read horoscope columns in newspapers and magazines, with their emphasis on the Sun signs, were the invention of the English astrologer R. H. Naylor. In 1930, he wrote an article about astrology for the *Sunday Express*, in which he appeared to foretell the crash of the airship R-101. This was considered so remarkable that he was invited to write a weekly column. To involve all his readers, he wrote about the 12 zodiac signs, for almost everyone knew their Sun sign. Within a few years, no popular paper or magazine could afford to be without its astrologer, and Naylor had single-handedly invented Sun-sign astrology.

The airship R-101 crashed in Beauvais, France in 1930. It was an event predicted by R. H. Naylor.

At the same time, there was a swing back from almost total scorn for astrology to a serious, speculative interest in the subject among educated people. The psychiatrist Carl Gustav Jung (1875–1961) published claims that zodiac types could be seen as archetypes of the human personality, displaying all its potentialities. The zodiac signs, he suggested, have a deeper significance than we know, and humans are conscious of them as archetypes when stirred by highly emotional circumstances, such as those that prompt people to consult astrologers.

JUNG'S STUDIES

In his clinical practice, Jung used the horoscope as a starting point from which to build a bridge of understanding between himself and his patients. He looked for common ground between his patients' birth charts and his own. Jung also interested himself in what he called *synchronicity*, or meaningful patterns of events. These, he believed, could be predicted, and often seemed to correlate with planetary movements.

As part of his research into astrology, Jung studied the birth charts of 483 married couples – 966 charts in all – not only in their original pairings but also in chance couplings. Altogether, 32,220 pairings were postulated and examined. He found that in the twinned

The German Kaiser's astrological chart was unfavourably assessed by Alan Leo during World War I.

charts of happily coupled people there was a statistically significant presence of the aspects, traditionally indicative of a satisfactory relationship. Jung's public standing did much to convince those naturally sympathetic to the subject that it was worth serious study and, in France and Switzerland in particular, such studies began.

PERSONAL COUNSELLING

Meanwhile, a renewal of interest was triggered in Europe and America by the founder of the Theosophical Society, Helena Petrovna Blavatsky (1831–91), and her American colleague Colonel Henry Steele Olcott (1832–1907). Soon consultant

astrologers began to use the language of psychology, and to turn away from *prediction* and towards encouraging clients to reach self-fulfillment by advising them how to make their lives fuller and more satisfying. The language of *the future* gave way to the language of character analysis and counselling. By the end of the century, all reputable astrological teaching bodies included courses in counselling as part of their training.

WORLD WAR I AND THE INTERWAR YEARS

During World War I, British and German astrologers took part in their own way and for their own sides. Alan Leo examined the horoscopes of King George V and the German Kaiser: not surprisingly, he found the first "magnanimous" and "peaceful"; the second "extremely unfortunate".

Between the wars, astrology was taken seriously in Germany. Herbert Freiherr von Kloeckler (1896–1950) pioneered astroanalysis as an aid to psychological analysis, while actor Karl Brandler-Pracht founded the German Astrological Society and started the *Astrologische Rundschau*, the most prominent astrological journal in Europe at the time. During the 1920s and 30s, no fewer than 400 specialist books and pamphlets on the subject were published in Germany.

Though the Nazi Party was initially drawn to astrology, in 1934 it banned all "fortune-telling" and made the publication of almanacs and astrological journals illegal. The German Astrological Society managed to survive, integrating with the establishment and giving some protection to astrologers.

THE THIRD REICH

There were some notable, high-ranking members of the Nazi Party who were enthusiasts of astrology, however.

Hess, Himmler, and to some extent Goebbels, were among them, and for a time Karl Ernst Krafft (who had correctly foretold an attempt on Hitler's life in 1939) was in high favour. Though the Führer himself remained uninterested in the subject, when war broke out Krafft was summoned to Berlin by Goebbels to translate the prophesies of Nostradamus and demonstrate that it was Germany's fate to conquer the world. Astrology was used as black propaganda by the British as well, and Churchill co-opted the part-German astrologer Louis de Wohl.

Nostrodamus' prophesies were used by Goebbels and Krafft to justify Germany's aggression.

Krafft, along with all German astrologers, was caught up in the panic that ensued when, in May 1941, Hitler's deputy Rudolf Hess flew to Scotland in an independent attempt to make peace with Britain. Hitler, who had always mistrusted

Himmler (to the left of Hitler) was one of several high-ranking Nazis who made use of astrology.

astrologers, immediately announced that Hess had been "crazed by astrology", and the Gestapo arrested a number of practitioners. Included among them was Wilhelm Wulff, who had been released from a concentration camp to work for Himmler as his private astrologer. Wulff survived the war, but Krafft died in 1944 in a train taking him to the concentration camp at Buchenwald.

A BURGEONING SCENE IN THE WEST

In America, there was the same blend of popular and serious astrology as in Europe. Evangeline Adams was a vastly fashionable astrologer in the 1920s, with syndicated columns and radio programmes, but in 1914 she had been prosecuted for "fortune-telling". The judge in the trial gave her an anonymous horoscope to interpret. Having done this, she was told by the judge that the chart was that of his son and that her interpretation had been spectacularly successful. He announced to the court that Ms Adams had "raised astrology to the dignity of an exact science", and so dismissed the case.

During the 1960s and 1970s popular interest in astrology ran rampant in the Western world: "What's your sign?" became a common question from stranger to stranger, and the most popular astrological journalists became millionaires, their columns syndicated through hundreds of newspapers and magazines. In 1960, a university student called Marcia Moore had no difficulty in finding 900 professional astrologers in Britain and America to question for a thesis, while in 1969 a journalist estimated that over 10,000 Americans were making a living from astrology. But more serious work

Evangeline Adams was a fashionable and widely popular astrologer in the 1920s.

continued, astrologers such as the American Dane Rudhyar and the English John Addey researching quietly, their work published only in specialist journals and books, the titles of which were familiar only to their peers. Addey's work on what he termed "the harmonics of cosmic periods" is among the most important of the second half of the last century.

ASSESSING THE FACTS

Contributing to the debate on the validity of astrology was Frenchman Michel Gauquelin, who, assisted by his wife Françoise, statistically tested several astrological propositions, using thousands of birth charts. He asserted that successful sportsmen tended to be born when Mars was dominant, while actors were born under a similar influence of Jupiter, and scientists and doctors under Saturn. Gauquelin's statistics were re-tested and approved by the scientist Hans Eysenck.

Meanwhile, many teaching bodies were established in Europe and America, tutoring students not only in basic astrology – the setting up and interpretation of charts – but also in specialist areas of the subject. The English Astrological Association and the American and Australian astrological federations hold regular conferences and publish papers and learned journals (such as the British *Correlation*). Courses in various aspects of astrology proliferate, as does a wide range of study. The American Robert Hand has intensely researched ancient astrological texts, for example, and

there has been renewed interest in many traditional tools of the astrologer – such as horary astrology (*see p294*). The Australian Bernadette Brady has renewed interest in the influences of the fixed stars, while others have explored the astrological significance of newly discovered stellar objects, devising new theories along the way. At Bath Spa University College in England it has even become possible to take a Master of Arts course in cultural astronomy and astrology.

It can scarcely be claimed that astrology has been returned to academic respectability. Yet the conviction that mankind has not yet discovered all the mysteries of the known universe continues to convince a growing number of people that it would be unwise to consign astrology to the dustbin of the cosmos.

THE REAGANS AND ASTROLOGY

As the Governor of California, Ronald Reagan signed a legislation legalizing the practice of astrology in the state. When he became the president in 1981, the astrologer Joan Quigley advised him (through his wife Nancy) on the timing of presidential travel and on his personal health. Furthermore, on Joan's advice, the successful US–Soviet treaty eliminating intermediate-range nuclear missiles was signed at precisely 1:30 pm on 8 December, 1987. Reagan himself wrote to the *Los Angeles Times'* astrologer Sydney Omarr, saying: "By promoting a greater understanding and appreciation of astrology you further the cause of science and inspire all stargazers to new levels of insight, discovery, and exploration."

Ronald and Nancy Reagan

The Twelve
SIGNS OF
THE ZODIAC

masculina. Orientalia.
Taurus.
Gemini.
Cancer.
Leo.
Virgo.
Libra
Julius.
Augustus.
September
Gemini
Aquarius.
libra. sunt calida et
humida masculina
sanguinea. meridionalia.

The TWELVE SIGNS OF THE ZODIAC

The zodiac's signs – Aries, Taurus, Gemini, and so on – derive from 12 of the many constellations. These 12 are unevenly spaced but give their names to 30° sections along the ecliptic – the imaginary path around the Earth through which the Sun appears to move. In the course of a year, the Sun passes in front of each of these sections in turn.

The origin of the association between the 12 "constellations" and animals and human heroes is obscure. However, we do know that the stars themselves were once regarded as living beings. The Greek philosopher Aristotle (384–322BCE), for example, believed this, while the first person to record it as a fact seems to have been Origen, the head of the Christian school of Alexandria, in about 200CE. So naturally, creatures such as the Lion, the Bull, and the heavenly Twins, which were assigned to the constellations, were also considered to have life and human characteristics too. In different countries these zodiacal creatures had different names – the Greek Tauros (the Bull), for example, was Tora in Iranian, Vrisha in Sanskrit, and Gud.an.na in Babylonian; similarly Scorpios in Greek was Gazdum, Vrischika, and Gir.tab.

The signs of the zodiac in this 15th-century illustration are not only shown in relation to their placing in the calendar, but also shown in respect of parts of the body – Aries being the sign of the head, for example, and Taurus being the sign of the neck.

For astrologers of both the ancient world and the modern, the constellations and their respective creatures exert an influence, somewhat mystically, over those born when the Sun was "in" their sign.

KNOWING YOUR SIGN

When someone asks, "what sign are you?", it is extremely likely that you will answer by telling them the Sun sign at the time of your birth. The fact that the Sun is said to be "in" a sign at any particular time does not mean that there is any real connection between the Sun and the constellations of Leo, Gemini, Pisces, and the rest. Rather it simply means that the Sun was in a position between the Earth and the section of the ecliptic named after its constellation.

The Sun sign is the astrological sign that we tend to most readily identify as ours, and almost everyone who picks up an astrology book automatically turns first to the Sun sign pages. A considerable number of the assertions the writer makes about the general characteristics of a Leo or a Virgo "the inward you" – the "you" only those closest to you would recognize.

The enormous publicity which Sun signs have received in the past 70 years or so seems to have thrown this rather out of kilter. Many people now know so much about their Sun sign that they unconsciously behave in the way the descriptions suggest, and the Sun sign now seems more accurately to portray the "you" people experience when they first meet you, while the Rising sign represents the "you" known by your parents or your lover. Experienced astrologers know how to make allowances for this ambivalence.

An 18th-century star chart with beasts and gods which lend traits, characteristics, and a living quality to the 12 constellations of the zodiac.

seem to be true; others do not. As the Earth revolves, so the 12 constellations on which the zodiac is based rise over the eastern horizon once a day, just like the Sun. The sign crossing the eastern horizon at the time of birth is known as the Rising sign, or Ascendant. Until about 80 years ago the Rising sign was considered probably the most important element of the birth chart, and was said to denote "the outward you" – the "you" recognized by the world. The Sun sign denoted

RISING & MOON SIGNS

What must be recognized is the part the Rising sign plays in portraying the whole individual. If you happened to be born at sunrise, then your Sun and Rising signs will be the same, and you will be instantly recognizable as a Sagittarian or a Libran. However, the position of the Sun at the time of birth is only one of many factors in the full horoscope or birth chart. We are all a subtle combination of all 12 signs, stressed in different ways, and overlaid by other important factors that combine to make our horoscope individual to us.

BORN ON THE CUSP

If you were born on a day when the Sun changes signs, do not suppose that you have the qualities of two Sun signs. Your sign will be one or the other, depending on the time of day when the Sun moves from one sign to the next (an ephemeris will give a precise time). If, reading the descriptions of both signs, you think, "yes, I'm just like that", it is probably because of the influence of Venus and/or Mercury, which can very often be in the sign immediately before or after your Sun sign. So if your sign is, say, Cancer, but you recognize the influence of Gemini or Leo, it may be because Venus or Mercury was in Gemini or Leo when you were born.

A Copernican depiction of the universe from 1708, using a heliocentric (Sun-centred) system.

As the Earth turns on its axis, a different degree of the zodiac rises and culminates roughly every three minutes. Therefore, for two individuals to have identical birth charts or horoscopes, they would have to have been born within three minutes of each other and in the same location. It can happen, but is very uncommon.

The sign the Moon occupies at birth is extremely important too. Traditionally, the characteristics shown by the Moon sign are those you have inherited from your parents, but the Moon sign also shows the way in which you instinctively react to situations in life. The appearance of all the planets in individual signs is significant and must be considered, but most astrologers would agree that these three basics – Sun sign, Rising sign, and Moon sign – are the most important when first looking at a birth chart.

Your Sun, Rising, and Moon signs can be found in an ephemeris – a book of astronomical tables (which is also used by mariners). These can be ordered from booksellers, but at the end of this book, you will find our own simple charts that are sufficiently accurate for anyone who wants to start discovering the mysteries of the full birth chart.

CATEGORIZATIONS

Finally, the signs fall into traditional categories that originated in the distant past. In a horoscope there are different emphases on the categories, and these form the beginnings of interpretation.

Among other traditional groupings, each sign is assigned an element, or triplicity. (The placing of the elements is summarized in our chart, above.) The theory attributing characteristics such as dry, hot, cold, and wet to elements was much used in medical astrology, and extended to the planets. Jupiter, Venus, and the Moon were said to be

THE ELEMENTS

The elements are fire, earth, air, and water, each operating through a different quality (or quadruplicity) three times to make up the 12 divisions of the zodiac. So each element has three signs attached to it: one cardinal (the realm of instigators), one fixed (indicating steadiness and determination) and one mutable (which implies an adaptable and flexible attitude). Of the elements, fire is said to be "hot and dry", earth "cold and dry", air "hot and humid", and water "cold and humid".

Element	Cardinal	Fixed	Mutable
Fire	Aries	Leo	Sagittarius
Earth	Taurus	Virgo	Capricorn
Air	Gemini	Libra	Aquarius
Water	Cancer	Scorpio	Pisces

"hot and moist", Saturn "excessively cold", and Mars "excessively dry". Fixed signs are said to be resourceful and persistent, but resistant to change; cardinal signs initiators of action and leaders; mutable signs are changeable, adaptable, and sometimes unstable.

Signs were also ascribed masculine and feminine qualities: traditionally, the signs in alternate order, starting with Aries and ending with Aquarius, are masculine, the others feminine. Ancient texts take these divisions of the signs much further – in the writings of the Greek astronomer and astrologer Ptolemy (c100–c178), for instance, we find Aries, Taurus, Leo, and Sagittarius described as "bestial"; Cancer, Scorpio, and Pisces as "fruitful"; and Gemini, Sagittarius, and Pisces as "common".

In astrology, there is also a very special and subtle relationship between each sign and its polar sign – that is, the one on the opposite side of the zodiac. It is a concept that derives from Aristotle's theory of the principles which ruled all matter – in this case, the principle of interacting opposites.

Ptolemy, the famous Greek astrologer of the 2nd century.

*"The Ram will ever cherish hopes; he will rise
from the sudden shipwreck of his affairs
to abundant wealth."*

Manilius, 1st century

Aries

The pioneering desire for personal achievement that is the hallmark of the Aries character is simple and straightforward – but they can often be accused of selfishness when ambition vies with home and family life. Patience is not a strong point, but lively and warm enthusiasm are the sign's endearing qualities.

ARIES AS A SUN SIGN

The Sun enters Aries, the first sign of the zodiac, on 21 March – spring equinox in the Northern hemisphere. This is the first day of the astrological year. Aries is the pioneer of the zodiac, and people who are born during the period when the Sun is in Aries certainly like to express an independent spirit.

Those who have Aries as their Sun sign have considerable resources of determination, but in their enthusiasm will often tend to rush into challenging situations regardless of possible problems. There is a strong need for achievement. If this is not attained, serious frustration will occur, sometimes leading to negative psychological or physical symptoms.

The worst Aries fault is selfishness, which is often due to a need to be out there, winning. "Me First," has long been an Aries motto! Lack of awareness of the need to achieve is often the root cause of selfishness. When confronted with this by, say, a parent or friend, the reaction is often one of disbelief. It is important that awareness of this negative trait is developed, so that it can be countered.

The traditional cardinal quality means that the individual is basically outgoing, ready to spring into action and to give encouragement as and

The illustration for April from the *Très Riches Heures du Duc de Berry* (1416), with the sign of the Ram shown in the astrological chart at the top of the image.

The Aries Ram, as depicted on the calendar page for April from the *Bedford Hours*, an illuminated manuscript produced in France in around 1423.

ARIES	
Symbol	The Ram
Sun Sign Dates	21 March–20 April
Ruling Planet	Mars
Element or Triplicity	Fire
Quality or Quadruplicity	Cardinal
Positive/Negative	Positive
Body Area	Head
Polar Sign	Libra

when needed. This combines extremely well with Aries' identity as one of the positive signs, which in many respects adds a psychologically strong, extrovert quality, doing much to propel these live wires of the zodiac towards the goal they most desire – the winning post.

The sign's symbol, the Ram, relates well to the characteristics of its denizens, and we think of the ram battling head to head with rivals. It is interesting, however, that as well as the positive, exuberant, and extrovert members of the sign, we do have a fair number of much quieter Ariens. In recent years, there has been discussion among astrologers of the typical Aries Ram contrasting with an Aries Ewe. The latter is much less likely to make a strong impact, but beneath a quiet exterior there is determination. They know what they want to achieve, but do not make such a song and dance about it as their more extrovert "cousins". Here, for instance, will be the young mother, having plenty of good ideas on nurturing her children, coping well with the heavy schedule of motherhood, and perhaps holding down a job as well.

Aries is depicted in a Turkish illuminated manuscript of 1550.

A Picture of Health

In terms of physical make-up, Aries Sun-sign types tend to be strong and healthy. By tradition, their body area is the head. Ask Ariens if they get headaches and they will either say they never get any or that they really suffer. When young they will often tumble from climbing frames and trees, and hit their heads much more than is common with those of other Sun signs.

It is important that Ariens take plenty of exercise, and many are very keen and active participants in a wide variety of sports. Heavy team games such as soccer and rugby attract Ariens, and Eastern martial arts are also popular for this Sun-sign type.

ARIES AS ASCENDANT

Many of the characteristics interpreted above will be present, but will be expressed rather differently when Aries is the Ascendant. The determination to win will again be extremely important, and physical and emotional energy will be exerted to this end – rather more so than with a Sun-sign Aries.

The direction the determination takes will rely on the individual's Sun sign and other areas of the birth chart. Restlessness may occur, but, if there is competition in the chosen direction, that will act as a great incentive to push forward and to succeed. In families where there is a child with an Aries Ascendant, these characteristics will emerge at a very early age, especially in competition with siblings. This instinctive "pushiness" can be lessened by encouraging Aries to care for and love other family members and pets.

The Social Environment

Ascendant Ariens can easily adapt to any kind of environment and social circumstance. There is a toughness which contributes to a natural resilience. There is also a strong tendency to be extremely high-key, not in a tense and nervous way, but in a more blustering and forceful way that can be exhausting for other people. It is excellent for Ariens to learn to be calmer and a little more philosophical, because in doing so they will express their natural powerful ability for self-analysis, without becoming too introspective.

Developing psychological balance in their lives is all-important if a tendency to go to extremes of action, and indeed inaction, is to be resisted.

In terms of health, the traditional vulnerabilities listed under the Sun sign are even more relevant. The possibility of headaches can be rooted in slight kidney disorders, and, as there is a tendency to have a somewhat slap-happy, devil-may-care attitude, there is a considerably increased vulnerability to being accident-prone.

ARIES AS MOON SIGN

The Moon in this sign gives the individual an extremely emotional and very quick response to all situations. Particularly in an emergency, a Moon-sign Arien will take charge and actually do something. When others are getting stressed out, and when action is called for (during boring meetings when decisions have to be made, for instance), here is someone who will take control and "cut to the chase". This quality also comes into its own on a personal level, when the individual is in a tight corner and has to make a snap decision.

The emotional content of the Moon in Aries is very high and needs positive expression through daily life, career, and sexuality. However, care is necessary that impulsiveness and an over-quick temper do not mar these very assertive and forthright responses.

The Moon-in-Aries type also has a liking for danger, and extreme sports are particularly attractive. The Aries' need for independence is important, especially in the young.

There are cases when, due to the influence of other planets on the Moon, these qualities are suppressed. It will be obvious from the individual's reactions and responses to situations if this is so. If it is, they should avoid bottling up problems and make an effort to live a lifestyle that is satisfying and right for them – even if it means making drastic changes or decisions concerning other people.

Charlie Chaplin demonstrated Arien determination and, as a performer, revelled in the inherent comedy of mishaps through slapstick humour.

Aries in Friendship, Love, and Permanent Relationships

The great thing about having Aries friends is that, basically, they are really cheerful types. They will encourage us all the way in our interests and our love life, and will make us get moving when, for one reason or another, we find ourselves procrastinating.

Remember, like members of some other signs, Ariens want everything here and now – and they want the same for their friends too. They are hugely encouraging, but tend to lose patience if a required response is not forthcoming.

A Simple Plan

When we have a problem that we cannot resolve, a wonderful Aries quality emerges in our friends – whether the Aries influence is from the Sun, the Moon, or the Ascendant. These people have the happy knack of simplifying even the most complicated

The Aries Ram appears in this mid-13th-century illuminated manuscript from Italy.

situation. They are adroit at coming up with a practical resolution in a matter of moments, and are able to do so without recourse to lengthy speeches.

It is worth remembering that while, on the whole, Ariens likes to do things on the spur of the moment, it is very often necessary to plan some events well in advance. Initially an Aries friend will gladly accept an impromptu invitation – yes, they will come, and look forward to it. However, we cannot totally escape from Aries selfishness, and nearer the proposed date we are all too likely to get word from them profoundly apologizing that they cannot make it. Their mother is sick, they have to work dreadfully late, and so on. Their story will be really convincing, and we will believe them; but, the more we get to know our Aries friends, the clearer it will become that, in such cases, they have simply had a better offer. They can be very tactful about this, but in the end they are transparent – especially if Aries is the Rising sign. It is here that the subtle influence of Libra – the polar, or opposite, sign across the zodiac – comes into play. Libra is all tact and diplomacy, and will tell untruths so as not to directly upset other people.

Overall, however, our Aries friends are fun, and we always have a good time when with them. Even if their interests are different from ours, their enthusiasm is in itself very infectious.

ARIES IN LOVE

Aries people are impatient, and will not be best pleased if their advances get insufficient encouragement, or, possibly even worse, a very slow, hesitant response. It is of above average importance to them to know how they stand – being "messed about" by indecisive types is anathema, and they will pretty quickly say goodbye.

With this in mind, Ariens do need to realize that, while someone may respond immediately to their attractive personality, the response to a romantic or even downright sexy approach is not necessarily immediate. If they do not show some patience, they may well miss out on a good relationship – whether it lasts but a few weeks or becomes something more long term.

To encourage a new lover, or someone who is being wooed, Ariens will very often ply him or her with little gifts. Thoughtfulness is not lacking, and neither is the variety of ways in which they will make life enjoyable for their lovers. Their enthusiasm for sex is abundant, and they need partners who respond to their exuberant approach. Someone who is sexually inhibited will not be tolerated for very long. Sexual compatability from an early stage is essential in a relationship, but here again the development of a certain amount of patience could be worthwhile.

ARIES FALLS IN LOVE

Aries falls in love very quickly and very often falls out of love with similar haste. These are among the most ardent and passionate lovers in the whole zodiac. Both men and women of the sign are, on the whole, highly sexed, and take sheer pleasure and enjoyment in the whole process – from the chase to the bedroom (or back seat of the car). They enjoy romps with their partner from youth through middle age and onward – indeed, if this is not possible both they and their partners will suffer.

Venus, the goddess of love, flanked by the Ram of Aries and the Scales of its polar sign, Libra.

Too Much Haste

It is also important that Ariens take on board the fact that many partners particularly enjoy foreplay as a sensual prelude to the sexual act. In their haste and natural exuberance, Ariens may be unconcerned with this kind of pacing. Developing a somewhat more gradual, romantic approach and technique is really very advisable.

All these indications will certainly not fade as Aries lovers grow older, when we can expect the same lively approach and enthusiasm for a sexual romp. Whether the actual performance will be as satisfying for both partners concerned is, of course, a moot point.

ARIES IN PERMANENT RELATIONSHIPS

Here we still see the same enthusiasm and exuberance for love and sex, but, once Aries has made a commitment to become a long-term partner and has taken time to be sure that this is what is seriously desired, all kinds of interesting qualities emerge.

They are great home builders, not only from the point of view of adjusting to a changed lifestyle, but also from a practical point of view. They have what it takes to develop all kinds of necessary skills for DIY projects, and, even if there is no serious lack of funds, many Ariens will simply prefer to get busy themselves rather than employ a professional. However, Aries' fiery enthusiasm can fade, so it is important that the partner gives continual nudging if the kitchen cupboard doors are not to remain piled up in the garage because the Arien is tremendously busy elsewhere!

Where long-term relationships can suffer is through Aries' selfishness. This can emerge in different ways.

An example might be that because Aries hobbies or spare-time interests are so engrossing, they lead to the neglect of the partner and his or her interests. Similarly, if their career is very demanding, and work is brought home to do in the evenings or if their job takes them away on frequent business trips, there can be trouble – even if the Arien motivation is to make a better life for the family. In addition, if the sex life is unsatisfactory, it will not be too long before Ariens start looking in other directions. Aries' restlessness can also be a problem, and to counter both this and any expression of selfishness, the development of joint interests with the partner will be an enormously positive step.

Polar Opposites

In permanent relationships, partners quite often respond to each other in the manner of their Rising sign's polar sign. For Aries, this is Libra. It seems almost unbelievable that any Aries would say, "Let's wait and see what happens," but within a close, permanent relationship this will indeed happen. A permanent partner will also bring out Aries' romantic side.

If children are planned, Ariens make excellent and very lively parents, and will shower children with encouragement. They can be a bit too forceful, however, and may not give enough attention to the child's own skills.

"A PERMANENT PARTNER WILL BRING OUT THE ROMANTIC IN ARIENS"

The youngest Aries will be excited and stimulated by the challenge of new toys, paints, and building bricks.

Aries in Education, Jobs, and Money

Giving the youngest Aries a feeling of independence is important. Even if parents are concerned about safety, it is a really good thing to allow the very young members of this sign to do their own thing, if only for a few minutes at a time. The chances are that they will love nursery school, and while their natural exuberance will be likely to make the teacher's life tricky from time to time, the challenge of new toys, paints, and building bricks will be exciting and stimulating for the child; and parents will soon see rapid developments.

This is the calendar page for March from the *Bedford Hours*, an illuminated manuscript made in France in about 1423.

When it comes to full-time day school, it is a good thing to encourage young Ariens to take some of their own toys with them, and if there happens to be a rather shy child in the class it will be advantageous to both of them if the Aries child can encourage the timid one to play with him or her. This will help develop a sense of sharing and rapport, and thereby help to balance any Arien selfishness and determination to win at all costs.

The Growing Rebel

As Aries gets older there will be restlessness, both at school and at home. However, if it is possible to sense the direction in which the child's potential lies, it will not be too difficult for the parents to give full support and backing. It should be remembered that Ariens hate discipline and will soon see through any stupid school rules, so it is essential that the reasons for rules are thoroughly understood. Young Ariens will definitely thrive if given their head; they will make mistakes, like all youngsters, but probably more often than most.

When it is time for further education or training, it can be all too easy for Ariens to change course in mid-stream. If changes are suggested, parents must do everything in their power to point out to their offspring that this will only slow down their progress in life, and that the prospect of their "winning" will recede into the distance. That is sure to be something they will not like.

Aries is the first of the three fire signs. Symbolically, we can say that the Aries fire is strongly charged with emotion, which starts to flare up and crackle at the least provocation. This can be evidenced in warm, lively, and positive enthusiasm. Conversely, however, petty annoyance can turn to fierce anger which, like sudden flames, soon burns out, but without resentment or sulkiness on the part of the individual. When the Aries fire dies on other occasions, it will be because Aries gets bored or feels that what is going on is unsatisfactory. It is their lively sense of immediacy, spurred into positive action, that is so admirable and infectious, and forms an important part of the Aries Sun-sign personality.

A 1920s image of Aries by Joseph Speybrouck shows the Ram placed beside the goddess of love, Venus, who rules Aries' polar sign, Libra.

ARIES AND CAREERS

Obviously one finds Aries Sun-sign people in all professions, but it is all-important that they are able to enjoy the right working atmosphere, that the demands put upon them and the amount of challenge they face stimulate their will to move ever onward and upward in their chosen profession or career. A boring, regular, soon decide which rung of the ladder to tackle next, and a new motivation will then grab their attention.

The Joy of Hustle and Bustle

Aries needs and will enjoy a busy, even noisy, working environment – either a frantic office or an energetic factory floor. Even if the basic work is predictable, Aries will soon become

"ARIES TYPES THRIVE ON COMPETITION"

predictable routine job is definitely not for them – nor will they tolerate an unapproachable, small-minded, or mean boss. A dreary working environment, such as one without good light and access to fresh air will also drive Ariens crazy.

There is no doubt that Aries people are ambitious; but more particularly it is the attainment of that ambition that is so important to them. Once they have achieved their goal, they will say, "okay, I've done that, so what's next?" The chances are that they will

involved in union matters and do everything possible to improve working conditions. They also thrive on competition and relish rivalry between colleagues. If work is arranged in teams, it is likely that the team with an Aries as a member will soon make its way to the front – and put distance between them and their rivals.

Engrossing and worthwhile careers for Aries fall into fairly specific groups. There are enormously successful engineers, including all kinds of jobs involving metal, such as automotive design and manufacture. On the artistic and creative side, we find sculptors and those using metals creatively in other ways. Aries artists tend to use bold techniques and strong brilliant colours.

A Head for Medicine

With the Aries body area being the head, we find there are clusters of Aries (whether this is their Sun, Ascendant, or Moon sign) becoming psychiatrists, psychotherapists, and brain surgeons. The armed forces have their fair share of Ariens too, and indeed any field work. Perhaps work with a charity that sends its staff to far-flung corners of the Earth will have its attractions, as it would chime with the pioneering spirit of the Aries mind. Many Ariens relish working in dirty, difficult, or even dangerous conditions. Becoming a war correspondent could be a possibility – especially if the birth chart also shows a flair for communications.

It is also fair to say that an above average number of Ariens make the grade as professional sports people, because here the desire to be first is paramount. It is, of course, very important to make sensible decisions when considering the long term future, and those Ariens who stay in the profession as trainers and coaches tend to do extremely well.

ARIES AND MONEY

The decision to buy something that is seen as absolutely vital to the Aries lifestyle will be taken in a flash – often to the surprise of astonished partners, who may have learned only a few minutes previously that a new, bigger, and faster car is really essential. Then there is the lawnmower: last weekend Aries was cursing because it did not work, and having tried unsuccessfully to fix it, got angry and kicked it.

Many Ariens find reward in sport, where they may fulfil their desires to be out in front and winning.

So coats on, and off to the showroom or garden centre to spend that money!

All this may well suggest that Ariens have absolutely no sense where cash is concerned, but in fact quite often the situation is very different. It seems that their constant quest to move on, and concomitant loathing for retreat, actually encourages a certain canniness when it comes to finance.

While the typical impulsiveness is never far from the surface, interesting investments will definitely attract Ariens. News of the development of mini-business – which no doubt will build into a plan for financial growth later in life when retirement looms. Retirement? Aries? Never! But a re-scheduling of their lifestyle, maybe. Then, of course, there is the all-consuming hobby to take into account, which could transform into a paying proposition later in life.

We must not forget the influence of the fire element on Aries, which can make gambling appear very attractive. It is usually the case, however, that due to other stabilizing

"IMPULSIVENESS IS NEVER FAR FROM THE SURFACE"

some original product which sounds like a good thing, and one can be sure that Ariens will be right there if there is any spare cash around. Being on the ball can at times pay off handsomely.

Other Sources of Income

The enterprising spirit of Aries is well known and, even if they are earning comfortable salaries, Ariens will very often decide to develop a second source of income. This can take the shape of a

planetary influences a compulsion to gambling can be countered (the Aries spirit responds to them rather more readily than some other zodiac types). Both Sun- and Rising-sign Aries will be more than likely to listen to and take notice of their partners' opinions on financial matters.

In financial matters, Sun- and Rising-sign Ariens are good listeners and will often take advice from their partners.

MIDHEAVEN SIGNS FOR ARIES

The influence of the Midheaven stems from the part of the zodiac that was immediately overhead at our birth – that is, the sign that was at the top of the celestial sphere (*for more detail, see pp304–6*). We relate to, aspire to, and identify with the qualities of the sign on the Midheaven, especially in relation to our careers. The Midheaven signs for Aries birth charts set out below are the only possible combinations of Ascendant and Midheaven signs in both the Northern and Southern hemispheres. To work out your own Ascendant and Midheaven signs at birth, see the charts on pages 344–7.

ASCENDANT ARIES
(WITH ARIES SUN SIGN)
with Midheaven signs:

Capricorn Aries' ambition will be very strong; identification with material progress and the aspiration to be very successful.

Aquarius Independence of Aries will be increased; there is also identification with the unusual and original, and perhaps an inner longing to follow an unusual profession.

ASCENDANT TAURUS
with Midheaven signs:

Capricorn Material security very important, and will strive to become wealthy; likelihood of musical talent.

Aquarius Ambitious; needs security, but independence also very important.

Pisces Identification with humanitarian problems which will motivate action; dislike of sudden changes.

ASCENDANT GEMINI
with Midheaven signs:

Aries Many changes of direction very likely in career.

Taurus Good business sense; particularly suited to working well in team situations.

Aquarius Needs considerable intellectual challenge; identifies with the unusual.

Pisces Will identify with the problems of others; quick to offer help and support.

ASCENDANT CANCER
with Midheaven signs:

Aries Will have great inner strength to devote to chosen profession with determination.

Taurus Will identify with beauty and antiques, and aspire to work in these areas.

Aquarius This combination often makes an enthusiastic and caring teacher.

Pisces An aspiration to help and encourage others – through sport or the arts.

ASCENDANT LEO
with Midheaven signs:

Aries The need to achieve is considerable and ambitions will be met.

Taurus As above but with a more materialistic outlook.

Pisces A sense of drama will colour aspirations; creative, and especially artistic.

ASCENDANT VIRGO
with Midheaven signs:

Taurus Identification with nature, agriculture, horticulture, and conservation.

Gemini Identification with, and talent for, all forms of communication and the media.

ASCENDANT LIBRA
with Midheaven signs:

Cancer Will aspire to the hospitality profession; travel guiding could be an option.

Leo Flair for and love of fashion, the beauty industries, glamour, and modelling.

ASCENDANT SCORPIO
with Midheaven signs:

Cancer Will help and heal others; medical and alternative therapies will be attractive.

Leo Dynamic and ambitious; needs total involvement in chosen career.

Virgo An aptitude for science; ability to research in universities or libraries will be evident.

ASCENDANT SAGITTARIUS
with Midheaven signs:

Leo Above average need to burn intellectual and physical energy in chosen profession.

Virgo An academic combination, with considerable aspirations in higher education.

Libra A philosophical attitude, with varied aspirations; highly ambitious intent.

ASCENDANT CAPRICORN
with Midheaven signs:

Leo The potential (and a possible aspiration) to become a tycoon.

Virgo Need for security in career, but satisfaction from growing things; interest in agriculture.

Libra Needs a dedicated business partner to develop joint interests.

Scorpio A hard worker; will relish difficult conditions in any atmosphere.

ASCENDANT AQUARIUS
with Midheaven signs:

Libra A romantic who may need to conquer a lackadaisical attitude.

Scorpio Determination and identification with important objectives; will succeed.

Sagittarius A natural philosopher, with possibly too many varied objectives.

ASCENDANT PISCES
with Midheaven sign:

Sagittarius Will have idealistic aspirations, but lack patience to fulfill them – good potential.

"*The sons of the Bull have a love of unsung excellence; in their faces dwells the boy-god Love.*"

Manilius, 1st century

Taurus

The steady tick of a reliable clock shows Taureans how to be happy. They need assurance, regularity, and stability. They have great patience and know that short cuts usually spell disaster. Their steadiness can bring material comfort, but they must learn not to regard their lovers as possessions.

TAURUS AS A SUN SIGN

Those who have Taurus, the second sign of the zodiac, as their Sun sign have some remarkably fine qualities. However, for Taureans to flourish, it is essential that they have security. While that may sound like a sweeping generalization (we all need to feel secure to a greater or lesser extent), security is paramount for those of this sign. The necessity does not end with a good house and a healthy bank balance; it is equally important for Taureans to have emotional security within their social relationships and family life.

The illustration for May from the *Très Riches Heures du Duc de Berry* (1416), with the sign of the Bull shown in the astrological chart at the top of the image.

Reliability, steadfastness, and the desire for a predictable routine are characteristic. Taureans like to know how and what must be done, and when. They have a very great deal of common sense, but in a situation where speed and quick responses are required they will not be at all happy. Haste is something that does not come naturally to Taureans, and they will be seriously stressed if pushed into an action which they have not had time to consider really carefully. To a lot of people this zodiac type may seem slow, and the impression they give is indeed to some extent the way they are. They inhabit a familiar and secure rut, are happy in it, and find it difficult to accept when it is time to move on.

The Taurus Bull, as depicted on the calendar page for May from the *Bedford Hours*, an illuminated manuscript produced in France in around 1423.

TAURUS	
Symbol	The Bull
Sun Sign Dates	21 April–21 May
Ruling Planet	Venus
Element or Triplicity	Earth
Quality or Quadruplicity	Fixed
Positive/Negative	Negative
Body Area	Neck and Throat
Polar Sign	Scorpio

Taureans absolutely love possessions. Their natural sense of beauty and identification with beautiful things enhance this love, but take this a stage further and we find the worst Taurus fault, possessiveness, which can cause a great deal of difficulty in relationships and among families.

The sign has the reputation of being the most good-looking of all 12, but Taureans really do need to watch their weight, as chubbiness can easily lead to obesity, especially with their love of chocolate and luscious desserts. Their body area is the neck, and sore throats are often a curse, especially to those who love to sing – and many do sing and perform extremely well.

Like the Bull of their sign, Taureans are calm and placid – until someone or something angers them; then they really let fly, and anyone in the vicinity should watch out!

TAURUS AS ASCENDANT

Reliability and common sense are as strong with Taurus ascending as when it is the Sun sign, but here the need for security is even more powerful. As the individual progresses in life, he or she becomes more and more attracted to possessions. Those with a Taurus Ascendant will make a special effort to get on the property ladder as soon as possible, seeing a house as the ultimate in physical and material security. Because of a love of creature comforts, Taureans will surround themselves with comfortable, heavy furniture on which to relax after a hard day's work. Their home displays obvious evidence of ever-increasing success, and with it greater security. On occasions when it is necessary to step outside their own domain, the Taurean sense of insecurity can become a problem.

The emotional level is higher than when Taurus is the Sun sign, and the temper can become more explosive, slower to subside and less easily subdued. An element of resentfulness can arise, and a kind of smouldering intensity akin to jealousy, especially if a partner is involved.

The vulnerability of the throat is considerably increased when Taurus is rising. Persistent problems may be related to the thyroid gland, which if it is malfunctioning has a direct

"WEIGHT-LIFTING AND BOXING OFTEN APPEAL"

influence on weight gain and lethargy.

Regular exercise is of above average importance. Young people with Taurus rising who are bulky and strong thrive on heavy team games where strength is an asset. Weight-lifting and boxing often appeal, while some will find that steady walking or working-out on machines at their own pace in a pleasant health club will be more acceptable.

The Taurus Bull is shown with a rider in this Turkish illuminated manuscript of 1550.

TAURUS AS MOON SIGN

There is an ancient tradition that says that the Moon in this sign is "exalted" and therefore rather special. It is always a very powerful element of the birth chart, but here it has a subtle added strength. It will bring with it the characteristics of Taurus, but, as must always be remembered, these will be expressed in the way in which the subjects respond to situations. For instance, if we consider possessiveness as an important part of the Taurean personality, those with a Taurus Moon will respond to certain situations in a possessive way. Later on, they may well dislike themselves for doing so, when their own Sun sign, Rising sign, and planetary influences take over and express counter characteristics.

Here, again, a secure background in life is definitely needed, and the individual will respond very defensively if this is threatened. Stubbornness and the tendency to be very conservative in one's opinions is encountered, but flexibility will occur on second thoughts if other

areas of the birth chart show, for instance, a more open mind. If in the full chart there are several other planets in the other "fixed" signs (Leo and Scorpio), the Taurean trait of stubbornness can, on occasion, become bloody-mindedness.

A Safer Option
The Moon in Taurus tends to encourage a conventional outlook. Anything new and untried may have an element of risk associated with it – and these individuals are all for self-preservation, not risk-taking; clinging to the known and well-tried is much safer. Despite other planetary and sign influences, the Taurus Moon will endow patience and a sense of discipline. If individuals are allowed to work at their own rate, which will be modified by the influence of the Ascendant and Sun signs, the end result will be excellent and supported by a real sense of dedication.

The individual will encounter similar health problems as when Taurus is in the Ascendant. Sore throats and the like can be provoked by environmental problems or allergies. It is advisable to control the consumption of chocolate and rich food to avoid weight gain.

Rich foods can be the bane of a Taurean's life.

The best bars and restaurants in town will tend to be the haunt of the Taurean.

Taurus in Friendship, Love, and Permanent Relationships

A Taurus friend is a friend for life. If you arrange to meet a Taurean, he or she will be on time, utterly reliable, and will always ensure they send a message if delayed in any way whatsoever. They are constant and faithful, and, as the Taurean becomes more successful, your joint outings will become more glamorous – but also rather more expensive, because Taurus always knows the best bars and restaurants in town.

This balletic depiction of the **Taurus Bull** comes from Southern Italy and was painted in 1240.

The Perfect Hosts

Although pretty shrewd about money, Taureans are not mean and are usually willing to pay for their less well-off friends. They make wonderful hosts, and entertaining is really high on their list of social accomplishments. They give delightful dinner parties, where the food is rich, delicious, and over-plentiful. I don't think that we have ever attended a Taurus dinner or lunch where, apart from lavish main courses, there weren't at least two, and often three, delicious desserts, usually created by the hosts themselves.

Taureans are good listeners and respect confidences. Any advice they offer will tend to be conventional, encouraging others to keep to the straight and narrow path and to "do the right thing" – which could well be very different from what certain other zodiac types might want to embrace.

Their liking for routine may be a source of trouble if one meets with them regularly and for some good reason the usual pattern is broken. We must tread very carefully when we plan to spend time with other friends –

especially when it is time we usually spend with a Taurean, for their possessive streak will come to the fore, together with a hint of jealousy, even if we are with friends of the same sex.

We will be doing our Taurus friends a service if we encourage them to get involved in new interests. Because they tend to become rather set in their ways, opening them up to new situations, ideas, and challenges is an excellent thing. It is as well to remember that they often have artistic leanings and are very appreciative of most art forms. They can be good at all kinds of carving, and have the patience for fine craftwork, such as embroidery and sewing. They frequently have a musical flair too. Their love of nature often leads them into horticulture. Taking an active part in any of these activities, as opposed to just an appreciative one, is really worthwhile for Taureans.

TAURUS IN LOVE

In many ways, Taureans are at an advantage when it comes to love. First and foremost, they have a great deal of irresistible natural charm, added to which Taurus is generally considered to produce the most handsome and beautiful people. Such traits are not handicaps, of course, when it comes to attracting lovers. Interestingly – as the decades mount up and provided they have avoided gaining weight –

a Taurean's sex appeal and charm will last effectively well into old age. Taureans are truly romantic, and will be more than generous when it comes to special dates. They are wonderful lovers, considerate, and sensual in bed, and one may be sure that the setting will be as luxurious as anyone could wish for – not for Taurus the quick fumble in the back seat of the car!

Taurean Possessiveness

Once the relationship has been established, one can encounter problems with Taurean possessiveness. So, in spite of good living and great sex, care is needed to ensure that the atmosphere does not become claustrophobic. It is important to get the relationship on the right level for both partners, with Taurus's lover explaining the problem quite clearly, so that they can come to terms with the difficulty swiftly – the difficulty often being that Taurus's lover may not want to be exclusively his or hers, 24-hours-a-day. Finding a suitable way round this is essential.

Possessiveness will particularly stem from the fact that Taurus is almost always ready for something really permanent, such as an engagement or even marriage. Partners have to decide whether this is right for them, and whether they are as ready as the Taurus man or woman to settle down. They must also understand that the

TAUREANS ARE STUBBORN

Once the Taurean mind is made up – that is it. This is a fixed sign, and a basic interpretation is that Taureans are people who are fixed in their opinions. Added to this, the sign has a reputation for considerable stubbornness. The influence of the earth element gives Taureans their practical ability and common sense outlook – they are in many ways very down to earth. Interestingly, too, many are dedicated and very talented gardeners. All this is excellent, of course, but it is all too easy for Taureans – especially those who are settled and contented with things as they are – to become very set in their ways and too resistant to change and new experiences.

need for security – a basic instinct in Taureans – develops fast. In spite of their usual ability to take their time over important decisions, Taureans can, on these occasions, jump the gun minds. The women in particular will – even more than most – look forward to their weddings and plan things down to the very last detail. While the sign is one that is financially shrewd, no

"WEDDING BELLS WILL BE GENTLY SOUNDING"

and go in for unsuitable relationships, which in all likelihood will end in tears. In such cases, the need for emotional security has got out of hand. Generally, though, they are good home-makers, and the sooner a Taurean can snuggle down with the right partner the better.

TAURUS IN PERMANENT RELATIONSHIPS

Most Taureans have a conventional side, which will be prominent when they are in the course of forming a permanent relationship. It is very likely that, from the start, wedding bells will be gently sounding in the back of their

expense will be spared when it comes to the big day and the beautiful dress.

However, warning bells may begin to be heard just as the sound of the wedding bells dies away. It is all too common to hear our Taurus friends refer to their partners as though they were possessions, like a car or a house. However loved a partner is, he or she will not like to feel owned, and with some Sun signs it will be anathema. In such cases it is very important that, right from the start, the partner makes it plain to the Taurean that he or she needs a certain amount of independence and freedom.

The Workaholic

Something else that must be considered is likely to be more of a problem with a male Taurean than a female (though a successful businesswomen can fall into the trap too). If he or she becomes overly involved with making money, they may find that they have very little time for anything else. The excuse will be – as in most cases of this sort – that there is a need to make more money to improve the home and standard of living, and eventually to be in a better position to educate any children they may have. With Taureans this can become an obsession, so that there is little space for quality time spent with a partner, and companionship can be seriously lacking.

The Taurean Bull is seen in the upper-left of a manuscript from Lower Saxony, painted in the late 13th century.

Musical ability is a common Taurean trait, and many Taureans become professional singers and musicians.

Taurus in Education, Jobs, and Money

Introducing Taurean children to nursery school may not be a very easy process. It will be most advisable for parents to take the child to visit the school together on a few occasions in order to get the young Taurean thoroughly used to the atmosphere. Any sudden change of location and environment will cause feelings of insecurity, and will probably lead to tantrums and a build up of stress for all concerned. Taking familiar toys to school will help, but the process in most cases is likely to be tricky until the child is thoroughly used to the place and the people in charge.

The calendar page for April from the *Bedford Hours* illuminated manuscript, c1423. Taurus is shown on the right.

A Need for Structure

It is important for parents to remember when deciding about the kind of education they want for their Taurean child that, while they themselves may well be attracted to schools where freedom of expression is allowed and where children are given challenging situations to develop independence, this may not suit the child. The Taurean child may do better with a rather more structured existence, where the school rules form safe boundaries, and they know what has to be done and when. Remember that Taurus needs and thrives on a certain amount of discipline, which in most cases will be understood and accepted. In this kind of atmosphere their child will thrive, given the sense of security which all Taureans need. Parents, then, should think carefully about settling their young Taureans into a school with a conventional, disciplined approach to education.

The Taurean child's potential is considerable, but throughout school, and indeed university years too, parents must remember that sudden progress is less likely than with many children. It is important to give lots of praise when

TAUREANS AND PARENTING

Taurean parents will do as much as possible to bring out the best in their children, and no money will be spared to that end. They need to be aware that they may be a bit too keen on discipline, and fail to allow the child's own individual interests to develop as well as they might. There is also a temptation that they may be rather too eager for the little ones to do well in subjects in which the parent had no opportunity to become involved: the "show business mother" springs to mind. This can cause the child to rebel, simply out of irritation with what he or she is being pushed into.

the child moves up two or three places in class at the end of term. Taurus is a plodder, but remember that, while unglamorous, plodding is the best way to succeed in exams and career. Things learned will stay learned – for life.

As for further education, as ever the scope is wide and the final choice, of course, up to the individual. If there is serious artistic talent, however, the Taurean might consider specializing in pottery, sculpture, architecture, or furniture design. If there is an attraction to a musical instrument, or if the young voice is particularly sweet or strong, such indications may well be the start of something worth nurturing. A music

Gardening is a popular pastime for Taureans, because they have a methodical approach and a keen eye for aesthetics.

college will, in such a circumstance, be something to consider. Agricultural college or business studies are other possibilities. The eventual chosen course will become increasingly engrossing, and young Taureans will stick to it – giving up a subject halfway through a course is less likely with this sign than with many others.

TAURUS AND CAREERS

Taureans are ambitious and will almost always work out a long-term plan for their lives. There can be problems when elements of risk-taking are built into a job, and these will be faced with considerable apprehension; Taureans function best when the work is steady and as constant as possible.

Though money-making is of great importance to this zodiac group, Taureans should think very carefully before taking a new position which is less secure than their present one, even if it pays more. The decision will not be an easy one and should be arrived at through careful consideration. There may be times when it will suit a Taurean to plod on in work that they do not really enjoy, accepting the dreary routine of commuting for the sake of security. For many, such a regime could well be detrimental to themselves and their families, but for other Taureans the monotony can be countered if they have an engrossing spare-time interest. This is especially the case if it takes them into the fresh air – a thriving garden, for instance, will be an ideal escape.

Taureans are extremely good at building their own businesses. They must remember to consider the risk level very carefully from the beginning, but they will work out a detailed business plan, and when the project is under way they will get extraordinary pleasure in seeing it grow slowly and steadily. If marketing or selling is involved, they may need a more extrovert partner – a lively Geminian, perhaps – to see to that side of things.

There are Taureans, of course, in all professions, but some areas of work are particularly well suited. Because Venus is their ruling planet (*see p211*), there is an emphasis on the beauty business, and we find that these zodiac types make wonderful beauticians and will

The Taurean child will happily put the odd pound or dollar into a prized piggy bank, and may be reluctant to spend any of it, going on to badger parents for more cash when some much-desired toy just has to be theirs.

Taureans know exactly where they are going as far as cash is concerned: they get enormous pleasure and contentment from seeing their bank balances and portfolio of shares – however small – gradually thriving and expanding. Starting off with a good high-interest bank account

"TAUREANS ARE GOOD AT BUILDING THEIR OWN BUSINESSES"

also enjoy working in the glamorous atmosphere of department stores. They make excellent horticulturalists, florists, and farmers too. The huge world of finance and banking is an option, and here also are an above average number of town planners, architects, and builders. Many make the grade as professional musicians and singers, while their patience is often expressed in spare-time hobbies such as embroidery and model-making.

TAURUS AND MONEY

When they hear the song lyric, "money makes the world go around", from the musical *Cabaret*, Taureans tend to sing along. The connection between this sign and finance goes way back to the ancient Egyptians, when the Bull was one of their most prominent zodiac signs at a time when cattle were used as currency.

Taureans make wonderful beauticians and will also enjoy working in the glamorous atmosphere of department stores.

(provided, that is, it is consistent with low or moderate risk) will get their financial life going, and they always enjoy investing in interesting companies – shares in a hotel or restaurant business is a high possibility, or perhaps in the construction industry. As a general rule, the bigger and longer-established the company, the more secure Taurus will feel.

Taureans take great pride in watching their investments gradually accrue value. They are clever with money, but enjoy expensive luxuries.

"TAURUS CAN ATTACH TOO MUCH IMPORTANCE TO MAKING MONEY"

An Ideal Home

Home ownership is of prime importance too, but some care is needed here that the temptation to own "the ideal home" does not result in Taureans taking on a much bigger mortgage than is wise. In theory, they will be aware of the danger signals, but the appearance – and more importantly the size – of the chosen house or apartment might turn out to be just too irresistible for them to turn down.

It can happen that Taurus attaches too much importance to making money – in spite of much-needed peace of mind and security. To get a different slant on this, if they realize they can get a great deal of aesthetic satisfaction from beautiful things, they might like to start a collection of, say, small pieces of porcelain, antique wine glasses, maybe copper items, or medals. That way, the Taurean will be simultaneously making an investment that will increase over time, and so contribute to their financial security.

MIDHEAVEN SIGNS FOR TAURUS

The influence of the Midheaven stems from the part of the zodiac that was immediately overhead at our birth – that is, the sign that was at the top of the celestial sphere (*for more detail, see pp304–6*). We relate to, aspire to, and identify with the qualities of the sign on the Midheaven, especially in relation to our careers. The Midheaven signs for Taurus birth charts set out below are the only possible combinations of Ascendant and Midheaven signs in both the Northern and Southern hemispheres. To work out your own Ascendant and Midheaven signs at birth, see the charts on pages 344–7.

ASCENDANT ARIES
with Midheaven signs:

Capricorn Much dedication given to secure a stable and prosperous life.

Aquarius Attraction to unusual occupations likely, but Taurean stubbornness is present.

ASCENDANT TAURUS
(WITH TAURUS SUN SIGN)
with Midheaven signs:

Capricorn Success will come with hard work and dedication; in this combination, a musical talent is very likely.

Aquarius Conflict likely between conventional issues and lifestyle, on the one hand, and attraction to what's trendy, on the other.

Pisces There will be a desire to do good and help those less fortunate; possible attraction to the caring professions.

ASCENDANT GEMINI
with Midheaven signs:

Aquarius Identification with the new and untried; attraction to modern technology or the media; good communicator.

Pisces Artistic ability; love of, and serious attraction to, dance, ice-skating, and poetry.

ASCENDANT CANCER
with Midheaven signs:

Aries An assertive attitude, with a shrewd and clever approach to future prospects.

Aquarius Identification with humanitarian problems; medical profession or charity work are considered likely.

Pisces Willingness to help others; a caring profession, such as nursing, is a possibility.

ASCENDANT LEO
with Midheaven signs:

Aries Very ambitious for desired objectives; possible ruthlessness.

Taurus The Sun and Midheaven are shared signs, so a big achiever likely; stubbornness a less admirable trait though.

ASCENDANT VIRGO
with Midheaven signs:

Taurus As above but a more flexible mind; caution and modesty are the watch-words.

Gemini A superb communicator; ability for media work, especially in magazines.

ASCENDANT LIBRA
with Midheaven signs:

Cancer Identification with luxury trades and good food; working with children; professional chef.

Leo Love of fashion and jewellery; identification with everything dramatic, artistic, and musical.

ASCENDANT SCORPIO
with Midheaven signs:

Cancer Attraction to the medical profession, finance, and the wine trade; emotional involvement in career is essential.

Leo Will aspire to become the boss of whatever chosen profession – especially if it is big business.

Virgo An inner desire to be a researcher, detective, or analyst; success in these professions.

ASCENDANT SAGITTARIUS
with Midheaven signs:

Leo An adventurous spirit with determination and stubbornness; surprisingly daring at times.

Virgo Aspirations to teach – probably at university level.

Libra Although security is important to these individuals, changes of direction will be anticipated and enjoyed; a varied career is likely.

Scorpio Sense of purpose very strong; an adventurous spirit, though not lacking direction.

ASCENDANT CAPRICORN
with Midheaven signs:

Leo A financial wizard seems likely; will need to be in control of all situations.

Virgo Conventional career with little risk-taking; security is all-important.

Libra A practical attitude with high aspirations; the ability to achieve may be marred by a lack of confidence.

Scorpio Will know what she or he wants and will go for it, and get it.

ASCENDANT AQUARIUS
with Midheaven signs:

Libra Many good plans and ideas will form, but laziness can weaken motivation.

Scorpio Strong determination to succeed, but stubbornness might cause eccentric changes of direction.

Sagittarius An inspired person, who may have too many ideas and tries to do too much with less success than hoped for.

ASCENDANT PISCES
with Midheaven signs:

Virgo Good communicator with high aspirations; must exert Taurus grit and discipline to achieve success.

"The life of the Twins is a life of ease and unfading youth spent in the arms of love."

Manilius, 1st century

Gemini

Versatility is the most recognizable quality of a Geminian; they refuse to be bored – or boring. Superficiality and a tendency to leave tasks unfinished can be a damaging trait, but a little structure in their lives will help overcome this. Doing several things at once is typically Geminian, and is not necessarily a bad thing.

GEMINI AS A SUN SIGN

The "heavenly twins", the symbol of Gemini, have a strong symbolic impact on the Geminian personality. We find Geminians always pursuing more than one project at a time, from those that are of great importance for their future lifestyle to simple domestic tasks such as spring cleaning. They commonly read several books at once, and their duality seems bottomless. Whatever they are doing, Geminians will more than likely have a telephone to their ear at the same time! The important thing for Geminians to remember is that they should try to complete everything they start if they are not to become restless and feel unfulfilled.

The illustration for June from the *Très Riches Heures du Duc de Berry* (1416), with the Twins of Gemini shown in the astrological chart at the top of the image.

The Gemini ruling planet, Mercury, is the planet of communication, and its influence is extremely marked in the Geminian personality, for here are the great communicators of the zodiac. If someone starts talking to you at the checkout queue, the chances are that he or she is a Gemini. They are also great writers to newspapers and love phone-in chats on the radio. The Internet could well have been created with them in mind! An above average number of Geminians work in the media (the others are probably Virgoans, for Virgo is the other Mercury-ruled sign).

The Gemini Twins, as depicted on the calendar page for June from the *Bedford Hours*, an illuminated manuscript produced in France in around 1423.

GEMINI	
Symbol	The Twins
Sun Sign Dates	22 May–21 June
Ruling Planet	Mercury
Element or Triplicity	Air
Quality or Quadruplicity	Mutable
Positive/Negative	Positive
Body Area	Shoulders, Arms, Hands
Polar Sign	Sagittarius

Geminians give the impression that they are very knowledgeable. While this may be true to some extent, their knowledge is quite often shallow. Actually, they know a little about a great many things. This leaning to the superficial is the worst Gemini fault. They are logical and rational, and their excellent minds work very quickly, which is an enormous asset. But Geminians need to realize that they should be sure of their facts, and should think before they speak or act. "Don't pull up the blind before there's something in the window" will be a good motto for them. Geminians can be extremely cunning and deceitful, and can tend to portray their qualities in a negative way. They also have the ability to talk their way out of the most difficult situations.

A heavy smoking habit is often the bane of a Geminian's life.

The Geminian Physique

Geminians are basically healthy and strong, many with a slim, wiry build. However, their arms and hands are vulnerable, and some tend to suffer from broken collar bones or dislocated shoulders. They also are more inclined to

Even in an impossible position, a Geminian will always do his best to talk his way out of trouble.

get addicted to smoking than others. They should put a stop to it as soon as possible.

GEMINI AS ASCENDANT

Those with Gemini as their Rising sign find it easier to be practical, and to keep their feet on the ground than their Sun-sign cousins. While they will be equally lively and versatile, there is a good chance that they will be less superficial, especially when dealing with subjects that interest them. Their ability to study a few chosen subjects in depth is a considerable asset, and often leads to life-long interests. They have tremendous enthusiasm for whatever they undertake, and are always happy to accept adventurous challenges. It is very much in their nature to question every concept that they come across, and to accept or reject it only after they have reached a satisfactory conclusion.

The Geminian Psyche

It is important that the Rising-sign Geminians are aware that they are more likely to suffer from nervous stress and tension than those who have it as the Sun sign. They may even have to seek professional help if the situation calls for it. Sometimes stress and tension can also exacerbate a vulnerability to asthma. Tackling the source of the tension may prove to be more satisfactory than attempting to cure the asthmatic condition itself.

Rising-sign Geminians are often keen to explore the depths of their personalities. However, they should be careful not to get too involved with the results of this discovery, as it may lead to questioning and re-questioning of their own motivations, only leading to further introspection.

They have an independent, freedom-loving quality about them, a desire for new experiences and travel – not only in the physical sense of the word, but intellectual, philosophical, and perhaps even occult journeys too. With proper guidance and care, the result is likely to provide satisfaction, a sense of fulfillment, and inner happiness.

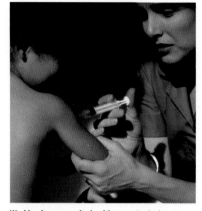

Working in community healthcare suits the lunar Geminian, who needs constant variety within a structured career.

GEMINI AS MOON SIGN

Those with the Moon in Gemini will have many characteristics of the Sun-sign Geminians. They will be versatile, good communicators, and will scurry around doing at least two things at the same time. But due to the lunar influence, responses to various situations will most likely be verbal.

birth chart may, however, come into play. They might feel guilty about their quick and often mendacious response, and decide that an apology is necessary. This usually works quite well, for there will be no lack of charm in the delivery of the apology.

A Restless Spirit

Those with a Geminian Moon have the same bright liveliness as apparent in the Sun-sign Geminians, but they will be restless. They may also have difficulty deciding the right path in life. Certainly, versatility is a blessing, but confusion often occurs when

"GEMINIANS ARE LIVELY AND VERSATILE"

Moon-in-Gemini types will have a quick, often amusing, but self-justifying answer – whether they have committed a dreadful mistake, have been rebuked, or simply wanted to get the better of a rival. It will be difficult for them to "see", much less admit, that they are wrong. They will talk their way out of difficulty with verbosity, impudence, and ease. Influences from other areas of their

important decisions regarding career or relationships have to be made. They may be attracted to one profession, but after a while, a certain boredom is likely. Dare we say that can be true of a relationship too? The lunar Gemini will need variety and change – like, for instance, being a general practitioner or nurse who deals with different types of patients, rather than a specialist in one area of medicine.

The latest exhibitions will draw in Geminians, who are always very keen to take their friends along too.

Gemini in Friendship, Love, and Permanent Relationships

For those of us who are laid-back about life – like to sit and linger over morning coffee, lunch, or a drink after work – our Geminian friends can, at times, be a little exhausting. Not just because we know they are anxious to get up and move on, but because sometimes they simply will not stop talking. They'll ask for our opinion and then, without listening to it, go on to deliver their own. But they are enlivening. Even if they are years older, they will encourage us to do things we have never considered doing – or thought we could possibly get away with. Their youthfulness will inspire us to climb out of our comfortable routine, and turn the clock back. In a friendship with a Geminian considerably older

A colourful, eclectic dress sense is characteristic of Geminians – their friends will need to be tactful if the effect starts to become comical.

than us, the age difference is soon obliterated. They try to keep up with the times, and even look younger than their age. They have excellent powers of persuasion, and their natural ability to sell comes into its own when talking us into going to see the latest movie or exhibition.

Tact and the Need for Common Ground

Apart from having the reputation for being youthful, Geminians are also the trendiest of the signs, especially when it comes to their image. Their appearance can, in fact, be a tad too colourful or piecemeal at times. We should be prepared, therefore, to do our bit, tactfully, when our Geminian friends turn up wearing different colours or styles, with no over-all look at all.

Sharing common interests is important in all bonds of friendship, but never more so than with Gemini friends. If they have nothing in common, there will be less to share and less to talk about. All too soon, the Gemini will get bored and say goodbye, or make excuses when the next meeting is suggested. But if there are shared interests, the feedback will be terrific. This will add vibrancy to the friendship that is both natural and very stimulating, and will result in years of fun. If by chance the friends cannot meet up for a length of time, they will take off from exactly where they had left off at the last reunion.

GEMINI IN LOVE

The Geminian ability to communicate readily and immediately comes to the fore when Geminians are attracted to a new love. Emails, text messages, and even old-fashioned letters will be dashed off. In fact, the Gemini will do everything possible to hasten the development of the affair. Sometimes, because they have so much to say in praise of their new partner, they may actually talk too much and too fast, thereby giving the impression that they are nervous. This will be unlikely, but they will do well to remember that others may get such an impression. If we find ourselves at the receiving end of this particular kind of voluble adoration, we should try to calm the Gemini and teach him to pace himself.

Pace and Timing

The "getting-to-know-you" period of a relationship will go on rather longer with a Geminian than with many other zodiac types, whose aim is simply to get their partners into bed as soon as possible. With Geminians it must be remembered that friendship – even in highly-sexed relationships – is very important, and must be soundly established right at the start.

Once the relationship has moved on sexually, the expression and style of lovemaking will be as lively as other

---

ONWARD AND UPWARD

Geminians enjoy, and in fact need, a lively and varied lifestyle. The one thing they cannot cope with is boredom. When they are bored, a blank look comes over them, and they start looking for someone interesting to talk to. Or else they will just stare blankly into the space with a glazed expression. They usually live life at a hectic pace, which means that they can build up a lot of nervous tension and stress. It is not easy for them to counter this – try telling a Geminian to slow down, or take things easy. It's not going to happen.

A blank look is typical of Geminians, to the extent that it looks funny.

---

spheres of the Geminian lifestyle. There will be no shortage of experimentation to keep the affair sparkling. Haste is sometimes apparent in bed, as elsewhere, and teaching the Geminian to slow down a bit may be necessary, especially in the case of Geminian men.

The Geminian Duality

Although Geminians are good communicators, many are taciturn as far as their emotions are concerned. In fact, at times when they realize that their emotions are beginning to take over, they may begin to question themselves and, in their eagerness to appear cool and logical, suppress their feelings. While this is likely to be most true with a Moon-sign Gemini, the tendency is also prevalent in both Sun-sign and Rising-sign people.

Geminian duality emerges in yet another aspect of their lives – they really do like to do more than one thing at a time. This tendency extends to their love lives more often than their partners may think desirable. They will date two people at the same time,

– and love them both, for different reasons. This will, of course, cause difficulties and complications usually, and it will take a lot of Geminian quick-wittedness to sort out the problem.

A partner may come to realize that a Geminian is unlikely to remain faithful to one person for a lifetime, and will be wise to come to terms with this early on in the relationship.

GEMINI IN PERMANENT RELATIONSHIPS

It is usually a rollercoaster ride for those with Geminians as permanent partners. There are highs and lows in every relationship, but here the switchback seems constant, and the change in directions dizzying. The partner needs to be very much on the ball to be able to cope with unexpected developments – they will certainly add zest to life, but may also be unsettling. For the relationship to flourish, it is essential that there is an extremely lively intellectual rapport between the Gemini and his or her

Expect a rollercoaster ride if you are trying to have a relationship with a Geminian.

partner. Both partners should have full say in discussions and decision-making, and the day-to-day problems of life should be resolved jointly. If the non-Gemini partner is too quiet and not very forthcoming, it is likely to frustrate the Gemini, who will in all sincerity want to know what is going on in his or her partner's mind. The key factor here is friendship – important in all permanent relationships, but absolutely vital with Geminians.

Flirtatious and Playful
The sex life of Geminians should continue to be lively and enjoyable for many decades. Sometimes Geminian flirtatiousness can get a little out of hand. This is one subject Geminians are not keen to discuss, although discussion may be called for when this happens. If possible, the partners should try to take this in their stride. As years go by, much can be done by partners by striving to maintain their looks, figures, and sex appeal. A bit of rivalry does no harm, and if the Gemini sees their partner getting plenty of attention, half the battle will be won. In such a situation, they are likely to feel flattered, because usually they are not jealous. In fact, they do not really know what jealousy is. They are not particularly possessive either, but sometimes a cross-influence from Venus (*see p210*) can cause a bit of seething.

Geminians find the challenge of parenthood exciting. They must be prepared for a certain amount of boredom during the early years, when their toddler's conversation is limited. However, once the children grow up and begin to respond adequately, they will always stimulate them and keep them busy. Most importantly, Gemini parents will always answer their children's questions to the best of their abilities. Moreover, they will even encourage them to refer to books or the Internet if they themselves are unable to come up with the answer.

The retail industry provides ideal jobs for lively Geminians – and any shop run by a Gemini is likely to be a colourful affair.

Gemini in Education, Jobs, and Money

If any child will benefit from listening to Mozart while still in the womb, a Gemini will. It will be worth remembering that stimulating the mind of the young Gemini is absolutely vital. Parents must constantly be aware that even from their baby's earliest months, the risk of boredom will be huge. Geminian babies will be fascinated by the shapes, colours, and movement of a dangling mobile. But if they have nothing to look at except a plain wall, they will get bored very soon and become tetchy. Even if his or her attention span is only average, the more stimulation the child receives, the better.

Geminian children will make quick progress once they get to nursery school. For instance, their vocabulary will soon surpass that of other children of the same age. They will be extremely talkative, and while this is to be encouraged, they must sooner or later learn that there are times when they just have to be quiet and listen.

The young Geminian needs a good variety of activity toys, or boredom will soon set in.

This is a lesson which should be instilled by the parents, so as to prevent upsets when it comes to more serious school days, and also for a bit of peace and quiet at home. Parents must also bear in mind that their child's questions must be answered as fully as possible. They will not be content with anything that seems illogical.

School Life

The Geminian child will thrive at a school that has a lively atmosphere, and believes in stimulating its pupils. The child will not like strict discipline, and the acceptance of rules will be easy only when their real reason is thoroughly explained and understood. Geminians are not shy about complaining if they think a rule is silly. Even if parents agree with them, the best approach is to try to find some reason why he or she should conform. Geminians are not rabble-rousers as children, but they will certainly use mischievous behaviour as a way to attract the attention of their classmates when they think the lesson is dull and the teacher boring. Actually, their progress will, more or less, depend entirely on the personality and approach of the teacher. If, for instance, the young Gemini falls a few places back in class, it will most likely be because their relationship with a teacher is not good.

Classes and Exams

Geminians are, on the whole, very bright children, but they can be extremely restless. It is absolutely no use telling young Geminians to do one thing at a time. This simply does not work. They must, however, be taught to complete every project and task they begin. If they are unable to do so, a trail of unfinished jobs is only likely to increase their feeling of restlessness, and eventually lead to unfulfillment. Praise for every painting finished,

Geminians are often happy as taxi drivers, because they generally enjoy driving and the chance to chat to people from all walks of life.

every piece of music thoroughly understood and performed, and so on, is essential.

When it comes to examinations, they must try to understand that a sound memory for boring facts is usually important. It is known for young Geminians to write pages of their own opinions, and never actually answer the question they were asked. All of this results too often in failure and frustration – a feeling of "not being understood". This can mar what should, in the final analysis, be a brilliant education, provided constant changes do not impinge upon it.

GEMINI AND CAREERS

As we have already said, because Geminians are such good communicators, the media is particularly well-suited to their talents. But it does not end there. They are great at bringing people round to their point of view, so they make excellent sales executives, who are able to convince the customers with their persuasive power,

as well as lively charm, that every proverbial Eskimo should own at least one refrigerator. Work in the retail trades is, therefore, ideal.

Going Places

Many Geminians are the happiest when driving. That chatty taxi driver one occasionally meets is more than likely to be a Geminian. Another area in which their best qualities can be rewardingly expressed is the travel and hospitality industries. Here, we have the particularly lively air steward, extremely eager to welcome us on board, and to convince us that theirs is the best or the only airline worth using. Or the travel guide, who constantly counts her flock, and is really excited about the sights of her own particular patch of touristic soil. Very different professions, such as the law, will be fascinating as well. Geminians can enjoy acting as go-betweens. So being an agent for writers, actors, musicians, or those in search of better jobs in most industries, or in finance can make for success. In calmer areas, because of the traditional astrological accent on the hands, those interested in the beauty industry will do well to consider a career as a manicurist or as a therapeutic masseur. Geminians also make inspiring and stimulating teachers – but they should think very carefully about the age group they want to work with, because they could become rather bored with nursery or kindergarten work.

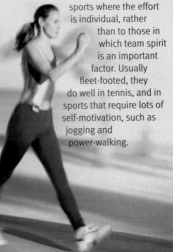

HEALTHY EATING AND EXERCISE

For good health, Geminians should maintain a fairly light diet. Heavy, stodgy food does not suit them. They will fare a lot better on salads, poultry, and fish, with some pasta to contribute carbohydrates. As far as exercise is concerned, they are individualists, and will be attracted to sports where the effort is individual, rather than to those in which team spirit is an important factor. Usually fleet-footed, they do well in tennis, and in sports that require lots of self-motivation, such as jogging and power-walking.

their own specialism might be. This will probably be English literature or its equivalent in other languages.

Chopping and Changing

Geminians make numerous changes in their careers, much more than other people. If they can be certain that the next change will be more lucrative as well as rewarding, the move is fine.

"GEMINIANS ARE SUCH GOOD COMMUNICATORS"

They will probably be at their best with children from about the age of seven or eight, through to year twelve. Geminian teachers are also likely to be very useful members of the school staff, because they will not find it difficult to fill in on a variety of subjects, whatever

But, they must always consider the possibility that they may be making a change just for the sake of it, and that it will not be beneficial in the long run. If they are fed up with their present situation, they should think of ways of making their work more satisfying.

The coolest club in town will attract the teenage or 20-something Geminian, who will also spend a lot of money on hip clothing and chart music.

GEMINI AND MONEY

Unless a Geminian's full birth chart indicates practicality and sensibility regarding money, the chances are that it will slip all too easily through lively fingers. When they are young, Geminians are particularly keen to keep up with, and even lead the latest trends in fashion and pop music. So, from pocket-money days, clothes and music will make gaping holes in their income. They must learn that they have to work for what they want. They are enterprising, though they will complain of boredom as they go off on their bikes to do a regular paper round. Their enterprising spirit can make them clever at buying and selling, and making a deal will really have its benefits.

Stretching student grants and credits is very hard for them, as is the sensible use of credit cards. Bills can very easily run right up to the limit if Geminians are not particularly careful.

The Work and Life Balance

Geminians will not want to spend their working lives just doing a job for the sake of money. In order to have real job satisfaction, they often go for a slightly lower salary. They believe that life is to be lived, and that working hours must be in line with this fact. Some Geminians are better at balancing books than others. We will go into these subtleties when relating the influences of Mercury and Venus (*see pp204–13*). These planets, more so with Gemini than with most signs, can make specific differences when it comes to the Geminian attitude and ability to cope with cash, material, and security.

"MONEY WILL SLIP ALL TOO EASILY THROUGH GEMINIAN FINGERS"

MIDHEAVEN SIGNS FOR GEMINI

The influence of the Midheaven stems from the part of the zodiac that was immediately overhead at our birth – that is, the sign that was at the top of the celestial sphere (*for more detail, see pp304–6*). We relate to, aspire to, and identify with the qualities of the sign on the Midheaven, especially in relation to our careers. The Midheaven signs for Gemini birth charts set out below are the only possible combinations of Ascendant and Midheaven signs in both the Northern and Southern hemispheres. To work out your own Ascendant and Midheaven signs at birth, see the charts on pp344–7.

ASCENDANT ARIES
with Midheaven signs:

Capricorn Serious attitude towards career, but Gemini will give the reverse impression.

Aquarius Need for a career that is anything but ordinary – television, or technology, very likely.

ASCENDANT TAURUS
with Midheaven signs:

Capricorn Flair for finance. Ability to sell. Clever in big business.

Aquarius Conflict between need for security and wanting something lively and fun.

Pisces Teaching, publishing, journalism, or horticulture. Psychic ability possible.

ASCENDANT GEMINI
(WITH GEMINI SUN SIGN)
with Midheaven signs:

Aries Will need speedy results in chosen career. A lack of tact, and impatience could mar progress.

Taurus Could do well in self-employment – an agency or real estate maybe.

Aquarius Technology, journalism, technical side of television, or film. A need to be "on the scene" in the career.

Pisces May work in radio. Caring professions or charity work.

ASCENDANT CANCER
with Midheaven signs:

Aries Chef, or the armed forces (choice of branch will be crucial).

Taurus Will have a desire to entertain, perhaps as a stand-up comedian. Good teacher.

Aquarius Possibly scientific; will want to express original ideas, but may lack confidence to do so.

Pisces Shrewd business sense, but will be attracted to caring professions and charity work.

ASCENDANT LEO
with Midheaven signs:

Aries A force to reckon with. Big achiever and show off. Will win arguments.

Taurus Stubbornness will pay off at times, but will learn the hard way. Will need challenge in career.

Pisces Very creative. Writing ability. Excellent for media work.

ASCENDANT VIRGO
with Midheaven signs:

Taurus A love of the land – agriculture, gardening, library.

Gemini Writing ability very likely. Media, journalism, or research work will be rewarding.

ASCENDANT LIBRA
with Midheaven signs:

Cancer Potential for hospitality industry. Chef, or beautician.

Leo Fashion, show biz. Will make selling a real "performance".

ASCENDANT SCORPIO
with Midheaven signs:

Cancer Finance, wine trade, or engineering. Shrewd business sense. Must not be hasty.

Leo Needs variety in career. Enormous drive and energy.

Virgo Suited for medical profession, scientific research, alternative medicine, or nursing.

ASCENDANT SAGITTARIUS
with Midheaven signs:

Leo Great flair and personality. Will do much to further career. Good talker and lecturer.

Virgo Teacher, critic, dietician, or horticulturalist. Literary talent. Must avoid being too self-critical.

Libra Publishing, law, travel industry, or language teacher. Will enjoy changes in career.

ASCENDANT CAPRICORN
with Midheaven signs:

Leo Will rise to a position of authority. Ambitious. Good sense of humour. Suited for politics.

Virgo Capable of detailed work. Researcher, real estate, land management, or architect.

Libra Will want fair play. Flair for fashion. Good business sense.

Scorpio The police, detective work, or in the Navy. Will have strong feelings, but will not show.

Sagittarius Sense of humour. Will disguise conflict between freedom and independence. Needs conventional, secure career.

ASCENDANT AQUARIUS
with Midheaven signs:

Virgo Very critical – of self and everyone else. Will make many career changes. Should exploit considerable originality.

Libra A glamorous combination. Will make most of self. Will aspire for the good life. Luxury trades.

Scorpio Antiques trade, motor or airline industry. Scientific flare. Good talker, stubbornness likely.

Sagittarius Flare for languages. Good teacher. Suited as a vet, or in law. Beware of restlessness.

ASCENDANT PISCES
with Midheaven signs:

Sagittarius Creative ability. May be psychic, but must express Geminian scepticism.

"The Crab risks money upon sea-winds to amass sudden wealth. His is a shrewd nature, ready to fight for profit."

Manilius, 1st century

Cancer

Claws will snap when a Cancerian is attacked; aggravate them or their family at your peril. Their emotions are powerful and can be smothering; they can be over-sensitive, and take offence easily. But their intuition is keen and rarely leads them astray — except when anxiety takes hold of them and refuses to be shrugged off.

CANCER AS A SUN SIGN

Here is a somewhat enigmatic zodiac type. On the first meeting, we may be greeted rather brusquely — especially if the individual is at all suspicious or the immediate impression of us is not completely positive. But very soon we will break through the protective Cancerian shell and find them full of kindness and helpfulness, with a warm, sympathetic, and loving nature.

Their emotions are very powerful, ebbing and flowing like the sea — and their intuition is paramount. If they instinctively feel that something's going to happen, that feeling is very strong and almost inevitably leads to worry, the Cancerian's strongest natural enemy. It is rare indeed to find a Cancerian with absolutely nothing to worry about — so much so that, in many cases, he or she will even worry at the absence of anything to worry about! Many, due to the influence of Mercury, will have more than a fair supply of logic, however, which can be appealed to. This is a great help when Cancerians are besieged with anxiety. Apart from which, more generally, they should listen to their intuition, which is also very powerful. These twin attributes are their guide, and this approach

The illustration for July from the *Très Riches Heures du Duc de Berry* (1416), with the Crab, symbol of Cancer, shown in the astrological chart at the top of the image.

Cancer's symbol of the Crab, as depicted on the calendar page for July from the *Bedford Hours*, an illuminated manuscript produced in France in around 1423.

CANCER	
Symbol	The Crab
Sun Sign Dates	22 June–22 July
Ruling Planet	The Moon
Element or Triplicity	Water
Quality or Quadruplicity	Cardinal
Positive/Negative	Negative
Body Area	Breasts
Polar Sign	Capricorn

is also excellent when decisions must be made. If they "feel" a certain action is called for, the chances are it will be the right one to take.

There is a delightfully sentimental quality in members of this sign. While they will probably disguise it when young because they feel it's uncool, it often emerges as a powerful feeling for the past – their own or maybe their family's. Their imagination is also extremely potent, and when, or if, it gets out of hand, it is often the source of a tendency to worry. However, if the imagination is used creatively here, we have the most inspired of novelists, and all kinds of artists and musicians – as well as cooks. Cooking is high on the list of Cancerian attributes.

CANCER AS ASCENDANT

While the individual's Sun sign will probably dominate the Cancerian Ascendant, there are many of the same characteristics present as in those with a Cancer Sun sign. When Cancer is rising, the individual – whatever the Sun sign – will get particular pleasure and inner satisfaction from caring for and cherishing those who are close.

The motivation to start their own families is very strong and they will work hard and with immense tenacity to see that family life is held together. Sometimes, a rather sterner attitude will emerge to this end, but after any crises the soft, melting quality common to all of this sign will come into its own and amends will be made.

Cancer's Vulnerabilities
We must remember that in all these situations the desire will be to *protect* – but this does not show itself as possessiveness. The influence of the cardinal quadruplicity emerges and plants a basic outgoing quality. There will be a great deal of ambition for the partner's progress in life, and, as a result of a keen desire to move up the ladder, a certain amount of social climbing will go on, perhaps through the giving of elaborate (home-cooked) dinner parties for the boss and his/her partner.

The basic health vulnerability is usually of the digestive system, which will be extremely sensitive and ignited by worry. If a Cancerian gets sick for no apparent reason, the digestion is nearly always at the root of the problem. As the breasts are the Cancerian body area, it is obvious that Cancerian women, like all women, should check them and have regular mammograms. But it should be emphasized that no one with a Cancer Sun, Moon, or Ascendant sign should

Ernest Hemingway was one of many great Cancerian writers.

"THE CANCERIAN IMAGINATION IS EXTREMELY POTENT"

think that the sign will make them more susceptible to breast cancer – or any other form of the disease – than those of any of the other 11 signs. There is no astrological reason to link the sign to the illness, nor research that suggests a connection of any kind.

CANCER AS MOON SIGN

The Moon is extremely powerful in Cancer because it is in the sign it rules. If by chance you were born at the time of the New Moon, bear in mind the fact that you are known astrologically as a "double Cancerian", and those born at the New Moon and at or near sunrise will be "triple Cancerians". In such cases, everything you read about Cancer will apply to you – you will be "like" your Cancer Sun and you will (like all who have the Moon in this sign) respond to situations in the manner of Cancer.

But irrespective of the Ascendant and the positions of the planets, when Cancer is the Moon sign, the influence of the Moon works overtime. This will bring about an instinctive and emotional response to all situations, and the individual will be very prone to worry. Sometimes there will be a tendency to overreact, but in such cases, other areas of the chart may act as a corrective.

Cycles of the Moon

This placing can have a rather negative effect on a woman's menstrual cycle, especially where PMS mood swings are concerned. Awareness and perhaps a little research into the pattern could be an enormous help in coming to terms with the problem. Comparing the cycle's phases with those of the Moon may well add another dimension. For instance, if one feels particularly energetic at full Moon, it is possible

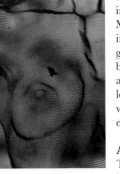

Breasts are the Cancerian body area, though this does not mean that Cancerians are more prone to breast cancer than anyone else.

to use exercise to help ward off depression or irritability; and if the Moon phases and the individual cycle coincide, greater allowances should be made by the subject, and the family should learn not to blame a woman for possible over-emotional responses.

Areas of Conflict

There may be conflict between wanting things to stay as they are and a certain restlessness and wish for change. These must be balanced, and there may well be problems: a strongly family-orientated Moon-in-Cancer person will have considerable difficulty when children grow up and want to move on to live their own lives. Fears – often irrational – for their safety and wellbeing will emerge, and special care will be needed so that far too many hints are not dropped to encourage the arrival of grandchildren.

A NEED FOR SUNSCREEN

Cancerians tend to have pale skins (whatever their ethnic background), and are extremely susceptible to sunburn – it is of above average importance for them to cover up in the sun and always use a high factor sunscreen cream, even in the winter sun.

Chatting about old times is a favourite activity of Cancerians, who tend to have terrific memories.

Cancer in Friendship, Love, and Permanent Relationships

Cancerians are one of those groups with whom friendships last for a very long time – and they will remember precisely what we were wearing and what was said when we first met, even if that first meeting was way back in kindergarten. Taking a stroll down memory lane with them will be delightful fun.

However, that excellent memory can work in other ways as well. Maybe we said something ages ago that upset a Cancerian, and while they will be unlikely to keep referring to it, it will be all too securely lodged in the back of their minds. But this need not be a problem: do them a good turn and they will repay several times over, expressing their caring kindness. Sometimes this will take the form of an unexpected present, or a meal they have specially cooked for

us, along with other friends they think we will enjoy meeting. Their intuition works very powerfully in friendship. They will be thinking about you and suddenly realize you need some kind of help, then will phone or text you.

A reassuring hug and maybe a shoulder to cry on are essential for the most sensitive Cancerians.

Ever-changing Moods

Cancerian changes of mood can cause a certain amount of stress between friends. In some extreme cases, having arranged to meet, we are just not sure whether we will be greeted with happy smiles and a well-worked out plan of events, or if clouds have gathered and we will need to work hard at cheering up, reassuring, and even providing a shoulder to cry on. But then there will be times when we may need such a shoulder – and we will certainly get it from our Cancerian friend.

We must be aware that these people will without doubt worry about us, so we really must make a special effort not to be late when we arrange to meet them, or be careful to send messages to tell them exactly where we are and why we are running behind schedule. If we neglect this, their imagination will start to work overtime and they will be absolutely sure that we have been run over, or mugged, or met with some other disaster.

While one can get along quite happily with Cancerians, just by respecting each others' interests, a shared pastime will further cement the bond, and if it happens to be one especially dear to a Cancerian, so much the better.

CANCER IN LOVE

Once Cancerians realize that they are in love, all their romantic and sentimental feelings will emerge, together with their sensitivity and powerful emotions. They will not be able to do enough for their lovers, and life will take on a very different and starry meaning. Cancerians tend to get carried away – rather more than a little – especially if the individual is beginning to be even slightly broody and keen to "settle down and start a family".

However, unlike some other romantic types, they are cautious and will not rush into a relationship, however strong their desire for a loving home life. Here, too, are true romantics who will use their imagination in a very special way; their lovers will have an extraordinary experience during the relationship. Because of their high emotional level and tendency to mood swings, partners must expect a few dramatic scenes from time to time. Whether they can cope with these outbursts will of course depend entirely on their own personalities and attitude.

Emphasizing the need for safety when crossing the road is the type of advice that will be dispensed by overzealous Cancerians.

> **A DEFENSIVE APPROACH**
>
> Challenge Cancerians in discussion or argument and a remarkable defensive system will spring into action – a strong instinctive urge to protect themselves and their family, signalled by a characteristic little frown which appears between the individual's eyebrows.

Doting Lovers

Cancerians make wonderfully sensual lovers, and while enjoying an expressive sex life, their caring and protective instincts can lead to a rather claustrophobic atmosphere. They can become something of a clucking hen, constantly asking their partners if they have everything they need, and if there is anything that can be done for them – even over-emphasizing the care needed when crossing a road, slicing bread, or staying out after dark. For a strongly independent partner who needs freedom of expression within a relationship, there will be differences that must be sorted before any attempt to deepen the commitment is undertaken.

It can be very difficult to end a relationship with a Cancerian. Their tenacity will prevent them from saying goodbye with any kind of resignation, or to accept the situation. They will cling on, hoping their partners change their mind, or even thinking that perhaps they did not mean what they said, that there isn't someone else, and that a little time apart will heal wounds. If this is the case, the Cancerian will be all forgiveness and ready for a fresh start, but the partner may need more freedom. This is hard for many Cancerians to accept. They just have to learn, probably the hard way, to make clean breaks; otherwise, both parties will suffer far more than is necessary, and the healing process will be seriously delayed.

CANCER IN PERMANENT RELATIONSHIPS

Here is a zodiac group which blossoms when settled into a permanent relationship, and whose members – more than many – will probably hope to be legally married eventually. Emotional security is important, mainly because Cancerians are eager to raise a family and build a stable family unit. This instinct is very powerful, and they do make excellent parents. But before that happy day when the first child arrives, the process of home building, in every sense of the word – but especially where atmosphere is concerned, as opposed to just having the right living conditions – is very important. This does not mean that their dream house, with the perfect nursery, lounge, bedroom, playroom, and study is not important too; it is, and the Cancerian dream will go on to visualize family dinners where everyone sits happily round the table discussing their day.

But of course reality kicks in, and it may well be that the Cancerian will be caring for an extended family, whose members come and go as they please, in freedom and independence. If this is a probability they should give extremely careful thought to the situation, for there is potential for a considerable build up of stress and worry, which will not be conducive to the serene family life of their dreams. If Cancerians have children of their own to add to the extended family, it seems unlikely that quite as much love and attention will be given to them as to the original family members; jealousy and resentment could soon begin to boil up.

Nurturing the Love

Where Cancerians really can score highly within a permanent relationship is in keeping the romance alive. In theory, because they are so caring and imaginative, they can do much more than just cook a special meal or bring home roses and chocolates. They will not forget the early days when they and their partner first met, and any excuse for a bit of sheer romance or a fun occasion will be welcomed. That is, just so long as they can really trust the babysitter … and that their partners can persuade them to leave their mobile phone at home … and that they can put aside irrational worries about the children for an entire evening.

In the long run, these contrasting qualities make them excellent partners and good, if over-anxious, parents.

Marriage is very important for Cancerians, who value emotional stability and mutual support as the foundation for happiness.

Young Cancerians may be reluctant to go to nursery school, preferring the security of staying at home with their mum or dad.

Cancer in Education, Jobs, and Money

The youngest Cancerians will, rather than most toddlers, tend to be clinging, and may well be quite frightened when introduced to nursery school. Obviously, the more they get used to this very different atmosphere before their parents leave them, the better. If it is at all possible for a parent to arrange a visit to the premises with their child before he or she starts attendance, it will be a great help – even better if the child already has a friend who attends the same school. But at all events, this first break with the established home routine is not going to be easy. However, once the initial shock has subsided, it should not be too difficult to ignite the young Cancerian's imagination, and as time goes on, the more he or she is allowed to help the helpers, the better.

Parents may face a similar situation during the first few days of kindergarten or reception class. Again, preparation is the key to smoothing the transition. Choosing a school where the Cancerian imagination is

A sudden burst of tears is not at all uncommon with Cancerian children.

immediately grabbed – probably by something as simple as a good display of other pupils' art work – will help enormously. Kindness is paramount, as is gentle, but firm, discipline. It must be remembered that here are sensitive children who will appear a lot tougher than they really are. When rebuked, their response will be to bite their lips and tell themselves they are not crying, but all too soon a torrent will burst forth, which, while it may be somewhat over-dramatic, will probably be for the best, with emotion allowed to flow rather than being bottled up.

Feeding the Imagination

The imagination of Cancerian children can be applied to any subject, and will emerge in science as well as art. History will be a popular subject, as will literature, and one will soon know which subjects are going to be the favourites for further study in greater depth when the time comes for choosing specialisms.

Becoming a chef is a popular career choice for Cancerians, who tend to excel at cooking.

Cancerians are endowed with great tenacity and determination. When the choice of subject for university arises, parents can be sure that the preference, once expressed, will be taken up with enthusiasm, and these qualities will come into their own, so the chances of a good degree will be excellent. If there is any indecision, a serious discussion, vocational guidance test, or perhaps a full astrological analysis will provide helpful information and guidance.

CANCER AND CAREERS

When one thinks of the most important Cancerian qualities, being caring and protective is what first springs to mind. There is also a quiet determination, tenacity, and natural shrewdness. When these are expressed through professional life and career, we will see a very fulfilled and successful individual. From the point of view of being caring, the medical profession has its own attractions, with gynaecology and pediatrics being the most popular options.

If we consider the caring quality in another way, we have airline stewards and those in the hotel and hospitality industries. There is often a great love of the sea, so the navy and merchant navy are rewarding careers. Many Cancerians are excellent cooks, so becoming a chef is an extremely popular choice. Eventually opening one's own restaurant and using the natural business skills is something that should be considered, and could work out extremely well. Interestingly, chefs have earned the reputation of being temperamental and moody, which are of course two very strong Cancerian faults.

Trading and Markets

The natural shrewdness of Cancer comes into its own in the banking, finance, and insurance industries, where Cancerians are often very clever at dealing with money, and their intuition can often be relied upon to predict market movements. These professions, along with accountancy, are excellent possibilities. Trading in antiques is also a viable option, and as far as the arts are concerned, the sign is well represented in most areas, with famous Cancerian singers and dancers dominating their fields.

Perseverance and Endurance

While on a superficial level there is a liking for change, in the long term the thread of a Cancerian's career will have good continuity. For instance, if one becomes really dedicated to antiques, the first purchase for one's own special collection will probably be made with pocket money or the very first earnings.

NATURAL BORN HOARDERS

Like the crab of their sign gathering food in its claws, Cancerians hoard – and how! They are reluctant to throw anything away, as it might come in handy – so much so that far too many of them, though not all, are chaotically untidy, with their homes full of clutter.

The business location may change from time to time, but the chances are that the individual's tenacity, knowledge, and love of the trade will be maintained. Most Cancerians have a collection of something rather unusual – a positive way of expressing their irresistable tendency to hoard. Continuity and a real sense of the past is important to them, and is an area that needs to be expressed; if in some way it can find an outlet within the confines of a career or serious hobby, this will be really rewarding.

Home and Family

The most important purchase for all of us is our home, and this is a sign whose members are particularly keen to own property. Budgeting for a mortgage will be very carefully planned – for on this planning will depend the security and protection of the individual and his or her all-important family.

Cancerian intuition and foresight will be of enormous help from the financial point of view. Buying stocks and shares needs a sense of timing –

"MOST CANCERIANS HAVE A COLLECTION OF SOMETHING UNUSUAL"

CANCER AND MONEY

As mentioned before, the Cancerian hoarding instinct is very strong, and in no other area of life is it more powerful than in finance. Cancerians often think themselves to be far less well-off than they actually are, and as a result, give the impression of being mean, especially when they have to give special gifts such as wedding presents.

Faced with natural disasters which call for donations to charity, there are two distinct possibilities. The Cancerian capacity for sympathy and identification with suffering will ignite the need to give help, and many will part with their last cent on these occasions – or even go to a disaster zone in person to offer help. The other possibility is that the Cancerian will recoil and fearfully decide that they simply cannot risk sending much, or anything at all.

Collections of an eclectic nature are quite typical of Cancer.

Studying the financial papers is indicative of Cancer's cautious approach to investment; their sense of timing will be a key factor if they are to be successful investors.

renewed determination and tenacity, start all over again, having learned the very hard way from the rash and stupid mistakes made in the past.

The Cautious Investor
Another Cancerian quality that can make its presence felt is the loathing towards risk-taking. While many Cancerians are brave and daring in other respects (they are the takers of calculated risks), the tendency is far less likely to grab them when it comes to hard-earned cash, as the thought of losing it through speculation is vehemently disliked. All in all, the poor unfortunate – who perhaps because of silly spur-of-the-moment investments or through lending cash to friends who cannot or will not pay it back – is, thankfully, few and far between among Cancerians.

something Cancerians have in money matters. In the long term, they should see their investments grow extremely well. It would only be a rush of emotion – most probably spurred on by the circumstances – that might cause a Cancerian to act rashly and lead to financial difficulty. In case this should happen, Cancer has what it takes to re-examine every past mistake, and in due course, with

"CANCERIANS ARE PARTICULARLY KEEN TO OWN PROPERTY"

MIDHEAVEN SIGNS FOR CANCER

The influence of the Midheaven stems from the part of the zodiac that was immediately overhead at our birth – that is, the sign that was at the top of the celestial sphere (*for more detail, see pp304–6*). We relate to, aspire to, and identify with the qualities of the sign on the Midheaven, especially in relation to our careers. The Midheaven signs for Cancer birth charts set out below are the only possible combinations of Ascendant and Midheaven signs in both the Northern and Southern hemispheres. To work out your own Ascendant and Midheaven signs at birth, see the charts on pp344–7.

ASCENDANT ARIES
with Midheaven signs:

Capricorn Will secure career and social progress with determination and tenacity.

Aquarius Strong humanitarian instincts. Caring professions or charity work.

ASCENDANT TAURUS
with Midheaven signs:

Capricorn Good business sense. Banking, finance, musician/singer.

Aquarius Restlessness in career likely. Archaeology, oceanography, shipping, interior decoration.

Pisces The navy, a ship's purser, baker, teaching or other work with young children.

ASCENDANT GEMINI
with Midheaven signs:

Aries Argumentative, restless; criminal/investigative journalism.

Aquarius Will possibly make a lot of money from unusual sources. Career changes likely.

Pisces Beauty professions, footwear trade. A talent for dance and poetry.

ASCENDANT CANCER
(WITH SUN SIGN CANCER)
with Midheaven signs:

Aries Determination and tenacity evident. Armed forces, engineering.

Taurus Catering, chef, agriculture, or horticulture. Security is extremely important.

Aquarius Excellent financial potential. Banking, detective work.

Pisces Needs spiritual development. Possibly psychic; charity work, beautician.

ASCENDANT LEO
with Midheaven signs:

Aries Good for self-employment. Hard worker, good organizer.

Taurus Determined. A secure and conventional career. Will be the boss.

Pisces Very creative. Likely to become a professional artist, designer, skater, or dancer.

ASCENDANT VIRGO
with Midheaven signs:

Taurus Garden designer, carpenter, banking, PR work.

Gemini Advertising, agent, journalism, a children's nurse. A lively and caring person.

ASCENDANT LIBRA
with Midheaven signs:

Cancer Will do well in the chosen career. Chef, dress designer, or hotelier.

Leo Luxury trades, entertainment, and fitness industries. Natural charm an asset.

ASCENDANT SCORPIO
with Midheaven signs:

Cancer Surgeon, wine expert, financier, stockbroker. Terrific shrewdness will be an asset in dealings.

Leo Export trade, travel industry, or research. A good organizer and a hard worker.

Virgo Criminal investigator or psychotherapist. Capable of arduous, painstaking work.

ASCENDANT SAGITTARIUS
with Midheaven signs:

Leo Fireman, professional sports, or adventurer/explorer. Possibly an actor.

Virgo Teacher, lecturer, or writer. Will inspire students.

Libra Lawyer, hair stylist, or dress designer. Good potential for extended study.

Scorpio Good sense of purpose; a vet or an in-depth interviewer who needs to expose facts.

ASCENDANT CAPRICORN
with Midheaven signs:

Leo Government official, surveyor, town planner; needs to work in partnership.

Virgo Concern for the environment; organic farmer, grocer, naturopath.

Libra Charm, sympathy, and a caring quality; funeral director, almoner, agony aunt.

Scorpio Dentist, osteopath, the antiques trade; needs to work in partnership.

ASCENDANT AQUARIUS
with Midheaven signs:

Libra A glamorous career, but hard working – fashion, jeweller, beautician, or PR work.

Scorpio Needs excitement and a secure job. Can cope with difficult conditions. Mining, the oil industry, engineering; possibly alternative medicine.

Sagittarius Personal trainer, lecturer, linguist, historian; good capacity for studies.

ASCENDANT PISCES
with Midheaven signs:

Sagittarius A sensitive individual; a powerful spiritual belief. The caring professions; good with the elderly. Possibly astrologer, tarot reader, psychic; must be well trained.

"They swagger about displaying the fruits of luxury – but the sentiments of their honest hearts are without guile."

Manilius, 1st century

Leo

Leo's assumption that the king of the jungle has the right to control all the other animals can be irritating – especially because they are so often right. Inspirational leaders they may be, but Leos need to cultivate tact, control their sometimes over-dramatic reactions, and throttle down their desire to take charge.

LEO AS A SUN SIGN

The power of the Sun is strongest in Leo, the sign it rules. Those born at the time of year when the Sun is travelling through its own sign will be powerfully endowed with its fine characteristics and qualities – and, of course, its faults. Organization is very important to Leos, who really feel the need to be fully in control of their lives. It is often the case that, when working or living with less well organized people, they will exert their influence over them. Leos will do as much as possible to encourage them, not only to sort themselves out, but also to develop their potential to the full. It is because of this tendency that many Leos are accused of bossiness – quite rightly so, but at least their attempts to dominate are made for what they believe are the right reasons. It is important that Leos realize they must avoid becoming dogmatic and fixed in their opinions, and instead develop flexibility of outlook. Otherwise a closed mind and the inability to accept others' opinions and lifestyles will cause unpopularity. However, the fire element of their sign burns very brightly, exuding warmth, generosity, and enthusiasm – both for their own interests and in the encouragement of all with whom they come into contact.

The August illustration from the *Très Riches Heures du Duc de Berry* (1416), with the Lion of Leo shown in the astrological chart at the top of the image.

LEO	
Symbol	The Lion
Sun Sign Dates	23 July–23 August
Ruling Planet	The Sun
Element or Triplicity	Fire
Quality or Quadruplicity	Fixed
Positive/Negative	Positive
Body Areas	Heart and Spine
Polar Sign	Aquarius

The Leo Lion, as depicted on the calendar page for August from the *Bedford Hours*, an illuminated manuscript produced in France in around 1423.

All Leos have their own kingdom. It may simply be a small area in which they work or live, or the office of the CEO of some huge company. They take great pride in their domain. Leos are highly motivated and hard-working. At the same time, they know how and when to relax in order to avoid stress.

LEO AS ASCENDANT

A certain well-known English astrologer always used to say "when Leo rises, the only thing to do is to keep it down", which was a considerable confession since it was her Ascendant sign. Everyone who knew anything about astrology was well aware of it working extremely powerfully in her case.

"ALL LEOS HAVE THEIR OWN KINGDOM"

Because they have special powers from the Sun – the source of creation – there is an element of creativity in this zodiac type. This does not mean that they are all actors or performers (although an element of "performing" does show up somewhere along the line). Their creativity is expressed in a great many ways – from a clever use of colour in a simple flower arrangement, right up to the practice of the fine arts. Many Leos will express their creativity in the joy of parenthood.

In Rising-sign Leos, some very strong characteristics are forcefully expressed, unless the individual's Sun sign endows them with a certain meek and mild quality, which counters the fiery qualities of Leo. While enthusiasm, optimism, generosity, and a certain amount of creativity is present, the tendency to be dogmatic and pompous is usually pretty much in evidence. In extreme cases, there is even a propensity for these people to assume that they know better than anyone else. It is vital that they become aware of this unlikeable trait.

The skyscraper is a natural domain of the most power-hungry Leos.

Material Success

The desire for material success is often stronger than in Sun-sign Leos, although here too we have those who love quality, and for whom only the best and most expensive is good enough. As a result, there is a tendency to ignore any inherent creativity. This is a pity because they could get psychological satisfaction from even the most simple expression of the creative urge. For those who have their Rising-sign characteristics in balance, psychological wholeness and inner security will be combined with a measure of humility. The strength of the sign will be expressed in ways that are beneficial and rewarding to not only the Ascendant Leo but also to others. Attainment of this balance is not always forthcoming, however, and sometimes it is difficult for Rising-sign Leos to learn from their own mistakes. Vanity and the conviction that they really are "the best", and that only they know what is right, can tend to hold them back.

LEO AS MOON SIGN

The immediate reaction of someone with the Moon in Leo is to take over. This is, of course, admirable in an emergency ("well, someone has to", they will say), but on a great many occasions the impression given is of sheer bossiness or a desire to get the better of others. However, this person's strong reactions can be quite differently founded – willingness to help, to listen, and to encourage are all part of the attributes of the Moon-in-Leo. These people give the impression that they are confident and capable, which in itself inspires confidence, and often puts them in a league of their own.

To the less enthusiastic types, this exuberance can be somewhat overwhelming and, at times, off-putting. However, there is no doubt that when combined with optimism, an intuitive instinct, and a creative

Conducting an orchestra is a profession that suits the inspirational leadership skills of Moon-in-Leo types.

imagination, Moon-in-Leos can potentially be really striking and supportive individuals.

Natural Show-offs

There is certainly a tendency to show off, whether these folks are young or old. There is always the temptation to top a rival in discussion: they have a superior car or a better-bred dog; or when their friend confesses she has just found a great bargain, it is difficult for Moon-in-Leo individuals to resist the temptation to appear in a spectacular designer outfit.

In spite of all this, their basic, instinctive, and most vital need is to make the right and most favourable impression. They want to be sincerely friendly, helpful, and encouraging, so awareness that they can go "over the top" in their immediate reactions is necessary. Here are leaders of the pack, with the strength to encourage others. This Moon sign is often in the charts of people in charge of large groups – many orchestral conductors and leading politicians are Moon-in-Leo types.

The Moon in Leo makes the individual extrovert, and can balance shyness, if it is in evidence due to other planetary influences. But, by making the less confident individuals assume an assured attitude, it may also make them talkative and all too obviously nervous or lacking in real self-confidence.

Family and friends will find themselves the beneficiaries of a Leo's desire to impress, whatever their age or financial position.

Leo in Friendship, Love, and Permanent Relationships

There is an element of youthfulness in the way Leos relate to their friends. They want everyone to enjoy being with them, and to join in everything that is entertaining, memorable, and rewarding. Outings will be planned with great enthusiasm and expectation, and in a certain Leo style. How this is interpreted will, of course, very much rely on the size of their budget – whether they are going to "treat" us or make the decision to "go Dutch".

Leo girls will always find ways to treat themselves on a modest budget, such as with a good coffee.

show off to their friends – though some would say so. It is far more likely that they just want to make sure that their friends are having a good time. They hate "making do", and will soon see to it that this does not happen: a typical girls' inexpensive morning out will be a small cup of coffee in the best coffee shop in town, followed by a wander through the mall with the famous designer stores – even though they know they can't afford to buy that Armani dress.

Life's Givers

Whatever their age or financial position, Leos really like to give pleasure – "better to give than receive" is one of their mottos. Even if they are on a tiny income, they will go for the best. It is not the case that they want to

Leo Flair

When funds don't allow Leos to spend with abandon, their creativity and inventiveness come to the fore. Leos will go to the market, buy a bargain length of fabric, and create something that roughly resembles the gown of their dreams. They will encourage their friends to believe that they too can have a unique garment, even if it is hurriedly thrown together, to be worn that very evening.

Friends Indeed

Leos are faithful friends, and will keep in touch over long years of absence and distance. They will always encourage their friends to get as much out of life as possible, but must be careful not to become dogmatic and bossy. Most importantly, they must learn not to be upset when their advice falls on deaf ears. The lack of positive response will irritate and frustrate Leos, as, in their own minds, they will know for sure that their words of wisdom were good.

Believing that they are always right is a problem for Leos – and their friends. They should think again, because occasionally they can be horribly wrong or inconsiderate of their friends' true needs and feelings.

LEO IN LOVE

When Leos fall in love, their inner psychological Sun shines brilliantly. They fall really hard and quite often. When things go wrong, we can see it in their faces – that inner Sun, which is so much a part of their personality, is suddenly wiped out by storm clouds. Their hearts are broken rather frequently, maybe because their partners find Leos simply too much to keep in step with.

However, once their love is reciprocated, Leos will go out of their way to make their partners happy. They will be showered with a plenitude of love, affection, and attention by the Leo.

Leos are generous to a fault in all respects, but they need partners who respond well to all this splendid treatment, otherwise the relationship will sink like a lead balloon. They are faithful, and they relish giving their lovers encouragement to be successful in their careers and hobbies.

THE SENSITIVE LION

Leos are far more sensitive than most people realize. When they are hurt, they do not make a fuss about it, but retire to their lair and lick their wounds in private while putting on a brave face outside. This does not, however, mean they are incapable of dramatic scenes – they are, and when the Leo roars, everyone knows about it. However, magnanimity is also a part of their make-up and the well-developed Leo is not averse to saying sorry – it would be undignified not to do so.

Leo's Sexual Appetite

Sexually, Leos are generous, and their warm hearts make them passionate and in need of full expression and satisfaction. Their partners must remember that they like the best of everything, and the setting for lovemaking must be as special and romantic as possible. Any chance of interruption, discomfort, or not feeling warm enough – anything lacking in the full romantic scene – will not favour a flowering of the Leo passion, which will inevitably have a measure of the dramatic about it.

When things are just right, Leos are extremely happy and that infectious happiness will result in a truly fulfilled partner and partnership.

Leos expect too much from their lovers, and when they fail to measure up to Leo's high standards – for instance not dressing in a way that pleases the Leo, being late, lazy, or forgetful – there is potential for trouble. Leos are not usually tactless, and should work out well in advance the best way of encouraging their lover to come up to their own high standards. If they do not, they will be at risk of making their lover feel small.

However, with encouragement from the Leo, improved standards will be acquired and then the pleasure of showing him or her off with true Leo pride will be achieved. In doing so, the lover will also be moving upwards and onward in life and career.

The best table in a restaurant is exactly what a Leo will plump for when they decide to treat their loved one.

LEO IN PERMANENT RELATIONSHIPS

Having decided to form a permanent relationship, the Leo partner must be aware that it is all too easy to take the lead and not pay enough attention to the actual partnership. If it is going to succeed, the relationship needs a strong element of sharing. In some cases, where the partner is less assertive, decisive, or ambitious, strong leadership may be necessary. If the Leo is astute, he or she will gradually and tactfully increase the partner's inner strength and confidence, without them actually realizing what is going on. Most Leos make sure that their partnership is fun and enjoyable, and that unexpected surprises occur from time to time, and not just on birthdays and anniversaries. In order to indulge their partners, chances are that the

Ballet is the sort of activity in which a Leo parent will over-encourage their child.

Leos will have booked at the best hotel or restaurant in town, or arranged a trip to a romantic location or an exciting city. And this is equally true whether they can afford it or not.

Leo's Strengths

What makes Leos good partners is the fact that they can be a real power behind the throne, because they can identify with their partner's ambitions. In most cases, in fact, they themselves would certainly have set their sights on something – probably creative – which is dear to them and that they know they will achieve in due course. At times like this, the Leo determination is certainly a force to reckon with.

Many Leos seem never to forget what it was like to be a child. How frustrating life became when their questions were evaded or unanswered by their parents, and how difficult it was to make even the most adored Mum and Dad really understand what they wanted, and what they had to say. It is because of this characteristic that Leos make excellent parents.

There is, however, one word of caution. While desperately wanting their children to be happy and to have everything they themselves lacked as children, Leo parents must be careful that they do not over-encourage their children to specialize in some activity simply because they had not had the opportunity to do so when they were young. Ballet and football are typical areas where this kind of over-zealous encouragement frequently takes place. Being certain of what the child himself or herself wants to do, and encouraging them in that direction would be far more rewarding in the long run.

A love of performing and a desire to take centre stage are typical qualities of Leo.

Leo in Education, Jobs, and Money

The Leo child (whether Leo is a Sun-, Moon-, or Rising-sign influence) should be happy and contented, and enjoy good food. The introduction to nursery school in most cases will provide few problems. They will soon discover the paints, and will delight in the brightest of colours, which will be splashed on with terrific gusto.

Quite soon, hints of Leo organizing ability and possible bossiness will emerge as the youngster tells her little friend that she should go over there, or that she's taking up too much room. This will be a source of considerable amusement to parents and those in charge, but the tendency needs to be watched because, while it's important to allow Leo's organizing ability to develop, bossiness needs controlling.

Here is a sign that loves to show off and to take centre stage. If and when they do, it is essential that praise is

Painting with the brightest colours will appeal to the young Leo.

given, and given freely. Young Leos thrive on it – but here again, encouragement to let others perform as well as encouraging the Leo to admire what friends are doing, is very important if young Miss or Master Leo is not to become a little show-off moppet.

Constructive Feedback

Once at school, young Leos must be encouraged by the teachers. Of course, like all children, they will need a lot of correction, but it must take the form of constructive criticism. Otherwise they can deflate all too easily and retreat into their own little lion's lair, and progress may come to a stop. They will really believe that their work and they themselves are "no good". When criticized, they do need to know why, and if what is good about their efforts is also pointed out to them, they will take corrective steps and make progress. Leo sensitivity must be recognized.

HEALTHY LIVING

Because Leo rules the heart and spine, it is important that Leos keep their cholesterol in check, and take care of their spine when sitting at desks for long periods of time. Because of their creative instincts, exercise will be more enjoyable if it is combined with some form of artistic expression – free dance, skating, sequence swimming, T'ai Chi, will be inspiring and extremely good for them. Those attracted to heavy sports will enjoy team games, but will aspire to be the captain. They will need to be aware of the vulnerability of their spines, and, to some extent, their ankles. Keeping warm is essential or circulation will suffer.

The practice of T'ai Chi

Further Education

University days will certainly be enjoyed, and, as ever, the level of achievement will very much rest on the inspiration gained from the lecturers. The choice of subject to read is, of course, a matter for the individual, but while Leos may be attracted to something simply to prove they have the capacity to attain a degree, it will be better for them to choose a subject that will help promote their eventual career. If they do this, their natural enthusiasm will get them off to a good start. However, it must be admitted that a lot of precious university

Studying at university or college will be most effective if the course is vocational.

time will be spent on the sports field, or enjoying the college's drama or arts clubs.

LEO AND CAREERS

Job satisfaction is of above average importance to this zodiac group. They are good organizers, disciplined, enthusiastic, optimistic, and like things to be right – all qualities which need full expression in the Leo career or profession.

As Leos are somewhat conservative and cautious in their outlook, they tend towards the conventional, but the influence of the Leo fire element comes into its own when new projects or productions are mooted, and they go with the flow. So, whether the choice is big business, politics, theatre, or the fine arts, here we have someone who will go far, be steadfast, and will not easily give up when facing challenges.

Leo determination is in a class of its own, and they will direct their physical and emotional energy to achieve their hearts' desire. It must also be said that Leo is a show-off, and will make a good but sometimes rather pompous boss, who will be a stickler for what he or she knows is necessary for the success of the company or organization. He or she will, however, be free with praise for employees.

Professionals
Through and Through

It is often said that Leos do not have hobbies, only careers. From time to time, a much-loved interest will be studied and practised in depth with a view to it becoming a profession in due course. They will often be eager to gain extra qualifications along the way, in order to prove to themselves and others that they can attain a high standard. In fact, if Leos are merely

Colourful bracelets and other trinkets will be attractive for a while, but Leo will soon want to move on to more sophisticated jewellery.

"LEO DETERMINATION IS IN A CLASS OF ITS OWN"

existing in a dull job simply to make money, they really should go in for some soul-searching in order to discover what they would really like to do during their working hours. Obviously there are limitations. For instance, if one is 30 and has never taken a ballet class, one cannot expect to dance *Swan Lake*, and it would be most inadvisable to give up a steady job to write a novel. But certain compromises can be made. A person with office experience could land an administrative job with a ballet company, or in a publishing house. Leos, when being interviewed, will show genuine enthusiasm and inspire confidence, and this is a great asset.

LEO AND MONEY

In theory, Leos need to make a lot of money, because they like to have the best and the most expensive of everything. For instance, it is interesting to notice that no matter how glamorous their costume jewellery may be, they will be eager to convert to the real stuff as soon as possible.

But they are in no way stupid with cash. Leos will be very good at saving for really important things in life, like a house or car. Starting off with an old banger, they will be keen to move on to something far more spectacular. Because they love their homes, the same attitude will apply. The tiny studio apartment will put them on the housing ladder, but they will be ambitious to move on to something more grand, where they can accommodate friends, not to mention a well-planned family.

Handling their Finances

Leos are generally good organizers, and this ability certainly applies to finance. When they have the cash to invest, they are cautious. They will take a slightly lower rate of interest rather than trusting an over-ambitious scheme. As investors, unless they are really impressed by a new enterprise, they will go for well-established, large organizations and for products and businesses of a type that interests them. Large department stores and five-star hotel chains will be popular, as will any industry where the products are of a high and extremely reputable standard.

Although they soon realize that get-rich-quick schemes are not for them, Leos do, occasionally, like to have a small flutter. For instance, the excitement of a glamorous casino will be fun, but we know many sensible Leos who put what they can afford to lose in one purse and their winnings in another, and so always go home without a damaging loss. Once their original stake money is gone – that is the end of it.

Other attractive risks include becoming an "angel" for a show or film. Here again, they must not be tempted to invest more than they can

Making videos for local broadcast may turn into a second income stream for resourceful Leos.

afford to lose. However, the temptation will be considerable for someone who is probably crazy about showbiz.

A Second Income
Somewhat like Aries – one of the other fire signs – they are enterprising, and with time, may well develop a second stream to their source of income.

Perhaps buying a high-quality video camera and getting their editing up to such a standard that a local cable company shows interest in their results; or they may sell paintings at a local art show. These kinds of enterprises are particularly good for Leos who are not expressing their creative talents in their careers. We seriously suggest they give this some careful thought.

"BECOMING AN 'ANGEL' FOR A SHOW OR FILM IS AN ATTRACTIVE RISK FOR LEO"

MIDHEAVEN SIGNS FOR LEO

The influence of the Midheaven stems from the part of the zodiac that was immediately overhead at our birth – that is, the sign that was at the top of the celestial sphere (for more detail, see pp304–6). We relate to, aspire to, and identify with the qualities of the sign on the Midheaven, especially in relation to our careers. The Midheaven signs for Leo birth charts set out below are the only possible combinations of Ascendant and Midheaven signs in both the Northern and Southern hemispheres. To work out your own Ascendant and Midheaven signs at birth, see the charts on pp344–7.

ASCENDANT ARIES
with Midheaven signs:

Capricorn Life and career will be taken seriously. Will "climb socially". Autocratic.

Aquarius Will have an original approach towards career. Could be attracted to self-employment.

ASCENDANT TAURUS
with Midheaven signs:

Capricorn Excellent business sense, needs security. Music will be very important.

Aquarius Stubbornness could mar progress. Must not suppress originality or inventiveness.

Pisces Conflict between a secure career and something creative but uncertain.

ASCENDANT GEMINI
with Midheaven signs:

Aries Restless. Will hate a static routine, and will need to be out and about.

Taurus Horticulture, selling, journalism, and fashion.

Aquarius Possible scientific flair; media and IT industries could be attractive options.

Pisces Creative flair for design, photography, or video. Must control restlessness.

ASCENDANT CANCER
with Midheaven signs:

Aries Clever business sense. Will make shrewd deals.

Taurus A conventional career; needs security. Agriculture, or perhaps nursing.

Aquarius Will make money possibly working from home in own business.

Pisces The caring professions – teaching, almoner.

**ASCENDANT LEO
(WITH LEO SUN SIGN)**
with Midheaven signs:

Aries Enthusiasm for career. Optimist, bossy, and risk taker. Has harm and charisma.

Taurus Good with creative work and big businesses. Needs security. Sensible with cash.

Pisces Attracted to showbiz. Will have talent and determination, whatever the chosen career.

ASCENDANT VIRGO
with Midheaven signs:

Taurus Good colour sense, interior decoration, theatre/film design, craftwork.

Gemini Journalism, fashion, retail selling, auctioneer.

ASCENDANT LIBRA
with Midheaven signs:

Cancer Hospitality industry, receptionist, public relations work.

Leo Career must have glamorous overtones. Needs to show off. Modelling, personal trainer.

ASCENDANT SCORPIO
with Midheaven signs:

Cancer Hard worker. Needs security. Antiques trade, mining.

Leo Potential for success in own business, finance, armed services.

Virgo Medical profession in specialist areas, pathology, brain or heart surgery, psychiatry.

ASCENDANT SAGITTARIUS
with Midheaven signs:

Leo Excellent organizer and good boss. Professional sports, lecturer, teacher, vet.

Virgo Librarian, scholar, literary agent, critic, researcher.

Libra A varied career in the arts, literature, music, or beauty trades. Travel important.

Scorpio Needs independence, and security. Has determination and discipline. Detective work and animals could feature.

ASCENDANT CAPRICORN
with Midheaven signs:

Leo Government official/civil service. Autocratic, a bit bossy.

Virgo Will make money through accepted channels – stockbroker, own business, financial advisor.

Libra Conventional approach towards creative work. Needs to be more innovative.

Scorpio Excellent sense of direction, ambitious, successful, whatever is chosen.

Sagittarius Enterprising and adventurous. Music and literature are important.

ASCENDANT AQUARIUS
with Midheaven signs:

Virgo Keen to make money. Hard worker. Suffers from too many changes of direction.

Libra Needs to work in partnership, but should take the lead. Beauty, fashion, or entertainment industries.

Scorpio Will pursue career with tenacity and discipline. Hard worker. Scientific flair. Astronomy, archeology, or antiques.

Sagittarius Slightly unpredictable, but superb teacher or lecturer. Writer, innovator and/or inventor.

Pisces Very creative and artistic. Career or hobby should involve the arts in some form.

"She has a tongue which charms, a mastery of words, and not so much wealth as the impulse to investigate the causes and effects of things."

Manilius, 1st century

Virgo

Natural reticence and a charming modesty can be mistaken for introversion in a Virgoan, while their discrimination and strong critical faculty can suggest a lack of emotional involvement. On the contrary, the right partners will find them delightful lovers. Among the busiest people in the zodiac, they will do anything for anyone.

VIRGO AS A SUN SIGN

Mercury, Virgo's ruling planet, is shared with Gemini, and its influence on both signs is clearly visible. Here are excellent communicators; they have bright, lively minds and are hardly ever still. In addition, Virgoans have enormous reserves of nervous energy, which need constant and regular expression through lifestyle, spare-time interests and possibly the working life.

The influence of the earth element makes Virgoans very practical and industrious. They flourish when they have set out the pattern of their day and can work to it. It suits them to know exactly what they have to do, and when. They need order in their lives, and a sense of security.

Unless other areas of the birth chart show that they have breadth of vision and can assess the overall picture, Virgoans have a tendency to get bogged down in detail and sometimes miss out on the wider concept of a project or plan. Awareness of this often helps them to balance what can be rather finicky over-planning with a view of the wider picture.

Virgoans are the natural critics of the zodiac; they see loop-holes in any and every situation, plan, or

The illustration for September from the *Très Riches Heures du Duc de Berry* (1416), with the Virgoan Virgin shown in the astrological chart at the top of the image.

VIRGO	
Symbol	The Virgin
Sun Sign Dates	24 August–22 September
Ruling Planet	Mercury
Element or Triplicity	Earth
Quality or Quadruplicity	Mutable
Positive/Negative	Negative
Body Areas	Stomach and Intestines
Polar Sign	Pisces

Virgo's symbol of the Virgin, as depicted on the page for September from the *Bedford Hours*, an illuminated manuscript produced in France in around 1423.

argument, and will be as quick as a flea to pick them up and point them out to whoever needs to know. Those who are less observant will be amazed at this facility, and will be thankful to their Virgo friends for saving them from making silly mistakes.

Like their Geminian cousins, Virgos are very talkative and enjoy communicating ideas and concepts to anyone who will take an interest. They will enthrall us with what they have to say, and by the lively, often bouncy way in which they express themselves.

Although their logic is of the highest quality, Virgos, nevertheless, still share with Cancerians the top prize for worry. Their apprehension is probably rooted in the fact that, since they look at every problem and situation from many points of view, the negative aspects of it are bound to present themselves along with the positive ones. Although they are generally not pessimistic, it does seem that the worst possible scenarios tend to dominate their thinking.

VIRGO AS ASCENDANT

When Virgo is the Rising sign, the sign on the Midheaven (see p283) is quite often Gemini. In such cases, the links between the two signs are considerably strengthened, as is the influence of the individual's Mercury sign.

Here we have a truly "mercurial" person – one who is very talkative and often unable to sit still for long, and

"EXERCISE IS ESSENTIAL FOR A VIRGO"

whose liveliness is more infectious than that of a Sun-sign Virgo. Rising-sign Virgos may become self-critical, sometimes to the point of undermining their confidence – which is not always particularly strong, whether the influence is from the Sun or Ascendant.

The Need for Exercise

We must remember that the nervous energy levels are extremely high when Virgo rises. Taking regular exercise is essential – tough workouts at the gym in the case of youngsters, and brisk walking, preferably in the country, if they are older. Interest in an active sport, such as tennis or netball, will be excellent; it is important to their general wellbeing that they keep moving. The most suitable sport for them is one which makes demands on their mind and intelligence.

While many may tend to underestimate their intellectual potential, and will go no further than becoming expert crossword addicts or getting hooked on "brain teasers", they are capable of stretching their minds and intellect in all kinds of directions. They should think, for instance, of always attending at least one demanding study course every academic year. The potential for communicating their ideas and opinions is very powerful in them, and there is a strong chance that they will find work in the media.

A Virgo's health is strongly related to the Rising-sign influence, and the traditional Virgo body areas are the stomach and intestines. More often than not, stress or a worrying problem will affect the stomach and result in bouts of diarrhoea, constipation, or indigestion. Worrying excessively can also cause a build up of headaches or migraines. Many individuals of this sign are vegetarians, and were so long before it became as popular as it is today; it particularly suits those with a Virgo Ascendant. We find that many are sensitive to conventional prescription drugs, to which they can be allergic. Homeopathic remedies are often more successful in such cases.

The Virgo symbol of a Virgin

VIRGO AS MOON SIGN

Perhaps, rather more than with most signs, we find striking similarities between the influence of the Moon, Sun, and Ascendant in Virgo. As ever, the Virgo's response to situations will be coloured by the Moon-sign influence, and it is here that the three governing influences tend to come together. They possess enormous resources of nervous energy, which, if channelled positively, can enhance the individual's generous supply of practical ability. Because of the speed of their reactions and responses, these people are in an excellent position to keep ahead of rivals. Their repartee will have a sharp, critical edge, and they will, more than they actually realize at the time, put many an erring person thoroughly in their place.

Yet in spite of these forthright qualities there is very often a lack of self-confidence. When meeting strangers or challenged in any way, the Moon-in-Virgo person will immediately become nervously talkative. They can nurse a conviction that they are in some way "not good enough", or "not clever enough". This can go really deep, and inhibition can restrict their progress in life and also preclude many enriching experiences.

A Nervous Stomach

The stomach upsets, which occur often with little or no apparent reason, usually spring from worry, especially if there is a sudden or unexpected problem. All this is further complicated because these individuals are extremely rational and practical. They should more often tell themselves to "go for it", and use all their strong, positive qualities with more determination. They do not lack purpose, but are often fearful of expressing it as forcefully as they should. They should learn to express their emotions and opinions sincerely, and not hesitate to say what they feel and what they think. When this happens (sometimes on the spur of the moment) it can have a stunning effect.

A vegetarian diet particularly suits Ascendant Virgos.

Sharing a common hobby with a Virgo can be a rewarding experience because of their natural enthusiasm.

Virgo in Friendship, Love, and Permanent Relationships

The lively activity of Virgos makes them fun, and also very useful. While they live extremely busy lives, we nearly always get a positive response if we ask for their help. Yes, they will manage to fit in feeding and walking our dog when we have to be out for longer than usual – even if their day is full of back-to-back appointments. If we are organizing a party or some event, they will again turn up trumps, and, provided they know exactly what we want them to do, their efficiency shows itself and blossoms. If they find a situation confusing, they can easily get rather worried and flummoxed, which causes them unnecessary strain.

Probably the best turn we can do for our Virgo friends is to help them build up their confidence. We should encourage them to think more positively about themselves, and to acknowledge and feel good about the depth and breadth of their skills and achievements. Many Virgos are genuinely shy, and if they become overtalkative in company,

the chances are that they are feeling somewhat ill at ease and endeavouring to cover up their nervousness.

Sharing Leisure Time

It is particularly rewarding to share a common interest with friends of this sign because they get tremendous satisfaction from their hobbies. Outside of their career, they will certainly have at least one really important spare-time interest which will be all-engulfing. If we share it with them, our own progress and involvement will develop considerably due to our friend's enthusiasm. Of course, we must expect them to criticize our inferior efforts – that is just the way they are – but the competitive element can be fun, as we assess each other's efforts.

Pleasing a Virgo friend is not difficult. They are nature lovers, so a surprise visit to a spectacular garden or arboretum will give enormous pleasure. The Mercury influence, which makes them good communicators, will ensure that we are kept in touch with their multitudinous activities, and that conversation is never at a standstill. If they are not into exercise we will do well to encourage them to get involved. They need regular workouts, and if bored with sessions at the gym, walking or cycling is ideal. Here too is potential for us to get moving along with our Virgo friends who really need to keep their high-keyed systems in balance to avoid restlessness or a build up of tension.

VIRGO IN LOVE

When Virgos realize they have fallen in love an all too common reaction is: "But what does he or she see in me?" The chances are that the admired one will see a very great deal that is lively, friendly, and – contrary to tradition – extremely sexy. What is also fascinating is Virgo's very natural and genuine modesty. It has a great deal of charm, but, like their initial self-questioning, can convince them that they are not really very attractive. They should remember that shyness can be a great aphrodisiac.

A Concerned Attitude

Virgos will be very concerned to do good things for their lovers, making sure of their creature comforts and

AN INTELLECTUAL BOOST

The Moon in Virgo adds a lively, colourful quality to the individual, whose talent and potential will be seen and expressed through his or her Sun and Rising signs. This placing will also give a tremendous intellectual boost which will increase the speed of understanding of subjects and areas where a Virgoan has real talent and potential. In certain cases a natural and animated scepticism will be present and counter that all too human failing, gullibility.

worrying about them. But it certainly can be the case that a concern about what their lover might think of them can dampen down the physical expression of love. In most cases Virgos come to terms with this, although perhaps more slowly than many other zodiac types. They learn to accept compliments graciously, and eventually welcome a more intimate development of the relationship. There is a romantic side to their nature which cries out for expression; it is up to the partner to recognize it and use it to help the Virgo to relax and enjoy their sex life.

Those Virgos for whom this is just too difficult will find expression of emotion in other ways. It may be through their interests or career, or perhaps by looking after an elderly relative for a long period of time. All this is very well-meaning, but Virgos should try not to spend too much time worrying about their partners, or whether they themselves are looking right for the next date, and just throw themselves into the experience of being in love. They should enjoy it in the conviction that with any luck it will go on for as long as they want it to. No problem about their being committed: they are very faithful lovers.

Virgos have genuine modesty and shyness, which can be very appealing.

We can always get a great deal of additional information about any sign's attitude to love and sex from the influences of Venus and Mars. For Virgos, the influence of Venus is of above average importance, so additional information will be gleaned from the Venus sign.

VIRGO IN PERMANENT RELATIONSHIPS

Partners of this zodiac group will be good friends and good talkers. The influence of Mercury is very strong, and Virgos are really good communicators who will freely express their opinions. They will do their best to encourage their partners to work hard and make rapid strides in their career or profession. This is wonderful when the exchanges are positive and constructive, but the main fault for

Being great communicators themselves, Virgos will encourage their families to talk freely.

Virgos in a permanent relationship or marriage is a tendency to nag and to be overcritical. They must learn to pull back, especially if a partner's little personal habits and mannerisms become disproportionately annoying to them. This can insidiously undermine and have a very disruptive effect on the relationship. After all, in most cases, the problems (even snoring) can be dealt with through practical action and making minor changes.

If Virgos becomes aware of the fact that they are really getting too preoccupied with their partner's alleged failings, they should go in for some self-analysis, and consider whether they are using their partner's weaknesses as an excuse for their own inhibitions and shortcomings. If they do become aware of difficulties in their relationship, they will find it easier than most people to discuss the problems frankly and openly with their partner, and sort out conflicts rationally.

Happy in Love

In all of this there is a stunning potential for Virgos to express elements of fun, and sheer happiness and liveliness. The rapport between them and their partners will increase, and they can very readily move forward together. This is particularly so where there are shared interests and work projects.

It is as well for Virgo's partner to be aware that, like the cat, they are very curious. Once this curiosity is ignited it can lead to entertaining and advanced sexual experimentation which will prove great fun and be extremely satisfying.

Parenthood will be undertaken with careful timing and much study, and while the Virgo parent will be extremely eager to encourage their child to read and develop a good vocabulary, warm affection and cuddling is important too, and special care really is necessary to see that on all occasions praise is given, and that criticism is kept to a minimum.

The Virgoan child will be in their element when developing their computer skills.

Virgo in Education, Jobs, and Money

Parents of very young Virgos will find their children talking much earlier than seems possible, and making themselves, and their wishes and protests, thoroughly understood. They will be somewhat shy during early nursery school days, and every effort must be made on the part of parents and teachers to boost self-confidence. Sometimes, grown-ups tend to tease children who appear shy. This is not a good idea with little Virgos, because their shyness is inherent; support, encouragement, and absolutely no teasing are very important. It is equally unproductive if the child hears parents say, "of course, you know she's shy." Such comments will only reinforce the tendency, and, more likely than not, Miss or Master Virgo will run out of the room; and who's to blame them?

Once there is an element of self-confidence present, Virgo children are at a considerable advantage at day school. Not only will their exercise books, course work, and handwriting be neat and tidy, but they will take to computer skills like a fish to water. Here we have thoroughly useful little people who will immediately want to help the teacher by giving out books or whatever and clearing up after class. This will often make them something of a teacher's pet, and result in a certain amount of teasing and even bullying. They must learn early on to stand up for themselves. They may well have to learn the hard way when told to stop talking. They are plodders, but their enquiring and lively minds will move them onward and upward.

Further Education

It is at university that the Virgos' naturally critical and sceptical minds will develop. They will enjoy debate and discussion, and if they have particularly good communicating skills, courses in media studies will be rewarding. Ecology will be attractive, as will agriculture, horticulture, business studies, and many other related areas. Creative young Virgos often take to designing pottery and craftwork, and in such cases, art college will be a good choice.

It is important to remember that worry will upset the Virgo stomach from the earliest of school days; the announcement of a tummy ache will

An attraction for books may lead a Virgo to become a writer, bookseller, or librarian.

be quickly followed by the plea: "Do I have to go to school today?" The pain will be due to some worry rather than anything that has been eaten, and it will be as well for parents to discover the real cause. They are also likely to take to a vegetarian diet from quite an early age.

LIST-MAKING FOR ANXIOUS VIRGOS

As with anyone suffering from anxiety, it is no use telling a Virgo to stop worrying, but there is an approach they should adopt which expresses both their logic and common sense. They should make lists of the pros and cons of every aspect of a problem and weigh one column against the other. Their natural logic will then kick in, and they will find it easier to reach a decision. Decision-making is actually not very difficult for Virgos – but the degree of ease depends on the sign Mercury was in when they were born.

VIRGO AND CAREERS

Here is the perfect and efficient personal assistant, the meticulous editor, the brilliant gardener, the hugely caring nurse, beautician, personal trainer, critic, and so on. The areas in which Virgos can find a rewarding niche are many and varied. Any job in which detailed work is called for, and where there is an element of service to others, will be rewarding. The immaculately dressed butler or housekeeper springs to mind, as does employment as an estate or any kind of agent. Acting as a go-between also has considerable attractions. Many are extremely bookish, and certainly there are more than a fair share of successful writers, librarians, and bookshop owners and assistants. Those connected with health, hygiene, and diet have also emerged from this zodiac group.

We must include the media here too. Remembering their communication skills, working in sound radio often has a strong appeal, as does any behind-the-scenes work for television. Appearing in front of the camera can have its problems, for if a tendency to self-consciousness is present in the individual this will immediately mar the performance. What is also important to them is to find a career that stretches them intellectually and includes a good level of variety – to offset any possibility of boredom in the daily rounds.

Problem-Solving

Virgos do need to be aware that they can become hypercritical, and should try not to lash out at colleagues. They can express this tendency toward pupils and students if they are in the teaching profession. If it is controlled they do make very good teachers – learning to criticize with a sense of humour is an enormous asset for them.

The Virgo tendency to worry will slow progress and is all too likely to bother them, from small day-to-day problems to whether they will still be in work this time next year. They should not get bogged down in the minute details of problems, but apply logic and common sense to keep the difficulty in perspective, and not allow it to mar their output or performance. They need to be kept busy, and if they are out of work, they should set themselves a schedule and keep to it. If they have been made redundant or dismissed, their self-esteem will have had a severe blow and

They will not squander cash or stretch their plastic to buy that expensive designer dress – rather a simple black number and a variety of accessories to make it look as varied as possible for all kinds of occasions. They sometimes give the impression that they are less well off then they really are. Having a healthy bank balance gives them additional security, whereas any overspending would increase the possibility of ongoing worries. Here is another zodiac group

"WORKING IN THE MEDIA APPEALS TO A VIRGO"

their confidence could well be at a low ebb. Sending out CVs, checking the Internet, reading the vacancies columns in the local paper, and doing everything else possible to find a job is really essential. This will be time-consuming but eventually worthwhile for them.

VIRGO AND MONEY

When Virgos have some cash to invest, it is unlikely that they will take risks by getting involved in get-rich-quick schemes. Once will almost certainly be enough; if they are trapped and fail, they will never be tempted again. The influence of the sign's earth element is in evidence here. Their natural instinct is to go for steady growth, which is precisely the right way for them, and they should always look for sound financial advice.

On the whole, Virgos are careful with money, partly because they hate showiness.

Behind-the-scenes work in the media will have a strong appeal for Virgos.

"VIRGOS WILL NOT SQUANDER CASH OR STRETCH THEIR PLASTIC"

who are enterprising. They should seriously consider taking advantage of one of their many hobbies by selling the results of their labours.

Wise Investments

If Virgos receive an unexpected boost to their bank account – maybe after a flutter on the lottery or as a result of an inheritance – they will definitely be among those who claim that "it won't change my life". That will at least be the basic idea; but pressures from their loved ones will in the end make them change their minds. In spite of this, their needs are often considerably simpler than with most of us, so if they really stick to their original reaction and do not let their increased bank balance affect their lifestyle, their best approach is to further develop their business skills and be more enterprising. Using their powers of communication on these occasions will also be a useful asset. They may well be inspired to give a large sum to a favourite charity. If this is the case they should also aim to get directly involved with the work the charity does; they will be fascinated to see where and how their endowment is being used.

Many Virgos enjoy organic food, and here is an area for potential investment. If finances allow, the actual growing of organic vegetables and fruit will be an extremely rewarding interest for them.

Growing vegetables or investing in organic farming will be of great interest to Virgos.

MIDHEAVEN SIGNS FOR VIRGO

The influence of the Midheaven stems from the part of the zodiac that was immediately overhead at our birth – that is, the sign that was at the top of the celestial sphere (for more detail, see pp304–6). We relate to, aspire to, and identify with the qualities of the sign on the Midheaven, especially in relation to our careers. The Midheaven signs for Virgo birth charts set out below are the only possible combinations of Ascendant and Midheaven signs in both the Northern and Southern hemispheres. To work out your own Ascendant and Midheaven signs at birth, see the charts on pp344–7.

ASCENDANT ARIES
with Midheaven signs:

Capricorn Hard working. Conventional career; finance, civil service, government occupations.

Aquarius Medical profession, caring for the elderly. Possibly unusual objectives/ambitions.

ASCENDANT TAURUS
with Midheaven signs:

Capricorn Strong urge to make money. Love of the land, ambitious, musical potential.

Aquarius Will need a career that is "different". Conflict between freedom of expression and conventional outlook.

Pisces Creative potential. Needs security, but will lack direction.

ASCENDANT GEMINI
with Midheaven signs:

Aries Impatient for success; needs travel, change of direction to avoid boredom.

Taurus Good communicative skills and business sense.

Aquarius Terrific originality, excellent communicative skills. Media, IT industries, airlines.

Pisces Possible work with under-privileged children. Lively kindergarten teacher. Love of chosen occupation.

ASCENDANT CANCER
with Midheaven signs:

Aries Quick-thinking, assertive business person; shrewd.

Taurus Extremely practical, but will love good living and identify with luxury even if unattainable.

Aquarius High emotional level. Humanitarian sympathies, charity work. Conflicting conventional and unconventional aspirations.

Pisces Nursing, beautician, naturopath. Marine biology. Emotional involvement in career.

ASCENDANT LEO
with Midheaven signs:

Aries Great enthusiasm for inner fulfilment, possibly through professional sport, creative work, or the car industry.

Taurus Finance, banking, insurance, accountancy. Bright, innovative ideas to make money.

Pisces The movie industry, possibly editing, research archive work; librarian.

**ASCENDANT VIRGO
(WITH VIRGO SUN SIGN)**
with Midheaven signs:

Taurus Needs emotional and material security. Agriculture, architecture, horticulture, garden design, sculpture, craftwork.

Gemini The media in any form; literary ability. Radio officer.

ASCENDANT LIBRA
with Midheaven signs:

Cancer Air steward, the hospitality industry, catering, chef. Hard worker.

Leo Creative potential for jewellery, good organizer, bossy. Needs glamour in career.

ASCENDANT SCORPIO
with Midheaven signs:

Cancer The Navy; will respond well to routine and discipline. Pathologist.

Leo Wine merchant, chemist, medical profession, banking.

Virgo Will enjoy considerable success, and possible fame. Detective work, medical research, psychotherapist.

ASCENDANT SAGITTARIUS
with Midheaven signs:

Virgo Teaching, university lecturer, the travel industry. A fulfiling, satisfying career.

Libra Considerable success; librarian, publishing, the law, working with animals.

Scorpio Excellent prospects; sense of direction plus breadth of vision. Town planning, editor, investigative journalism.

ASCENDANT CAPRICORN
with Midheaven signs:

Leo A good but somewhat relentless boss. Success in finance, banking.

Virgo Needs stability, restless but dislike of changes. Accountancy, own business.

Libra Outgoing, hard working, considerate, but critical. Retail trades, PR work.

Scorpio Intensive worker. Research, engineering, plumbing.

ASCENDANT AQUARIUS
with Midheaven signs:

Libra Will express charm during working hours. All luxury trades, television industry, beautician.

Scorpio Conservation, anthropology, astronomy, scientific research; fact-finding.

Sagittarius Airlines, travel industry; university lecturer, solicitor. Needs stability, but with freedom of expression.

ASCENDANT PISCES
with Midheaven signs:

Sagittarius Needs to work in partnership, possibly in small or shared business where hard work, inspiration, and creativity will blossom.

"*Whatever dispute needs resolution,
the Scales will see to it, well acquainted
with the tables of the law.*"

Manilius, 1st century

Libra

Balance and peace are the most important things in a Libran's life, and it sometimes seems that they try to achieve this simply by refusing to confront problems. Ultimately, it is fruitless to expect a Libran to make a quick decision, whether this involves a vast business takeover or the choice of a breakfast cereal.

LIBRA AS A SUN SIGN

Apart from being the only zodiac symbol that does not represent a living creature, the symbol of the Scales has an extremely interesting and important meaning for Sun-sign Librans. Balance and harmony are crucial to their lives, and it is vital for their wellbeing that they are as free as possible from upsetting arguments and from anything that seriously disturbs their peace and quiet.

In quest of the balance they consciously or unconsciously need, a great many of them will simply "wait and see" when it comes to decision-making – sometimes for so long that the problem goes away, unresolved. It is not without reason that they are often accused of "sitting on the fence"; when, for example, they are involved in a discussion that becomes an argument between two other people, the moment they realize they are going to be pressed to take one person's side against the other, they will simply refuse. Their reluctance to upset one of the two friends is total. But

The illustration for October from the *Très Riches Heures du Duc de Berry* (1416), with the Scales of Libra shown in the astrological chart at the top of the image.

they are natural diplomats, and if they do decide to intervene it will be as an honest broker, a go-between who will, in the end, probably be able to suggest a number of ways out of the argument or quandary, so that problems are solved in a highly civilized manner.

The Scales of Libra, as depicted on the calendar page for October from the *Bedford Hours*, an illuminated manuscript produced in France in around 1423.

LIBRA	
Symbol	The Scales
Sun Sign Dates	23 September–23 October
Ruling Planet	Venus
Element or Triplicity	Air
Quality or Quadruplicity	Cardinal
Positive/Negative	Positive
Body Area	Kidneys
Polar Sign	Aries

The theme of balance permeates the whole of the Libran's being. They have a strong need to relate to other people, and to a partner in particular. They feel only half alive when they are alone, and we find that requirement expressed in all areas of their lives. They like to work in partnership, and they like to have spare-time interests that involve working with another person. Loneliness really is anathema for the Librans – though this can be modified by the very powerful influence of Venus (the planet which also rules Taurus), for its influence adds several dimensions to the characteristics of the Libran Sun (*see p210* to discover the relevant Venus sign).

The influence of Venus – the most delightful of planets – is very powerful in the charts of Librans, and it endows them with a great deal of natural charm and sympathy. Here are excellent listeners who will gently make practical suggestions for friends in trouble, offering plenty of possible alternative solutions to their problems.

Due to their ability to relax, Librans are often wrongly accused of being lazy. In fact, when then do let up, it is in order to recuperate and to avoid a build-up of stress which might bring on headaches, to which they are vulnerable. An astonishing amount of activity forms an important part of the lifestyle of many Librans; it is through many varied interests that they get a great deal of inner satisfaction.

LIBRA AS ASCENDANT

Libra is not one of the compellingly strong signs of the zodiac, so it must be remembered that a powerful Sun sign will often overshadow some of the Libran characteristics when the sign is Rising. Nevertheless, here will be the

"LONELINESS IS ANATHEMA FOR LIBRANS"

same warm charm and need for a harmonious and well-balanced life, and particularly the need to relate in a full partnership. We deal with this all-important sphere of life in some detail below: suffice to say here that the psychological motivation towards partnership is probably at its strongest when Libra is the Rising sign. The influence of the assertive polar sign, Aries, comes into its own in this respect also.

There is a real sense of urgency in the search for a partner, and sadly mistakes will be made. One would think that the individual would learn the hard way, but this is not necessarily so, for the drive is very strong and, in most cases, overcomes the otherwise typical Libran indecision, so that the individual often dives prematurely into relationships. At such times there is a tendency to put the self first, which can be one cause of an equally speedy end to the relationship. Someone with Libra Rising must be aware of this tendency, which is most uncharacteristic of Sun- or Moon-sign Librans.

The Ascendant, or Rising sign, has a strong bearing on the individual's health. A vulnerability to headaches is marked with this sign. Libra, by tradition, rules the kidneys; therefore, it is advisable for them to see a doctor should headaches persist over any length of time. Libra is a sign that enables one in most cases to deal extremely well with stress or anxiety, so there should be few problems there. If problems do occur, chances are that the Libran is faced with a difficult decision which, even if hope springs eternal, just won't go away. At such times, those with a strong Libran influence should always confide in a sympathetic friend – in much the same way that their friends confide in them

Sport and physical fitness are important to those with Libra as their Rising sign.

when under stress. The need to talk important problems through is important to all of us, but under Libra one should never bottle up problems. Many with Libra as their Rising sign enjoy demanding and tough sports. They are motivated to use their physical energy in a dynamic and rewarding way, so sports, dance, and physical fitness are more important to them than to those Librans who are laid-back and who actually dislike exercise.

LIBRA AS MOON SIGN

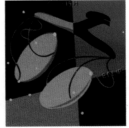

The Libran Scales is the only zodiac symbol that does not represent a living creature.

Moon-in-Libra people are the peacemakers of the zodiac. They express sympathy and kindness, with total awareness of what is going on in any situation: the immediate response to any tricky or difficult situation will be to attempt to sort things out quickly, quietly, and amicably. Libran tact and diplomacy, which emerges poignantly with the Sun- and Rising-sign people, is heightened when Libra is the Moon sign. However, in personal matters, the tendency to procrastinate over decisions will still be very much in evidence. It is necessary to look at the individual's Sun and Rising signs to see

A WELL-BALANCED VIEW OF LIFE

One particularly amusing way in which to recognize a Libran relates to the symbol of their sign, the Scales, and is likely to be noticeable whether they are Sun-, Rising-, or Moon-in-Libra types. In conversation, especially when they are listening to what we are saying, they will tend to move their heads from one side to the other, as if they really are weighing up our comments! The women often enjoy clothes which are asymmetric in design – but adding some pretty accessory to keep the overall appearance well balanced.

A Libran's hand gestures will emphasize the Libran love of weighing up and balancing out a discussion.

at what point, after the initial lunar uncertain response, stronger and more decisive or assertive characteristics take over. An emphasis on Leo, Scorpio, or Capricorn will offer few

if any problems, whereas Cancer or Pisces could increase the tendency towards uncertainty.

These individuals usually give the impression of being laid-back, and this is often indeed the case. The tendency is very much emphasized when those with the Moon in Libra speak in a rather slow and drawling manner, giving the impression that they have a relaxed lifestyle and live life at their own easy pace.

Bringing out the best in other people is something dear to the heart of the Moon-in-Libra person. Here are caring hosts who love to entertain, usually pretty lavishly. When guests arrive, they will immediately look after them, make them feel at ease, and make sure they have someone interesting to talk to. The food they offer will be delicious and rich. They will give the impression that absolutely nothing, whether it be time or money, has been spared to make any occasion thoroughly entertaining – lavish, memorable, and successful. Any Libran influence leads to a penchant for good living and luxury, and Libran Moon people respond very readily and willingly to this, wanting others to enjoy it as much as themselves.

Expect fine dining when you visit the Moon-in-Libra person.

Libran friends are easy-going, but find it hard to plan things far in advance, putting off decisions about where to go or what to eat.

Libra in Friendship, Love, and Permanent Relationships

There is always something particularly pleasant at the prospect of meeting up with our Libran friends. Whether we have arranged a splendid dinner at a favourite restaurant or are having a quick get together over coffee, their easy style will make for an interesting catch-up with our respective news and gossip. Having a lively exchange of opinions on joint interests will be fun, and we know that we will part feeling more light-hearted than when we met. We must, however, be prepared to be rather firm at times with their tendency to procrastinate. If we want to go to some event, for which its necessary to book in advance, we should get on and do the booking. A Libran is all too likely to put this off until all the best seats in the price category we want have been sold – or even until the show is completely sold out. Yes, they really would like to try a new skill and take classes, but, well, now isn't perhaps quite the time for it. We must contrive to keep one step ahead of them, offering lots of encouragement and gentle goading so that they don't go off the idea and waste what could turn out to be creative or innovative potential. Librans benefit from sharing interests with like-minded friends and generally discussing related problems, and this makes for really good opportunities to strengthen the ties of friendship.

Librans can be pretty resentful, and the chances are that, while describing someone's unwelcome reaction or behaviour, they will remark, "how can she treat me like that after all I've done for her?" They do like acquaintances to be openly and enthusiastically grateful for their kindnesses, and it is up to us to be tactful and ready with a believable excuse when we forget to be as gracious with our gratitude as we should. It is worth remembering, too, that they find it difficult to understand why some zodiac types are less outwardly expressive than they themselves are.

Libran men are romantic and will shower a new partner with wonderful bouquets and lavish gifts.

LIBRA IN LOVE

The skies are constantly blue for Librans when they're in love, and everything is sheer bliss. But how easily and frequently they fall! Their need to relate in partnerships is extremely important to them – to the point that they are unfulfilled until they find the right partner. And then each partner in turn starts out being the right one for them.

Here that typical Libran indecision and procrastination flies out of the window – they so often rush into a relationship, failing to wait for it to develop at a more natural pace. They need as soon as possible to be able to say "we" rather than "I". At times they will mistake polite flattery for a declaration of love, especially in a new relationship. Most learn through painful experience to be sceptical and build up a resistance to flirtation to help them avoid disappointment and heartbreak.

Librans are great romantics who want every stage of their relationship to be colourful, beautiful, and memorable. Women can expect wonderful bouquets and gifts from their Libran men, and men may safely look forward to enjoying specially fine candlelit dinners with their Libran hostess decked out in the most sexy outfit she possesses. When Librans realize the power and persuasiveness of this kind of treatment, they

make stunning partners who keep romance alive for a long time. But God help the poor partner who happens to forget an anniversary!

Librans too often fall in love with love, and sometimes need a partner without necessarily wanting what a true partnership entails – something to do and someone to talk to when they are not in bed. They can simply be unaware of the other elements in really successful bonding – the true compatibility and friendship which are so important if living together on a day-to-day basis is to be a happy and successful experience. It is only when they do learn this that they are really ready for permanent relationship or marriage.

LIBRA IN PERMANENT RELATIONSHIPS

"We're moving in together"; "Guess what? I'm engaged, and we're getting married." Librans will be almost more excited to tell us their news than they are by the news itself. If wedding bells are going to ring, the Libran woman will probably be more eager to spend money and time planning the big day than women of other signs. It can be the case that their concentration on the event itself will be more intense than any focus on the long-term future of her or her partner.

Once committed, they blossom and will attain a new and rewarding level of psychological wholeness and inner

A Libran bride will plan her wedding in great detail, whether or not she has fully considered her relationship.

satisfaction. But from marriage onwards, or from the time of setting up house together, Librans need to be continually reassured that they are loved, wanted, and desired. They can set about reassuring themselves by some odd tactics. They will, for instance, consciously pick quarrels to "rock the boat", because the making up process is so delightful and cosy to them. If this is the case, serious outbursts will occur, and if the partner doesn't recognize these tactics early on, the resulting conflict will be extremely uncomfortable. Even if the partner comes to know about what is going on, such tactics can become boring, and for no good reason can cause serious damage to the overall atmosphere of the partnership. This warning should be taken quite seriously: not simply because of the arguments and tensions that can arise, but because if the partner gives in to the situation and Libra is allowed to switch between nagging and smothering affection, it can become almost impossible to put up with.

Once they settle into a permanent relationship, it is all too easy for Librans to avoid decision-making even more

A Libran can be a good parent, although there may be a tendency to spoil the child at times just to get some peace.

Perhaps the most central decision for couples is whether and when they want to start a family. Librans are more than likely to say: "We needn't decide right now – let's wait and see – we'll cope when and if." All well and good, but it must be remembered that a Libran who has a child without feeling a strong need for one is likely to find parenthood an irksome and stressful business. When their desire for children is strong, Librans make good parents – though they tend to spoil their children in order

"LIBRANS OFTEN FALL IN LOVE WITH LOVE"

frequently than they do when they are on their own. Their reaction to almost every situation, from buying a house to deciding between tea or coffee, will be, "oh, you choose." Partners should watch out for this, and persuade them that certain decisions should be taken alone and – even more importantly – that mutual decision-making is the only sensible way of approaching other problems. Persuading a Libran not to avoid expressing what he or she really feels is really very important.

to get some peace and quiet. The child will be delighted, of course, and will exploit the situation. Librans must make sure that, uncharacteristically, they answer questions when a child asks them. Indirect answers to questions will be irritating, and cause frustration to the Libran as the child tries persistently to get a real answer. A Libran who answers "just because", when the child asks why, is heading for trouble – as is the habit of involving the other partner: "Oh, you must ask daddy/mummy about that."

Creative Librans often excel in careers such as fashion design.

Libra in Education, Jobs, and Money

The youngest Libran child will have a great deal of charm and will soon find that smiles and sweetness get them what they want. When it comes to nursery school, parents will see these tactics expressed even more successfully. There is a good chance that in such an environment young Librans are likely to throw a tantrum, especially if another child is playing with a toy that they want. In such cases, instructors can appeal to the little one's instinct for fair play and sharing by suggesting that the two children should enjoy playing together. This is the ideal solution, because here we already have the need to share and work in a partnership that is beginning to be developed and expressed in a positive way.

Libran children do their utmost to be indecisive. It is up to the parents to coax them about which colour they want or which toy they would enjoy playing with, and so on. Any response will encourage decisiveness.

Young Librans will work hard at school, but only in subjects that they enjoy. Consequently, reports will be mixed. If they fail to make progress in a particular subject, it will simply be because they do not like it, or maybe the teacher. Sometimes extra goading into action will be necessary.

At university, the laid-back Libran lifestyle may well come into its own. Librans will, however, procrastinate over revision for exams. They will concentrate far too much on their social and love life, so degree results may be disappointing. There are those who really enjoy tough sports, and many make excellent rowers, but these activities are also distractions from study.

The idea of sharing toys and taking turns will appeal to little Librans.

LIBRA AND CAREERS

It is in the luxury trades or those with an element of glamour that Librans really make their mark. Creative Librans often excel in fashion design or as beauticians and hair stylists. Interior decoration is attractive and financially rewarding to those with an aesthetic talent.

Many famous fashion models are Libran – but young Librans contemplating this career must be aware that it is tough and very physically demanding. It may look an easy and glamorous job, but it is not. Fortunately, most Librans are very competitive, and this will be an asset in all jobs.

Those with an ear for music will find their niche in a pop group, as part of a string quartet, or as a backing singer or an accompanist – musicianship on a small rather than symphonic scale.

DISCIPLINING THE LIBRAN CHILD

At school a Libran child's charm and winning ways will get them a very long way. The strictest, severest teachers are known to find them quite irresistible, so that punishments will be lighter and praise more forthcoming than for many other zodiac types. Because of these charming qualities it is extremely easy to spoil Libran children, and if they go through a stage of throwing tantrums for quite inconsequential reasons it will be because they have previously been allowed to get away with murder. It is, therefore, important that they are quite strictly disciplined early on.

"LIBRANS HAVE A LIKING FOR FAIR PLAY AND JUSTICE"

If attracted to millinery at art or fashion school, any Libran could certainly find considerable success in this rarefied area of fashion, and should not be put off because of the small number of opportunities available. Look to the theatre or film industry costume departments. Wig-making, too, might be worth consideration.

The theme of justice is central to Libra, and it is not surprising that many Librans are drawn to a career in law.

Librans whose success leads them to the top of a profession or industry may find it difficult to cope with the loneliness of a top job, and may not be as happy as they should be. In spite of all the benefits of privilege and increased income they will only really thrive if they can still relate to colleagues they have worked with along the way. Here their Libran tact must come into its own if they are not perceived to be leaning on their workmates and failing to assume the responsibility they have been given.

If working for large organizations in an office or department store (which they particularly enjoy), they will become disproportionately upset when there are squabbles, or if office politics cause problems. If this is the case their partners should try to distract them as often as possible from such annoying, time-consuming situations.

In some very interesting cases the influence of the Libran polar sign, Aries, makes its presence felt, and we find some famous generals who have

Libra prominent in their charts. The attraction to this kind of lifestyle may stem from the individual's need for fair play and a sense of justice, rather than the aggressive impulses, which are so much part of life in the armed forces. A liking for fair play and justice can also influence the Libran choice of career in other ways – the law in its various forms has its attractions, and Libran barristers and solicitors do extremely well.

LIBRA AND MONEY

Librans love to spend money, often shopping till they drop. Organizing their finances and filling out tax returns will be extremely boring for them, but they do have to keep the peace with the taxman, and will eventually get round to all that form-filling – or employ an expensive accountant to do it for them.

   When investing on the stock market, indecision could be their downfall because of missed opportunities, so they need a trusted advisor at these times too. If Librans invest in areas

Librans need good business partners when setting up shop together.

financial support than they should, and so risk losing a lot of cash by ignoring all practical aspects of the project. They should also be careful not to put all their financial eggs in one basket – there is a tendency to do so simply because it will save them having to make multiple decisions as to how to split up their capital.

   Should they have the opportunity to go into business for themselves, they should not do so alone. The need for

"LIBRAN INTUITION COMES INTO ITS OWN WITH INVESTMENTS"

that interest them, such as their favourite group of department stores or a large cosmetics company, they can get really involved. Libran intuition (a quality often ignored by astrologers) comes into its own when investing, and they should listen to what it is telling them – in most cases it is unlikely to let them down.

   As far as financial risk is concerned, there are times when they get rather too excited by a new business venture or project, and it is easy for them to get carried away and over-invest. If someone they know is starting a business they may become rather too soft-hearted and give them more

partnership in business is as important as it is in personal relationships. If, for instance, the Libran enjoys meeting the public and selling, that will be the best role for him or her. A "sleeping", behind-the-scenes partner will be ideal – someone who is firm; who will prevent Libra from getting carried away with expensive premises, advertising schemes, and the like; and who will see to the accounts and give strict advice as far as expansion or the employment of extra staff is concerned. This kind of partner is essential to take all the more boring aspects of the concern off the shoulders of the outgoing, charming Libran salesperson/joint owner.

MIDHEAVEN SIGNS FOR LIBRA

The influence of the Midheaven stems from the part of the zodiac that was immediately overhead at our birth – that is, the sign that was at the top of the celestial sphere (*for more detail, see pp304–6*). We relate to, aspire to, and identify with the qualities of the sign on the Midheaven, especially in relation to our careers. The Midheaven signs for Libra birth charts set out below are the only possible combinations of Ascendant and Midheaven signs in both the Northern and Southern hemispheres. To work out your own Ascendant and Midheaven signs at birth, see the charts on pp344–7.

ASCENDANT ARIES
with Midheaven signs:

Capricorn Very ambitious; excellent for own business, but in partnership.

Aquarius Will want the glamorous life. The luxury trades, cosmetic industry, modelling, scientific research.

ASCENDANT TAURUS
with Midheaven signs:

Capricorn Architecture, floristry, banking, finance. Musical talent.

Aquarius Archeology, television industry, working freelance, or own business in partnership.

Pisces Podiatrist, shoe design, dietitian, jeweller. Will work hard.

ASCENDANT GEMINI
with Midheaven signs:

Aries Art gallery assistant, manicurist. Needs challenge and change.

Taurus Creative work in own studio. Editing, dress design.

Aquarius The media, good television presence. The antiques trade.

Pisces Dancer, entertainer, make-up artist. Craftwork.

ASCENDANT CANCER
with Midheaven signs:

Aries The armed services. Determined business person. Will make money and enjoy it.

Taurus Children's nurse, kindergarten school teacher. Beautician. Needs security.

Aquarius Aroma therapist, masseur, midwifery, air steward. A caring individual.

Pisces Nursing, chef, restaurateur, interior decorator. Creative imagination.

ASCENDANT LEO
with Midheaven signs:

Aries Excellent communicator; the media. Needs to work in partnership.

Taurus The retail trade; good selling ability. Needs security.

Pisces Very creative. The fine arts, dance, luxury trades, modelling.

ASCENDANT VIRGO
with Midheaven signs:

Taurus Good business sense, quick mind, agriculture, possibly rearing unusual breeds. Horticulture.

Gemini Excellent at selling luxury goods, expensive cosmetics; good demonstrator. Lively personality.

ASCENDANT LIBRA
(WITH LIBRA SUN SIGN)
with Midheaven signs:

Cancer The caring professions: nursing, charity work, fund raiser. Emotional involvement with career.

Leo Good organizer; hotel work, receptionist, dating agency work.

ASCENDANT SCORPIO
with Midheaven signs:

Cancer Engineering, chef, bartender, medical profession. Psychic ability, but needs training.

Leo Strong desire to make money with excellent, shrewd business sense. Needs business partner; will show off.

Virgo Relationship counsellor, gardener, teacher, occupational therapist.

ASCENDANT SAGITTARIUS
with Midheaven signs:

Virgo The media, working with older people; needs challenge.

Libra
Success and possible fame in chosen areas. Work with animals; horse trainer. Has panache, could be daring.

Scorpio Tremendous sense of purpose. Criminal investigation, all kinds of research lecturer.

ASCENDANT CAPRICORN
with Midheaven signs:

Leo Banker, sculptor, builder, or architect. Needs to see good results from effort.

Virgo Osteopath, analyst, accountant. Needs security and regular pay cheques.

Libra Bookseller or publisher; real estate; auctioneer. Musical talent.

Scorpio Chemistry, museum curator, engineering; work with metals, restorer.

ASCENDANT AQUARIUS
with Midheaven signs:

Virgo Capable of detailed work; design with considerable originality.

Libra A successful career in the arts or fashion industry, possibly theatre.

Scorpio Brilliant but stubborn. Finance, the wine trade, the police.

Sagittarius An adventurous outlook on life. The travel industry, university lecturer, geographer. Needs constant intellectual stimulation.

ASCENDANT PISCES
with Midheaven signs:

Sagittarius Needs to be decisive and disciplined in attitude to career. Excellent potential, perhaps for creating original accessories. Photographer.

"*The Scorpion creates natures ardent for argument, and a spirit which rejoices in it.*"

Manilius, 1st century

Scorpio

The fund of emotional and physical energy at the disposal of the average Scorpio is almost alarming, and it must be extended positively if some kind of explosion is to be avoided. Their vigour must be joyously expended through their sex lives, but here, as in every other area, obsessiveness must be avoided.

SCORPIO AS A SUN SIGN

Over the years, Scorpio has had an indifferent reputation – it has even been considered "the bad sign". This is sheer nonsense. All signs have "good" and "bad" qualities, and Scorpio no more or less than the other eleven. In fact, this powerful sign bestows the highest level of physical and emotional energy of the whole zodiac. Those in whose birth chart it is emphasized – whether by Sun, Ascending, or Moon sign – are supported by strong resources which are the basis of great potential, and which can be expressed in countless ways.

It is their remarkable energy that singles out Sun-sign Scorpios. This energy must be positively channelled, and, if it is not expressed though a truly rewarding career or profession, or diversified in other meaningful directions, it stagnates, and the individual becomes vulnerable to feeling unfulfilled and restless, and suffering bouts of depression. In such cases these powerful emotions can be negatively expressed through the worst and most common Scorpio fault: jealousy (sometimes combined with resentfulness and brooding). In extreme cases, such negativity can lead to violence.

Most people born under this very impressive sign are big achievers.

The illustration for November from the *Très Riches Heures du Duc de Berry* (1416), with the Scorpion shown in the astrological chart at the top of the image.

The Scorpion, as depicted on the page for November from the *Bedford Hours*, an illuminated manuscript produced in France in around 1423.

SCORPIO	
Symbol	The Scorpion
Sun Sign Dates	24 October–22 November
Ruling Planet	Pluto, traditional ruler Mars
Element or Triplicity	Water
Quality or Quadruplicity	Fixed
Positive/Negative	Negative
Body Area	Genitals
Polar Sign	Taurus

Scorpios possess tremendous drive and a strong desire to "go places". Once they find the right goal for themselves in life, they approach it with determination and tenacity. They are capable of deep, incisive thought and sharp observation. In fact, their minds are rather like that of Sherlock Holmes' – they never miss a thing.

Scorpios have the reputation of being the sexiest among all the 12 zodiac signs. People tend to think that their preoccupation with sex leaves them with little time for anything else. However, this is not true. A detailed study of this sign often reveals that a Scorpio's positive energies usually find expression through a variety of ways. For instance, here is the dedicated homemaker, who works 24/7 for her family and keeps her home immaculate. Or the man who has a physically demanding job, but whose heart and soul is in his garden, boat, camera, or his model railway.

SCORPIO AS ASCENDANT

When Scorpio rises, it casts its influence on the entire birth chart. It energizes the individual's Sun sign and increases his or her emotional level, which, in most cases, is an asset. But, in the case of "cool" Sun signs – say Virgo, Capricorn, or Aquarius – there may be a conflict between expressing emotions and adopting a rational and logical approach. Scorpio will, however, add an element of get-up-and-go that will be especially valuable if it is in sync with other indications in the chart.

Rising-sign Scorpios are particularly keen to "know themselves".

Scorpio has the reputation for being the most sexy of the 12 signs – actress Goldie Hawn is herself a Scorpio.

In this pursuit, many even go through pyschoanalysis in order to "get themselves sorted". Their intention of untangling real or imagined complications in their lives is commendable, provided it does not turn into an obsession.

The Physical Being

The traditional Scorpio body areas is the genitals. It is probably due to this fact that Scorpio has acquired a reputation for being obsessed with sex. Be that as it may, the body area ruled by the Ascendant (and to a certain extent the Sun sign) is always vulnerable, so it is advisable that those who are sexually active do not take the risk of indulging in unprotected sex with new or casual partners. Women should get regular smear tests done, while men should regularly examine themselves for any signs of testicular cancer.

We cannot stress too strongly the

need for regular and demanding exercise – water sports, heavy team games, or martial arts are especially suitable. Physical energy must be properly used, if the typical penchant for rich food and good wine is not to lead to a dramatic increase in Scorpio's girth.

SCORPIO AS MOON SIGN

The Moon's influence over Scorpio is a potent and very powerful ingredient of the personality as a whole. It adds considerable depth to the individual, and takes his or her emotional energy to a very high level. The response to situations will tend to lean in one of the two directions. Either the Scorpio will become extremely quiet and brooding, holding back until he or she feels the time is right to take action, and to respond verbally. Or else, in the case of Aries, Leo, Sagittarius, or Taurus as their Sun or Ascendant signs, they will react immediately by flaring up, and putting everyone in their place with a display of anger. As emotions are heightened by the Moon, the tendency to overreact and dramatize situations is considerable. When stressed, the individual may also suffer from jealousy, or may become resentful. Sulkiness can also occur.

Determination

The Moon will encourage the Scorpio to always see a project to its end. Scorpios will be eager to get to the root of everything that involves or interests them. Being perfectionists, they have to "get things right", and they will rest only when they have done so. An element of possessiveness can occur, but this will usually emerge only as an immediate response to a particular situation. This possessive streak can be countered by the presence of other planetary influences in the chart.

This planetary placing may at the same time emphasize sexual needs, as well as a tendency to be sexually impulsive. This, of course, can be good fun and hence delightful; but, if the urge is particularly potent, the individual can be susceptible not just to choosing the wrong partner, but to life-threatening ailments as well. At its best, this sign placing will pleasantly enhance the sexual impulse and response, and make for an excitingly erotic sexual partner.

The Effects of a Fixed Sign

Faced with an apparently lazy child, parents with a Scorpio Moon may well resort to a very strict disciplinary régime. They might even attempt to bully the child into action. In other ways, there can be a fairly harsh reaction to anything the Moon-in-Scorpio individual considers reprehensible. Such a person will, for instance, favour strong curbs on criminals or illegal immigrants, to the extent that others may find it difficult to argue with him or her, let alone convince them that they are overreacting. Scorpio is a "fixed" sign, and flexibility of thought and opinion does not come easily. In fact, in most situations it is difficult for anyone to change the minds of people who have their Moon in Scorpio.

The exhilarating and physical demands of surfing will help a Scorpio burn off some of his or her huge energy.

Have an energetic game of squash with your Scorpio partner to keep your relationship as well as your bodies in good health.

Scorpio in Friendship, Love, and Permanent Relationships

Scorpios are cautious about making friends. Before upgrading someone from an acquaintance's position to that of a friend, they will carefully take a look at the individual's lifestyle to make sure there is something in common to help seal the bond. Once the chord is struck, their friends will thoroughly enjoy the time spent together. Scorpios tend to go the whole way, and will inspire their friends to make a greater effort in their careers, or in any interests or hobbies (especially if they are shared with the Scorpio). They also love good food and wine, and often entertain lavishly.

Sharing a sporting activity with a Scorpio may be a good idea, not only because they will inspire us into action, but also because it will help the Scorpio use his or her physical energy in a satisfactory manner. Sessions at the gym, on the sports field, at the pool, or on

the dance floor are likely to end with a lively but exhaustive talk about their current preoccupation.

Trust and Confidence

If Scorpios become uncommunicative or moody, it may be because they have some problem about which they find it difficult to open up and talk. Friends will need to assure them of their trustworthiness before Scorpios can confide in them. It is relatively easy to encourage them to discuss any day-to-day family or work problem. But if they are troubled by some long-standing and perhaps deep-rooted psychological trouble, we need to do everything we can to encourage them to seek therapy. It is all too easy for a problem of this sort to seriously injure a Scorpio's psyche.

Tact is necessary if one has to split time between Scorpio friends and others, who they may or may not know well. Scorpios can get jealous very easily, and then one will have to do a lot of careful explaining, lest the friendship takes a permanent hit. The suggestion of a get-together with other friends will, however, be a good litmus test. If the Scorpio clams up, then the problem is unresolved; if there is a happy grin, then the case is won. If they are truly delighted, they will suggest uncorking another bottle of champagne. Scorpios love good wine and to have fun; they also like to make a good impression.

Champagne, with its image of sophistication and fun, is the perfect tipple for Scorpio.

SCORPIO IN LOVE

When Scorpios fall in love, they fall really hard. They are not just sexually, but psychologically passionate – often with an almost obsessive affection for the partner and a hope that it is reciprocated with equal fervour.

An unrequited love will often act as a considerable challenge for Scorpios. They will not give up easily, and will pursue their admired one doggedly, using every trick in the book until they get the desired response.

Scorpio affairs will not be placid like a pleasant drift on a moonlit lake; they are better described as a highly enjoyable storm. There will be moments of blissful happiness, but their relationships will also be marred by upsetting quarrels and difficult moments. If the relationship

is going to continue or develop into something permanent, these difficult moments need to be faced and resolved along the way.

Unfortunately, jealousy is very often the cause of problems where a Scorpio partner is concerned. They tend to draw the net even more tightly at such times, and become extremely possessive. They want to know every detail of the time that the partner did not spend with them. As a result, the partner may start feeling claustrophobic, and unable to do his or her own thing freely. Scorpio fears are, of course, frequently unjustified, but proving this can be quite difficult and tiresome. Their suspicious nature will need a lot of convincing that nothing untoward is going on.

Break-ups

It can be very difficult when one wants to end a relationship with a Scorpio. They will cling on in the hope of making a fresh start, especially if they have been at fault and are nursing guilt. On the contrary, if they feel that they have had enough, the end may come as a short sharp blow to the partner. At a time like this, the partner will do well to remember that the

---

ENERGIZING EFFECT OF PLUTO IN SCORPIO

Serious studying is a must for Scorpios born in 1984–95, or their energy and potential might be misdirected.

Between 1984 and 1995, Pluto travelled through Scorpio, the sign over which it rules, enhancing and strengthening the characteristics of the generation born in this period. They have Scorpio as their Ascending sign, and find their Scorpio characteristics considerably increased because Pluto is on or near their Ascendant in their birth chart. This adds greatly to their potential, although they will need to get involved in demanding studies or active sports to make the most of their high energy potential. If this is not done, the energy could be misdirected, and even be expressed negatively.

Scorpio will definitely not be interested in healing wounds. The affair is over, and that is the end of it. As for the reason – it will probably be because the Scorpio has become attracted to some new, and perhaps in their eyes, even more desirable partner.

SCORPIO IN PERMANENT RELATIONSHIPS

Scorpio determination and sense of purpose are more vehemently expressed when they decide that they are ready to settle into a permanent relationship. They will do everything possible to make it a success, and will work really hard on practical problems such as finding a place to live and making the home comfortable.

If both partners are working full-time, they will need to lay down some clear-cut ground rules. Otherwise, a Scorpio's naturally suspicious mind will go into overdrive when, for instance, the partner is home late from work. In this zodiac type, fears about the partners wellbeing are rare. Rather, the question playing on their minds will most likely be, "who are they with?"

Togetherness

Spending quality time together is extremely important for all relationships, but in Scorpio's case, it is of above average importance. There should ideally be a compelling shared interest – either physical, through sports or exercise, or something creative, such as photography, video-making and editing. The tie could also be non-physical in nature, perhaps like genealogy or some other kind of research. However, adequate space must

"SEXUAL COMPATIBILITY IS PARAMOUNT FOR SCORPIO"

be provided in all such activities so as to prevent any feeling of claustrophobia. If such feelings do emerge during the early stages of an affair, even before the commitment has been made, the chances are it will recur or simply persist. A lot of "talking through" will be essential, and the partner may have to accept the fact that the leopard does not change its spots.

Sexual compatibility is of enormous importance in a permanent relationship. It is, of course, important in all cases, but for Scorpios it is paramount. Any settling into routine is to be avoided at all costs, and the partner should be as interested in a varied sex life as the Scorpio. A partner who finds any area of sex obscene or repugnant is unlikely to be happy with a Scorpio, for whom experiment and change are a matter of course in this area.

Emotional outbursts will be apparent in a Scorpio from a young age.

Scorpio in Education, Jobs, and Money

Parents will soon notice that their Scorpio child has plenty of energy, and, when uncomfortable or distressed, tends to respond rather more emotionally than other children. It will be interesting for parents to see how fascinated their infants get with anything that catches their eye. The attention span of Scorpios can be surprisingly long for their age.

When they first go to nursery school, there could be some problems as the Scorpio child may feel insecure. He or she will certainly become very possessive of the toys they are playing with. On the other hand, their phenomenal energy will far exceed that of any young Taurean or Sagittarian.

Scorpio children should be given small, regular tasks to do, since they respond well to routine. This will be useful both at the nursery school and at home, especially if another child is going to be born in the family. Getting the child involved as early as possible, before

Possessiveness over toys is a certainty with Scorpio children.

the baby is born, is advisable. This group of zodiac children are far more prone to jealousy than any other. Encouraging them to be little helpers, at bath time and so on, will help prevent trouble.

If young Scorpios become quiet and moody, they are usually facing some problem. However, it could be extremely difficult to get them to talk about it. When asked how they got on at school, they may brush it off by saying, "oh, all right", and walk away. But there could be some problems which parents will probably need to sort out with teachers, sooner rather than later.

The Importance of Structure

One must always keep in mind the fact that children of this sign like to have a structured life. Scorpio children almost welcome discipline, so a school where there is plenty of freedom may not be quite as suitable for them as one that tends to be more conventional in its approach towards teaching.

In theory, Scorpios rank high as hard workers. Therefore, they will not shirk from study and revision at exam time. However, getting really involved with a few choice subjects will be their real key to success.

Their sexual needs and expressions will be both vital and time-consuming, and balancing these, along with the pressures entailed by university life, will require some effort. However, Scorpios do not lack common sense, and while curious for life's experiences, they should not lapse into laziness or absence of application.

SCORPIO AND CAREERS

Whether they aim to become high-powered financiers or plumbers (their choice of possible careers is very wide), emotional involvement is extremely important for Scorpios. If, for some reason, they find themselves stuck in a dull and uninvolving job, it will be especially important for them to have an extremely stimulating leisure interest. As opposed to this, some Scorpios are highly motivated to make money and, therefore, devote all their energy towards this end. Such people find fulfilment in the growth of their bank account. But in far more cases – although prosperity is

important because they love to spend money on as lavish a lifestyle as possible – it will be their actual work or irresistible spare time interest that provides the focus.

Specialists

While selecting various possibilities for a career, we must remember that Scorpios are motivated to delve deeply into what fascinates them. While some have breadth of vision, many are specialists and supreme fact-finders. Here are the natural detectives, researchers, forensic surgeons, psychotherapists, and criminal investigators – or even criminals.

Choosing different paths in life, we find many Scorpios enjoy the national and merchant navies. They make superb engineers, and often, either as an occupation or serious hobby, they become wine specialists. Overall, their involvement in a career in which expert knowledge and research is essential will be more than merely satisfying.

Many Scorpios are extremely ambitious. They can carry considerable responsibility, and rather differently, also cope well with tough

Engineering is an excellent choice of career for many Scorpios.

HEALTHY LIVING

Scorpios work hard for their families, to make life good for their partners and their children. They make demanding parents who, in their eagerness to have successful offspring, tend to push their children too hard. They should know that they can discipline rather too strictly. They will encourage their children to be active, and will be at their best on the sidelines. But while they remember to cheer, they should not shout criticisms to deflate the youngster. If they praise enthusiastically, they will be expressing their Scorpio emotion in the very best way possible.

A "work hard, play hard" ethic will dominate family life if one parent is a Scorpio.

working and living conditions, such as those which may be experienced on a construction or engineering site, or on an offshore oil rig.

When they assume a top job, they become very demanding bosses – extremely strict with employees and subordinates. However, they will set

always bear this in mind, especially after forming a permanent relationship or starting a family.

SCORPIO AND MONEY

Scorpios who follow their intuition where money is concerned are usually on the right track. A knack of

"SCORPIOS TEND TO BE OBSESSIVE"

a good example by often arriving at work before anyone else does, and will notice and reward dedication, good work, and the right kind of attitude. This keenness will bring about benefit for the rest of the team as well.

Scorpios tend to be obsessive about their careers. So, while they go all out for success, they can end up not spending as much time with their families as they should. This is something that will, no doubt, be pointed out to them when the partners can no longer put up with their preoccupation with work. It is advisable, therefore, that Scorpios

Born on 27 October 1914, the writer Dylan Thomas famously had the passion and energy so typical of a Scorpio.

investing shrewdly and wisely will be present due to the Scorpio influence as Sun, Rising, or Moon sign. They are generally interested in finance, and enjoy watching stock movements. They often intuitively know precisely the right moment at which to step into the market in order to buy or sell stocks. There are always some members of this sign who will risk all their capital, and as a result, lose everything. At such times, Scorpio individuals will turn to another facet of their personalities which will tell them that the problem is water under the bridge, and that now is the time to start to begin building their financial empire all over again. Not hankering after the past is what keeps them focused on the long term future.

A Secretive Nature

We must accept the fact that Scorpios are not the "open book" kind of people that we find in other signs. Their secretiveness will sometimes be expressed through their attitude towards money. They are often reluctant to talk about their financial situation, even to partners. They may also conceal the extent of their regular income. Money is the most likely source of conflict between couples, and can very easily become extremely disruptive.

While Scorpios are known to have pretty strong views on what, where, and when to invest, some traditional indications have been proven to be worthwhile over time. These include mining, coal and oil, heavy engineering, armaments, fisheries, the wine trade, and catering. All these sectors have seen some successful investments by this zodiac group. Others, who feel that the stock markets are too risky for investment, will do well to settle for long-term insurance policies. Regular saving in accounts where the element of risk is less will prove much more rewarding in the future. On completion of the policy, the individual will be in a good position to reassess and make changes to his or her lifestyle.

"SCORPIOS ARE OFTEN RELUCTANT TO TALK ABOUT THEIR FINANCIAL SITUATION"

The harvest from prestigious vineyards, like in the Loire Valley, will be of interest to the Scorpio who wants to make a sound investment in fine wine.

DOMAINE R COULY

Clos de l'É

MIDHEAVEN SIGNS FOR SCORPIO

The influence of the Midheaven stems from the part of the zodiac that was immediately overhead at our birth – that is, the sign that was at the top of the celestial sphere (*for more detail, see pp304–6*). We relate to, aspire to, and identify with the qualities of the sign on the Midheaven, especially in relation to our careers. The Midheaven signs for Scorpio birth charts set out below are the only possible combinations of Ascendant and Midheaven signs in both the Northern and Southern hemispheres. To work out your own Ascendant and Midheaven signs at birth, see the charts on pp344–7.

ASCENDANT ARIES
with Midheaven signs:

Capricorn Ambitious. Can get aggressive while making business deals.

Aquarius Will have an original approach to career. Will be successful, but stubborn streak will inhibit progress.

ASCENDANT TAURUS
with Midheaven signs:

Capricorn Affinity with land or the sea. Hard worker. Would benefit in business partnerships.

Aquarius Excellent sense of direction. Will resent any forced changes. Can do well in retail trade and banking.

Pisces Should work in small, friendly atmosphere. Potential for painstaking creative work.

ASCENDANT GEMINI
with Midheaven signs:

Aries Career may change. Restless, good communicator. Suitable for the media.

Taurus Suited for medical profession, alternative therapies. Musical talent is also possible.

Aquarius Hard worker; original approach to daily work. Will do well in airline or IT industries.

Pisces Quick mind, but deep thinker. Detective work, research.

ASCENDANT CANCER
with Midheaven signs:

Aries Shrewd, financial flair; risk-taker. Armed services, nursing, or professional sports.

Taurus Has talent to build family business in partnership. Would thrive in an office at home.

Aquarius Caring professions like medical research; archeology.

Pisces Midwifery, kindergarten teacher, historian, the fishing industry, boat building, or sailing.

ASCENDANT LEO
with Midheaven signs:

Aries Can cope with difficult conditions. Excellent leadership ability. Brave and daring.

Taurus Stubborn and conventional. Excellent business sense. Banking, management. They can also be creative; talent for music is possible.

Pisces Customs official, prison services, vet, or zoologist.

ASCENDANT VIRGO
with Midheaven signs:

Taurus Wine merchant, grocer, estate agent; good at selling.

Gemini Will reveal facts. Good for the media, investigative journalism, detective or spy work.

ASCENDANT LIBRA
with Midheaven signs:

Cancer A connoisseur, curator, obsessive collector; will make money and spend it.

Leo Arts oriented. Talented, but may not develop it fully.

ASCENDANT SCORPIO
(WITH SCORPIO SUN SIGN)
with Midheaven signs:

Cancer Medical profession, Navy, cruise operator, or police. Will be determined and dedicated.

Leo Will succeed. Excellent business sense, but stubborn and dogmatic. Very hard worker and good organizer.

Virgo Medical research, surgeon, psychotherapist, computer programmer, detective. Possibly obsessional attention to detail.

ASCENDANT SAGITTARIUS
with Midheaven signs:

Leo Will take many intellectual journeys. Appetite for study. Will be a good teacher.

Virgo Librarian, accountant, literary agent, or a role in the publishing industry.

Libra Will be fair. Can be good at sports, law, diplomatic services, or as a vet. Can be cunning.

Scorpio Will prefer to work behind the scenes. Clever, with good intellectual powers.

ASCENDANT CAPRICORN
with Midheaven signs:

Leo Excellent business person. Politics will attract, or can be a government official.

Virgo Town planning, architect, builder, or dentist.

Libra Success in self-employment – as a beautician, optometrist, chemist, or PR work.

Scorpio Possible fame in any typical Scorpio career. Skills for raising funds for charity.

ASCENDANT AQUARIUS
with Midheaven signs:

Libra Modelling or advertising. Creative; will enjoy a "different" kind of job.

Scorpio Cosmetic surgery, or scientific research. Good sense of direction, but somewhat eccentric.

Sagittarius Hospitality industry, law, or geographer. Will not take directions easily. Stubborn, but can be very successful.

ASCENDANT PISCES

Sagittarius Needs to travel. Success abroad very likely. Interest in spiritual matters.

"The Centaur imparts strength to limb and keenness to the intellect, swiftness of movement and an indefatigable spirit."

Manilius, 1st century

Sagittarius

"Freedom" is more than a word to Sagittarians – they simply cannot be without it. They also need continual challenge, at work and in their relationships. They love life, hate claustrophobic conditions, and get very bored indeed with anyone lacking a sense of fun. Partners must realize that they mustn't be fenced in.

SAGITTARIUS AS A SUN SIGN

The Centaur – the mythological animal with the body of a horse and the torso of a man – is the symbol of Sagittarius, always shown as an archer. This is an interesting and potent clue to the Sagittarian personality, because those of this sign constantly shoot arrows of challenge – challenges for themselves or for other people to take up.

The point where an arrow lands represents the latest trial that they want to confront; when they have completed it, off they go to concentrate on the next target. The arrow can take the form of a provocative remark in an argument or discussion, maybe an inner challenge to improve a sporting personal best, or eagerness to get involved in some large and important project – even perhaps the challenge of deciding which of two flies on the wall will take off first: bets may be made or taken!

Sagittarians are basically lively, positive, and optimistic people to be around. Natural enthusiasm for their own concerns are dominant, but these lively qualities will also be fully expressed when they are used to encourage other people. Rather like their fire-sign cousins Aries, they are prone to take risks, though usually only while they are relatively young.

The illustration for December from the *Très Riches Heures du Duc de Berry* (1416), with the Sagittarius symbol of the Centaur shown in the astrological chart at the top of the image.

SAGITTARIUS

Symbol The Centaur
Sun Sign Dates
23 November–21 December
Ruling Planet Jupiter
Element or Triplicity Fire
Quality or Quadruplicity Mutable
Body Area Hips, Thighs, Liver
Polar Sign Gemini

The Sagittarian Centaur, as depicted on the page for December from the *Bedford Hours*, an illuminated manuscript produced in France in around 1423.

completely different one. This sometimes causes frustration, because in the end they might not be able to complete any project. This realization can also make them restless. In order to get the best out of their versatility, Sagittarians need to work carefully on one project or scheme, and complete it, before starting the next one. This way they will be able to achieve far greater satisfaction from their work and avoid the dreaded restlessness, which can be a source of considerable stress for them.

SAGITTARIUS AS ASCENDANT

The need for challenge is increased in the case of those who have Sagittarius as their Rising sign. These individuals have the ability to exploit the potential of their Sun sign to the fullest, provided they control their enthusiasm, which can get out of hand all too easily. If they have been encouraged to be self-confident during their upbringing, they will constantly be able to move forward and achieve their desired ambitions.

As with the Sun-sign Sagittarians, these individuals have considerable versatility. If this is under control, it can be a great asset which will enliven their outlook, and will be expressed through a lifestyle that is full of varied interests and commitments. It may also encourage fairly dramatic changes in their career or profession. While their involvement in a project is often total for as long as it lasts, once it is over, Rising-sign Sagittarians are keen and enthusiastic to take up the next challenge.

Rising-sign Sagittarians are very eager to learn more about themselves and about factors that motivate them. They are able to look at their personalities objectively, but by no means obsessively. Their natural breadth of vision will set them on a journey which will take them beyond the confines of their own personality, and lead them to a greater understanding of human nature in general.

Fast sports cars are attractive to many signs, but for Sagittarians they are a source of vulnerability.

Sagittarians are most vulnerable when they are on the sports field, or are driving fast cars. The more they develop their intellectual potential, the more this "devil-may-care" element of their personalities will decrease. In fact, it is often said that there are two kinds of Sagittarians: the sporting, risk-taking kind, and the intellectual type. While many remain one or the other for the whole of their lives, a far greater number will make a gradual change from the former to the latter. Once this transformation takes place, they are able to express the best of all of their positive qualities, and live life to the fullest.

Sagittarius is one of the "dual" signs of the zodiac, along with Gemini, the twins, and Pisces, the fishes. Duality is a strong characteristic of this sign, and it gives its inhabitants tremendous versatility. As a result, they have a tendency to move rather too quickly from one kind of task to another,

The Downside
It is when they have little or nothing to challenge them that their ebullient personality begins to slump, and Rising-sign Sagittarians become depressed and restless. However, when they hit a low, they do not sit around idle for very long. If out of work, they will do everything possible to find a job. If their depression is due to the end of a relationship, they will soon go out "hunting" for a new partner. Even if they do not find someone interesting, hope will spring eternal, and they will force themselves to enjoy life.

Sagittarians who find themselves out of work will put a lot of effort into searching for a new job.

SAGITTARIUS AS MOON SIGN
Individuals with their Moon in Sagittarius will respond to any and every situation with optimism and enthusiasm. They have an extremely broad and immediate grasp of

influence of other planets, Moon-sign Sagittarians must be aware that their exuberance can easily turn into blind optimism, which is a negative trait.

Moon-sign Sagittarians have a tendency to react in a somewhat offhand manner to ideas, suggestions, or problems put to them by others. This can be quite disconcerting, and gives the distinct impression that they want to concentrate only on their own agenda. This is something that should not be ignored by those at the receiving end. Once the Moon-in-Sagittarians realize that they have given such an impression, they will immediately want to put things right.

A Restless Spirit
When the Moon is in Sagittarius, it increases the possibility of restlessness and a constant desire for change. It leads to deep inner discontent, which

"SAGITTARIANS LOOK ON THE BRIGHT SIDE OF LIFE"

situations, although sometimes, they will ignore problems and complications, or simply gloss over them. They do not like dealing with details, and will leave that to other, more meticulous people. The urge to constantly move forward is well marked by their somewhat impatient driving technique – they loathe waiting about at traffic lights, for instance – and their drive to achieve their career and personal ambitions.

Up, Up, and Away
Of all the Moon signs, Sagittarius encourages high hopes and optimism the most. "Always look on the bright side of life" sums them up well. While this is admirable, they do need to keep a balance. If some necessary counter-indications do not emerge from the

is tinged with negative emotion and a feeling of helplessness, or even a temporary loss of self-confidence.

Sagittarians should always aim for consistency of effort. If they are able to do so, there will be considerable development of intellectual capacity and all their inherent potential will be unleashed.

Waiting in a queue at traffic lights is anathema to the forward-looking Sagittarian spirit.

Sagittarius in Friendship, Love, and Permanent Relationships

Having a Sagittarian friend is always fun. They are very good at encouraging and helping us to feel optimistic about the future development of our proposed ideas.

Even if there are no common interests at first between a Sagitttarian and his or her friend, there will be soon enough. This is because Sagittarians have good powers of persuasion, and their enthusiasm for their own preoccupations will spark friends off along the same trail.

Sporty or Intellectual

The fact that there are two distinct types of Sagittarians is nowhere more evident than in their ties of friendship. Again, here are the sporty and the intellectual types. If we prefer the outdoor life, and like to hike, bike, or go camping outdoors, then our sporty Sagittarian friends will be favoured. Perhaps one of the greatest challenges we can enjoy with them is to keep fit. Therefore, sessions at the gym will have quite an edge as we try to do our best in going faster and longer on the cycle machines, or hold difficult yoga poses for longer durations, and so on. By tradition, Sagittarians are the archers and riders of the zodiac, and if they are interested in these sports, they certainly will become extremely proficient.

However, the more bookish kinds will enjoy mixing with intellectual Sagittarians. Friends of such people will soon realize that there is an element of the eternal student about them. Even if they are not our teachers or lecturers, we will learn from our intellectual Sagittarian friends. They will provide us with their own special brand of encouragement, as well as some lively mini-challenges along the way to help us progress. Travelling along with Sagittarians will be memorable, although rather spartan, for they would not want to spend too much money on luxury hotels. They prefer, instead, to travel further afield, perhaps camping in some remote spot far from civilization. But we must also remember that their journeys will often be of the mind, satisfying their need for new and fascinating learning experiences.

Trekking to remote places, far from the luxuries of civilization, is the way Sagittarians like to travel.

SAGITTARIUS IN LOVE

Sagittarians are passionate, and will have no difficulty in expressing their feelings. In their enthusiasm, they may attempt to develop a relationship rather too quickly as compared to many other zodiac types. Should they do so, while the admired one will be flattered and probably even come around eventually, the eager Sagittarian will have to show a little patience to avoid a cold shoulder early on.

Sagittarians are flirtatious and generally will not take their love life very seriously. Indeed, much like their polar sign, Gemini, it will not be unusual for them to have more than one lover from time to time. While they are good talkers and will have plenty of excuses ready in case they are discovered, this tendency can complicate their lives and cause unnecessary problems for them.

It is extremely important that, apart from their passion and desire, Sagittarians have much in common with their lovers so that they can have enjoyable and stimulating conversations, evening outs, and so on as a prelude to passionate lovemaking. Sagittarians are generally energetic, and being in a relationship with one will be intellectually and physically demanding. They keep their lovers on their toes, and if the partner does not measure up to the pace, the Sagittarian will move on to new relationships.

New Territories, No Possessions
Sagittarians have a very strong liking for new pastures in whatever sphere of life they happen to be involved. As far as their love life is concerned, it is important that they really understand that the grass is not necessarily greener over the hedge, no matter how lush it may appear.

HIPS, THIGHS, AND THE SAGITTARIAN HANGOVER

The Sagittarian body areas are the hips and thighs, and the women of the sign especially tend to put on weight in these areas. Both sexes have a love of good, rich, and hearty food, which obviously encourages corpulence. The emphasis on the liver is highly relevant, as rich food is usually complemented with strong drink. Those with more than just a liking for the occasional glass of wine must be aware that their livers are somewhat vulnerable. The Sagittarian hangover can be particularly nasty.

A love of hearty food encourages weight gain, especially in the hips and thighs.

It is rare for Sagittarians to be jealous or possessive lovers. This may be because they like to feel unencumbered by their partners, and to keep that sense of freedom for themselves they are reasonably relaxed in their attitude towards relationships. If their partner becomes jealous, the Sagittarian will seriously dislike it and, all too soon, put an end to the relationship.

SAGITTARIUS IN PERMANENT RELATIONSHIPS

Perhaps the most important element necessary in a permanent relationship with a Sagittarian is shared interests. This can take any form, ranging from participating in a joint business partnership to sharing some kind of specialist expertise, preferably not so much in precisely the same field as in a complementary one. If the areas of interest are too close, mutual rivalry can become an ongoing problem. There is potential for a very great deal of happiness, liveliness, and fun in a permanent relationship provided there is a strong bond in some form, apart from sex. It is a truism that to keep their relationships sparkling and moving forward, members of this zodiac group really do need stimulating ties of friendship, as well as love. Any form of boring dreariness will not be tolerated.

Breathing Space

Claustrophobia is perhaps the one thing that Sagittarians really cannot cope with. If a claustrophobic net begins to close around them, they will struggle and rebel. Being constantly questioned about where they have been, or why they are preoccupied with some hobby when they should be paying their partner more attention, will drive them crazy. In such cases, dramatic and highly emotional scenes

"IF A PARTNER BECOMES JEALOUS, A SAGITTARIAN WILL SERIOUSLY DISLIKE IT"

will be inevitable and frequent. Indeed, Sagittarians are unlikely to withstand such a situation for very long, and will simply get out. In the same vein, a dreary round of housecleaning or sacrificing a successful career for one's lover will make for an equally claustrophobic and unchallenging lifestyle for Sagittarian women. In the end it will prove intolerable, no matter how dedicated she is to her partner's career. She will feel frustrated that she is not moving along at the same pace. This seems to be about the only time in a Sagittarian's life when jealousy is likely to surface, unless such a tendency is emphasized in the birth chart.

A dreary round of housework will soon become intolerable to a Sagittarian.

Sagittarians are happy babies who love to smile and engage with everyone.

Sagittarius in Education, Jobs, and Money

From the earliest days, parents of a young Sagittarian will realize that they have an extremely lively and demanding child on their hands. However, their demands will not very often be due to bad temper or tantrums. Sagittarians, on the whole, are happy babies who love to grin at everybody and everything, especially when they are old enough to sit up and take notice. Many have the tendency to throw small toys out of their buggies in order for us lesser mortals to pick them up, only to notice as we walk on that the small Sagittarian is playing the same trick on the next passer-by.

Sagittarians will respond really well to nursery school, and may be ready for it somewhat earlier than a lot of children. From as early an age as possible, these children need to know the difference between enthusiastic, energetic play and boisterousness. If the latter is not firmly controlled, it will be far more difficult to discipline later on, when it can turn to wilful wildness, even if it is accompanied with broad smiles and giggles of mirth.

School Days

A school that has sensible rules and is quick to recognize individual potential and talents will be best suited to a Sagittarian child. If the young Sagittarian thinks a rule is silly, the chances of his or her abiding by it are nil. Therefore, careful explanations are essential, even if boredom sets in during the lecture session. During school days some specific areas of potential will emerge, and teachers will do well to carefully encourage the children towards these areas so that progress is made. While this may sound like a generalization, it is essential for these children because once their symbolic inner fire is ignited, it will burn strongly and brightly. It is in this way that their lifelong fascination with specific subjects is born.

A careful explanation of the correct way to do things and the reason for rules is important for young Sagittarians.

Sagittarian children will have to be made aware that lack of attention to detail can hold them back. They will almost always be very cavalier over revisions during exams, and this should be corrected.

Sagittarians will have the potential to really shine during university education, and the tendency to become an eternal student will more than likely take root. Even if they are more attracted to sports than studies, the benefits of university education will rank above average. Time spent abroad as part of their course will also be most welcome and extremely beneficial.

William Blake demonstrated the Sagittarian flair for versatility, creating combined works of literature and art.

SAGITTARIUS AND CAREERS

When Sagittarians set about choosing a career, an important factor that works in their favour is their ability to clearly see every step of the way, which will lead them to their ultimate goal. For instance, if they choose the law, they will realize that a long road of study and examinations lies ahead of them, but that the final goal will be well worthwhile. However, they also need to realize that a career involving claustrophobic conditions will severely hinder their feelings of job satisfaction.

For individuals with this sign, challenge is all-important, as is the opportunity to use initiative and to feel unburdened by petty matters. There is a need for an element of adventure in all things, and even uncertainty of tenure can be faced with a certain tense excitement.

Individual Sagittarians who decide to work for themselves must ensure that they are disciplined enough not to go off at tangents, because chances are that some new idea or a proposed project will have great appeal. At such times, Sagittarian enthusiasm can carry them away.

Career Selection

As with all signs, the choice of professions is extremely wide for Sagittarians. Many, who have a love of sport, can do extremely well as coaches, instructors, or sports journalists. Others, who have a great love of horses and dogs, will find a niche working with animals, or perhaps becoming vets.

SAGITTARIANS AS PARENTS

Because of their ability to stimulate their children from the earliest age, Sagittarians make superb parents. It is often the case, however, that a lone Sagittarian parent will get bored with the limitations of a young toddler's conversation. So, as soon as is practical after the arrival of a baby, the parent should make quite certain that he or she has time for her own stimulating interests. In contrast to this, however, the child's development will be especially fascinating for Sagittarian parents. They will study it with great curiosity, and encourage the child to talk and respond to every kind of stimulation.

The publishing world is also a popular vocation for them, as is library work and bookselling.

Sagittarians also find teaching attractive. Generally speaking, they are less well-suited to kindergarten work than to instructing children of about 11 years of age, and older. Ideally, a post as a university lecturer or other work in some area of further education would be most suitable for them. Many have a flair for foreign languages and find them suitable for specialization.

If a Sagittarian has a talent for the fine arts, his or her inherent versatility will be of enormous help. Painters and designers, singers, and musicians will work in a great variety of styles. The media also attracts Sagittarians, as does the scientific world and the travel industry.

Over the centuries, there has been a strong connection between the church and this sign. Those with a strong faith and who wish to take training as priests will gain inner

"SAGITTARIAN ENTHUSIASM CAN CARRY THEM AWAY"

The church has a strong attraction for Sagittarians.

fulfilment and joy from the help they can eventually give their parishioners or to humanity in general.

SAGITTARIUS AND MONEY

While a fair spattering of Sagittarians will be fascinated by the actual process of making money, far more will enjoy work that involves more than just keeping track of boring stock market movements. However, as this sign has a more-than-normal tendency to take risks, gambling instincts are seen to be quite strong in Sagittarians. One will find them taking a chance on some promising share, regularly buying lotto tickets, or enjoying the excitement of betting on the result of a big race. If this trait is kept under control, and they do not allow themselves to lose more than they can afford, all well and good. But compulsive gambling can become a serious addiction when Jupiter, their ruling planet (*see p226*), influences them from certain positions in their full birth charts.

Whatever their financial background or attitude towards money, when Sagittarians decide to invest in a particular business, their natural enthusiasm will spring into

"SAGITTARIANS WHO GO INTO BUSINESS SHOULD HAVE A PARTNER"

action. It is not a good idea for them to lack enthusiasm for the company they have chosen to invest in, and to be uninterested in the progress of their hard-earned money. The Sagittarian will usually turn up at the annual general meeting, make suggestions to the board and probably get approval, if not from the company's officers, then from the other shareholders present.

Sagittarians who go into business for themselves are advised not to do so alone. They should have a partner – preferably one who will be in charge of the finances – while they go about drumming up the business by selling products or services.

Areas of Investment

What then are the areas from which members of this sign can hope

The travel industry will be an interesting investment choice for Sagittarians.

to get a good return, and which ones will they find interesting? The travel industry and hotel groups should prove both interesting and lucrative. If fuel prices do not escalate, investment in the airline industry can be rewarding. Sagittarians might consider discovering more about large publishing press or media companies. Tin is the metal of both Jupiter and Sagittarius, so an interest in tin mining is another suggestion.

Going back to the Sagittarian gambling spirit, if these individuals enjoy the theatre or the cinema, putting some cash up front for a film or play will be fun. But serious financial investment in such chancy enterprises should be reserved for those who have large quantities of money which they can afford to lose.

MIDHEAVEN SIGNS FOR SAGITTARIUS

The influence of the Midheaven stems from the part of the zodiac that was immediately overhead at our birth – that is, the sign that was at the top of the celestial sphere (*for more detail, see pp304–6*). We relate to, aspire to, and identify with the qualities of the sign on the Midheaven, especially in relation to our careers. The Midheaven signs for Sagittarius birth charts set out below are the only possible combinations of Ascendant and Midheaven signs in both the Northern and Southern hemispheres. To work out your own Ascendant and Midheaven signs at birth, see the charts on pp344–7.

ASCENDANT ARIES
with Midheaven signs:

Capricorn Serious towards studies; ambitious. Suited for law or as a lecturer.

Aquarius Needs adventure. Will be brave. Travel is important. Airline pilot or the media.

ASCENDANT TAURUS
with Midheaven signs:

Capricorn Finance, banking. Needs security. Talent for music; farming.

Aquarius Creative design, fashion, or furniture maker. Successful all round.

Pisces Research work, librarian, museum curator, or art restorer.

ASCENDANT GEMINI
with Midheaven signs:

Aries Risk taker. Wants quick results. Career changes likely. Good at selling.

Taurus Adept at complementary medical techniques; dietician, or a beautician.

Aquarius Needs glamour and excitement. Suited for television, film work, or as a tour operator.

Pisces Needs variety. Caring; might work with animals. Good in small business partnership.

ASCENDANT CANCER
with Midheaven signs:

Aries Shrewd business sense, but prone to risks and gambling. Sports, the armed services, medicine, catering, hospitality, or public relations work.

Aquarius Suited as a researcher, teacher, nurse, or translator.

Pisces Work abroad, perhaps in the developing nations.

ASCENDANT LEO
with Midheaven signs:

Aries Leadership skills present. Sportsperson, actor, auctioneer, or barrister. Likes to show off.

Taurus Needs to make and spend a lot of money. Banking, property developer, or architect.

Pisces Creative, literary, or poetic flair. Can work with children.

ASCENDANT VIRGO
with Midheaven signs:

Taurus Horticulture, personal assistant, interior decorator, or language teacher.

Gemini Journalist, writer, or researcher. Good communicator, and good at selling.

ASCENDANT LIBRA
with Midheaven signs:

Cancer Will be successful in joint business. Fashion, cosmetic business, or personal trainer.

Leo Jeweller or model. Scattered energy, but determination will be necessary for success.

ASCENDANT SCORPIO
with Midheaven signs:

Cancer Will like making money. Finance, banking, or real estate.

Leo A force to reckon with. Very ambitious; will be successful, autocratic, and strict, but with a sense of humour.

Virgo Research, detective work. Literary ability. Analyst, surgeon.

ASCENDANT SAGITTARIUS
(WITH SAGITTARIUS SUN SIGN)
with Midheaven signs:

Leo Enthusiastic and optimistic. Will be successful. Needs powerful or creative exercise – heavy sport, yoga, or free dance.

Virgo Highly motivated. Excellent for media work, capable of detailed work. Might enjoy riding.

Libra Restless. Needs pushing to reach potential. Enjoys good things in life.

Scorpio Broad vision. Capable of intellectually demanding work. Researcher, biographer, or linguist.

ASCENDANT CAPRICORN
with Midheaven signs:

Leo Very ambitious. Good organizer and a demanding boss. Suited for law or as lecturer.

Virgo Farming, caring professions. May have musical talent. Offbeat sense of humour.

Libra Thoughtful, indecisive, versatile, sensible with money. Success comes with determination.

Scorpio Needs to concentrate on one subject with many aspects. Archeology, anthropology, or Egyptology.

ASCENDANT AQUARIUS
with Midheaven signs:

Libra Travel industry, entertainer, or beautician. Will want to see the world in comfort.

Scorpio Conflict between modern and conventional attitude to life. Hard worker. Engineering, motor industry, or mining.

Sagittarius Will be successful. Must develop potential. Original approach towards career. Lecturer, media, films, or airline work.

ASCENDANT PISCES
with Midheaven signs:

Sagittarius Will be successful and even famous in career. Must not make too many changes, and should ensure that they are meaningful.

"*To pry for hidden things, to smell out riches hidden in the veins of the earth — these skills will come from you.*"

Manilius, 1st century

Capricorn

Pessimism can grab Capricorns by the throat and throttle all their desires which otherwise impel them toward their goals. At their best, however – and with the support of family and friends – they are sure-footed enough to attain their aspirations. They are not generally emotional, but loyal and have a saving sense of humour.

CAPRICORN AS A SUN SIGN

While not generally considered one of the dual signs of the zodiac, Capricorn is a very strong contender for this grouping – the symbolic creature of the sign being half-goat and half-fish. The contrasts between the two very different beasts is obvious, and the interpretation of a well-known British astrologer was that here are the "giddy mountain goats" and the "wet fish". Indeed it does sometimes seem that more contrasting qualities can be seen in Capricornean individuals than in people of any other sign.

The Capricorn potential for success is enormous, but, even when successful, many are prone to a pessimistic outlook. In contrast to their successful and confident brothers and sisters, Capricorneans who have not fulfilled their ambitions despite years of hard work are dedicated grumblers. They will often blame their background, their un-cooperative partners, or an impossible boss for their relative failure to move on and up in the world, as they had hoped to do.

To further complicate matters, there are not only the successful pessimists but the unsuccessful optimists! The latter are to be admired in many ways: they simply refuse to give up, whatever discouragement hits them – yet they simply refuse to make the

The illustration for January from the *Très Riches Heures du Duc de Berry* (1416), with the Capricorn symbol of a Sea-goat shown in the astrological chart at the top of the image.

CAPRICORN	
Symbol	The Sea-goat
Sun Sign Dates	22 December–20 January
Ruling Planet	Saturn
Element or Triplicity	Earth
Quality or Quadruplicity	Cardinal
Positive/Negative	Negative
Body Area	Knees and Shins
Polar Sign	Cancer

The Capricorn Sea-goat, as depicted on the page for January from the *Bedford Hours*, an illuminated manuscript produced in France in around 1423.

"CAPRICORNS HAVE A WONDERFULLY OFFBEAT SENSE OF HUMOUR"

Comic actor Rowan Atkinson
exemplifies the typical offbeat
humour of Capricorns.

kind of drastic change of direction
which might benefit them. Instead,
they grasp at straws as and when
they can, smile resolutely, and plod
on along the same furrow.

Many Capricorns who lack
self-confidence will feign laziness
as a cover-up. But when they do spur
themselves into action, they are
supported by a great deal of practical
common sense and patience, which
stands them in good stead as they
resolutely and nimbly climb the
upper slopes of the mountain that
they aspire to conquer.

There are very few Capricorns
who do not have an offbeat sense of
humour. We see it beautifully illustrated
in the work of the British actor and
comedian Rowan Atkinson, a Sun-sign
Capricorn. Older Capricorn men often
do not realize that they are making the
rest of us laugh, or if they do, they will
tend to return our smile with the
corners of their mouths turned down.

CAPRICORN AS ASCENDANT

At times, those with a Capricorn
Ascendant will be extremely self-
confident; at other times, they will
find it very difficult to be assertive at
all. They certainly have what it takes
to make their mark and attain success,
but their wavering attitude will
seriously hold them back, especially
when they are faced with important
interviews or examinations. As a

result, frustration builds up when
they realize that they have made a
mistake, or did not succeed in making
the right impression. When they seek
astrological help, the consultant
will need to carefully examine other
areas of their birth chart to help them
come to terms with this tendency to
be indecisive.

Capricorn's ruling planet, Saturn,
has a lot to answer for in this respect.
Its influence is all too often found in
an inner voice which inflicts a series
of "put-downs". Individuals will tell
themselves not to be so silly as to
contemplate this or that difficult task;
they continue to underestimate
themselves, and their achievements,
talent, and general ability. If, by chance,
the subject had very strict parents or
teachers, the tendency will be even
more marked. Rising-sign Capricorns
must learn to readily accept praise and
compliments, and believe that those
who bestow them are being sincere,
and are not exaggerating.

Mind and Body

Rising-sign Capricorns will share
the sense of humour of the Sun-sign
people and, in addition, will be
somewhat more practical and
commonsensical. Many with
Capricorn Rising will also be

more sensitive, and have a delightfully caring quality which will be freely expressed from time to time.

The traditional Capricorn body areas – the knees and shins – are vulnerable, and in addition, this group will be rather prone to worry, which can have a negative effect on their digestion. Their skin and teeth are sensitive, so regular dental check-ups and a powerful sunscreen are of above average importance. Physical activity out and away from the daily round are vital; far too many will remain tied to their office computers when they have a great love of sweeping landscapes, mountains, and fresh air.

Regular trips to the dentist are essential for Capricorns.

While so many of these individuals aim for material progress, they should also realize that involvement with

Walking in the hills will greatly appeal to Capricorns – if they can tear themselves away from their desk jobs.

some form of spiritual development acts as a wonderful balance and will contribute a degree of inner calm, which is often lacking in them. They will probably benefit from yoga; its physical exercises will help to keep Capricorn joints in good condition.

CAPRICORN AS MOON SIGN

The immediate reaction of someone with the Moon in Capricorn will be very cool, and the impression given will be that they are extremely aloof. Whether this is really the case will, of course, depend on their Sun and Ascending signs and other areas of their full chart. However, the Capricorn sense of humour will emerge with great spontaneity, and can do a very great deal to counter what may be an unfortunate first impression.

The tendency to grumble or carp will emerge, usually over small matters – for instance, not being able to get exactly the right kind of detergent, or because a particular dish is off the menu. Again, such a strong reaction could well be a cover-up for the lack of self-confidence, or a desire to impress other people or to put them in their place.

Advanced driving skills are often mastered by Moon-in-Capricorn individuals.

A Head for Business

The Moon in Capricorn will endow a person with a shrewd business sense. These individuals are quick to recognize opportunities, and it really is up to them to take full advantage of these, with a view to possible progress. They should not put up barriers of excuses, such as that they are insufficiently qualified, or wouldn't be able to take the pressure or responsibility. If they can avoid making such excuses, there is no reason why their Capricorn Moon should not serve them extremely well. It will give them the ability, along with dedication and clear vision, to scale any peak they care to attempt. In addition, all the strong, powerful, and practical qualities of Capricorn will emerge at a moment's notice, together with great determination. The Moon's influence will further ensure that the individual inspires confidence.

Steadfast Companions

Capricorns often aspire to partners who are more successful and possibly further up the social ladder than themselves. However, they are really faithful in their relationships, be they personal or business. They like to stand by their lovers and colleagues, especially if the latter are coping with difficult problems.

There is a powerful instinct for self-protection when the Moon is in Capricorn, so the risk-taking factor is low in these individuals. They often learn advanced driving techniques (which is to be encouraged in the young), and are sensible in emergency situations. They are usually sure-footed and walk well – the women often wearing the highest of high heeled shoes without difficulty.

"CAPRICORNS MAKE VERY TRUSTWORTHY COLLEAGUES"

Oliver Hardy, the Capricorn, is glum, while Stan Laurel waits patiently for him to cheer up.

Capricorn in Friendship, Love, and Permanent Relationships

Capricorns are like the salt of the earth when it comes to forming friendships. They are constant, true, and faithful, and for the most part we can have a great deal of fun when we get together with them. If we have known them for long, we can reminisce about old times. However, while Capricorns will delight in recalling amusing anecdotes, we can sometimes find them in a depressed mood. Then nothing is right with the world: they have had a dreadful day, or the current political situation is dire, or their kids have run wild, and so on. On such occasions, we must simply allow them to have their moan; if we dare to interrupt, they will grumble even more. Let them get their complaints off their chests, before we come up with suggestions as to how to spend the rest of the day together in an enjoyable

The sure-footed goat is the traditional symbol of Capricorn.

way. This will put them in the mood to express their delightful sense of humour.

Perennial Doubters

Capricorns need encouragement, and the more we can appeal to their sense of ambition, the better. Even the most ambitious of them will have doubts. Very often they tend to take themselves far too seriously and negatively. These are difficult barriers to break down, but the slightest chink in their self-defensive and self-denigratory attitude will be a help. While there is an element of the "wet fish" in all of them – or to put it in another way, a hint of the domestic goat glumly tethered to his post – there is also much of the giddy mountain goat, ambitious and often successful, with a capacity to enjoy life.

Capricorns are reliable and have a great sense of pride. They will turn up on time and dressed exactly right for whatever the occasion is planned. When going out with a Capricorn, who pays for what will often be amusing. If they are in the mood to impress, they will generously pay for dinner without hesitation. But if they are in a practical frame of mind, expenses will be scrupulously shared, probably down to the last cent or penny.

CAPRICORN IN LOVE

Capricorns fall very deeply in love. However, before they express their emotions, they will rationalize their feelings and make sure they are not putting themselves in a vulnerable position. Rejection hits everybody hard, but with Capricorn it goes deeper, because it deals a severe blow to their confidence and self-esteem.

Their approach, then, will be cautious, and they can give the impression of being cold and even uncaring. Capricorn aloofness is formidable, and it may seem that they are trying to decide whether a prospective partner is good enough for them – which may be the case. This can throw up barriers that must be broken if the relationship is to develop.

Signs of Affection

Capricorns will want to impress their lovers, and will vacillate between spending more money on them than they can actually afford and penny-pinching, when conscience strikes and common sense is the order of the day. Their partners will have to accept this quirk as part of their cautious nature.

Many Capricorns have a somewhat old-fashioned attitude towards love. They will always want to behave towards their partners in what they deem to be the correct manner. While this is fine, it can give the impression that they are somewhat older than they really are. Sometimes, especially when Capricorn has had a strict and maybe oppressive upbringing, it is necessary for their partners to encourage them to relax and free themselves in order to enjoy sex to the fullest.

Once committed and sure of their feelings, and sure, too, that these are reciprocated, they will move fast. Then they are anything but cool and distant. There is a relationship between this sign and the god Pan, who was highly sexed. Pan has a potent influence on the Capricorn sex life, turning these individuals into virile and lively partners. Then they get, and give, great pleasure, and bring a surprising amount of spontaneity and amusement into their relationships.

Strong-willed and aloof, actress Marlene Dietrich, born on 27 December 1904, was a renowned Capricorn.

CAPRICORN IN PERMANENT RELATIONSHIPS

Once committed to a permanent relationship, Capricorns will take it very seriously. If partners are free to marry, they will – more often than not – want to tie the knot. Seeing that everything is done the "right and proper way" is important to them, and they will take the view that the official piece of paper linking them together is vital – to a far greater degree than most.

Their attitude to finance is usually also very formal, and many Capricorns will seriously consider making a pre-nuptial agreement, which appeals to their practical and rather severe attitude to money. It does not, however, chime well with their equally strong and far more endearing qualities of faithfulness and a strong belief in the sanctity of marriage. Here is a conflict that the individual must resolve; while the non-Capricorn partner must make of it what they will.

Working on Relationships

Capricorn will do much to make sure a relationship works and becomes more meaningful over time – not least by making more money to improve the home. The family cars will get bigger, and the garden will grow prettier.

Taking the relationship so seriously, Capricorns must guard against working so hard that they miss out on enjoying life with their partners. Working extra hours to further ambitions and earn more is admirable, but Capricorns must remember that they need to live and have fun too. Even though they are forever getting nearer to the peak of their own special mountain, it is all too easy for them to neglect the delightful "giddy goat" side of their nature. Keeping a balance is important, and there's no denying that goats are good at it, but it may be a tough battle for the partner to impress upon the ambitious Capricorn that there should be time for fun in life.

CAPRICORNS DO THE RIGHT THING

Sun-sign Capricorns have a conventional outlook on life. No matter whether the individual is young or old (though the young may not readily admit it), they are the most conformist of all 12 zodiac signs, with an inner voice which tells them always to do "the right and proper thing". Here is a possible source of conflict, because their neighbouring sign in the zodiac is Aquarius – the least conventional. So for many Capricorns there is a contrasting influence from the position of Mercury – because that planet can often be in Aquarius, and at times they will be caught between acting in a conventional manner or taking a more original line of action.

A traditional wedding appeals to Capricorns, who like to follow the rules.

Capricorn Parents

When Capricorns become parents, they will be very keen for their children to have every advantage that they did not have themselves. While most parents feel this way, there is more to it with this particular sign. It will give them an enormous sense of pride as they take their children out in the family car, wearing the smartest uniforms, to the best school in the neighbourhood. Snobbishness? Possibly! What the scene does is inform everyone, and mostly Capricorns themselves, that they are getting near the top of their own Capricorn mountain – and at the same time, are ambitious to climb further still.

A Capricorn child may be happier staying in to read a book than going out to play with other children.

Capricorn in Education, Jobs, and Money

From a very early age young Capricorns will be more able and content to amuse themselves than children of many other signs. Once at nursery school, the little one may have to be encouraged to mix with other children. Because there is a tendency for Capricorns to be loners, encouraging them to join in from the start is a very good thing.

Parents will do well to start a little library for their children, as Capricorns are the bookworms of the zodiac.

When young, they respond happily to being read stories, and many learn early on to read for themselves.

Fun Time

The Capricorn offbeat sense of humour will soon make its presence felt, and should be encouraged. It will be an enormous asset and a good confidence-builder at school, and may possibly bring popularity. In sports, there may be a dislike of team games. Capricorn legs are strong, and athletics – running, long jumping, and so on – will be an area that they enjoy and in which they can be successful.

Slow and Steady is the Way

Capricorns are plodders and, once settled, will make slow and steady progress at school, with end-of-term results showing a gradual increase of a place or two in the class position. This is the way they function, and they should not be pushed or nagged if they do not seem to be working fast enough.

Strong legs and self-motivation are qualities that give Capricorns a great advantage on the athletics field.

It is worth remembering that they are thorough, and that once something is learned it will be remembered.

Many Capricorns have a flair for science and mathematics. When it comes to further education, these are the subjects worth considering. Chemistry and physics are also popular, as is archeology. Young Capricorns should be encouraged not to underestimate their ability and achievements, as the tendency to self-deprecation is common among them.

CAPRICORN AND CAREERS

A sense of continuity is something that is appreciated by this zodiac group. If the experiences and qualifications gained at university can be put to good use from the outset of the career, it will make good sense to young Capricorns on the brink of their life in the adult world. They have a driving ambition, but lack of self-confidence often seriously hampers fulfilment, and so getting to the top remains a far-off dream for many. Self-belief comes hard, and in extreme cases personal development courses will be of great benefit.

Finding the right niche in the right firm is as important to Capricorns as to most of us, but because they are self-contained, they can cope with working conditions that may not be acceptable to many. To counter the stuffiness of a city, time spent in the country on farms, rock-climbing, or mountaineering will be enjoyable, satisfying, and restorative.

Getting to the Top

The many Capricorns who achieve their ambitions will almost inevitably acquire a top job, and this is likely to place them in a very lonely position. They can cope with this, but considerable care should be taken that, when they move up, they do not become the strict boss who seems aloof and even unapproachable to their ex-colleagues – now their subordinates. When this top position is achieved, the Capricorn sense of pride is activated, and,

A NEED FOR STRUCTURE

It is important for forward-looking parents to remember that while they may be attracted to the type of school that is modern in outlook and its objectives, and more experimental and free in discipline, their Capricorn child will be more conventional and may thrive far better in a school with a traditional outlook and attitude, and somewhat more structured discipline. This kind of background will give the child a sense of security, whereas in a freer atmosphere confusion and shyness might become a problem.

although they are not the type to show off, they can become isolationist, despite fulfilling their chairman's expectations down to the last detail.

The Career Path

As to the choice of profession, working for local government may suit them, and if political leanings develop, here we have many successful politicians. The traditional Capricorn relationship between teeth and bones would suggest dentistry and osteopathy as possible occupations. Capricorn is an earth sign, so attraction to the land is pronounced, and here too we have farmers, estate managers, and town planners. The building trades are also popular, especially with those who want to establish their own company. Ambitious Capricorns can also find work in a large finance company or in banking, and we must not forget that here are many famous musicians as well.

CAPRICORN AND MONEY

Very young Capricorns will be delighted to put coins into their piggy bank and find it getting heavier over time. But parents must not be surprised if their offspring are reluctant to use that special hoard for a new toy or game that they so want to have. These early actions will soon show that this sign can be very clever with money, and will often seem rather mean – though they will probably describe their attitude as

The piggy bank of a young Capricorn is rarely emptied.

come through these years in as reasonable a financial position as possible. Later, their somewhat pessimistic outlook will encourage them to put money aside for dire emergencies, which is very sensible and practical.

The Lure of Collectibles

Rather differently, there are those Capricorns who develop a taste for antiques, and who, after serious study will perhaps make investments in beautiful furniture, silver, or the portrait

"CAPRICORNS ARE TRADITIONALISTS"

"careful". From time to time, however, they will splurge to impress someone who might come in useful to them.

Many will start to invest when they are very young, and while student debts are widespread, they should

of a fake ancestor from the 18th century. These things will give the Capricorn great pleasure, with the additional bonus that if it is ever necessary to sell such treasures, the collection is likely to have greatly increased in value.

Quality Counts

Capricorns are traditionalists and appreciate quality. They will, unless very young, prefer a few designer outfits to a large wardrobe of trashy, ill-made garments, even if these are eye-catchingly fashionable. Every purchase, not only of clothes but items for the home, the family pet, and so on, must be practical and hard-wearing, and in the long run it is the most practical course that is right for the upwardly mobile Capricorn.

They have an inherent dislike of risk-taking, and this is especially so when they are making financial arrangements. They will favour the safest bonds, as low risk as possible; but if they can accrue enough capital they are likely to buy investment properties, let them, or simply restore and resell at a profit.

Antique furniture and old paintings can be a great investment for Capricorns.

MIDHEAVEN SIGNS FOR CAPRICORN

The influence of the Midheaven stems from the part of the zodiac that was immediately overhead at our birth – that is, the sign that was at the top of the celestial sphere (*for more detail, see pp304–6*). We relate to, aspire to, and identify with the qualities of the sign on the Midheaven, especially in relation to our careers. The Midheaven signs for Capricorn birth charts set out below are the only possible combinations of Ascendant and Midheaven signs in both the Northern and Southern hemispheres. To work out your own Ascendant and Midheaven signs at birth, see the charts on pp344–7.

ASCENDANT ARIES
with Midheaven signs:

Capricorn Very successful. Assertive, hard working. Should choose typical Capricorn careers.

Aquarius Possible success working abroad. Conflict between conventional and less obvious type of career.

ASCENDANT TAURUS
with Midheaven signs:

Capricorn Practical application will lead to considerable success. Farming, horticulture, politics; possibly musician/singer.

Aquarius Stubborn, will resist change; charities or the caring professions will be satisfying.

Pisces Creative. Would do well working with natural materials, wood, stone, clay, silk. Nursing.

ASCENDANT GEMINI
with Midheaven signs:

Aries An outgoing Capricorn, good at PA work; receptionist, the hotel business.

Taurus Will enjoy working behind the scenes or perhaps from home. Agent, beautician, editor, magazine journalist.

Aquarius Scientific skills likely and will attract. Will make money somewhat unconventionally.

Pisces Archivist, curator, furniture or fabric restorer. Good at selling.

ASCENDANT CANCER
with Midheaven signs:

Aries A formidable business person. Will make money in partnership. Not a loner.

Taurus Shrewd; needs security. Antiques trade, chef; very entertaining. Farming, rural life.

Aquarius. Fascinated with the past and future. Archeology, computer programmer; possible talent for science fiction.

Pisces Good imagination, creative, and sensitive. Teacher or children's nurse.

ASCENDANT LEO
with Midheaven signs:

Aries Bossy, good organizer, leadership qualities. Perhaps professional sports person.

Taurus Excellent business sense, banking and finance, estate agent, auctioneer.

Pisces Will be attracted to and have possible talent for the fine arts, pottery, architecture, the wine trade, the fishing industry.

ASCENDANT VIRGO
with Midheaven signs:

Taurus Ambitious, cautious, and has good business sense. Gardening, mining, talent for pottery-making and carving.

Gemini Financial organizer or journalist. Personal trainer, solicitor, researcher.

ASCENDANT LIBRA
with Midheaven signs:

Cancer Home lover, caring, well organized. Interior decorator, upholsterer, cook. Children's nurse, midwife.

Leo Good chance of success but will underestimate achievements. Career needs elements of glamour; hotel industry, cosmetics, fashion.

ASCENDANT SCORPIO
with Midheaven signs:

Cancer Success abroad, talent for teaching, the law. Clever with cash.

Leo Good, but autocratic. Armed services, mining, the oil industry.

Virgo Needs emotional involvement in career: doctor, analyst, or literary critic.

ASCENDANT SAGITTARIUS
with Midheaven signs:

Leo Very ambitious, good leader. Money and success. Own business, work abroad.

Virgo Hard worker, very critical; the media, financial journalist.

Libra Likely to squander money. Selfish, good at languages.

Scorpio Needs an area where specialization is essential – pathology, criminal investigation.

ASCENDANT CAPRICORN
with Midheaven signs:

Leo Success in business, enjoys making money and showing off possessions. Restoration work.

Virgo Will own/manage country estate or historic buildings.

Libra Fashion industry, small unique business in partnership.

Scorpio Determination. Wine trade, entertainment manager.

ASCENDANT AQUARIUS
with Midheaven signs:

Libra Travel important. Possibly astronomy or archeology.

Scorpio Hard working, stubborn. Successful; money important, and spent on glamorous items.

Sagittarius Needs intellectual stimulation. Excellent at research and languages. Sociable, trendy.

ASCENDANT PISCES
with Midheaven signs:

Sagittarius Probably psychic. May study mythology. Possible writing ability on occult subjects.

"A gentle sort and a lovable breed – no meanness of heart is theirs, and of riches they have neither need nor surfeit."

Manilius, 1st century

Aquarius

No two Aquarians are alike. Tremendous individualists, they build their lifestyles without reference to anything but their own inclinations. All of which means that they can have difficulty relating to other people, for they hate to hand over any part of themselves, emotionally, to someone else.

AQUARIUS AS A SUN SIGN

Independent, original, individualistic, idealistic – these are the sometimes enigmatic qualities of Aquarians. It is essential that they evolve the individual and unique lifestyle that is right for them. While this is an air sign – which would usually indicate a free-flowing mind – it is all too easy for Aquarians to be extremely stubborn. This is related to the traditional influence, which tells us that Aquarius is a fixed sign, somewhat in contrast to what we might expect of them. It does not, however, mean that they are predictable. Quite the reverse in fact: they are often extremely unpredictable. This tendency usually emerges in the course of a discussion, when they will express an opinion very much out of line with current views – especially on controversial matters. They may voice an argument that seems very conventional, and in total contrast to their reputation for being avant garde. All this is due to the influence of their traditional ruling planet, Saturn, which represents the status quo and everything traditional, correct, and conservative in life and outlook. Aquarius's modern ruler, on the other hand, is Uranus, whose influence offers more unconventional and independent qualities.

The illustration for February from the *Très Riches Heures du Duc de Berry* (1416), with the sign of the Water-carrier shown in the astrological chart at the top of the image.

The Aquarian Water-carrier, as depicted on the page for February from the *Bedford Hours*, an illuminated manuscript produced in France in around 1423.

AQUARIUS	
Symbol	The Water-carrier
Sun Sign Dates	21 January–18 February
Ruling Planet	Uranus (traditionally Saturn)
Element or Triplicity	Air
Quality or Quadruplicity	Fixed
Positive/Negative	Positive
Body Area	Ankles, Circulation
Polar Sign	Leo

The Aquarian need for independence is extremely powerful. Once they leave home they will gradually begin to build a lifestyle to suit themselves. We must accept that they are very private people. If we think about it, do we really know our Aquarian relatives and friends? Probably not – partly because their sudden unpredictability makes us think again, but more importantly, because of their desire to be private. This is not because they are secretive (as might be the case with, say, Cancer or Scorpio), but because they sincerely feel that there are certain things about themselves which are of absolutely no concern to anyone but themselves, and they want to keep it that way.

Aquarius is a friendly sign, and those born under it tend to be great companions.

A Helping Hand

Of all signs, Aquarians are in fact the friendliest. If we need help they will give it – no matter how busy they are – with much practical advice, and suggestions for action which they

and probably send more cash than they can actually afford.

Aquarians are positive as well as optimistic, even when things get tough for them and their friends. They think well ahead, and will not dwell on good or bad times that have gone by.

AQUARIUS AS ASCENDANT

Many of the qualities listed above will definitely apply to those with Aquarius as their Rising sign. Here is the same independent spirit, the need to be individual and live life the way one wants. However, the difference between independence and isolation must be recognized, and the way this group comes to terms with it will very much depend on their respective Sun and Moon signs. The emphasis on an outgoing fire sign, or the other air signs, will help enormously, while the water and earth signs may in some cases cause a certain conflict between doing one's own independent thing and becoming lonely and isolated.

"OF ALL SIGNS, AQUARIANS ARE THE FRIENDLIEST"

themselves will carry out. Their reaction is not, "oh poor thing – what a mess", but a totally rational approach: "Help is needed, so I shall do something about it." This quality chimes with their powerful humanitarian streak. Hearing news of a disaster, they will catch the next flight to the scene, if they can possibly do so. If that is not possible, they will immediately reach for their credit card

Introspection

Here are people keen to understand themselves, but who at times find it difficult to accept their failings. When they do learn to recognize their faults, it will be a good thing and they will be well on the way to psychological wholeness.

Aquarian friendliness is much in evidence, and these people will give help freely too. But when thanks is given in return, they should accept it gladly and in a gracious manner, rather than retreating behind a cool and distant facade.

When Aquarius rises and the question of commitment to a partnership is voiced, be it emotional or more practical (say, at work), they will realize that they have to make certain sacrifices to their all-important independence. This will provoke a real inner battle, and a compromise will be freely accepted only when they totally respect the other person involved and know that in some way the respect is reciprocated. Attempting to get the better of the other person may well be a temptation, but people with this Aquarian influence must really realize that they are not at their best when appearing aloof, stubborn, or even vain.

Health Implications

While the traditional indications concerning health apply in general, whether the Aquarius influence is from Sun, Moon, or Ascendant, they seem to be at their most potent when Aquarius rises. Most of these individuals prefer cold rather than hot weather, but even so, their circulatory system is extremely vulnerable. They need to keep warm and move fast, which will be good for their heart. It is equally important that they watch their cholesterol level to prevent the arteries from getting clogged. The ankles are the traditional Aquarian body area, and many suffer from broken or turned ankles, especially when they are skiing. Most importantly, women wearing fashionable high heels need to be constantly careful.

AQUARIUS AS MOON SIGN

Those with this placing have a strange magnetic appeal. They are typically friendly Aquarian characters, but our first impression is that they do not want us to come too close. They appear somewhat aloof and even respond slightly frostily at times –

Skiing will hold an attraction for Aquarians, but when out on the slopes they'll need to take care of their vulnerable ankles.

in a way because they are on the defensive. They also do not want to give the impression that they are being cautious. Or it is possible that they may want to appear somewhat mysterious, enigmatic, and secretive.

The unpredictability of Aquarius is usually present, and sometimes these individuals may even act perversely to surprise and shock other people, or just to amuse themselves (occasionally both). Playing devil's advocate in a discussion is a common expression of this tendency. Children with Moon in Aquarius will be sure to try this on with their parents, and do exactly the opposite of what is demanded of them. Clever parents need to get wise to this ruse, and should tell them to

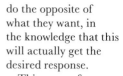

The razzmatazz and romance of the theatre will provide plenty of appeal for Aquarians.

do the opposite of what they want, in the knowledge that this will actually get the desired response.

This group of Aquarians will frequently come up with some particularly brilliant and very original ideas. More often than not, they themselves will dismiss them, or, if they do give them a second thought, will leave it at that and the idea will be forgotten. They should train themselves to stop and carefully think through these sudden inspired ideas. All too often they have potential which will be well worth developing, and could culminate in successful projects.

Glitter and Sparkle

The Moon in Aquarius strongly underlines everything glamorous. Women under this influence, for instance, will love the glitter and gleam of sequins and beads, and will usually choose evening clothes that seriously sparkle. Men are often particularly interested in making the artificial lighting of their homes different and interesting.

In spite of attempting to be cool, calm, and collected, and very independent, Aquarians have a wildly romantic streak that is often expressed through a love of romantic films and theatre. They enjoy their love life and will make any excuse for a big romantic night out, knowing full well that they don't find it difficult to attract the opposite sex. How they go on from there to compromise or even sacrifice their all-important independence will be expressed through their Sun and Ascending signs.

Dresses that sparkle and other shiny adornments are hallmarks of the Aquarian woman.

Aquarians are loyal and considerate friends, and we can expect a cheery call from them at any time of the day.

Aquarius in Friendship, Love, and Permanent Relationships

Those of us who have an Aquarian friend are fortunate indeed. Here is someone we should treasure and respect. They are extremely faithful, and once the bond between us has been sealed we have a friend for life. The chances are that even if we do not get together for ages, when we do meet up again, we will simply pick up from where we left off. Even if there is a huge distance between us, our Aquarian friend will make full use of all forms of communication and we will find our birthday greetings arriving on the exact day, as well as unexpected phone calls at any time.

Aquarian symbol of the Water-carrier

If we are in need of help Aquarians will spring to our assistance – almost before we actually tell them in detail what is wrong. Their suggestions will be extremely practical and there will be no hanging around feeling sorry for us; just a great deal of practical help and the appliance of a logical and common sense attitude to our problem.

Parties and Clubs

Aquarians are extremely sociable. They love to give parties and will entertain royally. These occasions are always very enjoyable because we know that the other guests will be interesting. Even if they come from different backgrounds, and we don't have anything in common with them, they will all be intelligent company – they wouldn't be friends with an Aquarian if they were bores! In spite of the need for privacy, Aquarians are members of specialist clubs and societies where they can enjoy their varied hobbies and interests. Here they come into contact with a great many people and have a wide circle of acquaintances, in addition to their special friends.

Because of their extreme kindness and willingness to help, it does happen from time to time that someone takes quite serious advantage of them. At such times, it is up to us to confront these individuals, and to suggest they back off at least for the time. We do, however, need to be especially tactful, as we would not want our Aquarian friend to think we are interfering – even if we are.

Perhaps there is one thing that can dampen friendship with an Aquarian: when we do something special for them or give them a present, they often do not seem particularly grateful or even really pleased. That is the way they are, but it is nice if they realize this and try to be somewhat more forthcoming.

AQUARIUS IN LOVE

Aquarian powers of attraction are at their most powerful when they have admirers, and when Aquarians are equally attracted their response can be compared to a magnetic force. A kind of film star or pop star glamour comes into play. They will dazzle their admirers, but they will also be metaphorically saying (and in no uncertain terms) "keep your distance. You can admire but don't come too close."

They know that to develop the relationship too soon – if they allow it to develop at all – will seriously conflict with their unique free lifestyle, and they will have to sacrifice their beloved independence. This attitude of theirs can also be rooted in a deep psychological desire to protect themselves from other people, or a fear that they may not be able to relate totally to a partner. However, when Aquarians do fall in love they fall heavily. There is a tendency for them to be attracted to a partner who is "different" in some way. Perhaps he or she has a particularly intriguing career, or – as is often the case – comes from a different ethnic or cultural background. This is sufficiently challenging to add a certain frisson to the relationship. When the romantic side of their nature is fully expressed it can take on the atmosphere and feeling of a

Hollywood film icon James Dean demonstrated the kind of magnetic appeal that Aquarians can possess.

romantic novel. At times Aquarius will tend to get more than a little carried away, but eventually they will vacillate, and their doubts can have a disastrous effect, so that the balloon, instead of continuing to soar up towards the sky, is punctured and falls (sometimes ungracefully) back down to earth.

Expect plenty of disagreements, as well as amicable discussions, in a relationship with an Aquarian.

AQUARIUS IN PERMANENT RELATIONSHIPS

So at last Aquarians have reached the point where they are ready to deepen an existing relationship into something permanent, or even to seal the knot by getting married. To get this far they will have experienced a very great deal of soul-searching, summing up their prospective partners, and making quite sure that the sacrifice of their independence will be at a minimum. Aquarians need partners who will allow them to do their own thing. The couple should have a great deal in common, but it will be as well if they are not, for example, both doctors. If they do share the same profession, their fields of specialization will need to be very different.

Love and Friendship

The most important element in a partnership with an Aquarian is friendship. There must always be plenty to talk about, to discuss, and to argue over; but if there has been a row, cool indifference – even in a serious disagreement – is likely. Somewhere along the line it may be necessary for the non-Aquarian partner to find ways of thawing out the chilly one. The thaw will happen over time – and so it should, for otherwise the feeling that the couple are moving in opposite directions will have a damaging effect. Even if "togetherness" as a slightly gooey and sticky concept is not an especially cosy element of their relationship, a warm, glowing friendship and good sex should be.

However, those who share a long term relationship with an Aquarian will certainly experience great joy and happiness because of their consistent kindness and consideration. They will help their partners achieve much in life by showing them different approaches to, for instance, career problems. They will encourage and challenge their partners, and with understanding on both sides the couple will move forward in life together.

THE SOUL OF DISCRETION

The question of sex is very important when dealing with an Aquarian. They are happy and eager to experiment in bed, and will enjoy lively and experienced lovers. There is usually no hint of shyness in their attitude, and they often get their fullest satisfaction in bed from a partner who is free of commitment. It is not for us to intervene or offer an opinion to the Aquarian, and asking questions is a no-no as they are, to repeat, very private people.

Experienced lovers who are not shy to experiment sexually will be the most satisfying partners for Aquarians.

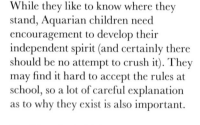

Many Aquarians have a scientific bent, and go on to follow science-based careers.

Aquarius in Education, Jobs, and Money

Parents will very soon realize that they have a lively child who will become fascinated by things like flickering reflections or rays of sunshine on a wall, and as soon as the baby starts to move around, the famous Aquarian independent streak will be much in evidence. Crawling off on an adventure into another room will be the first sign, but once there they won't just sit around – they will attempt to make a phone call or turn on the television.

Nursery school should be no problem for them. They will make friends very quickly, but both parents and teachers should be aware that if young Aquarians go off by themselves or stand in a corner looking glum, then something is quite seriously wrong. Maybe they have been asked to join in some simple team activity like "ring-a-ring-o'-roses" and just don't want to. Not forcing them is the best way, and giving them a different toy to play with by themselves is ideal.

Young Aquarians will be more than willing to speak up in class.

While they like to know where they stand, Aquarian children need encouragement to develop their independent spirit (and certainly there should be no attempt to crush it). They may find it hard to accept the rules at school, so a lot of careful explanation as to why they exist is also important.

Finding their Voice

Young Aquarians do well when being allowed to express their opinions; however, when exam time comes around they must learn to revise carefully and be sure of facts. This will be both boring and difficult for them, but if they go off at tangents, spurting their own opinions, the chances are that they will not get good grades.

At university they will do well to make sure that the subjects they read will be useful to them in their career. So if they can concentrate on these and master them, their subsequent career will get a good kick-start.

The social life at university will hold above average attraction. Aquarians are the type to join the astronomy club, the drama group, or something else, and such activities will become central to their lives. Similarly, if they are interested in sport, this can become more important than their studies. While the young women – and to a certain extent the young men too – will like glamorous, trendy clothes, and be eager to show off at every opportunity, they are not stupid with money. In theory, they should leave university with manageable debts.

AQUARIUS AND CAREERS

Aquarians are "people people", so a career where there is direct contact with others will be rewarding. Their caring qualities will be fully expressed when they opt for any area of the medical profession, or for work as tour guides, air stewards, or on cruise lines. In fact the range is extremely wide and very varied.

Because of their free spirit they should try to avoid a simple nine-to-five routine, the predictability of which would drive them crazy, even if the actual work is extremely interesting. Shift work, or being in a job that takes them out and about will be appreciated and satisfying.

To get the best out of Aquarian employees, superiors will soon discover that they need to give them the opportunity to work in their own way. Aquarians do not need the chatter or interference of a niggling boss or colleague. Once they know what they have to do, they will work very hard and all will be well – provided that they are interested in what is going on.

Team Player

Aquarians like working on their own in their own way, but can work on a joint project in tandem with others, or as part of a team. Indeed, they can do a great deal to encourage team spirit and improve products, because, their lively, original, and inventive minds often find new approaches to old problems, or areas where production can be either simplified or speeded up.

Many Aquarians have a scientific bent, and follow a science-based career involving research and experimentation. Others are the inventors of the zodiac. There is a general rule that a fascination with the deep past and the distant future is common. We have found this to be so, and here we have the archeologists, paleontologists, astronomers, technocrats, futurists, and so on. There is a zany quality to Aquarians, who like to have careers that are out of the ordinary.

Nature Lovers

It is also good if, in some way, they can become involved in ecological matters, the world's resources, and climate

PROGRESSIVE PARENTS

Aquarians make lively parents. They will encourage their children to read, and take notice of nature and their surroundings. They need to think more carefully than most parents about the way they educate their children, as they are extremely forward-looking people, and may well be attracted to a school which is equally progressive in outlook. But it may be that their child will do better at a school with a more conservative structure. Some children like this as it gives them a greater sense of security than a freer environment, which can be confusing.

Studying climate change or a similarly ecologically-based career will suit many Aquarians.

change, either through a career or as a spare-time interest. When speaking up for these issues, they make considerable impact and can contribute a very great deal. Humanitarian work for charities will also be extremely rewarding, not only to the Aquarian individual, but also for the organization as a whole.

AQUARIUS AND MONEY

Very few Aquarians like to spend time studying the markets in order to make money or deciding how to invest their capital. To keep boredom at bay, and to make sure that their cash is safe, they should opt for a savings account at a bank which offers a reasonable level of interest, or perhaps an investment bond where the interest level is low but offers no serious risks.

With their liking for the glamorous side of life, an Aquarian may be tempted to become an "angel investor" when production for a stage show or film is under way. They will find this hard to resist, and will have fun if they go ahead – but must be sure they invest an amount they can afford to lose, and should be strict with themselves at such times.

A Business of One's Own

Because they are individualists, many will want to start their own business. This they will do extremely well, enjoying the unpredictable ups and downs and varied working hours. However, Aquarians can get carried away and decide on a wild scheme, like

"AQUARIANS NEED A DOWN-TO-EARTH BUSINESS PARTNER"

While for the most part Aquarians are not serious or compulsive gamblers, they may succumb to risks. For instance, if asked to put up money to back the development of a new product, they can easily get swept away by enthusiasm and fail to pay attention to the practicality of the product, and could thus lose a lot of cash. They will probably get their fingers burnt only once; with rather more thought they will fail to lose out at all.

starting a vineyard in Australia (because they love Australian wines) when they have spent all their working life on a car production line in Coventry.

When running their business they need a down-to-earth partner to tackle the business side of things. They'll need to apply the iron hand in the velvet glove when the Aquarian gets carried away with the next big thing before checking the state of the first year's profits.

MIDHEAVEN SIGNS FOR AQUARIUS

The influence of the Midheaven stems from the part of the zodiac that was immediately overhead at our birth – that is, the sign that was at the top of the celestial sphere (*for more detail, see pp304–6*). We relate to, aspire to, and identify with the qualities of the sign on the Midheaven, especially in relation to our careers. The Midheaven signs for Aquarius birth charts set out below are the only possible combinations of Ascendant and Midheaven signs in both the Northern and Southern hemispheres. To work out your own Ascendant and Midheaven signs at birth, see the charts on pp344–7.

ASCENDANT ARIES
with Midheaven signs:

Capricorn Ambitious and successful; good business sense. Practical, determined. Suited to own business.

Aquarius Very successful, impatient. Will need glamorous or unusual career. Fashion, television; possible fame.

ASCENDANT TAURUS
with Midheaven signs:

Capricorn Good business sense. Will make money, enjoy creature comforts. Organic farmer, horticulturist, beautician.

Aquarius Successful, but possibly resistant to new developments. Must counter this by expressing natural originality and creative flair.

Pisces A varied career with many changes of direction. Creative talents, caring. Florist.

ASCENDANT GEMINI
with Midheaven signs:

Aries Will relate to speed. Professional sport. Needs quick results; should develop patience.

Taurus Will take intellectual journeys; good student. Teacher; will enjoy working/living abroad.

Aquarius The media, law; successful in journalism. Needs excitement, must be stable.

Pisces Possible flair for poetry and writing. Could be psychic; if so must find good teacher and resist experimentation.

ASCENDANT CANCER
with Midheaven signs:

Aries Will have excellent business sense, but must not be led away by grand sounding schemes which could fail. Good at working for the self, establishing own business.

Taurus Possible flair for cooking and entertaining; the restaurant and hotel business. Will take good care of clients.

Aquarius Shrewd and successful; will be dedicated to chosen profession. Perhaps museum curator, historian.

Pisces Working in art shops or owning a gallery. The navy or cruise lines. Instructor for sailing, swimming, or skiing.

ASCENDANT LEO
with Midheaven signs:

Aries Keen to travel; possible work abroad. Good at sport, bossy, good organizer; teaching.

Taurus Needs more than a conventional career. Excellent business sense. Makes money to enjoy the high life. Big spender.

Pisces Extremely creative; good dancer, actor. Needs to work in partnership if in business.

ASCENDANT VIRGO
with Midheaven signs:

Taurus Complementary medicine. Homeopathy, horticulture; needs security – both financial and emotional.

Gemini The media, journalism – gossip or scientific magazines.

ASCENDANT LIBRA
with Midheaven signs:

Cancer Receptionist, PA; public relations. Sympathetic. Self-confidence will waver at times.

Leo Anything glamorous where the person can show off. A need to make other people enjoy life a bit more.

ASCENDANT SCORPIO
with Midheaven signs:

Cancer A good researcher, historian. The antiques trade. Archeology, interior decoration.

Leo A private person. Police or detective work. Great potential; big achiever. Conflict between home and professional life.

Virgo Scientific research. The medical profession. Critical, demanding, eccentric.

ASCENDANT SAGITTARIUS
with Midheaven signs:

Virgo Publishing, law, teaching. Excellent communicator.

Leo A great enthusiast, with zest for life and many varied interests. Eternal student; also lecturer, linguist, sportsperson.

Libra Changes of direction in a varied and ever-evolving career.

Scorpio Will fully research any problem or injustice, and bring it to public notice. Green activist.

ASCENDANT AQUARIUS
(WITH THE SUN IN AQUARIUS)
with Midheaven signs:

Virgo Should achieve potential steadily; no short cuts to fame, fortune. Changes of direction.

Libra An image maker, cosmetic surgeon, fashion expert.

Scorpio Stubborn, will go own way, not keen to take advice. Determination an asset in career.

Sagittarius Inventive, original; breadth of vision. Astronomy, scientific research, film industry.

ASCENDANT PISCES
with Midheaven signs:

Sagittarius Fascination with the unusual. Science facts/ fiction. Will work alone; photography.

"*The children of the Fishes are endowed with a friendly disposition, swiftness of movement, and lives in which everything is ever apt to change.*"

Manilius, 1st century

Pisces

The emotional response of a Piscean is immediate, generous, and sometimes overwhelming. They can easily become carried away and unable to see reality within the beautiful pink cloud with which they have surrounded it. The shock of finding that some things aren't what they would like them to be can sap their self-belief.

PISCES AS A SUN SIGN

The traditional symbol for this sign has always been illustrated with fishes swimming in opposite directions, but with a cord joining them. This image makes a very potent statement about the Piscean personality: so often Pisceans will decide on one line of action, then, for deep-rooted reasons known only to themselves, will do exactly the opposite.

Here are some of the kindest and most sympathetic of all zodiac types, extremely self-sacrificing and very charitable. But it is often the case that they find it difficult to face up to reality, so others who are stronger and rather more assertive should give them support and encouragement. When they do, Pisceans will be eternally grateful and become friends for life. The kind, charitable spirit of Pisceans will sometimes interfere with the full development of their own potential. They are usually talented in a creative way, but due to a lack of self-confidence will justify themselves by helping others – perhaps looking after a sick relative or simply helping someone long-term rather than seriously getting down to expressing their own natural talents.

They have enormously colourful imaginations and are extremely intuitive. When these qualities are

The illustration for March from the *Très Riches Heures du Duc de Berry* (1416), with the sign of the Fishes shown in the astrological chart at the top of the image.

The Fishes of Pisces, as depicted on the March page of the *Bedford Hours*, an illuminated manuscript produced in France in around 1423.

PISCES	
Symbol	The Fishes
Sun Sign Dates	19 February–20 March
Ruling Planet	Neptune (traditional ruler, Jupiter)
Element or Triplicity	Water
Quality or Quadruplicity	Mutable
Positive/Negative	Negative
Body Area	Feet
Polar Sign	Virgo

working positively, expressed through the individual Piscean's chosen art form – craft or perhaps dance – they are at their best, and will feel considerable inner satisfaction.

The Piscean symbol of the Fishes

The Poetic Tongue

Pisces has nearly always been known as the sign of the poet. This has a ring of truth to it, and if they are not actually poets, there is certainly a tendency to look at life in a very poetic and romantic way. If their imagination is suppressed, their natural romanticism, along with their other intuitive gifts, will turn to apprehension and a tendency to depression. Many Pisceans do not respond well to medically administered drugs, let alone recreational ones. When negative escapism catches up with them – which sadly it does for many – their lives can easily crumble if they start to rely on the latter. They will definitely need a lot of support and encouragement to overcome any addiction.

PISCES AS ASCENDANT

Perhaps the most important failing of Rising-sign Pisceans is the fact that they tend to undervalue themselves. They will brush off praise for their efforts, since they are sure that they are unable to cope, and lack the necessary ability or experience to do what is asked of them. In reality, they are often extremely talented people who are quite capable of putting their rivals in the shade. This self-critical attitude is a direct influence of their polar sign, Virgo, which has the reputation of being the most critical sign in the zodiac.

Sun-sign Pisceans, when asked if they really want to know themselves and their true motivation, usually say they doubt it. With Rising-sign Pisceans this tendency is even stronger. However, once

they have gone through a certain amount of self-analysis, much confusion and doubt about themselves will be resolved. Consequently, being stronger in self-knowledge, they will be able to express their varied talents more positively.

Those with Pisces Rising are very much prone to anxiety. Of course, it is fruitless to tell someone simply to "stop worrying", but if they can use their intuition and couple it with some logical thinking, they may well get their concern into a more rational perspective. This will not be easy, but is well worth the effort.

Sensitive Feet

The traditional Piscean body area, the feet, shows vulnerability. Although this is likely whether the influence is that of the Sun, Ascendant, or Moon, it is at its most potent when Pisces is the Rising sign. Those for

High heels can be a problem for Pisceans, who often have sensitive or troublesome feet.

whom this sign is emphasized will either have a lot of trouble with their feet, or, if fortunate, have beautiful and trouble-free feet. With women in particular, such difficulties are often due to their fascination with beautiful and fashionable shoes. That is all very well, but probably sooner or later, they will find that they have to wear simple flats instead of the glamorous footwear that they desire. However, if they ration the length of time when they wear high heels, they can avoid a lot of damage. Interestingly, the eminent British astrologer John Addey observed that people who stand with their feet crossed, imitating the look of a fish's tail, tend to be Pisceans.

Ice-skating could be a calling for Moon-in-Pisces individuals.

PISCES AS MOON SIGN

A lot has been written and observed about Piscean eyes, which are usually large and beautiful. They always seem to be on the brink of tears – not only of sadness, but also of great joy. This is particularly so with those who have a Pisces Moon, as their responses to situations will be emotional, activated very quickly when, for instance, clips of suffering are seen on television, or they are enjoying a "weepy" movie.

This placing adds sensitivity to the Piscean creative talent, or to activities in any of the caring professions, so suitable for those of this sign. But astrologers working on the charts of this zodiac group will look for other indications which help strengthen the individual. Otherwise, the Moon will tend to weaken the personality, making the line of least resistance the immediate reaction to difficulties.

A Life of Dedication

The Piscean Moon encourages a sense of vocation and dedication to what is important to the individual. In the past, this has often been expressed through allegiance to religion, with many Sun- and Moon-sign Pisceans taking to a monastic life. Nowadays, this dedication is more likely to take different forms, ranging from working for large charity organizations to becoming a dedicated nurse or vet. Due to the sign's association with the feet, dancers and ice-skaters spring to mind. Indeed, they are prominent among Pisceans – especially in the discipline of classical ballet, where they really need to have a sense of vocation and dedication if they are to survive the rigours of this beautiful but demanding art form.

To this we can add the concept of sacrifice. The lunar responses are so powerful in Moon-sign Pisceans that many will sacrifice their potential fulfilment for a good cause. If challenged, they will say that they are fulfilled by the work they love.

Nurturing a Piscean

Parents, especially those of Moon-sign Pisceans, must make sure that their child knows it is wrong to be deceitful. Otherwise it will be very easy for the child to come up with some plausible, over-elaborate, imaginative, and totally untrue excuse, simply to get themselves out of trouble as quickly and easily as possible.

Pisceans are kind friends, with great generosity of spirit.

Pisces in Friendship, Love, and Permanent Relationships

Our Piscean friends are extremely kind, and are very generous with their time and energy. Every now and then they will present us with little unexpected gifts, often having made them themselves. In return, we can and should do much to encourage them, and give them moral support when they are worried or more apprehensive than usual.

We know that those with the slightest artistic talent or creative instinct are capable of really brilliant work. Telling them time and time again that they can do it – whatever "it" might happen to be – is an important part of our role. If our Piscean friends become overly self-critical, lightly teasing them will sometimes make them snap out of any downward spiral of depression and discontent.

Home-made gifts often play a part in the way Pisceans demonstrate their friendship.

A typical scenario would be if we have a Piscean friend who perhaps makes pretty scarves or bags, and maybe we know a shop somewhere that would sell them for him or her. For certain a Piscean will find it difficult to go to the shop on their own, but, if we can make an arrangement for them not only might Pisces get an ego boost, but they also might end up making a little money.

Spinning a Line

We must be aware that everything our Piscean friends tell us may not be precisely true. From time to time they can make up some fantastically improbable excuse for not turning up when and where we had arranged to meet. More importantly, many will make life very complicated for themselves simply because they have not been straight with their partners, having told a few too many white or perhaps grey lies. If they tell all to us, we will have the task of trying to get them sorted out, and that may not always be very easy.

Outings with Piscean friends will be most enjoyable. They will inspire us by taking us to art galleries we have not been to; or if they are spiritually inclined, introduce us to all kinds of philosophies and disciplines. They might read our tarot particularly interestingly, or perhaps be students of astrology. If they claim to be psychic, the best advice and encouragement we can give them is to work with someone who is really experienced and knows what they are doing. Otherwise their talent or gift can all too easily be misdirected.

Pisceans are great charmers, though they do tend to come on a bit strong and are not averse to a little deceit.

PISCES IN LOVE

The high emotional level of Pisceans will be fully expressed when they fall in love. There will be no holding back on their generosity of spirit. But they need to be aware that many other zodiac types will favour a rather cooler approach, and find the Piscean tactics rather cloying or even metaphorically claustrophobic.

There are many Pisceans who are unattached for too long. When this happens, they will go all out to search for a partner. When they find a likely candidate, they will shower him or her with such love and affection that the poor individual all too often gets rather scared and backs off, leaving the Piscean heart broken once more. Their approach is not overtly sexual, but they do come on strong. Hope springs eternal, but, too often, they fail to learn how to pace themselves.

In all of this, will our Piscean lovers be faithful to us, or will the Piscean penchant for telling lies spoil everything? Good question. We do have to be somewhat sceptical, especially if we have not seen them for longer than usual, and their excuses seem somewhat far-fetched. They often think they are better at telling lies than they actually are, and partners who are quick-thinking may easily catch them out. However, all too often their charm at such times is particularly endearing and they get away with their misdemeanors.

Big Romantics

Those who enjoy a touch of real romance in their love affairs will certainly get a share of it when attracted to a Piscean. They are big romantics, and will spend more than they perhaps should on flowers, a special bottle of perfume or wine, or some innovative way to make the time spent with their lovers memorable. They are passionate, but will pace themselves according to their partner, and because they are sensitive and

LIES, EVASION, AND PREVARICATION

Pisceans really need to be on their guard against self-deception, and at times will fall into the trap of being not just evasive but deceitful. They do this for two reasons. One is that it is usually an easy way out of a difficult situation, and the other – equally strong – is that when other people are involved they do not want to hurt them. But lies simply make for extra complications. They must learn to develop minds of their own, and the more straightforward they can train themselves to be, the less complicated their lives will be. This is a difficult concept for them to grasp, but nevertheless it is very true.

A romantic setting by a river or lake is well suited to the Piscean sensibility, with its aquatic leanings.

A Need for Decisiveness and Action

Partners should encourage their Pisceans to become practical and decisive. If not, there is a strong tendency for Pisceans to procrastinate. They tend to leave it to their partners to take action, and so should learn that in successful relationships decisions big or small, important or trivial, should be shared. They ought not to try to get out of them – which they will often do by asking,

"THERE IS A STRONG TENDENCY FOR PISCEANS TO PROCRASTINATE"

caring, are unlikely to be rough or want to be rushed. They will enjoy as much sensuality of approach and foreplay as possible, and like to be comfortable in a setting where there is perhaps a view of the sea, a lake, or a river – in fact anywhere with more than a touch of pure romance. If this is not possible, they will, for instance, drape some silk over a rather garish bedside lamp or hang a sexy but beautiful picture in full view of the bed – anything to make the right kind of atmosphere, not forgetting the exotic aroma of joss sticks.

PISCES IN PERMANENT RELATIONSHIPS

Once committed, the Piscean individual will make a very loving and caring partner, and the romantic atmosphere and level of consideration, which developed when he or she was first in love, will remain when the relationship has moved on to a more permanent footing.

Pisceans want their loved ones to be happy and contented, and will intuitively know if anything is upsetting them. When it comes to assessing what their partner is thinking, they will almost psychically read their thoughts, even if a new topic is being discussed.

"but what do you think?" If something needs doing around the house, which they are totally capable of coping with, it will be the Piscean's instinct to (maybe conveniently) forget all about it.

Pisceans can become extremely evasive when things go wrong, which can be a far greater cause for tension than they realize. It can drive their partners crazy in attempting to pin them down and keep them to the facts. Again, an element of not wanting to hurt the partner is part of the reason for this vagueness. For most other zodiac types it hurts far more; they would much rather know what is going on so that they can come to terms with the situation.

If something needs doing around the house, Pisceans often leave it to their partners.

Pisceans are water lovers, on the whole, and most will enjoy swimming from a very early age.

Pisces in Education, Jobs, and Money

From their earliest days, Pisceans can be divided into those who never want to get out of the bath and those who never want to get in. However, generally they are water lovers, and taking them to mother-and-baby classes in which they learn to swim should find young Pisceans in their element.

Piscean children may be apprehensive when they first go to nursery school, but they take in impressions very quickly and should not be difficult or stubborn once they see other children at play. Their imagination is powerful: for them simple toys will become wonderful, strange, and fascinating objects.

Music lessons and being part of an orchestra or band will be important to young Pisceans.

Right and Wrong

The most important thing to develop in the Pisces child is honesty. The slightest fib or evasiveness should not be tolerated, and, along with this, a gradual but firm introduction to what is right and what is wrong is equally important. Parents must not give way to the sad look in those beautiful Piscean eyes. All this sounds very strict, but it will give the little one far greater strength of character when they are older and when there is great temptation to take the easy way out of tricky situations.

The sort of schools at which Piscean children flourish are those where creative activity is encouraged. General art lessons and being a member of a choir, an orchestra, or a dance group will be important to them. Subjects in which they are likely to do well, apart from art, will be those which capture their imagination – such as history and geography. Literature and poetry will be popular. Maths and science may not hold much appeal but will have to be tolerated.

Higher Education and Training

University, and art or theatre school will be very much enjoyed. If a young Piscean has a talent for dance, theatre, music, or any other art form, parents

"PISCEANS WILL MAKE MANY CHANGES OF DIRECTION IN A VERY VARIED LIFE"

Michael Caine, one of the most successful Piscean actors, has taken on a wide range of roles throughout his film career.

child is smoking – marijuana or cigarettes – they really have to be on their guard to make sure that the habit does not lead on to harder drugs.

PISCES AND CAREERS

In all probability, Pisceans will make many changes of direction in a very varied life, and that in itself brings considerable satisfaction to many. When getting on in life, being able to remember that they have done a considerable number of different things will be its own reward. Following their nose in the direction of whatever life offers and opportunity suggests is right for most Pisceans.

Pisceans, on the whole, are not the most disciplined of all zodiac types, but their fascination and enthusiasm will see them through. A film-making or media course at university will stand them in good stead, and will probably move them into photography or the editing side of film and television work. This is because Pisceans are usually at their best when working behind the scenes, often in their own studio, office, or study at home.

Hiding Behind a Mask

To suggest that Pisceans are at their happiest working behind the scenes may sound odd when one considers those who have been stage-struck and gone on to become successful dancers and actors. Research into their motivation for choosing a very public career and sometimes achieving fame (quite the reverse of those Pisceans who work away unseen or unheard-of) is very revealing. It seems that they are not

will become aware of it well before their child becomes a teenager. While the difficulties of a dancer's or actor's career must be made perfectly plain from the start, if overwhelming passion is present, they will have what it takes to stick to it and, if necessary, take menial jobs when work is short.

Parents will have to face up to the fact that, as with most young people, there will be the temptation to experiment with recreational drugs, to which Pisceans are extremely susceptible. If there are signs that their "putting themselves forward" when they perform, but actually hiding behind the character they are portraying. This is particularly true of many actors. Costumes, make-up, and the required characterization provide a carapace within which the Piscean can hide his or her own real personality securely.

A desire for expensive shoes is one of the many reasons why Pisceans are all too easily parted from their money.

about working professionally at channelling, tarot, or any "occult" discipline, real study and training are essential. If there is a flair for astrology, it should be remembered that it takes at least four years to attain a reputable diploma from an acknowledged school.

Tenderness and Acute Sensitivity

The caring instinct is strong in many Pisceans, and they make superb nurses, either for babies or in hospices with the very old. Working with animals, which also needs dedication, presents the individual with experiences that bring them inner satisfaction and fulfilment.

A great many Pisceans claim psychic gifts; those for whom this takes the form of premonitions must develop a sceptical streak to put their instincts to the test and prevent themselves from losing touch with reality. (Testing themselves by carefully noting a premonition, getting it dated, sealed, and posting it to themselves or to a friend sorts out the wheat from the chaff, for if the premonition is fulfilled they have actual proof that the psychic instinct was correct.) If they are serious

PISCES AND MONEY

Pisceans must face the fact that they are not at all good at coping with their finances. Cash slips through their fingers with fluid ease, and all too often there is nothing left with which to pay the rent, the phone bill, or the taxman. This may just be because the Piscean has been enjoying too many concerts, or having drinks at a favourite bar, or buying scores of pairs of shoes (many of which will never be worn because they hurt). Their credit cards are all too easily stretched and broken by the strain.

Get Rich Quick

There will be times when Pisceans are tempted into investing in get-rich-quick schemes. However, care should be taken if this is the case. Then there is the Lotto, and the temptation to buy a scratch card at the newsagent's.

A SOFT TOUCH

When Pisceans become parents they will be kind and very soft-hearted, and as a consequence will tend to spoil their children. They will give in to whims or demands simply for a bit of peace and quiet. As their children get older they will suffer from a certain amount of frustration due to their parents' Piscean evasiveness or indecision, and inability to be as simply honest with their children as they should. If there is something they do not want their children to know, they may fob them off with an untruth, thinking that perhaps the child is not ready to handle the real facts. Maybe they should think again; they could easily be underestimating their children's comprehension.

Well, Piscean intuition is not by any means always wrong, and they certainly can win from time to time, but the buzz it gives should not encourage them to spend that windfall on yet another scratch card or an extra row of numbers for a Saturday night draw.

It is obvious from all this that Pisceans are easily parted from their money. Unless they have inherited a shrewdness and are naturally artful, they can all too easily get into difficulties.

Piscean Nat King Cole achieved financial success through his brilliant musical talent.

Creative Worth

Obviously we do not mean to suggest that there are no wealthy Pisceans: there are many. But those who really make high incomes are usually those who are successful due to their creative talents – for instance, successful photographers, film-makers, models, writers, and dress designers, or rather differently, medical practitioners.

So, when success comes to Pisceans, they should get a good accountant and financial advisor and rely on their judgement, and think carefully about restricting spending limits on credit cards. If coping with finances without professional advice, the best thing for them is to go for a simple investment such as a savings account with interest at a low risk rate. When making really important purchases, such as a car or an apartment, they need to be realistic about repayments. Finding cash for the mortgage is a real burden, and the money due every month needs to be carefully managed.

Finally, if a friend comes asking for a loan, Pisceans will be generous. Of course the loan will be repaid, won't it? Not necessarily so. The chances are that the money will not be seen again.

"CASH SLIPS THROUGH PISCEAN FINGERS WITH FLUID EASE"

MIDHEAVEN SIGNS FOR PISCES

The influence of the Midheaven stems from the part of the zodiac that was immediately overhead at our birth – that is, the sign that was at the top of the celestial sphere (*for more detail, see pp304–6*). We relate to, aspire to, and identify with the qualities of the sign on the Midheaven, especially in relation to our careers. The Midheaven signs for Pisces birth charts set out below are the only possible combinations of Ascendant and Midheaven signs in both the Northern and Southern hemispheres. To work out your own Ascendant and Midheaven signs at birth, see the charts on pp344–7.

ASCENDANT ARIES
with Midheaven signs:

Capricorn Ambitious, hard working; will work behind the scenes. Photography, archeology.

Aquarius Originality; will enjoy change. Astrology, dancing or skating. Designer: fashion, cars.

ASCENDANT TAURUS
with Midheaven signs:

Capricorn Potter, horticulturist, farmer, confectioner. Will need, and achieve, financial security.

Pisces A successful career. Hotel industry, public relations, shoe design, and selling.

ASCENDANT GEMINI
with Midheaven signs:

Aries A fast worker, but restless and impatient. Needs careful thought in choosing jobs/career.

Taurus Friendly, kind, and outgoing. A good agent; the caring professions, dietitian.

Aquarius A successful and rewarding career. The travel industry, airlines, possibly teaching, and working abroad.

Pisces Media/magazine work. Must consciously learn to be more self-confident to succeed.

ASCENDANT CANCER
with Midheaven signs:

Aries A very shrewd and canny Piscean. Will make money and maybe work in finance.

Taurus Hard worker, needs security. Chef, sculptor, architect.

Aquarius Good at research and detective work. Studious, with a focus on favourite subjects.

Pisces Travel industry. Translator – good with languages. Study of primitive cultures.

ASCENDANT LEO
with Midheaven signs:

Aries Forthright and energetic. Very creative, involvement in the fine arts, dance, or sport.

Taurus Needs financial and emotional security. Attraction to wine and cosmetics industries. If creative, jewellery is an option.

Pisces Successful if grounded. Actor, dancer, magician, investigative work, modelling.

ASCENDANT VIRGO
with Midheaven signs:

Taurus Creative craftwork with natural materials. A need to work in partnership.

Gemini Media: talent for creative writing; good at selling.

ASCENDANT LIBRA
with Midheaven signs:

Cancer Kind and sympathetic. Beautician, hair stylist, caring professions, children's nurse.

Leo Perhaps lazy. Won't want to be rushed; must be confident to develop latent creative potential.

ASCENDANT SCORPIO
with Midheaven signs:

Cancer Secretive, with powerful emotional energy. Must have total career involvement. Surgeon, detective, police; MI5 or FBI.

Leo Intuitive. Will make money, take financial risks, but beware excessive gambling. Lecturer.

Virgo An analytical and critical mind. Librarian, researcher, museum curator, literary talent.

ASCENDANT SAGITTARIUS
with Midheaven signs:

Leo Dedicated; possible sports person – swimming, skiing.

Virgo Possible conflict between career and home/family life. Should try to work at home. Any Pisces occupations will be good.

Libra Ambitious, but lacks determination. Likes change.

Scorpio Will want to go it alone; needs peace and quiet to succeed. Photography, design.

ASCENDANT CAPRICORN
with Midheaven signs:

Leo Determination and organizing ability will develop. Conventional career: banking, retail trade; clever accountant.

Virgo Farming and work in the countryside; growing organic vegetables. Journalistic ability.

Libra Fair play vital. Social worker, solicitor. Good communicator.

Scorpio Very hard working. Complimentary medicine. Homeopath, dietitian, podiatrist.

ASCENDANT AQUARIUS
with Midheaven signs:

Virgo Individualist. Critical, is less independent than thinks. Original. The fitness industry.

Libra Loves beautiful things and people. Starry-eyed, charming; a looker, but needs discipline.

Scorpio Stubborn but kind. Hard worker, will go own way. Possible scientific flair; chemist, biologist.

Sagittarius Free spirit; breadth of vision and love of study. Good teacher. Will live or work abroad.

ASCENDANT PISCES
WITH THE SUN IN PISCES
with Midheaven signs:

Sagittarius Imagination, creative talent which will find own niche. Possibly psychic. Should write a regular diary and/or poetry.

The
PLANETS

INTRODUCING THE PLANETS

Astrologers for the past 70 years or so have used 10 planets in their work. The Sun and Moon continue to be referred to as "planets" in modern astrology. To them are added Mercury, Venus, Mars, Jupiter, and Saturn – the traditional seven visible lights observed for thousands of years – and Uranus, Neptune, and Pluto, the so-called "modern planets".

P lanets with orbits outside that of the Earth are known as the "superior", or "outer", planets; those within the Earth's orbit are called the "inferior", or "inner", planets. It is the view of astrologers that each of them has a distinctive influence on the Earth and the creatures living on it, and that it is possible to study this influence and use it. The planets affect humankind in different ways, depending on their relationship to each other and their position relative to the 12 zodiac divisions.

Mercury will still have its own particular influence when it is in Aries, for example, but this can be seen to be quite different from the influence it will have when it is in Cancer. This effect has been compared to a light shining through a stained glass window: the source of the light is the same, and it will still illuminate what it shines on – but its effect will differ according to the colour of the glass through which it passes.

An artist's impression of the planets in our solar system

The relatively modern division between astrologers and astronomers has meant that, while the former still take the view that the planets – in a mysterious way – illuminate, influence, and comment on life on Earth, the latter regard them merely as lumps of matter circling the Sun. This has recently been illustrated by the "demotion" of Pluto, in the sphere of astronomy, from a planet to a mere "dwarf". Happily astrologers can claim that, whatever one chooses to call Pluto, its effect remains as it has always been – the astronomical definition or classification is immaterial.

Other heavenly bodies are also used in astrology. Chiron, a comet discovered in 1977 moving in unstable orbit between Saturn and Uranus, is considered of great importance (*see p239*). Many astrologers also use some asteroids, notably Ceres (which is associated with mothering and compassion); Pallas (associated with surprise, a "maker of change"); Juno (inner personal power, pride, and glamour); and Vesta (dedication, service, and sacrifice).

"*At the moment of birth there bursts from the seven planets a whole complex of rays that bear on each part of man.*"

Berosus, c.260 BCE

The Inner Planets

Traditionally known as the "inferior" planets, the inner planets are those that in orbit are placed between the Earth and the Sun. There are just two such planets in fact, Mercury and Venus, and their close connection to the Sun means that any interpretation of their influence is inextricably linked to that of the Sun.

MERCURY AND VENUS

The orbits of Mercury and Venus are nearer to the Sun than to the Earth. Consequently, the two planets always appear from Earth to be quite close to the Sun – hence they are known as the Sun's family. When placed in the birth chart, Mercury, Venus, and the Sun form a close cluster, which is known astrologically as a stellium.

Mercury, the planet nearest the Sun, can never be more than 28° from it, and so can only fall in the same sign as the Sun or in one of the signs either side of it. If the Sun sign is Gemini, for example, Mercury will be in one of three places: in Gemini with the Sun, in Taurus, or in Cancer.

Venus's orbit is between the Earth and Mercury, and it cannot be more than 48° from the Sun. In the birth chart, it can only fall in the same sign as the Sun or in one of the two signs on either side of it. If the Sun sign is Aquarius, for example, Venus will be in one of five places: in Aquarius with the Sun; in Sagittarius or Capricorn; or in Pisces or Aries.

Because of the close proximity of Mercury and Venus to the Sun, it is always relevant to relate the influences of these planets to that of the Sun sign.

Nicolaus Copernicus was the first scholar to formulate a heliocentric, or Sun-centred, theory to explain the workings of our solar system.

"Celestial Map of the Planetary Orbits" from *The Celestial Atlas* (1661) by Andreas Cellarius. Here, Earth is shown at the centre, encircled by planetary orbits and the band of the zodiac.

SPHERES OF INFLUENCE

Though the planets of our solar system have been known, astronomically, as superior and inferior planets, astrologically this has nothing to do with the power or nature of their influence. Whatever its position in the solar system, any planet can dominate a birth chart because of its individual relevance in that chart. The influence of the inner planets, however, does often blend with the qualities of the Sun sign.

The Mercury Factor

Below and on the following pages, we have summarized the effect of Mercury for each Sun sign. In each case, the planet can occupy only one of three places: in the Sun sign itself, or in one of the signs on either side of it.

Mercury, the innermost planet, is a small, rocky world named after the fleet-footed Roman god.

SUN SIGN: ARIES

MERCURY IN PISCES

This placing sensitizes Aries' quick decisiveness and makes individuals far more thoughtful and less prone to selfishness. They often get quite confused over small matters and can, especially when concentrating on something really important to them, become amazingly forgetful. They have considerable intuition, which they should not dismiss – it is something worth cultivating.

Planetary symbol for Mercury

MERCURY IN ARIES

The mind will work extremely quickly; there will be a sharp decisiveness which is usually accurate, but can lead to premature action if the

individual is being particularly assertive. The broad picture will be considered, but details can be overlooked. These people will not have time for trifles; hastiness may make them appear very off-hand at times.

MERCURY IN TAURUS

The mind will work slowly and steadily, with the individual being thoughtful and deliberate. The Aries temper will be slow to ignite, but is far more stormy, and will not subside particularly quickly. There is good concentration and memory, and generally the impetuosity of Aries will be stabilized by this Mercury influence.

SUN SIGN: TAURUS

MERCURY IN ARIES

Mercury works speedily and decisively from Aries, which will be an asset to the slower, more

Children take time to assimilate facts when Mercury is in Taurus.

deliberate Taurean. Individuals will express themselves persuasively and come out with bright ideas. However, if these individuals are accused of undue haste at times, they should take note.

MERCURY IN TAURUS

The individual will be patient and show great common sense, with slow but thorough thinking processes. Mercury will increase the Taurean

MERCURY AT A GLANCE
Distance from Sun 58 million km (36 million miles)
Orbit around Sun 87.9 Earth days
Rotation on Axis 58.5 Earth days
Satellites None
Keyword Communication
Rules Gemini and Virgo

tendency towards stubborness.
Children take time to assimilate facts,
but what is learned will be retained.

MERCURY IN GEMINI

This adds a sparkle to the way
Taureans express themselves.
Geminian duality enhances the
ability to do two things at once.
Taurean patience and skilful
Gemini-influenced hands can
make one adept at craftwork.

Weaving is an example of a skill
found in Taureans who had Mercury in
Gemini at the time of their birth.

SUN SIGN: GEMINI

MERCURY IN TAURUS

This powerful placing of Mercury
does much to control Geminian
superficiality, adds stability to the
thought process, increases common
sense, and instills a practical outlook.
There is more consistency of effort,
and less tendency to become restless.

MERCURY IN GEMINI

All the basic Sun-sign characteristics
of Gemini will be present, with duality,
restlessness, and the inability to cope
with boredom very much emphasized.
The mind will work extremely quickly,

darting from one aspect of a subject to
another. There is natural intelligence
and a tendency to give the impression
of knowing more than they actually do.

MERCURY IN CANCER

There is considerable intuition in this
group but a proneness to quite serious
worry from time to time. This will
be tackled with Geminian logic, but
can cause a certain amount of inner
conflict. The placing will add a fertile
imagination and increased sensitivity,
but logical reasoning may lead to the
suppression of inner feelings.

SUN SIGN: CANCER

MERCURY IN GEMINI

This combination will allow the
powerful Cancerian emotion to be
tempered by a strong shot of
Geminian logic, which will emerge
when individuals are plagued with
worry. This will help restrain their
fertile imaginations and prevent them
getting out of hand; they should then
retain a sensible perspective, even
when conditions are seriously stressful.

MERCURY IN CANCER

The Cancerian imagination should
be creatively expressed, and good
solutions will be found to personal

MERCURY: PLANET OF THE MIND

Mercury is often described
as the planet of the mind.
It affects the way we
think – rationally,
intuitively, slowly,
or swiftly.

problems after much soul searching. A tendency to look to the past will be somewhat style-cramping. Tenacity is very strong in this grouping, and goes in tandem with steadfast determination, so that these Cancerians may well not know when enough is enough. The memory should be excellent, but sometimes resentfulness can mar friendships.

MERCURY IN LEO

This sign placing adds inner strength and much-needed organizing ability. These individuals really can take charge, if and when necessary – sometimes to the point of becoming quite bossy. Leo will increase confidence and broaden the outlook, along with thinking big, while the Cancerian worry factor will be reduced.

SUN SIGN: LEO

An artistic Leo will get a creative boost if Mercury was in Cancer at the time of his or her birth.

MERCURY IN CANCER

This placing adds sensitivity, intuition, and a certain shrewdness to the Leo characteristics. Cancerian imagination will be a considerable boon to artistic Leos, allowing full flights of fancy to work on whatever the individual is creating. There will be an above

average tendency to worry, and the renowned Leo magnanimity will be considerably less in evidence.

MERCURY IN LEO

There may well be a reluctance to change opinions once they are formed, together with increased determination and possible bossiness, but superb organizational and leadership abilities. The powers of concentration are excellent, and, though the Leo tendency to show off and exaggerate will also be present, generosity and big heartedness make good counters to these negative traits.

MERCURY IN VIRGO

This gives a critical edge and a quickness of mind, which adds common sense, so that, when Leo wants to put big ideas into action, an inner voice will encourage restraint, both in concept and where finances are concerned. These Leos are hard-working but often less self-confident than they seem to be.

SUN SIGN: VIRGO

MERCURY IN LEO

This influence increases Virgo's self-confidence, and adds determination and breadth of vision. These individuals will be far less inclined to worry, and will be optimistic in their outlook. The tendency to nag and carp, common to this sign, will also be less of a problem – but any hint of bossiness will have to be controlled.

MERCURY IN VIRGO

Those with this placing who read descriptions of their Sun sign will agree with everything that is written. They will work hard and in great detail, analyzing problems and being ultra-logical. They should, however, consciously develop self-confidence, for their nervous haste can cause careless mistakes, shyness, or over-talkativeness.

MERCURY IN LIBRA

This placing will considerably help individuals to worry less and take life as it comes, but it will increase a tendency towards indecisiveness. The Virgo inclination to be querulous is not diminished – any accent on Libra encourages quarrels, just because of the pleasure of making up afterwards.

> **FINDING MERCURY**
>
> Mercury is difficult to observe in the sky because it is always near the Sun. Look out for it very near the horizon at twilight.

However, the influence of Venus on the Virgo Sun-sign people (*see p214*) will certainly make an impact.

SUN SIGN: LIBRA

MERCURY IN VIRGO

Libran indecisiveness will be very much countered by the strong, logical influence of Mercury from its own sign, Virgo. But, in being graced with this blessing, Libra must also consciously control the Virgoan tendency to nag, especially their partners. They have excellent minds and if inclined to intellectual pursuits, should become really involved. Mental cobwebs are not good for them.

MERCURY IN LIBRA

This placing will increase Libran indecisiveness and tend to encourage mental laziness. Drifting and day dreaming or being over-relaxed as the television chunters on is not to be encouraged. Here is tremendous sympathy, understanding, and kindness, for these individuals are superb listeners; but pinning them down to take action is extremely frustrating for family and friends.

MERCURY IN SCORPIO

This adds considerable inner strength to the somewhat languid characteristics of the Sun sign. Here is determination and deeply incisive thought processes. Jealousy and resentfulness can occur, often without good reason, but the natural Libran charm will as ever be in evidence. Here is also a liking for gossip and a tendency to enjoy plotting and scheming.

SUN SIGN: SCORPIO

MERCURY IN LIBRA

The natural sex appeal of Scorpio will be enhanced by the equally natural, pretty Mercury-in-Libra speeches which will enhance the Scorpio approach to prospective partners. This placing will soften some of the harsher expressions of Scorpio characteristics and adds sympathy, understanding, and empathy. Here too, are good listeners.

MERCURY IN SCORPIO

Intensity, determination, and a sense of purpose will be heightened by a mind that will retain everything and forget nothing; but in extreme cases a destructive urge can emerge.

If this enormous cavern of thought and intuition is expressed positively here we should see a sleuth-like mind capable of solving the most enigmatic problems.

Being a good listener is typical of Scorpios with Mercury in Libra.

MERCURY IN SAGITTARIUS

The optimism, breadth of vision, and all-round positive outlook of Mercury from Sagittarius makes for a fascinating counterbalance to the depth and intensity of Scorpio.

These contrasting qualities will give the best of two very different worlds, and because Scorpio has such inner strength and Sagittarius gives excellent intellectual capacity and potential there should be no conflict.

SUN SIGN: SAGITTARIUS

MERCURY IN SCORPIO

This placing counters the somewhat carefree attitude of breezy Sagittarian Sun-sign types, giving them great intensity and depth of thought which will often contribute considerable success for them. Here, the individual will take time to think through plans and projects and feelings regarding other people. The ability to cope with detail, often seriously missing with this zodiac type, will be well countered.

MERCURY IN SAGITTARIUS

Sagittarian intellectualism is further enhanced when Mercury joins the Sun in this sign. There is a wide breadth of vision but very little ability to see fine detail, which is often overlooked.

The Sagittarian broad and rather jokey sense of humour will be present, as will terrific optimism, enthusiasm, and a near fear of claustrophobic psychological or physical living conditions.

MERCURY IN CAPRICORN

The influence of Mercury in this placing will tend slightly to sober up the exuberance of Sagittarius. There will be increased thoughtfulness and better powers of concentration with less blind optimism, and an element of caution. Interestingly, the wonderful Capricorn offbeat sense of humour will make its mark and chime in quite interestingly with Sagittarian wit. A love of literature is usual.

SUN SIGN: CAPRICORN

Heaven of Mercury from an illuminated manuscript (1440) by Giovanni di Paolo of Dante's *The Divine Comedy*.

MERCURY IN SAGITTARIUS

Mercury will lighten the serious side of the Capricorn personality and will enhance the "giddy goat" (*see p167*) in all of them. There will be increased optimism and the ability to grasp concepts quickly, a fair measure of versatility, and less single-mindedness. The thought processes will be quicker than when Mercury is in other signs.

MERCURY IN CAPRICORN

The Capricorn dry sense of humour can get no better expression than when the two planets share this sign. But here is determination and ambition at its peak. These individuals can achieve a very great deal if they will free themselves of unnecessary worry.

MERCURY IN AQUARIUS

An element of stubbornness and mild eccentricity will be expressed from time to time, and these individuals will have a less conventional outlook on life. But, at times, there will be conflict between deciding to take a conservative or radical line of action. Bright and original ideas should *not* be ignored.

SUN SIGN: AQUARIUS

MERCURY IN CAPRICORN

Here are two rather chilly sign influences getting together. These individuals' minds will be practical, logical, and inventive, with a tendency to stubbornness. There will be a very clear concept of what should be undertaken in a very conventional way and where greater freedom of expression can be expressed. If these two extremes work well – excellent; if not, a certain amount of inner conflict will have to be resolved.

MERCURY IN AQUARIUS

Aquarian Sun-sign characteristics will be further enhanced by this placing, as will increased stubbornness and unpredictability. Inventiveness and considerable originality will be expressed, and independence will be of prime importance. Freedom of expression to get on with their work and life in their own individual way is necessary.

MERCURY IN PISCES

This placing will add sensitivity and greater consideration of other people, so that the Aquarian independence is somewhat softened. The Aquarian humanitarian quality will be markedly strengthened, and the emotional impact of Pisces, through Mercury, will add an interesting and warm dimension to these individuals.

SUN SIGN: PISCES

MERCURY IN AQUARIUS

Mercury will add strength of mind to the Pisces Sun. There will be an element of determination and stubbornness which will also be extremely positive. The caring elements – so strong in this Sun sign – will be further increased, and originality and inventiveness will add considerable sparkle and a touch of glamour to Piscean creative interests.

MERCURY IN PISCES

Here are very Piscean individuals. They often find it difficult to keep both feet on the ground. When they take off – if they can allow their incredible imaginations to take off with them and *eventually* give their ideas life and creative form – they will do extremely well. They are gullible and must try really hard to develop an element of sceptism at all times.

MERCURY IN ARIES

This placing gives Pisceans a lively and energetic intellectual boost. Their mind will work quickly and, for the most part, decisiveness and a direct approach to problems will be present, as will optimism and enthusiasm. At times they will waver and fall into a less assertive mood. They must realize that they need not feel negative and can always assess their problems in a positive frame of mind.

A touch of glamour is characteristic of a Piscean with Mercury in Aquarius.

The Venus Factor

Below and on the following pages, we have summarized the effect of Venus for each Sun sign. In each case, the planet can occupy only one of five places: in the Sun sign itself, or in one of the four signs closest to it.

Venus, named after the goddess of love, is the brightest planet in the sky.

SUN SIGN: ARIES

VENUS IN AQUARIUS

Venus adds a mysterious glamour to individuals. Aries independence relates to relationships and other spheres. Often a final commitment to marriage or a relationship is delayed due to a need for independence. Individuals will be highly sexed, but may be emotionally distant. They often waste money on silly, trendy things.

Planetary symbol for Venus

VENUS IN PISCES

Aries selfishness will be considerably lessened, replaced by a loving and caring attitude. The passionate fire of the Aries Sun and the sensitivity of the water element of Venus blend perfectly to make an ideal lover, one attuned to the partner's concerns and interests. Charity can sometimes be carried to excess.

VENUS IN ARIES

These individuals love passionately. They make lively partners who fall in and out of love very quickly, and once

A need for freedom occurs when Aries people have Venus in Aquarius. These people are likely to delay marriage and other major commitments.

tired of a partner will hastily move on. Aries selfishness will emerge out of the need to put the self first and to always take the lead. A good measure of independence is vital within their relationships, and they spend freely.

VENUS IN TAURUS

Venus is very powerful from its own sign and will complement Aries passion, but these individuals will be slower to arouse than many of this Sun sign, and be somewhat possessive. There is a touch of the pure romantic, and a love of the finer things in life, especially good food. They are also enterprising and clever with cash.

VENUS IN GEMINI

Geminian flirtatiousness adds an interesting perspective to the Aries individual, who will be especially brilliant at chat-up lines. The temptation to have more than one lover at a time will often prove irresistible. Here there is less passion and a greater need for friendship within a love relationship. A lively business sense is usual but there will be difficulty in saving cash.

VENUS AT A GLANCE

Distance from Sun 108 million km
(67 million miles)
Orbit around Sun 224.7 Earth days
Rotation on Axis 243 Earth days
Satellites None
Keywords Harmony, Unison
Rules Taurus and Libra

SUN SIGN: TAURUS

Taurean passion and sensuousness is noticeable with Venus in Pisces, Aries, and Cancer.

VENUS IN PISCES

Here we have the pure romantic – the nostalgic and sensual lover. The emotional content of relationships will be very high, and usually beautifully expressed both in and out of bed. Taurean possessiveness will be expressed with loving care, but will nevertheless make some partners feel claustrophobic. Money will be generously given to charity – and spent on good living.

VENUS IN ARIES

While passionate, these individuals will pace themselves – Taurus does not like to be rushed. However, once aroused, there will be a great deal of enjoyment and sexual fulfillment for both partners. Taurean possessiveness will not be pronounced, as Venus adds an element of independence to the attitude towards relationships. Taurean business acumen combines with Aries enterprise to offer excellent potential for financial success.

VENUS IN TAURUS

All Taurean characteristics will be enhanced. While there is sincere love, affection, and sexual passion, possessiveness will also emerge, and the partners' reaction to it will vary according to their particular birth charts. Thinking of the partner as a possession ("she's mine") must be countered. There is brilliant business sense and a strong desire to make and spend a lot of money.

VENUS IN GEMINI

A need for friendship within a love relationship will encourage a light-hearted atmosphere, while Taurean possessiveness will be weakened by Geminian logic. Some conflict can occur when the Taurean Sun-sign qualities are ready for a permanent relationship while the Geminian Venus wants to continue to play the field. Expenditure will be considerable – justified by regarding purchases as "good investments".

VENUS IN CANCER

The psychological need for family life and a permanent relationship will be a powerful force. Here are wonderfully sensual lovers, but those who, while creating a beautiful home, will be extremely possessive both towards partners and children. They are brilliant business people, who can make a fortune yet are not particularly generous. There is a tendency to be over nostalgic for the past.

VENUS RULES TAURUS

Irrespective of the five possible Sun signs, a powerful show of Taurean characteristics will be present in the individual, who will be affectionate, sexy, and passionate. Taurean possessiveness will occur to a lesser degree, unless Taurus is the Sun sign, when it will be strengthened. If this is the case, food will also be central – teasing them about their love of eating is worthwhile, especially if they are good looking. This sign is known for its looks, but weight gain often has a disastrous effect. When love goes wrong, the Venus/Taurus influence takes solace from comfort eating.

SUN SIGN: GEMINI

VENUS IN ARIES

Geminians with an Aries Venus are the most passionate of their sign. This adds an interesting perspective to the personality, and enquiring Geminian minds will become even more sceptical than usual when they read about their Sun sign, which will have no mention of a deeply passionate and highly sexed attitude to love. Here are big spenders – even if they are not big earners.

Expensive boutiques will be the haunt of Geminians with Venus in Aries.

VENUS IN TAURUS

This placing stabilizes the light-hearted Geminian attitude to love, and will encourage faithfulness, a deeper expression of feeling, and a warm and loving attitude. The sex life will be fun, and sheer enjoyment and pleasure will be both given to and readily received from the partner. A love of beautiful things will prove expensive, but there is usually a talent for selling.

VENUS IN GEMINI

Here are the flirts of the zodiac, with a natural gift for expressing their love – romantically and sexily or with the best chat-up lines ever. They can enjoy more than one relationship at a time, but have the knack of talking their way out of difficult situations. Money? They will make it one way or another.

VENUS IN CANCER

Here is the poetic Gemini – a romantic lover and the least flirtatious of the sign. Great tenderness and sensitivity is beautifully expressed, and there is a tendency to worry about partners, often with less Geminian logic than might be expected of this very rational type. They have an excellent and shrewd business sense but are not always good at saving.

VENUS IN LEO

This placing will bring constancy to the Gemini who, while still enjoying flirting and giving new acquaintances a come-on, will have a desire for true love and affection, which will be warmly expressed. Here are Geminians who tend to collect broken hearts, but eventually find true love. They need to make a lot of money because of their love of the beautiful and the expensive.

SUN SIGN: CANCER

VENUS IN TAURUS

Here is a potentially caring and loving parent to whom family life will be extremely important. But we also have here one of the most sensual and responsive lovers of the whole zodiac. This can result in possessiveness and a tenacity which sometimes becomes overwhelming. The break-up of a relationship will be incredibly painful and difficult for both partners. There is considerable flair for business.

VENUS IN GEMINI

When logic and intuition meet, as they do in those that have this combination, individuals are canny enough to keep several steps ahead of others – especially when it comes to matters of love and sex. They know where it is that they are going and precisely what they want out of life. Friendship for them is as important as passion. They have a knack of managing their finances very well.

VENUS IN CANCER

Love will be expressed tenderly and cherishingly. Cancerian anxiety will seriously emerge where lovers are concerned, and the imagination will take off if the partner is not home when expected. These Cancerians epitomize kindness, but moodiness can mar their love and sex life. They are very clever at making their bank balances grow.

VENUS IN LEO

This placing gives a certain panache to these individuals, who love enthusiastically and are highly sexed. Venus adds fiery emotion to their sensuality, and they make each romantic encounter

something of a special occasion. They have a sense of style and a liking for luxury, and appreciate beautiful things, which means they tend to be considerably more extravagant than most Cancerians.

Protectiveness over children is likely to be heightened in a Cancerian with Venus in Virgo.

VENUS IN VIRGO

Cancerian anxiety is considerably heightened, and likely to be centred on the partner (or on children). The tendency to criticize and nag needs conscious controlling if it is not to have a negative effect on the caring and sensitive expression of love and sex. Venus in Virgo will lower and cool the powerful Cancerian emotion. A careful attitude to money is usual.

SUN SIGN: LEO

VENUS IN GEMINI

This placing adds a light-hearted and enthusiastic attitude to love, but with a considerable need for love and affection. The early stages of a relationship are especially enjoyable when a battle of words adds spice to the encounter. Leonine passion is present, and real friendship in the relationship is essential. There will be a logical approach to problems, and cash will usually be available when unexpected bills arrive.

VENUS IN CANCER

This adds considerably to Leo sensitivity – which is far more potent than many realize. Here the extravert Leo Sun will conceal injury and Cancerian worry will exaggerate the problem. Sensuality plus passion will enhance the love and sex life, making for exciting and responsive partners. A love of works of art or antiques will lead to good investments for this canny group of Leos.

Prestigious art exhibitions will be naturally attractive to Leos who had Venus in Cancer at the time of birth.

VENUS IN LEO

Here we have the full Leo drama queens, who will do everything possible to enhance their relationship by expressing their fire-sign passion with gusto. They will give enormous encouragement, but, when breakdown occurs, the damage will be well above average. Money is important to pay for a much-enjoyed expensive lifestyle.

VENUS IN VIRGO

Leo's enthusiasm for love and sex is restrained, and a bit of sexual inhibition is present – often expressed through criticism of a partner. Awareness of this should allow the warmth of the Leo Sun to counter the coolness of Venus. Circumspect attitude towards cash.

VENUS IN LIBRA

Sexual passion will be enjoyed in as much opulence as can be afforded. A lasting relationship is important, and may lead to putting too much expectation on partners. Leo's tendency to put the loved one on a pedestal is present, as is Libra's to pick a quarrel because it's nice to make up afterwards. Money will not be kept for very long.

SUN SIGN: VIRGO

VENUS IN CANCER

This placing increases Virgoan emotions and makes for rewarding love and sex. Here is a joint tendency to worry from the two signs most prone to it. When Venus gets out of hand, Virgoan logic and common sense will be expressed – which is not easy, as a lot of concern will be focussed on the partner. Money is handled practically and carefully.

VENUS IN LEO

Venusian fire will add enthusiasm for love and sex, and sexual fulfillment should not be a problem; neither should Virgoan modesty, which Venus will mitigate. The Virgoan critical attitude will be expressed in a domineering way, and awareness of this is necessary. Friendship within the relationship is important. Guilty feelings will occur when this group is extravagant.

Having good business sense is a noticeable trait in Virgos with Venus in Virgo.

VENUS IN VIRGO

The need to relax in relationships is necessary if shyness is not to inhibit a rewarding sex life. A lack of self-confidence and thoughts of inadequacy, or feelings that sex is "dirty" can be the cause. Awareness that natural modesty and charm is present and attractive to the opposite sex will be a great help. Here is a good business sense.

VENUS IN LIBRA

Venus from its own sign is particularly powerful, and creates a strong desire for a rewarding relationship. But Virgo shyness and inhibition will inhibit desire. These individuals must stop thinking that they have nothing to offer to partners when, in fact, they have a great deal. Here is an excellent blend of common sense and the enjoyment of hard-earned cash.

VENUS IN SCORPIO

This is a very meaty placing for Venus, which will considerably increase emotion and sexual desire. The sex drive is powerful, but seriously conflicts with Virgo inhibition. These individuals are extremely sexually attractive, but may not want to appear so. Relaxation in sexual enjoyment is essential, then huge pleasure and fulfillment results. There is a considerable ability to make money.

SUN SIGN: LIBRA

Libra is flirtatious when Venus is in Sagittarius, which can cause conflict in relationships.

VENUS IN LIBRA

Harmony, balance, fairness, and romantic love are at their strongest here; Librans are at their most complete, and have the ability to relax in love and sex. Life, then, is beautiful – unless the balance is upset. Searching too hard for the ideal partner can cause problems, as can overspending.

VENUS IN SCORPIO

The influence of the Sun plus emotional strength from Venus provides a force which will be useful in furthering all spheres of these people's lives, and in enhancing the sex life. Provided that jealousy is guarded against at all times, here are exciting individuals who will be considerate towards their partners. A flair for making and spending money.

VENUS IN LEO

Here the need for romance is more powerful than the desire for sexual fulfillment. These individuals will generally spend money freely – at times being accused of "buying" love. They are fun-loving people who need their partners to think well of them.

VENUS IN VIRGO

This influence of Venus will dampen the desire for a permanent relationship. A psychological breakthrough will be needed if Libran qualities are to be fully developed. The critical tendencies of Virgo will sometimes be used to cover up sexual insecurity. A careful attitude to money is common.

VENUS IN SAGITTARIUS

Venus is in a lively, flirty, and frivolous mood in this sign, so the Libran love of romance and longing for a partner may conflict. If these individuals realize that a certain amount of independence is enjoyable they will do extremely well.

TWO TRICKY CONFIGURATIONS

Although Venus is a very beneficial planet, we have two combinations that are potentially stressful. When Libra is the Sun sign and Venus falls in Virgo, the acceptance of much-wanted love and affection is thwarted by Virgo's acute critical sense. This will undermine a free flow of affection and add an element of uncertainty, especially when the individuals are self-critical.

When the Sun sign is Virgo and Venus is in Libra there are other complications: Virgos are known for their modesty, but the powerful Venus in Libra gives them a throbbing need for a beautiful relationship. To get full benefit from the glory of Venus in Libra, they will have to free themselves of their Virgoan lack of self-confidence.

Expensive gifts will be well-intentioned from a Libra with Venus in Leo, but might be seen as "buying" love.

SUN SIGN: SCORPIO

VENUS IN VIRGO

The Venus influence from Virgo will cool Scorpio's ardour and add modest Virgoan charm. It can cause inhibition, but, in some cases, can also encourage an obsession with sex. The Moon and/or Ascending signs will usually counter such problems.

VENUS IN LIBRA

This is a good placing for intensive, passionate Sun-in-Scorpio types who will be romantic and sensitive with partners. These individuals are capable of true love, which will be expressed in long relationships. However, there is a need to control the mix of Scorpio jealousy and Libran resentfulness.

VENUS IN SCORPIO

Everything written about Scorpio sexuality will have a ring of truth; but even so there are those with this placing who will express their energies in other directions (*see p140*). Prospective partners will be greeted with seductive charm, and will not put up much resistance – but should be aware that the green-eyed monster will be lurking in the wings.

VENUS IN SAGITTARIUS

While this adds Sagittarian fire to Scorpio passion, the Venus influence will lighten intensity, bringing a more relaxed attitude and a need for good intellectual rapport within relationships. Sometimes the Sagittarian need for independence will conflict with Scorpio jealousy. There is an ability to make money, but a tendency to gamble too.

VENUS IN CAPRICORN

This influence adds constancy to relationships. It also enhances the ability to have an objective outlook on love. A tendency to find a partner who is of a higher educational or social standing is likely. These folk will get what they want, not only in love and sex, but also in other ambitions.

Scorpios with Venus in Capricorn usually end up getting what they want in love and life.

SUN SIGN: SAGITTARIUS

VENUS IN LIBRA

This is an excellent placing for exuberant, sexy Sagittarians who can be blustering in their approach. Venus adds a lovely attitude and increased consideration of the partner. The need for good intellectual rapport is present, but the Libran romantic flair combines well with Sagittarian bright sexiness, and here are responsive lovers who are flirtatious and do not necessarily take their relationships particularly seriously.

VENUS IN SCORPIO

The fiery emotion of the Sun sign is merged with the deep-water emotion of the Venus sign. Feelings will be intense and passionate and clash with a Sagittarian need for independence and love of freedom. These people will fall in love hard, but somewhat less often than most of their Sun sign. Venus will install an above average interest in financial advancement and gain.

VENUS IN SAGITTARIUS

There is need for love, romance, and good relationships – but these individuals may give the impression that they do not care very much about this sphere of their lives. Sagittarians are the hunters of the zodiac, and while unlikely to go off with the hounds, they frequently move on in love, and the grass is always greener over the hedge! Gambling must be controlled.

A glamorous attraction often marks out Sagittarians with Venus in Aquarius.

VENUS IN CAPRICORN

These Sagittarians will take their love and sex lives rather more seriously than most. A tendency to have more than one relationship at a time will not be their scene, and while the sexual impulsiveness of the Sun is definitely cooled, enormous pleasure will still be enjoyed. Sagittarian gambling instincts combined with Capricorn business instincts can work extremely well.

VENUS IN AQUARIUS

These Sagittarians will so enjoy their freedom and independence that they will put off a serious commitment for a very long time. They have a kind of magnetic attraction which they will use to immense effect, and the ardent passion of the sign will be cooled. However, once committed they will be faithful. They may waste money on glamorous, trendy things.

SUN SIGN: CAPRICORN

VENUS IN SCORPIO

The love and sex life will be taken very seriously, and the Venus influence will definitely add passion and very powerful feelings with an above average desire for sexual fulfillment. A final commitment may be delayed because of the need to experiment sexually and emotionally in order to choose the "right" partner. Here is considerable business ability.

VENUS IN SAGITTARIUS

The love and sex life will be spiced with enjoyment and fun. Capricorn loyalty and faithfulness will be less evident. An element of independence is also present, and very freely expressed. However, the partners of this group will be expected to encourage and give support to the aspiring Capricorn ambitions and appreciate their ever-increasing bank balance.

VENUS IN CAPRICORN

Faithfulness and loyalty will always be in evidence, and the need to look up to the partner is important. The expression of love will be very cool, but because of the influence of the god Pan, who is related to Capricorn, sheer fun and a lively sexiness is present when the mood takes them. A canny and shrewd business sense is usual.

VENUS IN AQUARIUS

This is about as cool as any expression of love can be, with all the glamour and magnetism that Venus always bestows on Aquarius. Here is a need for independence and a sense of freedom, but at the same time a conventional style of relationship is also important. Flair for the new and original when investing can cause losses.

VENUS IN PISCES

The serious Capricorn exterior reveals an "old softie" within when it comes to love. There will be confusion and amazement when these individuals fall in love, and while enjoying every romantic encounter, they may well tend to tell themselves to pull themselves together. One minute they assiduously save, while the next they spend freely.

SUN SIGN: AQUARIUS

VENUS IN SAGITTARIUS

Both these signs are known for their love of independence, so commitment to a permanent relationship will be considerably delayed. Enjoyment of doing their own thing in their own individual way is crucial, while at the same time there will be an equal enjoyment of love and sex and no lack of willing partners. Serious saving schemes may tend to be very boring.

VENUS IN CAPRICORN

Aquarians always enjoy their unique and independent lifestyle and are reluctant to sacrifice it. With Venus in this sign, here is discretion personified; only when the individual is attracted to someone they know to be "right", socially as well as romantically, will their pursuit of love be thorough and enthusiastic. Cash will be well invested in antiques and works of art.

VENUS IN AQUARIUS

Here is glamour and a kind of star quality that magnetically attracts but also says, "keep your distance". However, these individuals are very romantic beings, who may well long for a partner but not a partnership. Aquarian independence will rule, but sometimes an inner longing causes conflict which may or may not be resolved.

An Aquarian with Venus in Sagittarius will be happiest when single and in a job that allows great freedom.

VENUS IN PISCES

The romantic inclination of the Sun-sign Aquarian will dominate over the independent lifestyle. These individuals will fall in love frequently and may well suffer from an above average number of broken hearts. They will tend to take off to cloud nine when falling in love, and ignore lessons learned from past experiences; but they make lovely partners once committed. They probably need professional help with their finances.

VENUS IN ARIES

Here is a warm, passionate, and forthright attitude to love. These individuals will get a great amount of pleasure from love and sex, and be ready to move on to new relationships once even an iota of boredom sets in; it is at that point that Aquarian independence emerges. Commitment? That will happen in due course. Here are big, impulsive spenders.

Art and antiques shops are of interest to Aquarians with Venus in Capricorn.

SUN SIGN: PISCES

VENUS IN CAPRICORN

This group of individuals will have a down-to-earth attitude towards their love and sex life. They are sincere, constant, and very loyal. This is a rather cool placing for Venus, but with the very sensitive and emotional content of a Pisces Sun sign it is an excellent stabilizer, and so there will be far less heartache than is often the case. Here is an intuitive and clever business sense.

VENUS IN AQUARIUS

The need to feel free and independent of lovers, but an equally powerful need for meaningful relationships is a problem that often has to be resolved by those of this group. Creating a balance – a certain amount of freedom – expressed perhaps through some absorbing interest will help, provided there is always warm love and sex to come home to. Will spend too freely.

VENUS IN PISCES

Here is a most romantic lover who will get carried away at the least encouragement. Life will be total bliss until they fall back to Earth with a resounding bump. They must develop an element of scepticism when approached by members of the opposite sex, and not look too hard for new partners. There is need for professional help in all financial matters.

Expect luxury and an aura of blissful relaxation from a Piscean with Venus in Taurus.

Shopping sprees are commonplace for a Piscean with Venus in Aquarius, and can cause financial problems.

VENUS IN ARIES

Here are ardent and passionate lovers who will fall in love very quickly and enjoy sexual fulfillment along with a considerable measure of romance. Their emotional intensity is very strong and will sometimes confuse and even surprise them. While their desires are powerful, a lack of self-confidence may cramp their style. They are enterprising and good at making money.

VENUS IN TAURUS

Venus will add depth, constancy, and stability to the emotional Piscean heart. Here are some very romantic and beautifully sensual lovers, but they need to be aware that possessiveness can mar their relationships. They will do much for their partners and will create a wonderfully comfortable and relaxing atmosphere. There is a common attitude towards money and a liking for luxury.

"Ever consider this Universe as one living Being, with one material substance and one spirit. Contemplate the fundamental causes, stripped of all disguises."

Marcus Aurelius (121–180)

The Outer Planets

Traditionally known as the "superior planets", the outer planets are those with orbits outside that of the Earth. Mars, Jupiter, and Saturn were the furthest prominent lights recognized by man in ancient times. Saturn, the most distant from the Sun, was seen as the ultimate outpost, marking the end of the Universe.

MARS, JUPITER, AND SATURN

Mars, in orbit between the Earth and Jupiter, resembles Earth more closely than any other planet, though it is only half its diameter. Its two satellites or moons, Phobos and Deimos, are named after the children of Ares and Aphrodite; Ares is the Greek name for Mars. The names mean "fear" – hence "phobia".

Jupiter's orbit lies between Mars and Saturn. It was aptly named after the Father of the Gods, for it is the giant of the solar system, with a diameter 11 times that of Earth. It has 16 known satellites: one of them, Ganymede, is the largest satellite in the solar system. In mythology, Ganymede became the cup-bearer to Jupiter under his Greek name of Zeus.

Saturn, almost the same size as Jupiter, has many moons, including Titan, the only known satellite in the solar system that has an atmosphere. Eighteen of the satellites have been named, though after running a gamut of mythical personalities, astronomers ran out of steam and retreated to a system of numbers such as S161980S27.

Mars, Jupiter, and Saturn take considerably different periods of time to orbit the Sun. Like the other planets, they travel through the 12 signs of the zodiac; as they do so their influence is exerted on the signs and also in the way they form and break away from angular relationships with each other – this is known as the Aspects (*see pp264–83*).

According to Greek mythology, Aphrodite bore two children by Ares, Phobos and Deimos, and the two moons of Mars were named in their honour.

Saturn with Dione, one of the planet's many moons, in the foreground.

THE STAR OF BETHLEHEM

From time to time, two large planets such as Jupiter and Saturn appear close to each other in the night sky. It was probably the sight of such a spectacular conjunction that alerted the biblical Magi to an extraordinary event, and made them follow the star of Bethlehem to the manger in which Christ was born – there was a conjunction of these two planets in March, 6 BCE, and it was particularly brilliant in those latitudes.

The Mars Factor

On an orbit that varies between 208 and 248 million kilometres from the Sun, Mars is the fourth planet in our solar system and the first of the outer planets. Below and on the following pages, we have summarized the influence of Mars on each of the 12 signs of the zodiac.

Mars, the red planet, is approximately half the size of Earth; like our planet, it has polar ice caps and seasons.

ASTROLOGICAL SIGNIFICANCE

While Mars is at its most potent in the signs it rules, its influences are a powerful marker by which an astrologer can determine the level of the subject's physical energy, assertiveness, and sex drive. The way the planet manifests its influence is geared to the sign it is in, and we are able to discover whether the energy is high or low, whether it will have immediate impact, giving the subject a rush of adrenalin and sudden anger, or whether the energy flow is controlled and burned up in a regulated way, perhaps through regular exercise.

These indications are further modified by the house position of the planet and the influences of the other planets by way of the various aspects it receives from them. When Mars is on the Ascendant (near

Planetary symbol for Mars

nine o'clock on the chart) and about to rise, it will considerably colour the characteristics of the Rising sign, strengthening them and giving the individual additional assertiveness and a powerful driving force which will be blended with the Rising sign's accepted characteristics. It will also have an impact on the general health and wellbeing of the individual.

If Mars is placed high in the sky (on the Midheaven) in the birth chart, the planet's influence will be expressed through hard work and the will to get on in life in the chosen career.

While accepting that Pluto is the modern ruler of Scorpio, astrologers will still consider the special relationship between Mars and Scorpio. If Mars happens to be in Scorpio, the planet's placing will considerably strengthen the influence of that sign – to a far greater degree if Scorpio happens to be the Sun, Moon, or Ascending sign in the chart under consideration.

Levels of sex drive can be interpreted through the position of Mars in a birth chart.

MARS AT A GLANCE		
Distance from Sun 228 million km (142 million miles)		
Orbit around Sun 687 Earth days		
Rotation on Axis 24 hrs 37 mins		
Moons Deimos and Phobus		
Keywords Physical energy, sex drive, and assertiveness		
Rules Aries (and traditionally Scorpio)		

MARS THROUGH THE ZODIAC

MARS IN ARIES

Here is Mars in the sign it rules. The planet will be of increased importance and a focal point of the birth chart. It gives an energy force which will need to be burned positively through daily physical work, sport, and exercise. These individuals will in some respects show certain characteristics of Aries. They will want to be out in front and way ahead of any rivals. They are also likely to put themselves first, so an element of selfishness can sometimes emerge.

Accident-proneness when exercising or driving too fast, plus a vulnerability to burns and cuts is ever present, and the sex drive is considerably increased.

MARS IN TAURUS

Mars will make the individual a passionate, sensual, and romantic lover who will give considerable pleasure and satisfaction. It is a powerful energy source which gives skill at team games such as soccer and rugby.

Taureans are placid until aroused, when they become a force to be reckoned with. This is exactly the way Mars operates from Taurus, giving a calm exterior until individuals explode.

When this happens they may not always fully realize the severity of the impact they are making. Very often stubbornness is present.

MARS IN GEMINI

This placing adds considerable mental stimulus, so these individuals are always mentally as well as physically busy. Their alert minds move energetically about, surveying and preparing the next project, and solving problems. Mars has the reputation for not being particularly well placed in this sign, and certainly there is a vulnerability to restlessness and inconsistency of effort; however, any Gemini influence adds versatility. The need for constant intellectual challenge is present, and there is often an evident talent for athletics, tennis, and dance – all of which will be enthusiastically practised.

MARS IN CANCER

The Martian energy is expressed emotionally and passionately. There is enormous tenacity, which will be applied

The romantic nature in a Taurean will be emphasized with the placing of Mars in Taurus.

to all spheres of life, especially the career and parenthood. Sensuality and caring qualities will be very much part of these individuals' attitude towards their partners, but a tendency to create a somewhat claustrophobic atmosphere can have a negative effect. It is important that encouragement is given to get them to talk through their problems.

There is great capacity for hard work, sometimes carried out in difficult or even dangerous conditions. The ideal exercise for those of this sign placing are all kinds of water sports.

A talent for painting is a noticeable trait when we have Mars in Leo.

MARS IN LEO

The energy Mars brings when in Leo will do much to encourage these individuals to be physically healthy and strong, and positive and enthusiastic in outlook. They need to enjoy exercise, and finding a sport or some interest which makes a demand on their energy level is important. The back and spine are vulnerable, however, so care must be taken to give support to this area of the body.

They have excellent if somewhat domineering powers of leadership, and their emotions will flow positively and be expressed through enjoyment of sex and the other pleasures of life. Here too is creative flair, with a talent for painting.

MARS IN VIRGO

This placing gives a tremendous ability to work hard, and a need to do so. If for some reason this is not possible, the individual will suffer from restlessness. Here too are considerable reserves of nervous energy, which, if expressed through a rewarding career or study, will facilitate excellent results; but awareness that stress and tension easily catches up with them is important: early symptoms emerge as indigestion or stomach upsets. To counter this, yoga or some other relaxing discipline is advisable, and

Yoga is advisable for those who have Mars in Virgo, to channel nervous enery.

sporting activities where quick movement is necessary – tennis, squash, or even tap-dancing are all enjoyable.

MARS IN LIBRA

Mars complements the Libran need for love and adds pleasure to a rewarding sex life. The tendency to fall in love at first sight can be attended by an equally sudden falling out, so heartbreak is frequent. The planet in languid mood encourages a tendency to say "I can't be bothered", and excuses will be made to delay getting moving – especially when it is time to go to the gym or it is going to rain. Here is good perception and a surprising level of intuition, which should not be ignored. A preponderance for headaches, damage to the head, and slight kidney upsets can also be present.

MARS IN SCORPIO

Mars is the traditional ruler of this sign, and its influence is particularly strong. It will considerably increase the emotional and physical energy, giving drive, determination, and strength of will to succeed. An element of stubbornness is present, and should be countered.

While sexual fulfillment is important to all of us, for those with this placing it is extremely important, and any problems of a sexual nature should be resolved, if necessary through therapy. Here are individuals who need emotional involvement in their careers, because working in a dead-end job will be a source of considerable frustration.

MARS IN SAGITTARIUS

This is a happy placing for Mars: it increases physical energy, and involvement in a demanding sport is essential for these individuals' wellbeing, and there will be no lack of enthusiasm. The sex drive is strong, positive, and uncomplicated, so hang-ups and inhibitions are unlikely. However, restlessness will occur when individuals are prevented from using this energetic force, which also contributes considerable intellectual energy and versatility.

An element of recklessness is often present together with an inclination to take risks – not only physical risks but perhaps gambling too. This needs controlling if disaster is to be averted.

MARS IN CAPRICORN

There will be high aspirations and determination to achieve them, with the Mars influence to win and come first much in evidence. If the career makes physical demands on these people they will cope extremely well and flourish, accepting hardship as a formidable but surmountable challenge. There is also the ability to cope with working in dangerous conditions. The risk-taking element, usually present with a Mars influence, is minimal when the planet is in this sign. Sex will be taken very seriously, though it is not necessarily of paramount importance since energy is often burned in other directions.

A demanding sport such as rock climbing will be essential for those with Mars in Sagittarius.

MARS IN AQUARIUS

A need for independence and freedom of expression is very much in evidence. There is also a considerable element of stubbornness and perversity, which at times can be extreme. (In children, it is as well to tell them to do the opposite of what is desired, then parents will get the result they actually need.)

There is a decidedly unconventional streak, and true originality, often expressed creatively, or in science or technology. Energy levels are somewhat erratic, but dance or winter sports will be satisfying. Here too is humanitarianism and a desire to relieve suffering.

MARS IN PISCES

Here, emotional energy is increased to a near torrential force. This needs to be expressed positively, for if there is no outlet for it there can be psychological problems which may need professional help. These individuals will be very easily moved by suffering, and have enormous sympathy for friends and relatives in trouble, helping out as much as possible.

There is often impressive creativity which may be suppressed due to a lack of belief in their own ability. Encouragement must be given to them to carry on working. Physical energy will be best expressed through dance, skating, and water sports – maybe synchronized swimming.

The Jupiter Factor

On an orbit of about 779 million kilometres from the Sun, Jupiter is the fifth planet in our solar system, and the second of the outer planets. Below and on the following pages, we have summarized its influence on each sign of the zodiac.

Jupiter is the largest planet in our solar system; its atmosphere is mostly made up of hydrogen.

ASTROLOGICAL SIGNIFICANCE

Jupiter's influence is at its strongest when it is placed in Sagittarius, the sign it rules. Because it is the traditional ruler of Pisces (now ruled by the modern planet Neptune), the planet also has a somewhat more pronounced effect on those individuals who have it in that sign.

Planetary symbol for Jupiter

It is not surprising that the main keyword of Jupiter is *expansion* – it is after all the largest planet in our solar system. It is totally gaseous and with no solid core, and has a delicate and mysterious appearance. Known to the Greeks as Zeus, Jupiter was the chief immortal, whose numerous amorous conquests are recalled in the names of some of the planet's moons – among them Ganymede, Io, and Europa.

Jupiter's relationship with Sagittarius is particularly interesting: it has an influence on the acquisition of knowledge. Here, expansion takes the form of breadth of vision, increasing one's experience of life, often through travel and understanding of foreign countries and cultures. It can also bestow a flair for the study of languages. There is also a philosophical side to Jupiter's influence, and when aware of it, our attitude towards life and its problems will more readily fall into a logical perspective. Traditionally, the planet has for centuries influenced those who are drawn to conventional religion and the law.

The planet encourages optimism and hope – it is often necessary for the astrologer to warn against the dangers of over-optimism which, in its most exaggerated form, can turn into blind optimism. This tendency, for example, can be expressed through compulsive gambling. The negative influence of Jupiter also encourages exaggeration, extravagance, wastefulness, dare-devil risk taking, and foolhardiness.

Due to the physical manifestation of expansion when Jupiter is prominent in our charts, we have a strong tendency to put on weight.

A desire to travel and learn about different cultures is typical of the combined influence of Jupiter and Sagittarius.

JUPITER THROUGH THE ZODIAC

JUPITER IN ARIES

Jupiter's natural optimism and fiery enthusiasm sits comfortably and positively when the planet is in this sign. It adds an independent and freedom-loving quality to the nature. Here too is adventurousness, and a pioneering spirit which will also encourage sportsmanship and the Aries need to win, to be first, to be way out in front of one's rivals.

There will be a quality of quick decisiveness which can sometimes lead to premature action. There is increased accident-proneness and a tendency to sometimes take unnecessary risks; but equally the intellectual and studious side of Jupiter will find fascinating expression.

A freedom-loving nature is engendered by the placing of Jupiter in Aries.

JUPITER IN TAURUS

Here Jupiter contributes bonhomie, a great love of good food and wine, and a taste for comfortable and sometimes extravagant living. Jupiter will also encourage investment – these people are ambitious for a healthy bank balance which will give them an added sense of security and, of course, an increasingly comfortable lifestyle. If they are not careful all that good living will inevitably have a negative effect on their waistlines, hips, and thighs.

Here Jupiter is not usually in an intellectual mood, but as these individuals grow older a philosophical attitude to life will develop.

JUPITER AT A GLANCE
Distance from Sun 778 million km (484 million miles)
Orbit around Sun 11.86 Earth years
Rotation on Axis 9 hrs 51 mins
Satellites 16
Keywords Expansion, optimism
Rules Sagittarius (and traditionally Pisces)

JUPITER IN GEMINI

Jupiter often causes intellectual restlessness, along with vacillating opinions on important matters or, during further education, changes of study courses. Consistency of effort is something that should constantly be strived for, otherwise what potentially is a very good mind will not develop as fully as it should, thereby cutting down on the chances of success. Here are clever individuals who are broad-minded and versatile, and who will take a tremendous interest in everything going on around them. They can play Devil's advocate in discussions, getting away with outrageous comments simply to stir up other people.

JUPITER IN CANCER

Here Jupiter is beautifully spiced with Cancerian intuition and emotion. These people are extremely kind and sympathetic, with an understanding of human nature and of others' problems. The imagination is increased and can be used in ways that emerge from other sign and planetary influences; sometimes there is a talent for writing. Cancerian changeability causes opinions to alter considerably from time to time, but, at its best, this trait encourages flexibility and an open-minded attitude.

Home and family life will be of above average importance, and these individuals make excellent, if sometimes worrying, parents, who will be keen to stretch their children's minds.

JUPITER IN LEO

The Leo influence on Jupiter adds optimism, enthusiasm, cheerfulness, and ambition. It injects a sense of drama and showiness, which if controlled adds effervescence, but if allowed to get out of hand can become bombastic. Here too, is generosity and a liking for the best of everything. Leo is a sign of creativity and this will be expressed in any number of ways – acting, dance,

An appetite for life's luxuries is a hallmark of Jupiter-in-Leos.

creative writing, and film-making. There are powers of leadership and an excellent organizing ability. These individuals often do great work with children and young people.

JUPITER IN VIRGO

The key here is breadth of vision – absorbing the big picture in situations and projects – even though Virgo is actually the sign of detail and the close examination of facts. If those with this placing are aware of this conflict, it is possible to make it work extremely well, so that they attain the best of the two extremes. One thing is certain: the mind will be brilliant, with a quick grasp of an intellectually demanding situation. Provided that Virgoan inhibition or lack of self-confidence does not block the flow of practical and lively thoughts and ideas, success is assured.

JUPITER IN LIBRA

This placing endows individuals with sympathetic friendliness and natural empathy. There is a great desire to please, especially lovers, and considerable generosity will be showered on them. Libran charm will be present, and altogether these are lovely people to be with. There is a huge love of luxury and keenness to make money. A tendency to procrastinate will definitely be present, and if we chide them for a somewhat languid attitude they will in turn chide us for being in too much of a hurry! These individuals might well make *"que sera, sera"* ("whatever will be, will be") their motto in life.

JUPITER IN SCORPIO

Both planet and sign encourage individuals to live life to the full, and these two powerful forces will be the

Film-making is possible as either career or hobby with the Jupiter-in-Leo combination.

source of considerable incentive to live a consistently hard-working and busy life, so that psychological fulfillment grows and energy is burned up in a very positive and rewarding way. There is immense depth and an intense sense of purpose with any Scorpio influence, and when Jupiter's breadth of vision is added these individuals can have the best of both worlds. The tendency to work too hard and too fervently, however, can lower their reserves, resulting in burn-out.

JUPITER IN SAGITTARIUS

This is the sign Jupiter rules, so its influence is considerable. Here is breadth of vision, optimism, enthusiasm, and the need to look ahead. A brilliant mind; all intellectual powers should be used and enjoyed. Here are "eternal students", moving on from one subject to the next for the sheer enjoyment of learning. There is a poor grasp of detail, as it is felt to be boring and best left to those who enjoy intricacy. Blind optimism, risk taking (sometimes financial due to gambling), and participating in dangerous sports need to be controlled.

Volunteer work, such as joining a mountain rescue team, will hold a strong attraction for individuals with Jupiter in Aquarius.

JUPITER IN CAPRICORN

Here we have a classic blending of positivity and negativity – of extraversion (Jupiter) and introversion (Capricorn). Not that all those with a Capricorn influence are shrinking violets; far from it! These individuals are ambitious and determined to achieve objectives. Challenges will be considered in a practical and common sense manner, and enjoyed. Responsibility will be gladly accepted, and one thinks of these people as perhaps the quintessential good boss or senior lecturer who knows how to keep a distance, but will be there to help and encourage staff/students as and when necessary.

JUPITER IN AQUARIUS

This interesting placing for Jupiter endows individuals with humanitarian qualities and a strong need to express

them in whatever way possible. Aquarian independence will be in evidence, but these are extremely friendly people who enjoy a rewarding social life with a great many friends and acquaintances. Impartiality, tolerance, and a good understanding of human nature make them sympathetic yet unbiased in outlook and opinion. There will be an abundance of originality, and enthusiasm for scientific interests and technology – often for astronomy and space. Jupiter in Aquarius tends to suggest a picture of a zany professor.

JUPITER IN PISCES

The traditional ruler of Pisces will contribute a philosophical outlook with strong spiritual beliefs, whether associated with an accepted religion or New Age concepts. There is a very great deal of intuition which, while these individuals must listen to it, must be balanced with logic and common sense to prevent emotions being over-dramatically expressed. There is a compassionate spirit and tremendously sympathetic and caring rapport with other people. There are those who have genuine psychic powers; it is essential that they work with someone experienced in these disciplines to prevent negativity or misguided use.

The Saturn Factor

On an orbit of about 1,426 million kilometres
from the Sun, Saturn is the sixth planet in our
solar system, and the third of the outer planets.
Below and on the following pages, we have
summarized its influence on each sign of the zodiac.

Saturn, like Jupiter,
has an atmosphere
made up almost
entirely of hydrogen.

ASTROLOGICAL SIGNIFICANCE

Before the integration of the
modern planets into the
astrological discipline, everything
that was stern, negative, and
ominous was attributed to Saturn.
The emphasis has now changed,
and Saturn is associated with
authority, and provides a severe
inner voice which controls and
sometimes limits our self-
expression. Here is our inner father, or
authority figure, which will either
inhibit us by uttering countless put-
downs, telling us that we are no good at
anything or will give us the
kind of sensible advice
we might expect of a
strict, but by no
means negative,
parent or teacher.

**Planetary
symbol
for Saturn**

Often our Saturn influence relates to
our parents when in a heavy-handed
mood, telling us we must work
harder at school or that we must
break off a relationship with
someone "unsuitable".
While the influence of Saturn
can inhibit or become a source
of depression, more often it adds
stability. The planet contributes
the ability to discipline ourselves and will
control and guide, although sometimes it
may be a source of frustration and delay
to many of our ideas and projects –
which are probably not as well thought-
out as we think. We learn lessons under
this planet's influence, and can rest
assured that we rarely make serious
mistakes when Saturn is about (although
we may well not think so then). In short,
Saturn usually says, "*Thou shalt not*",
but from time to time changes
the instruction to, "*Thou shalt*" –
usually encouraging us down a
difficult, perhaps unexpected
path. If we take that path the
long-term future will be all
the more successful for us.

The authority figure or inner father is associated
with Saturn – an influence that provides stability.

SATURN AT A GLANCE
Distance from Sun 1.4 billion km (887 million miles)
Orbit around Sun 29.46 Earth years
Rotation on Axis 10 hrs 14 mins
Satellites Complex ring system with at least 34 moons
Keywords Limitation, self-control
Rules Capricorn (and traditionally Aquarius)

SATURN THROUGH THE ZODIAC

SATURN IN ARIES

The energetic qualities of Aries are at variance with Saturn's restraint, so at times these individuals will move forward with confidence and at other times hold back, lacking the necessary drive to see through situations and challenges. Frustration at lack of achievement may be due to an imbalance of energy. If so, individuals should review their lives and not blame externals; a reassessment of personal attitudes could free up the way forward.

SATURN IN TAURUS

Taurus has a reputation for caution and patience. Saturn also encourages caution, common sense, and circumspection. Jointly they increase the need for both emotional and financial security. So these individuals have Taurean patience, will cautiously build up their financial reserves, and will wait for the right moment to finalize important decisions. This placing will slow them down, and they will at times have to be encouraged to get on with what they must do.

SATURN IN GEMINI

This is a good placing for the mind. Saturn will stabilize and organize the somewhat

The need to relax and unwind is essential for those with Saturn in Cancer in order to express their emotions more fully.

chaotic Gemini thinking patterns and discipline verbal expression, so that these individuals, while still being talkative, will make pertinent comments which other people will be glad to hear. Sometimes, however, there is a hard edge to their opinions and remarks, with hints of satire and cynicism. Children with this placing may be rather slow to speak. They must not be rushed or hassled, otherwise impediments could occur which will be difficult to counter.

SATURN IN CANCER

Here is a particularly strong need for emotional security; a formal contract of marriage will be more desirable than co-habitation. Many of these individuals will be especially keen to build a sound family background for themselves, their partner, and children. The Cancerian tendency to worry will be pronounced, even if the dominant signs of the individual's chart show otherwise. Any hint of depression must be talked through with a sympathetic partner or friends. Often there is restraint in the expression of emotion. They need to relax as this helps counter the tendency.

SATURN IN LEO

This placing brings determination, strength of will, superb organizing ability, and loyalty. These individuals take life very seriously, and the usual sunshine of Leo will not be particularly noticeable. Here we have some really splendid but sometimes autocratic and bossy people. Many will be very strict with themselves, imposing a particularly rigid discipline of sergeant-major proportions, excusing themselves when challenged to loosen up a bit by asserting that they are "setting a good example".

SATURN IN VIRGO
Saturn from Virgo gives a strong sense of duty, especially when it comes to family loyalty or loyalty to career commitments. The thinking processes are very well ordered, and life must run like clockwork. In relationships, or with anyone working for them, these individuals can be over-critical and tend to "pick holes" at the least provocation. Virgoan worry and obsession with detail is usually present, with little ability or desire to grasp the broad perspective of any aspect of a project, or of life in general. Here is a need for high standards and perfection in everything that is undertaken.

SATURN IN LIBRA
A very powerful need to see fair play is present – not only in these people's own lives but on behalf of others within

their circle or even internationally. Here are kind, practical people, always willing to help, who are also practical enough to give just the kind of support that is needed for someone who is bereaved or emotionally upset in any way. Saturn will encourage the formation of a permanent emotional relationship, and some will feel more comfortable with a much older partner, who may be a father- or mother-figure to them – perhaps countering a psychological gap from their childhood.

SATURN IN SCORPIO
Emotional energy can be suppressed, and there is a dark intensity which gives the impression that these individuals are pondering on the great problems of the universe. Determination and a sleuth-like talent for research are present, as is an excellent business sense and the ability to make a great deal of money.

A certain hardness or coldness may be a cover-up for sexual inhibition, and any problem in this area needs therapeutic resolution. But here too is the ability to enjoy all the good things of life – added to which there is also a Saturnine offbeat sense of humour.

Life must have structure and order, and run like clockwork for Saturn-in-Virgo individuals.

SATURN IN SAGITTARIUS

Jupiter and Saturn are opposites in their fields of influence. So when Saturn is in Sagittarius, we get a meeting of contradictory influences – even though Jupiter is represented by its ruling sign, Sagittarius. There will be a considerable emphasis on the intellect, with Saturn steadying and adding the ability to cope with detail as well as seeing the broad perspective of situations and projects.

The powers of concentration are good, and there will be a practical approach too. Positivity of outlook will be spiced with Saturnian caution and common sense, and Sagittarian natural enthusiasm; optimism will be "controlled".

A good imagination is common for those with the placing of Saturn in Pisces.

SATURN IN CAPRICORN

This placing will be an extremely powerful influence. These individuals will have strong elements of the Capricorn personality (*see p162*); they will be ambitious and determined and will set their sights on some impressive goals. With Saturn's positive back-up it is most likely that they will attain them. The Capricornian sense of humour will strongly feature, and in most cases, influences from the inner planets will ease the element of coldness and stand-offishness which sometimes occurs.

Capricorn's characteristics are magnified with the placing of Saturn in the star sign.

Stiffness in the joints can become a serious problem, so it is important that these people should be encouraged to keep up regular exercise.

SATURN IN AQUARIUS

Saturn is the traditional ruler of Aquarius, so its influence is increased from this sign. Here it is in a positive mood and as light-hearted as is possible with this dour planet. It encourages independence and strength of will. These individuals are usually self-contained, but, as is the case with any Aquarian emphasis, very friendly and helpful. The humanitarian side of the sign will be pronounced. There is considerable originality, but stubbornness can be a problem at times. Any Aquarian eccentricity is very subdued and will only very rarely emerge. Discipline is another positive Saturnine influence from this sign.

SATURN IN PISCES

The sacrificial tendencies of Pisces will be increased with this placing. Individuals will go for a job which they know will help those in need, rather than one which will develop their own potential and give inner satisfaction. Sometimes there is a lack of self-confidence. It is often the case, however, that a certain shyness plus an attractive self-effacing quality – which many of these individuals will be quite unaware of – will add charm and considerable sex appeal. A powerful imagination is usual and should be allowed free-flowing expression in any kind of creative form.

"*The universe begins to look more like a great thought than a great machine.*"

Sir James Jeans (1937)

The Modern Planets

The planets beyond Saturn were not known in ancient times. Uranus was discovered in the 18th century, Neptune in the 19th, and Pluto in the 20th. The discovery of Uranus and Neptune confused astrologers at first, but eventually it was shown that the "modern planets" are part of the system.

URANUS, NEPTUNE, AND PLUTO

On 13 March 1781, the astronomer William Hershel unexpectedly spotted a new planet – Uranus – which is barely visible without a telescope. In September 1846 the discovery of Neptune was announced by astronomers who had been looking for a distant planet whose gravity was affecting the path of Uranus. Tiny Pluto was not found until 1930, after a long quest for "Planet X".

Percival Lowell was convinced of the existence of a planet beyond Neptune, but he died in 1916 before it was found.

For some astrologers, the modern planets appeared to invalidate the whole astrological system. Others have undertaken detailed research to define the influence of each new planet, and the sign it should rule. Such research is ongoing as other bodies are identified (*see box*) and the significance of objects such as asteroids (*see p199*) is considered. One approach is to examine geographical and political conditions dominating at the time of the planet's discovery. The 1700s, when Uranus was found, were a time of unrest and scientific development – hence the eventual connection between Uranus and the scientific qualities of Aquarius. In the 1860s gas was first used for lighting, and there was a fascination with spiritualism – such matters relate to the qualities of Pisces. The placing of Pluto is most revealing: the time of its discovery coincided with the rise of Fascism, the crime wave linked to prohibition in the USA, and the brutality of Stalin's Russia. These events complement the darker side of Scorpio, hence Pluto became the modern ruler of Scorpio.

Neptune is the second of the "modern planets"; Triton, the largest of the planet's two moons is shown in the foreground.

CHIRON AND OTHER BODIES

The half-comet Chiron was discovered in 1977 and has since been shown to have great astrological significance (*see p239*). Since then, many other small bodies have been observed far beyond Pluto. Sedna was identified in 2002; Eris (which is larger than Pluto) in 2005. Small worlds such as these remain in each sign for hundreds or thousands of years, and their astrological significance (if any) is under consideration.

The Uranus Factor

Uranus takes seven years to travel through each sign of the zodiac, and is in the same sign for everyone born in that period. It is important for those who have Aquarius as Sun, Moon, or Ascendant sign, when it becomes a "personal" planet.

Uranus is circled by five major moons and many smaller bodies.

ASTROLOGICAL SIGNIFICANCE

Astrologers consider Uranus as one of the generational planets, though its influence springs into action for all of us at certain times of our lives, most notably when we are 21, in our early forties, and when we reach 84. These potent transits are described in The Returns (*pp284–9*). It is also of increased importance when it forms a strong aspect to another planet. There was a powerful conjunction with Pluto during 1963–9, which was shown in the charts of everyone born then, and had a strong effect on those in whose birth charts it was in a prominent position. Its more recent influence was during 1996–2003, as it travelled through its

Planetary symbol for Uranus

own sign, Aquarius. For those of this sign it will have meant some important, possibly disruptive events, and/or new beginnings.

Uranus relates to things ancient or futuristic. It encourages an interest in archeology, geology, and paleontology at one end of the scale, and space travel, computer technology, and futuristic projects at the other. In between are many Aquarians – or those with a Uranian influence in their birth charts – who become good astronomers and/or astrologers. When forming relationships to some planets it will also encourage the individual to be glamorous and sexy, but with a magnetic, cool, and distant charm.

URANUS THROUGH THE ZODIAC

URANUS IN ARIES

Uranus works well from this sign, when the positive flow of Aries energy will be expressed with originality. It increases self-confidence and the ability to achieve objectives in an unusual or offbeat way.

Discovering treasures of the past is likely to have considerable appeal for those influenced by Uranus.

If these individuals are creative, this placing gives them a lively sense of colour, and if powers of leadership are hinted at in other areas of the birth chart, Uranus in this sign will enhance them. Uranian stubbornness will be in evidence, and possibly a rather quirky foolhardiness, which can lead to risk-taking that will need controlling.

URANUS IN TAURUS

Uranian stubbornness combined with the Taurean "fixed" quality is a powerful force. Many individuals will say, "I've made up my mind – and that's it." This can be a help if indecisiveness is shown in other areas of the chart; but flexibility of opinion is often lacking. This placing adds stability, and Uranian originality will be expressed with common sense and logic. Sometimes there is a daring attitude to money. Care is needed that cash is not lost on unsound projects.

URANUS IN GEMINI

This is a very lively placing for Uranus, especially if the chart also shows intellectual capacity, perhaps with powerful influences from Mercury, Jupiter, or Sagittarius – or if there are other planets in Gemini with Uranus. Eccentricity will be present and sometimes too, perversity – just to shock. There are quick responses in argument and debate, and many will be successful in the media. The flirtatiousness of Gemini plus the magnetism of Uranus will be an advantage.

URANUS IN CANCER

Any Cancerian influence brings moodiness and changeability, and this will combine with Uranian unpredictability. This can cause problems, according to whether anxiety, concern, or indecision is shown in other areas of the chart. However, other planets and combinations can mitigate the negative influence. Originality will be present, resulting in very lively expression, either creatively or scientifically, when applied to research. There will also be a caring, humanitarian streak.

URANUS IN LEO

Leo energy and powers of leadership are increased. Sometimes there is a liking for power and an attraction to politics. If this is expressed positively and not dogmatically others will be willing to follow. Leo – a fixed sign – plus Uranian stubbornness can cause

Scientific study appeals to many, as Uranus imparts a fascination with the future as well as the ancient past.

problems, perhaps also bringing pomposity. There is always warmth with a Leo emphasis but Uranus cools it. Nevertheless this combination brings a pleasant friendliness. Self-confidence is considerably helped from this placing, especially if shyness or inhibition is shown in other areas of the chart. Any Leo creativity will have a dashing and original flair.

URANUS IN VIRGO

This generation also has Pluto in Virgo with Uranus. Here is a potential source of tension, but the analytical qualities of Virgo plus Uranian originality are excellent for scientific or literary research. There may be clashes between the desire to take a conventional line of action (Virgo is an earth sign) and the very unconventional input of Uranus. It is up to these individuals to be aware of this conflict and learn to rationalize it.

URANUS AT A GLANCE	
Distance from Sun	2.9 billion km (1.8 billion miles)
Orbit around Sun	84.1 Earth years
Rotation on Axis	17 hours, 24 minutes
Satellites	Five main moons and a faint system of ice rings
Keywords	Change – disruptive or sudden
Rules	Aquarius

A natural sense of fun and humour is typical of people who have Uranus in Sagittarius.

URANUS IN LIBRA

Here the romantic facet of Uranus shines strongly, adding glamour and magnetic charm. But if there are other planets in Libra, a conflict may occur between needing independence and the equally powerful need for settled relationships. Uranus is also in a sexy mood, and there is a desire for sexual experimentation. Here too is tremendous friendliness, and someone who is sympathetic, easy to talk to, and willing to help others. Uranus will steady people who have powerful emotions by adding a cool, rational quality to their personalities.

URANUS IN SCORPIO

This is an extremely dynamic and powerful placing for Uranus. While Scorpio is an emotionally charged sign, the cool detachment of Uranus will encourage these individuals to restrict any display of emotion, resulting in a calm exterior when inwardly the emotions are volcano-like. They should learn to release their emotions in a controlled manner, and not allow Vesuvian eruptions to occur.

URANUS IN SAGITTARIUS

Uranus will add originality to the intellect with plenty of fresh ideas which will be acted upon with enthusiasm. Uranus travelled through this sign between 1981 and 1988 during which time its ruler Jupiter joined it, giving individuals a very positive outlook on life and a natural sense of humour. Here too are some really good brains with fantastic potential which must not be wasted or allowed to lie dormant.

URANUS IN CAPRICORN

Here the common sense and logic of the sign will complement the originality and dynamic influences of Uranus; but there will be conflict between Capricorn's conventional attitude and Uranian unconventionality. Capricorn will want always to be seen to do the "right" thing, while Uranus is more daring. Hopefully, these individuals will take a sensible line of action and not cause embarrassment to themselves or other people. It must be remembered that this is a generation influence, and the characteristics will be modified by other more powerful planetary placings.

URANUS IN AQUARIUS

Because Uranus is in its own sign, it would be quite wrong to think that everyone born during the seven-year period will be an archetypal Aquarian. But the generation as a whole has a particularly independent streak, and will want to go its own (stubborn) way. If other planets are in Aquarius, the best qualities of the sign will emerge – humanitarianism, friendliness, and sympathy for Earth's problems such as global warming. It is up to these people to bring about greater awareness of them in others (*see also p234*).

URANUS IN PISCES

Uranus will complete its journey through Pisces in March 2011. Children born before that time have the planet in Pisces. This generation will have the hope and optimism of Uranus, and will be eager to take action where older people have been recalcitrant. These indications chime in very well with those born since 1996, when Uranus entered its own sign, Aquarius, and while the expression of international concerns will be different, there should be good results as these young people reach maturity.

THE CHIRON FACTOR

Chiron was discovered on 1 November 1977 by Charles Kowal, an astronomer at Palomar Observatory in California. Initially labelled an asteroid, it is now classified as a half-comet, with an orbit between that of Saturn and Uranus. It rotates on its axis in just under six hours and orbits the Sun in 50.7 Earth years. Because of eccentricities in the orbit, Chiron spends varying lengths of time travelling through each sign.

A sign rulership has not been finalized for Chiron, and keywords are still debatable, although most astrologers favour "self-healing". When a new planet is discovered, astrologers discuss and research for a very long time before coming to definite conclusions as to its influences. Some totally favour a symbolic approach, while others consider the conditions and events of the period when it was discovered. Here we are compromising, but in our personal research we have discovered that Chiron tends to "highlight" and "invigorate" the characteristics of the sign in which it falls.

CHIRON IN ARIES

Considerable hastiness and enthusiasm is present, as is a desire to discover new challenging projects to burn up energy. Accident-proneness is likely, and little notice will be taken of cuts and burns, which will be left to heal alone.

CHIRON IN TAURUS

The Taurean need for financial security is highlighted: these individuals will not be totally happy until they attain this state. They have to guard against possessiveness towards partners, which otherwise will cause psychological difficulties that will be difficult to heal.

CHIRON IN GEMINI

This placing gives mental ability and often a brilliant mind which will be logical, sceptical, and constantly questioning. There is a natural urge to bring about changes of opinion regarding man's cruelty and a desire for a more humanitarian attitude.

CHIRON IN CANCER

Belonging to a family is important, and the cherishing attributes of Cancer will blossom when these individuals settle and have their own children. But belonging to a larger universal family is also important – a church or some society, for instance.

CHIRON IN LEO

Here Chiron will bestow elements of Leo sunniness, and these individuals will attract attention. Sometimes the negative side of the planet's influences occurs, and they will tend to complain – about their parents, lack of education, and lack of cash.

CHIRON IN VIRGO

These people are very hard and compulsive workers who are sticklers for regular routine and always strive for perfection. They are vulnerable to considerable stress and must always counter it by practising a relaxing discipline such as yoga.

CHIRON IN LIBRA

Resentfulness is common, and these individuals should avoid saying, "if only..." and make an effort to put the past behind them. There is need for them to develop a sympathetic rapport with partners and to counter occasional selfishness.

CHIRON IN SCORPIO

This brings a clear-cut attitude to life. Everything is black or white. Here is decisiveness, but also extremes of moodiness which may cover doubts and inadequacies. There is considerable competitiveness and often a flair for business.

CHIRON IN SAGITTARIUS

Here the influence of Chiron and Sagittarius complement each other. The aphorism that "the grass is always greener over the hedge" is very relevant as these individuals seem always to be searching to find the right direction in life.

CHIRON IN CAPRICORN

This adds reliability, and these people seem to have the happy gift of making other people feel confident. There is an above average need for financial security and material success, which can become over important to them.

CHIRON IN AQUARIUS

Chiron here helps individuals to cope with serious illnesses. Their attitude towards it is positive and they will remark, "Well, I have been ill but I'm better now" – even if they are not. Aquarian resistance to a committed partnership is often present.

CHIRON IN PISCES

This is a marvellous placing for those who enjoy studying – they are often "eternal students", with the more practical elements of life being much neglected. Here too is creative potential, especially for decorative design and clever use of colour.

Palomar Observatory, California

The Neptune Factor

Neptune is the second of the
modern planets. It takes 164 years to complete
a journey through all 12 signs of the zodiac.
Because it is in each sign for 14 years at a time, it
is possibly the most potent generation influence.

Neptune is a gas giant, whose
blue colour comes from methane
in its upper atmosphere.

ASTROLOGICAL SIGNIFICANCE

There is never a time when
living people have Neptune
in each of the 12 signs. So while
we interpret signs here for
the very elderly and for those
about to be born, do not be
misled by our not covering
Aries, Taurus, and Gemini.
These people have long since
departed, and Neptune will not
be active in Aries again until 2025.
For that reason we begin our
interpretations with Cancer (*below*).

Neptune is the accepted ruler of
Pisces, and this is a perfect placement
for the planet, though until the middle
of the 19th century Jupiter reigned
supreme over this sign. Neptune will
become a personal planet for those
who have Pisces as their Sun, Moon,
or Ascendant sign, and in spite of
its generation influence, sensitive

**Planetary
symbol of
Neptune**

Piscean types will find the
planet's influence to be
very potent.

The subtle influence
of this planet works in two
distinct ways. It has a personal
influence on all of us, even
though it is in the same sign
for everyone born within its
14-year journey through one
or the other of them. From a universal
point of view it seems to set markers for
each successive generation, adding
subtle colour and emphasis on certain
spheres of life and the attitudes of all of
us, irrespective of our age and the sign
Neptune was in when we were born.
While the universal influences are
general, they are clear-cut enough to be
more than just noticeable. Therefore, in
this section (and for Pluto), we set out
both general and personal influences.

NEPTUNE THROUGH THE ZODIAC

NEPTUNE IN CANCER
Neptune was active in Cancer from
1901–2 (the double year is due to
retrograde motion, *see box on p243*)

to 1915. Cancer being the sign of home
and family, here was Neptune's main
influence during the period that began
with the Boer War in South Africa,
and ended with the
First World War still
raging as the planet
completed its
journey. Children
born then suffered
again as grown-ups,
facing the equally
dreadful conditions of
the Second World War.

World War II was the terrible prospect that
awaited those born when Neptune was
active in Cancer at the 20th century's start.

While Neptune increased these individuals' powerful emotions, it added to the tenacity (a powerful Cancerian trait) they needed to keep going while under privation. The placing also increased sensitivity and intuition. This worked well in some circumstances, such as when a dreaded telegram arrived announcing the death of a husband or son, yet the recipient instinctively knew that the message was wrong. Similarly, some expected bad news even before the telegram boy knocked on the door.

NEPTUNE IN LEO

Neptune entered Leo in 1915 and continued through to 1928–9, when it overlapped with Virgo.

It was during these years that the popularity of cinema considerably increased. Millions of people visited the cinema each week to see the great silent movie epics. Here was escapism from the aftermath of the First World War and the financial disasters of the Depression, into a wonderful world of make-believe.

The Neptune generation influence added a sense of drama and a need for glamour – traits still present with its remaining members. If Leo or Pisces are accented by Sun, Moon, or Ascendant, these individuals will have a really creative imagination which can be expressed through any art form. Maybe they danced, and still paint or create beautiful embroidery, or take photographs. Their potential was and still remains considerable.

NEPTUNE IN VIRGO

When Neptune entered Virgo, the sign of communications, in 1928–9, cinema leapt ahead with the advent of "talking pictures", television was developed, and in 1936, the British Broadcasting Corporation started its first transmissions.

While Virgo is the sign of the Virgin, and Neptune is connected with spirituality and faith, the critical side of the Virgo influence began to be expressed on religion by this generation.

The golden era of cinema arrived in the 1930s and corresponded to the period when Neptune was in Virgo.

The imagination can be considerably stimulated by this placing. If either Gemini or Virgo is emphasized by Sun, Moon, or Ascendant, the influence is helpful and strong. It can also give the potential for writing or craftwork. Neptune from this sign tends to sap self-confidence, and this should always be carefully considered, in spite of it being just a generation influence.

NEPTUNE IN LIBRA

The planet was in Libra from 1942 to 1956–7. Think of the romantic songs of the 1940s and the war – full of longing and regretful separation,

NEPTUNE AT A GLANCE
Distance from Sun 4.5 billion km (2.8 billion miles)
Orbit around Sun 164.79 Earth years
Rotation on Axis 14 hours
Satellites Triton, Nereid, and others
Keywords Confusion, cloudiness
Rules Pisces

with lovers parted and not knowing when or where they would meet again. All this was emphasizing Neptune confusion and the total lack of Libran togetherness. During this time the flower-power generation of the 1970s was born.

Here Libran principles and characteristics are merged with the sensitivity of Neptune, but the illusion of love is unrealistic, and it will be emphasized when the Venus signs, Taurus and Libra or Pisces, are prominent in this generation's charts. From Libra the planet adds kindness, generosity, and willingness to make sacrifices for loved ones. However, if these signs are not prominent by Sun, Moon, or Ascendant, this generation influence will not be very noticeable.

NEPTUNE IN SCORPIO

The difference between the softness of the Neptune-in-Libra generation and the punk rock generation of the Neptune-in-Scorpio (1956–7 to 1970–1) people is unmistakable. The latter have a hard and aggressive image: their drug scene was not the peaceful drifting of Neptune in Libra, but something far more intense and often extremely dangerous.

As Scorpio is an intensively emotional sign, Neptune's journey through it increases this powerful force, especially if Scorpio is Sun, Moon, or Ascendant. But sometimes, even with the strength of Scorpio giving tremendous back-up, there is uncertainty and confusion present. While this is a generation influence, many individuals born during this period tend to lack the usually disciplined attitude of this powerful sign.

NEPTUNE IN SAGITTARIUS

Jupiter, the ruler of Sagittarius, used to be the ruler of Pisces (now ruled by Neptune), and that traditional ruling seems to have an effect here. The 1970–1 to 1984–5 generation is more idealistic and hopeful, and will do much to save the Earth's resources. Those who get the best out of Neptune are idealistic and express hope, even if they have to cope with cynicism and bureaucracy.

Neptune in Sagittarius is a lovely influence for those who have this sign or Pisces prominent by Sun, Moon, or Ascendant. Many have a special love and respect for animals, and this is one reason for increased vegetarianism; but when the influence works negatively, there is a near gluttony for junk food, resulting in increasingly dangerous obesity.

NEPTUNE IN CAPRICORN

At the time of writing, many of the Neptune-in-Capricorn people (1984–98) are still very young, and it must be hoped that time will have not run out for saving the Earth's resources. This generation, if any, has what it takes to actually do something about this, and hopefully the negative escapism of the drug scene will begin to diminish.

The flower-power generation grew up under the influence of Neptune in Libra.

will surely assist those in medical research – the relief of suffering is very Neptunian and will complement the humanitarian side of Aquarius.

As we see things at present, this area is moving fast and will continue to do so – especially as these young people reach maturity and take their places in their various professions. The arts and medicine will dominate, while other branches of science, space travel, and knowledge of the universe will receive considerable attention too.

If the rather dreamy idealism and creativity of Neptune can be channelled and given form, so that despite cloudiness and confusion there are inspired but constructive results, then there is hope. Here is a greater sense of direction and caution, not only for those who have Capricorn as Sun, Moon, or Ascendant, but more generally. Many will be less inclined to take the easy way out of difficult situations and will see the stupidity of taking drugs.

NEPTUNE IN AQUARIUS

Currently active, Neptune entered Aquarius in 1998 and will remain there until 2010. At the time of writing, only children under 10 have this interesting generation influence. The general effects have barely started, but there are distinct characteristics. Here is Aquarian idealism and humanitarianism heightened by Neptunian sensitivity and emotion. Those with an Aquarius Sun, Moon, or Ascendant will have considerably increased emotions which will be expressed as suggested above. We can expect a certain amount of quirkiness in their self-expression, but there is a huge amount of originality which will be expressed through scientific development. The influence

Victorian Gothic was one of the defining architectural styles the last time Neptune was in Pisces.

NEPTUNE IN PISCES

Following its current position in Aquarius, Neptune is due to be active in Pisces from 2011 to 2025. It was way back in the 1860s that Neptune last visited Pisces, and while we could study its influences from that time, is it worth doing so? The world is a different place, and becoming increasingly so in the 21st century. One thinks of that age of regular churchgoing and sexual repression – but also incredible progress in engineering and grand Victorian Gothic architecture; of the horrors of the American Civil War, but the end of slavery... How will these influences be reborn, if at all?

RETROGRADE MOTION OVER THE YEARS

Owing to the visual phenomenon of retrograde motion (*see glossary*), in which the planets can appear to be moving backwards when viewed from Earth, it can take a couple of years for Neptune and Pluto to settle down into each new sign. Some people born within the changeover period will have, for example, Neptune in Cancer, while others will have it in Leo, and so on.

The Pluto Factor

Because of Pluto's extreme distance from the Sun, it has moved through only six signs in the past century. Its generation influence is not so pronounced as Neptune's. When entering a new sign it heralds changes in the emphasis of worldly problems.

Pluto, a tiny world of rock and ice, is smaller than the Earth's Moon.

PLUTO THROUGH THE ZODIAC

PLUTO IN CANCER

The First World War began not long after Pluto settled down to its slow crawl through Cancer (1912–3 to 1937–8), emphasizing fruitless effort and death on an appalling scale. As with Neptune (in that sign at roughly the same time), here the disruption of home and family life was almost worldwide, and those born during this period suffered again during the Second World War.

Astrological symbol for Pluto

When Cancer is a person's Sun, Moon, or Ascendant sign, the powerful emotions of that sign are further heightened by Pluto's compulsive and intense presence. These individuals have particularly powerful and determined responses, which will either make them pull right back or cause them to explode emotionally. This influence is increased when supported by other planets in water signs.

PLUTO AT A GLANCE

Distance from Sun 5.9 billion km (3.7 billion miles)
Orbit around the Sun 247.7 Earth years
Rotation on Axis 6 Earth days, 9 hours
Moon Charon, at half of Pluto's size, is the largest moon relative to its planet
Keyword Elimination
Rules Scorpio

PLUTO IN LEO

The Second World War broke out as Pluto settled into a new sign (in Leo, 1937–57) and emphasized the concomitant disasters. But here there was a much more acceptable reason for war, and it was successful in spite of the appalling suffering and elimination of millions of innocent people. The good that came out of this influence was in the formation of the United Nations, which has very Leonine overtones.

When Leo is a person's Sun, Moon, or Ascendant sign, a power complex can develop. Generally a spark of Leo big-heartedness is present, especially if there are planets in other fire signs, but the enthusiasm of the fire element is suppressed. Here are people who were the first computer buffs, and who, because of Pluto in Leo, knew when to pull the plug to stop the machine from taking over.

The United Nations, founded at the end of World War II, when Pluto was in Leo, has very Leonine overtones.

PLUTO IN VIRGO

Pluto was in Virgo from 1957 to 1971. Also, Uranus and Pluto formed a conjunction in Virgo for several years at this time. There was much student violence and criticism of the older generation's values. This generation has a very special power, still expressed by more extreme politicians and the uncaring attitude of many others.

Virgo as Sun, Moon, or Ascendant sign plus Pluto adds an obsessive tendency which needs countering by seeing the broad picture of situations and projects. More generally, the influence heightens the ability to specialize in chosen subjects. Healthy eating is essential for this generation.

PLUTO IN LIBRA

After Virgo, Pluto entered Libra in 1971 and remained there until 1983–4. The 1970s saw an increase in sexual permissiveness, mostly due to the free availability of the Pill. Here were the Neptune-in-Libra people doing their own thing and enjoying freedom of expression and experimentation with drugs.

Author George Orwell's prophetic novel *Nineteen Eighty-Four* drew attention to state control over individuals in society.

Pluto puts a brake on the romanticism of Libra, but adds heightened sexuality, especially when Libra is the Sun, Moon, or Ascendant sign. Generally the influence adds a spicy sex appeal. While a Pluto influence tends not to favour free discussion of problems, this generation will not find it difficult to do so.

PLUTO IN SCORPIO

Nineteen Eighty-Four, the novel by George Orwell, made a lot of people apprehensive as that year loomed. Astrologers discussed Pluto's entry into its own sign at the time (1983–4), and the phenomenon became the

---

PLUTO'S ECCENTRIC ORBIT

Classified as a dwarf planet in 2006, Pluto has a very different orbit to the big planets. It takes an elongated path around the Sun, tilted at 17° in comparison with Earth's orbit, and for 20 years at a time it comes inside the orbit of Neptune. This eccentricity means that Pluto spends differing lengths of time in each sign of the zodiac. Like Neptune, the phenomenon of retrograde motion (*see p243*) means Pluto can take a couple of years to settle into a new sign.

---

theme for astrological conferences. It was evident that Pluto was signalling the development of HIV and AIDS.

This illness is extremely Scorpionic in character, and it was not difficult to predict the devastation it would cause as the planet progressed through its own sign (until 1995).

While its influence from Scorpio will increase the Scorpio characteristics of those with a Scorpio Sun, Moon, or Ascendant sign, there is no added danger of these individuals contracting the illness.

PLUTO IN SAGITTARIUS

Pluto was in Sagittarius from 1995 to 2007. It is too soon to assess the influence of Pluto in Sagittarius, either generally or personally. The two entities are totally opposite, with Pluto being an extremely intensive, secretive influence, and Sagittarius being more open, enjoying breadth of vision and freedom. If we can get the strength and passion of Pluto working with determination, plus the openness and vision of Sagittarius, we should get a very great deal from the influence; but sadly, crime, terrorism, and the hugely negative drug scene are very Plutonic, and seem to be winning. All this will radically change when Pluto enters Capricorn in early 2008.

The
HOUSES, ASPECTS,
& RETURNS

"*The skill of the astrological art and the complex reckoning of the horoscope require the laborious investigation of the expert.*"

Aldhelm, c.700CE

The Houses

Following the 12 signs of the zodiac, the 12 houses form the next layer of the complete birth chart, and are represented by the large segments in the centre of the chart. It is fair to say that, just as the planets make us what we are and the signs show how we will express ourselves, so the houses represent the various spheres of human life.

THE EMPTY HOUSE

The first six houses have a personal implication; the rest relate to external matters. Often there are no planets in a sign or house, but the sign and planetary ruler covering the house will give a good indication of the subject's attitude and concerns for matters relating to the house in question.

When interpreting the sphere of life as indicated by the empty house, it is necessary firstly to relate it to the influences of the Sun and Ascendant. Then we must consider the position of the ruling planet of the sign covering the house. Take, for example, a situation where there are no planets in the Ninth House (the house of further education and long-distance travel) and the sign covering the Ninth House is Virgo. Virgo is ruled by Mercury, so look to Mercury's sign. Mercury is the planet of the mind, but does the planet accentuate logical or intuitive thinking, or does it make the individual indecisive?

In answering this question, it is also necessary to consider the influence of the Moon, which will show how the subject will respond to those Ninth House matters. If the Moon sign is Cancer or Pisces, the chances are that the individual will be apprehensive about travelling and lack confidence about further education. But if the Moon sign is Aries, the individual won't be able to wait to get a round-the-world ticket and will be enthusiastic about college.

A zodiac chart with the Sun in his chariot at its centre. The chart comes from Ptolemy's *Tetrabiblos* (*see p20*), an influential textbook on astrology.

HOUSE SYSTEMS

There are several different house systems, including Placidus, Koch, and Campanus. The Equal House System – the oldest and simplest – is the one we use throughout this book, with the exception of the Horary Section, where we employ the Regiomontanus System (*see p297*).

Venus is the goddess associated with the Second House (the house of security and possessions) and the Seventh House (the house of relationships).

Defining the Twelve Houses

While the planets represent our motivation and the signs show how we direct it, the houses represent the areas of our lives where that motivation will be manifested. The first six houses have a personal implication; the second six mirror the first, in a sense, but relate to external matters.

THE FIRST SIX HOUSES

FIRST HOUSE

THE HOUSE OF ARIES AND MARS

This is the house of the Ascendant, or Rising sign, which, along with the Sun sign, is the most important area of the birth chart. It represents the lifestyle, health, wellbeing, and physical and psychological characteristics of the Ascendant. A planet in this house will modify these characteristics and often alter the appearance of the individual.

SECOND HOUSE

THE HOUSE OF TAURUS AND VENUS

Here is the house of emotional and financial security through earnings. There is often a tendency to think of a partner as just a treasured possession, and it is well to be aware that there is a close relationship between money and love, especially when relationships break down.

THIRD HOUSE

THE HOUSE OF GEMINI AND MERCURY

This house represents our school days and general education, and our relationships with our brothers and sisters, cousins, aunts, and uncles. Our mode of transport is highlighted. We consider the Third House when we want to buy or sell our bikes, motorcycles, cars, and so on. The house also rules short-distance travel and the media.

FOURTH HOUSE

THE HOUSE OF CANCER AND THE MOON

This house shows how we relate to our family and domestic life, and how we see our parents, especially our mother. It can also be accentuated when we wish to start or extend our family. It is to this house that we will look when wanting to make changes to our home – moving house, buying and selling, redecorating, or building extensions.

FIFTH HOUSE

THE HOUSE OF LEO AND THE SUN

This is the house of creativity, which can be expressed in all kinds of ways, and how we relate to children. It is the house of the father and how we see him. Love affairs begin here, and our optimism and exuberance for life is shown, plus our predilection for risk-taking.

This star chart highlights the 12 houses, which are represented with their ruling planets placed within them.

SIXTH HOUSE

THE HOUSE OF VIRGO AND MERCURY

Here is our attitude toward health
and the way we look after ourselves –
or not – through diet and exercise.
This is the house of the daily round
of work, routine, and discipline in our
lives. It will also suggest the kind of
hobbies and spare time interests we
might feel inclined to pursue.

THE IMPORTANCE OF TIMING

Unless the birth time is known to within
two hours, we are unable to integrate the
houses into our astrological interpretations
because we will not have the all-important
Ascendant. Nevertheless, a great deal of
information can still be gleaned from the
positions of all the planets in all the signs,
and the relationships that they make to
each other. This area of astrology is known
as the aspects (see p265).

THE SECOND SIX HOUSES

SEVENTH HOUSE

THE HOUSE OF LIBRA AND VENUS

Just as the First House is the most
personal of the 12, so its polar house
(the Seventh) relates to our attitude
toward partners – not only in love
but also in business. A planet here
will be a big factor in our attitude.

EIGHTH HOUSE

THE HOUSE OF SCORPIO AND PLUTO

The Second House rules security
through earnings, and in the Eighth
House the accent is on inheritance,
investment, unearned income, and
insurance. Negative emotions, such as
jealousy and resentfulness, can emerge,
often countered by self-analysis and
soul searching. Sexual instincts and
fulfilment are also focused, as is the
individual's attitude toward death
and the afterlife.

NINTH HOUSE

THE HOUSE OF SAGITTARIUS AND JUPITER

This is the house of higher education,
of college and university life. Here we
have the individual's attitude towards
long-distance travel and exploration –
geographically and intellectually.
Idealism, optimism, and our ability
to communicate are accentuated, as
is emigration. It is also known as the
house of dreams, wishes, and desires.

TENTH HOUSE

THE HOUSE OF CAPRICORN AND SATURN

This is the house of aspiration and
ambition – the need to achieve, to set
goals, and how we set about reaching
them. As a balance to the Fourth House
(the one of home and family life), the
Tenth House has the career to the fore.
It is also the voice of the "inner father",
who either encourages or puts us down.

ELEVENTH HOUSE

THE HOUSE OF AQUARIUS AND URANUS

The creativity of the Fifth House shows
what we can do for ourselves, while this
house accentuates our attitude towards
friends and what we can do for them.
It is also concerned with our social life,
how we spend our leisure time out of
the home, our humanitarianism, and
how we cope – psychologically and
practically – with world disasters.

TWELFTH HOUSE

THE HOUSE OF PISCES AND NEPTUNE

This is the house of seclusion and
escapism. This house shows how we
cope with being alone and what work
we can do "behind the scenes". Here
hospitals, retreats, and prisons are
accentuated, as is the need for peace
and quiet, whatever that means to each
individual. A sense of vocation or
psychic ability can be present.

The Planets through the Houses

The placing of the planets within the 12 houses adds another dimension to the horoscope, sometimes accentuating and sometimes softening traits, depending on the combination of house and planet.

FIRST HOUSE: THE HOUSE OF THE ASCENDANT

SUN The strength of the Sun on the Ascendant characteristics will make individuals a *double* Cancer, Leo, or whatever. Both positive and negative qualities will be present, and the aspects the Sun receives will also be important. Back problems are likely.

MOON Here the individual will respond and react in the characteristic manner of the Ascendant. This is another kind of "double", according to the sign involved. Digestive upsets, and worry. But increased intuition and emotion.

MERCURY This planet will add a lively, intellectual quality, mental brightness, and quick thinking to the Ascendant characteristics. There will be an element of duality present, also

> **PLANETS IN THE FIRST HOUSE**
>
> Any planet that is placed in this house will considerably influence the characteristics of the Ascendant, or Rising sign.

Mercury in the First House adds intellectual acuity to the Ascendant characteristics.

artfulness, cunning, critical acumen, and vulnerability to nervous stress and tension.

VENUS Here, Venus will soften but sometimes weaken the characteristics of the Ascendant, adding charm and some possessiveness. There will be kindness, sympathy, empathy, and often extravagance. Sore throats are likely.

MARS Here Mars is "at home" so its influence is powerful, whatever sign is involved. Individuals will find that it contributes increased physical energy, assertiveness, elements of selfishness, hastiness, and a flair for sport. They have a tendency to take risks and are also prone to headaches.

JUPITER The planet adds breadth of vision, optimism, enthusiasm, an intense love of travel, and a gambling instinct. There is, potentially, a brilliant mind which requires stimulation. Weight gain to hips and thighs is likely.

SATURN Will sober the Ascendant characteristics. Often causes inhibition, lack of self-confidence, and bouts of depression. A conventional outlook, with determination and ambition. These individuals will take life seriously. The knees and shins are vulnerable.

URANUS Will contribute unpredictability, originality, independence, and often stubbornness. There can be a tendency to be unconventional and perverse, along with flashes of brilliance and original ideas. Above average periods of stress and tension are likely.

NEPTUNE Here, Ascendant characteristics will be weakened, especially for Libra and Scorpio. The planet adds kindness and tenderness, but self-deception and a tendency to take the easy route is common. Possible foot problems.

PLUTO A dynamic force. Sweeping changes will be made and psychologically needed too. The individual must learn not to bottle up problems. A seeker with detective instincts. Can be obsessive – especially over self-analysis. Possible genital problems.

CHIRON Will add energy, daring and panache to the characteristics of the Ascendant, along with the ability to self-heal physical, emotional, and psychological wounds.

SECOND HOUSE: THE HOUSE OF TAURUS AND VENUS

SUN The ability to make and spend money will be very important in this case, as will a liking for sumptuous things. Possessiveness will occur, and self-indulgence is likely.

MOON The Moon's influence will work strongly from this house. A hankering for the good things of life will be matched with possessiveness, which could lead to regret. Shrewdness in financial matters is common.

MERCURY People with this combination will enjoy making money – and spending it quickly! Financial situations will therefore fluctuate, while the speed of Mercury thought will be slowed.

VENUS Venus is powerful in this, the Taurus house. There will be Taurean characteristics in the personality – modifying them by the Venus sign or enhancing them if also the Sun sign. Very loving, but possessive.

MARS A passionate person who will want and get a lot of everything. There will be masses of strong feelings which need an outlet, and a keenness to make money. Physically tough, especially the men.

JUPITER Will work well from this house, contributing *bonhomie*, a sense of fun and humour, and a need for good living and comfort. Tendency to weight gain due to love of rich food and wine.

SATURN Here there will be a tendency to work extremely hard for every penny earned, and as a consequence

Money is a key theme of the Second House, and each planet gives its own distinct nuance to the theme.

will have a sensible attitude to finance. Somewhat restrained expressions of feelings are likely.

URANUS An erratic attitude to money is common. A steady income may be elusive, and money will often be spent unwisely, possibly in unlikely get-rich schemes. Will express feelings dazzlingly and with flattery, but may not be totally sincere. Freedom loving.

NEPTUNE Emotions, with perhaps a tad of possessiveness, will flow towards those whom these individuals admire. Very generous, hopeless with cash, and will over-spend and usually need help with finances. Will love beautiful objects.

PLUTO A control of finances and a flair for making money is very likely indeed. A similar attitude is often the case when expressing feelings – will hold back at first, then sweep admired ones off their feet.

CHIRON A free-wheeling attitude to finances and possessions is common here – won't particularly care for either, but will soon recover losses. Will express feelings in a bright, slightly off-hand and maybe jokey way, but will be good company.

THIRD HOUSE: THE HOUSE OF GEMINI AND MERCURY

Investigative journalism is a possible career for those who have Pluto in the Third House.

SUN Excellent powers of communication. Versatility and Geminian traits will be present, especially if this is the Sun sign. There will be erratic progress at school; consistency of effort must be learned.

MOON The Moon accentuates a lively mind, but these individuals will have extremely changeable opinions. An instinctive need for knowledge is present but is often superficial. Shrewdness, cunning, and cleverness are usually present. A caring sibling.

MERCURY Here Mercury, in its own house, is powerful, and a quick-thinking mind is present. Changeability and inconsistency of effort must be controlled. These individuals will be artful and sometimes duplicitous.

VENUS The planet Venus will encourage these individuals to win their way into prospective lovers' hearts through eloquence. Sympathetic communication with others is usual, as is charm and youthful looks.

MARS A sharp, quick mind, and argumentativeness and sometimes aggression – but the bark may be worse than the bite. School is enjoyed and good progress in studies is generally made.

JUPITER Mental challenges will be particularly enjoyed here. These individuals will always be at least one intellectual step ahead of rivals, especially at school. Breadth of vision is excellent, but a grasp of detail may be lacking.

SATURN Here is a good, retentive mind, though the thinking processes will be slow, as will be progress at school. These individuals should be let to pace themselves. A responsible sibling.

URANUS A brilliant and original, but stubborn mind – and one that needs constant stimulation. There will be erratic progress at school, with a tendency to shock, just for the hell of it!

NEPTUNE Children with Neptune in the Third House will take a while to settle at school. While fertile, their imagination will need guidance and encouragement. Singing potential may exist.

PLUTO A conflict will occur between the need to communicate and secretiveness. Encouragement in talking over problems is necessary if things go wrong at school or with siblings. Good prospects for investigative journalism.

CHIRON There will be a bright and lively mind with Chiron in the Third House, but often a tendency to be sceptical about their ability to cope. Encouragement must be given when original or imaginative ideas emerge, then confidence will build.

Singing potential may be present in children who have Neptune in the Third House.

FOURTH HOUSE: THE HOUSE OF CANCER AND THE MOON

SUN These individuals are very family oriented, and need its support and security. Above average closeness to the mother, or perhaps specific problems concerning her, are likely. A strong desire for parenthood.

MOON The strength of the Moon is considerably increased from this house, accenting all the characteristics of its sign, expressed through reactions and emotions. A love of, or work with, children is a special characteristic.

MERCURY The influence of the Mercury sign will be related to home and family. An individual here will worry too much about the children (if Cancer or Virgo), stimulate them mentally (if Gemini or Sagittarius), and so on.

VENUS A relaxed attitude towards home and family, peace, and harmony will be desired, and children may be spoilt to achieve this. These individuals will be keen to make their homes beautiful and very comfortable.

MARS Here, energy will be spent on DIY home improvements. Partnerships may be rushed into through an enthusiasm for family life. Parents will expect their children to be fun-loving and noisy, and lively arguments will often occur.

JUPITER As parents, these lively souls will do much to further their children's education, and the home will be full of books and intellectually stimulating games. Enthusiasm for family participation in sport and exercise is likely.

SATURN This placing very often shows that the father was either particularly strict or absent. The childhood might have lacked warmth and comforts, with importance paid to discipline and following rules instead.

URANUS Here conflict occurs between the need for a conventional family life and personal freedom and self expression. Within the family unit, those with this placing tend to be "different", with others making allowances for them.

NEPTUNE An over-idealistic attitude towards home and family life is common, with individuals often deluding themselves as to what is going on. Love and affection will be present, and possibly problems with alcohol or drugs.

PLUTO Frustration during childhood and youth is common here. Perhaps parents have stopped these individuals from doing what they really want, and thereby blocked potential talent. Intuition is increased and used to overcome parental conflicts.

CHIRON With Chiron placed here, there is a tendency to be intense and brooding, along with a nervous disposition. Self-confidence needs to be built, perhaps through sports such as swimming or yachting.

Yachting is a way to build confidence for those with Chiron in the Fourth House.

FIFTH HOUSE: THE HOUSE OF LEO AND THE SUN

SUN Here the Sun's usual strength, whatever its sign, takes on certain leonine qualities. These individuals have a happy disposition, are ambitious, extrovert, creative, and good organizers; they make lively, if bossy, parents.

MOON There is usually creativity, a powerful imagination, and intuition. Often the creative urge is expressed through having children, and here we often see very young parents. It is also common for great pleasure to be taken from lovemaking.

MERCURY Here are clever minds who enjoy risk-taking – maybe gambling or dangerous sport. Creativity is sometimes expressed through writing or painting. Assiduous lovers, who plan their approach to prospective partners.

VENUS Appreciation of all art forms is likely, as is support for the arts. A laid-back attitude may diminish an otherwise creative output. Here are passionate lovers who will have many affairs.

MARS The energy level is considerable, and enthusiasm for sporting activity – from the bedroom to the sports field – is certain. A tendency to take risks is very likely, and often money is wasted on gambling.

JUPITER The gambling spirit is very strong here, and needs to be consciously controlled. Broadmindedness, optimism, and enjoyment of life and love is very much part of these individuals' personalities.

SATURN Here is a "put-down" effect on individuals who suffer, or have suffered, a strict father. Creativity and joyfulness may have been inhibited, causing frustration and pushing them in unwanted directions.

URANUS This brings originality and flair to all creativity, and so makes for brilliant cooks as well as painters, and writers. These people will enjoy an exciting love life with their partners, but will delay commitment.

NEPTUNE The permutation adds imaginative creativity and an extremely romantic and over-idealistic nature. There is a tendency to drift up to cloud nine every time these individuals are even slightly attracted to a new partner.

PLUTO These individuals will strive to develop their potential in whatever area attracts them. Determination to win prospective partners is present, and a passionate sex life follows. However, some suffer sexual frustration and inhibition.

CHIRON The childish enthusiasm for life that Chiron engenders may be crushed by strict parents demanding maturity. This can dampen expressions of love and sex.

Casinos are likely to be highly attractive if Mercury, Mars, or Jupiter are in the Fifth House.

SIXTH HOUSE: THE HOUSE OF VIRGO AND MERCURY

SUN Whatever the Sun sign, here is dedication to work and the need for a predictable routine. Health indications emphasized according to the Sun sign; vulnerability to stress and worry.

MOON Diet is of above average importance and, if the Moon sign is sympathetic, vegetarianism could appeal. Relaxation techniques are advisable to counter stress, nervous tension, or digestive upsets.

MERCURY The planet's influence is increased in this, its own house. A lively and sharp mind, and critical acumen will be pronounced. Considerable attention to detail and a strong tendency to worry.

VENUS There will be lack of motivation to exercise and generally a laid-back attitude to routine work is common. A certain predilection for sweet, rich food can cause weight gain and a loss of physical attractiveness.

MARS Here, Mars will invigorate the nervous system and encourage a lively mind that particularly enjoys verbal battles. Hasty decision-making can cause premature action. Stress should be worked off with exercise.

JUPITER There will be breadth of vision and optimism. It is important that these individuals really watch their diet, as the *expansion* influence of Jupiter plays havoc with the figure, resulting in a *lot* of weight gain.

SATURN There is an ability to work hard in a disciplined way with this permutation, but this quality can turn into an obsessional need, with the individual neglecting family life in the pursuit of riches.

URANUS Uranus will contribute originality and innovation, and these qualities will be incorporated into the working life. Scope for freedom of expression is necessary if life's routines are not to become a bore. Regular, sensible eating habits are advisable.

NEPTUNE A tendency to hypochondria often mars the sense of wellbeing. Medically prescribed drugs can have a negative effect, and homeopathic remedies are a useful alternative. Recreational drugs and smoking are particular dangers.

PLUTO Routine is important – especially if Pluto is in Virgo. Being too hard on the self, as far as work patterns are concerned, can lead to stress and overworking. Bowel complaints are common.

CHIRON These individuals can be obsessive over even minor inhibitions. A rational and logical attitude will enable the individual to avoid stress and self-doubt which may otherwise occur.

SEVENTH HOUSE: THE HOUSE OF LIBRA AND VENUS

SUN Here is a strong need to relate to others, not only on a one-to-one basis, but also more generally; good relationships with business partners and colleagues is important too. The Venus sign/house placing will be very significant in this case.

MOON The Moon increases the ability of these individuals to respond sensitively and well to their partners' needs. A tendency to attempt to be wholly at one with the partner results in suppression of individuality.

MERCURY In this case, a lively intellectual rapport will be necessary within all permanent relationships, as too a strong level of pure friendship. Shared interests, along with empathy, will make for great understanding and successful relationships.

VENUS There is a tendency to fall in love with love, which can lead to above average heartbreak. But here is potential for a superb relationship, provided that friendship and good communication are not ignored.

MARS A vibrant and long-lasting sex life is important here. There is also a great willingness and determination to work together for the relationship's future stability. However, a quarrelsome temperament is likely, which could be disruptive.

JUPITER There is a positive and enthusiastic attitude towards relationships, but often these individuals have unrealistic expectations of their partners. A tendency to give up too soon is common, especially if they are young.

SATURN Relationships will be taken seriously and delayed because of a need for certainty. There is a preference for partners who are older, and who can be looked up to – perhaps a "mother" or "father" figure.

URANUS A strong desire for a fulfilling relationship may clash with an inherent need for independence and a desire for freedom of expression. These individuals will have an extremely romantic streak, with the power to exert great charm.

NEPTUNE These people will experience terrific highs and lows in their relationships. Care is needed that they do not make commitments prematurely; they can easily lose touch with reality when under the spell of love.

PLUTO With Pluto in the Seventh House, there is a tendency to dominate relationships; this should be corrected before the other partner crumbles. The emotional content will be high; if it is expressed positively, all will be well.

CHIRON Here is a tendency to merge with the partner and lose all individual identity. By telling themselves that this is what they want most, these people are almost certainly deluding themselves, and will only learn the hard way in the long run.

Gifts of champagne and other romantic gestures are typical of those with Uranus in the Seventh House.

Sexual expression is very important in the Eighth House, especially if the Sun, Mercury, Venus, Mars, Jupiter, Uranus, or Neptune is present.

EIGHTH HOUSE: THE HOUSE OF SCORPIO AND PLUTO

SUN There is emotional intensity here, and sexuality needs to be an important outlet for self-expression. Here too is ambition; the individual will be very successful if emotionally involved with the chosen career.

MOON Here the Moon's emotional force will be intensified. There is often a sixth sense as the intuitive powers are also heightened, especially if the Moon is in a water sign. Jealousy can occur.

MERCURY This placing adds investigative powers to the mind; here are the sleuths and researchers of the zodiac. Sometimes psychic powers are evident, as is a rich sexual and fantasy life, but there is a tendency towards brooding and moodiness.

VENUS This placing encourages a rewarding sex life, with increased emotions and intuition. Here is a financial influence, making these individuals big spenders but with a gift for making money, often through shrewd investments.

MARS Both emotional and physical energy are strong here. The sex drive needs above average fulfilment. Aggression is evident and should be burned up through martial arts or heavy team games. Obsessive behaviour can be a problem.

JUPITER These individuals have good business sense and the ability to make money through clever investments. There is a lively and exuberant expression of sexuality, and lovemaking will be considered fun and not taken too seriously.

SATURN Here is a placing that adds the powers of concentration and determination. There is a responsible attitude towards finances, and a career in banking is likely. Possible sexual problems may need resolving.

URANUS This is not a good placing financially, as the attitude can be uncaring. There is need for a lively sex life with partners who enjoy experimentation. If there are sexual problems they will be self-analysed, but often remain unresolved.

NEPTUNE This is a meaningful placing for those with Neptune in Scorpio. It will enhance their emotions, encouraging a rich and rewarding sex life. But it will also increase the temptation to escape problems through recreational drugs.

PLUTO With the planet in its own house, Pluto's influence is increased. There is often interest in metaphysical subjects and the occult. Here too is a preoccupation with the afterlife. Financial acumen and business sense are common.

CHIRON A preoccupation with sex and a craving for material progress and power often occurs here, sometimes with a tendency towards self-seeking. Psychic ability is occasionally present; if so, careful training and guidance from experts is recommended.

NINTH HOUSE: THE HOUSE OF SAGITTARIUS AND JUPITER

SUN Here is a need for intellectual growth and mind expansion. The acceptance of challenge and a need to move on in all spheres of life is important. These individuals are optimistic, positive in outlook, and generally enthusiastic.

MOON These individuals' minds seem to work intuitively here, and with forever broadening intellectual horizons. An understanding of different cultures is possible, and both intellectual and geographical journeys will be undertaken.

MERCURY Here is an eternal student on a quest for knowledge. The mind will need constant challenges, and questions will be asked and the answers assiduously sought out. However, the powers of concentration are not particularly brilliant.

VENUS This is where we find the lover of long-distance travel, with living and working abroad, or emigrating, being distinct possibilities. Love affairs often occur when travelling. There is motivation to study, undermined by laziness.

MARS This placing leads to an energetic and adventurous spirit that will engage in extensive travel. There is intelligence, but hastiness in speech and a hurried approach to study does not bode well for examination results.

JUPITER Jupiter will exert its best influence in this permutation. There is considerable intellectual potential, which will be expressed through the influence of the Jupiter sign. Communication skills are good and people with this configuration are often able to speak several languages.

SATURN Here we have the serious thinkers of the zodiac, who will concentrate on, and attempt to alleviate, important world issues and suffering. Travel is not usually enjoyed, since these individuals may have a fear of flying or be reluctant to journey far from home.

URANUS This placing adds brilliance to the mind. Original ideas will happily be passed on to others for development, while these individuals take upon themselves the challenge of further invention.

NEPTUNE Dreams and wishes are ruled by the Ninth House, and when Neptune is there it will bring these fantasies to the conscious mind. This means that it will be all too easy to drift up to cloud nine at almost any eventuality.

PLUTO Here is a mind that works compulsively, with a strong desire to study in-depth and to accept mental challenges. These are often more complicated than assumed at first, resulting in a considerable build-up of stress, frustration, and anger.

CHIRON The Chiron influence will encourage these individuals to seek out new, fascinating, and daring challenges, which they will blithely work their way through to a satisfactory conclusion. Extreme opinions will need to be modified.

Interest in travel, different cultures, and foreign languages are common themes of the Ninth House.

TENTH HOUSE: THE HOUSE OF CAPRICORN AND SATURN

SUN These individuals will be ambitious and usually successful, with good powers of leadership. They will carry responsibility well, and often have a great sense of the dramatic.

MOON The potential for fame is evident with this positioning. It is often the case that these individuals will be responsible for large groups of people.

MERCURY Changes of direction in life will be enjoyed, with possibly a variety of jobs or professions. As a result, ultimate real success may prove elusive.

VENUS Here is good potential for developing rapport and empathy with colleagues; a sympathetic and understanding, but possibly indecisive, boss.

MARS Energy, enthusiasm, and the ability to work hard and aggressively are all present, as is a sense of urgency for progress. The armed forces could be a likely career path.

JUPITER Success, with fortunate "lucky" breaks, will help these individuals progress in their profession. This placing is common among successful actors.

SATURN These individuals will eventually have to carry considerable responsibility, and will do so well and loyally. A tendency to distance themselves from their employees or families in pursuit of, and dedication to, their objectives often occurs.

URANUS There is attraction to technology here, or to an unusual occupation. The airlines and space industries offer possible occupations, but sudden and unexpected changes of direction in career are also likely.

Acting is a distinct career possibility if Jupiter is placed in the Tenth House.

NEPTUNE This is a placing indicative of a very varied career with quite decided changes – possibly within various art forms or different branches of science.

PLUTO Emotional involvement with one's career is essential here. A power complex will exert itself – especially if Pluto is in Leo – perhaps fanatically, with the individual being obsessionally involved in his or her work or with a "message" that they wish to convey.

CHIRON This placing encourages individuals to be constantly looking to the future, and to do things differently; originality needs to be expressed positively.

MIDHEAVEN AND THE EQUAL HOUSE SYSTEM

When using the Equal House System, the Midheaven does not always fall in the Tenth House of the chart, as it does with other house division systems. If you have a planet in conjunction with your Midheaven, you will find it revealing if you read the interpretation for the Tenth House; it will have considerable relevance. However, do not forget to integrate the planet's original house placing, as well as this one, into your interpretation.

Eating out and socializing, often in glamorous places, is typical of those with the Sun in the Eleventh House.

ELEVENTH HOUSE: THE HOUSE OF AQUARIUS AND URANUS

SUN Here are friendly and often glamorous people who enjoy a vibrant social life. They also make excellent members of committees – particularly those that are involved with fundraising for charitable causes.

MOON Humanitarian qualities and great sympathy for suffering are usually present. The need to be an active member of a group or society is sometimes psychologically linked to lack of acceptance as a child.

MERCURY Meaningful friendships formed early in life by these folks will usually last. These are very sociable individuals, and the type who'll make sure they have their say at committee meetings or parties.

VENUS The social life will be extremely important to these individuals, who will often opt out of working hours to attend social functions. There is a sincere need to please friends, and to entertain lavishly.

MARS Here is the pack leader among friends – the organizer of long Sunday hikes or bike rides. Here too is the stirrer, the devil's advocate of the committee, and one who will get things done *right away*.

JUPITER These people have a wide circle of friends and even more acquaintances. They have an interesting way of enthusing others, and will organize outings and memorable occasions, usually to raise cash for charity.

SATURN The social life is taken seriously, with regular visits to familiar venues. The circle of friends is small, and often consists of people older than the individual. Interests developed when young will last a lifetime.

URANUS Here are very friendly people who in a subtle way like to keep their distance, not wanting to get too close to anyone. They are free spirits and independently minded. Sudden breaks with friends tend to occur.

NEPTUNE The social life will be full and greatly enjoyed, but these people are gullible and can be easily taken in by friends and associates who will sometimes exert a negative influence or take advantage of them.

PLUTO These individuals will have extremely powerful ties of friendship and may have a tendency to become obsessed with particular friendships. Other people's attitudes will be considered seriously.

CHIRON This placing adds dynamism and verve, and also considerable charm. There is a distinct need for personal space and a hatred of clutter and being smothered or under too much of an obligation to friends. Doing their own thing is important.

TWELFTH HOUSE: THE HOUSE OF PISCES AND NEPTUNE

SUN Here are private people, who are at their best working behind-the-scenes. They need peace and quiet – in whatever form suits them as individuals – and their own space; this is especially important to them if they are creative.

MOON Even if these individuals are extrovert they must recognize the need to refresh their spirit. A discipline such as yoga will be restorative, as will going on retreats or taking up an engrossing hobby.

MERCURY Conflict can occur between the logic of Mercury and the emotional and spiritual content of the Twelfth House. However, the two can come together if there is a love of poetry and literature, or indeed a talent for writing.

VENUS Secrecy is common, especially if these individuals are involved in love affairs. Sometimes there is inhibition and shyness – often in respect of their own creative work – designs, fashion, and so on.

MARS Here is secretiveness and difficulty in unburdening problems; as a result, anger and stress will tend to build up. If there is indication of a naturally sympathetic nature, these people do well in the caring professions.

JUPITER Here is a sense of vocation that can be directed towards religion, or perhaps dedication to the study of music, dance, or a sport – any subject that needs hours of regular practice. There is a very philosophical attitude to life.

SATURN There is a tendency towards isolationism here. These individuals will go to their place of employment and work hard, but then will be in a rush to return to their pad to restore themselves for the next day. Music and books will be important.

URANUS The contrasting zodiac entities come together through humanitarianism. These people have the potential to do a lot of good for humanity, as the sharpness of the planet will ignite action from the somewhat complacent attitude of the Twelfth House.

NEPTUNE Here is Neptune in its own place, bringing a genuine, meaningful faith, perhaps dedication to a cause, an esoteric subject, or to animals or the sick. A talent for poetry, dance, ice-skating, or singing is very possible and should be developed.

PLUTO This tends to make individuals extremely secretive, with an inability to open up and talk when things go wrong. Sometimes there are deep-rooted psychological problems that are difficult to resolve and from which there is no attempt to move on.

CHIRON At times these individuals feel frustrated or inferior. Care is needed to avoid escapist drugs when this happens. The Chiron energy will, however, stimulate the imagination which should be given concrete and creative form.

Yoga helps in revitalizing one's spirits, especially if you have the placing of the Moon in the Twelfth House.

> *"Man, like a tiny universe, is sustained by the everlasting fiery movements of the five planets and the Sun and Moon."*
>
> Firmicus Maternus, 4th century CE

The Aspects

The angular relationships formed between the planets
when they are viewed from Earth are known in astrological
terms as the aspects. Planets are said to be "in aspect"
when there are a certain specific number of degrees
of the zodiac between them around
the circle of the horoscope.

In this 17th-century chart by
Comte de Gabius, eclipses and
other conjunctions are plotted
and charmingly illustrated.

INTRODUCING THE ASPECTS

The aspects have different names, according to
the relationship between them, which, in turn, is
governed by the degrees between them. These
relationships are of considerable importance: from
them an astrologer can learn much about the
subject of a birth chart. According to the aspects
formed, one planet will either enhance the qualities
of the other or considerably inhibit its influence –
either contributing power (through a *conjunction*),
harmony and ease (when the aspect is *positive*),
or stress and inhibition (when *negative*).

The aspects are divided into two groups, major
and minor. The major aspects are the conjunction,
positive aspect, and negative apect (*see p266*), with
the conjunction being the most powerful. The
commonly used minor aspects are the semi-square,
semi-sextile, sesquidquadrate, and quincunx. They
are formed when there are 45°, 30°, 135°, and 150°
separating the planets concerned.
Of this group the semi-square is the
strongest and most stressful.

Within this book we can only deal
with the calculation of the major
aspects. The minor aspects, which
will appear in a more detailed birth
chart, tend to follow the negative
interpretations of the major aspects
but are far less potent.

**The planetary aspects, oppositions, and
conjunctions** are the subject of this plate from
the *Harmonia Macrocosmica*, a beautiful celestial
atlas drawn up in 1660 by the Dutch-German
cartographer Andreas Cellarius.

ALLOWANCES FOR ORBS

While an aspect is exact when two planets
are separated by a specific number of
degrees, astrologers still consider its effect
when there are a few degrees more or less
than the precise number between them.
This allowance is called an orb. If we take
the example of a square (a commonly used
major aspect), to be exact the planets should
be 90° apart, but an orb of 8° is allowed.
So if, for instance, Venus is on 15° Virgo
and Mars on 18° of Gemini, they will still be
"in square aspect". In this book, because
of the limitation on our calculations, it is
unnecessary to allow orbs; but with further
study you can learn how to use them.

Understanding the Major Aspects

On the following pages are the characteristics
of the major aspects, including, on pages 282–3,
the aspects to the Ascendant and Midheaven.
To calculate the aspects on a birth chart, see page 304.

**The orbits of seven
planets** are shown
on this 19th century
mechanical model.

THE CONJUCTION

Of the major aspects, the conjunction
is the most powerful. An exact
conjunction takes place when two
planets inhabit the same degree, but
it will still be operative when there is
up to 10° of the zodiac between them.

THE POSITIVE ASPECTS

The positive aspects are the trine and
sextile, formed when there are 120°
and 60° separating them respectively.
These are helpful, and generally will
not be a flashpoint for stress or
difficulty. The trine is far stronger
than the sextile.

THE NEGATIVE ASPECTS

The negative aspects are the square,
quincunx, and opposition. Here we
have angles of 90°, 150°, and 180°
separating the planets. Both square
and opposition are very powerful.
The square is nearly always stressful
or inhibitive, while the opposition is
seemingly so, but can very often act

as a good anchorage for an individual
personality. The quincunx is considered
by some astrologers to be a minor
aspect; we, however, think it is of
considerable importance. A quincunx
indicates a point in the chart where
something stressful may occur.

CONVENTIONS IN DESCRIBING THE ASPECTS

Once you have worked out your chart
and begin to interpret the aspects,
you will immediately notice that the
sections on the following pages
decrease in length as we move from
the Sun's aspects to those of the Moon,
then the other planets. This is because,
in astrology, we always put the planet
nearest to us on Earth first, so that by
the time we reach the aspects of Pluto,
we only show its aspects to Chiron.
The golden rule is that we do not refer
to Pluto's aspect to the Sun, or any of
the other planets; we look at the Sun's
aspect to Pluto. Similarly, we do not
refer to Saturn's aspect to Venus, but
always Venus's aspect to Saturn. This
can be a bit confusing at first, but it is
a formality we always use, and one
soon gets used to it.

**Conjuctions of the brightest
planets** can be easily observed
with the naked eye, or in more
detail with a pair of binoculars.

THE GLYPHS OF THE ASPECTS

In astrology, the signs, planets, and other
essential elements are often depicted
on charts with shorthand symbols, which
are called glyphs. The aspects have their
own set of glyphs, shown below. These
are worth committing to memory as
soon as possible.

Glyphs of the Major Aspects	**Glyphs of the Minor Aspects**
☌ Conjunction	⚺ Semi-sextile
□ Square	∟ Semi-square
☍ Opposition	⚼ Sesquidquadrate
△ Trine	
✳ Sextile	
⚻ Quincunx	

THE ASPECTS OF THE SUN

SUN AND MOON

CONJUNCTION This will mostly occur when both planets occupy the same sign, and always at new Moon. Individuals will not only have the qualities of their Sun sign, but will respond and react to all situations in the manner of that sign. Their intuition and instincts will serve them well.

POSITIVE ASPECT A harmonious relationship between the outward expression of Sun sign and the natural responses of the Moon. If the Moon is in a water or fire sign, the emotions will be considerably increased.

NEGATIVE ASPECT Restlessness, and in constant need of change. This is particularly so for the opposition, which occurs at full Moon. An ongoing inner discontent is then often present, as is the inability to rest content.

SUN AND VENUS

CONJUNCTION Love and affection will be expressed through the influence of the Sun sign. Individuals will love and express their feelings in the manner of that sign.

POSITIVE ASPECT No positive sextile or trine aspect can be formed in this placing.

NEGATIVE ASPECT The minor semi-square – revealed in a detailed birth chart – is the only possible negative aspect. It can sometimes cause stress and problems between partners.

SUN AND MARS

CONJUNCTION Here is a powerhouse of energy, which must be expressed through physical activity. The

Power and vigour result when the Sun and Mars are in positive aspect – separated by 60° or 120°.

individual's vitality is also increased considerably by this placing. Emotions are extremely powerful, especially if the conjunction is in a fire or water sign. He or she will take risks and be impetuous.

POSITIVE ASPECT A well-directed energy force, but it provokes less impetuosity than the conjunction. These individuals are endowed with good physiques and will be keen to keep fit.

NEGATIVE ASPECT High energy, but stress is likely to be present. These individuals will be easily angered, very impatient, and sometimes ruthless. They are also highly sexed individuals, and need more sexual fulfillment than most.

Expressions of love, affection, and sexuality are marked in the conjunction of the Sun and Venus.

SUN AND MERCURY

Because these two bodies cannot be more than 28° apart, the only aspects they can form is the conjunction or the very weak semi-sextile. A detailed interpretation of Sun and Mercury in the same sign is on pp203–9. Use this as your guide, as in most cases it will apply and be very relevant.

A happy, carefree attitude is typical for the conjunction of the Sun and Jupiter.

SUN AND JUPITER

CONJUNCTION A lively, carefree influence which will bring optimism and a spirit of good fortune to the individual. Usually a liking for fine food and wine can bring about Jupiterian expansion – to the waistline. A jolly sense of humour is present.

POSITIVE ASPECT A basically happy and contented individual who is not particularly competitive; can be sometimes interested in religion, the law, or publishing.

NEGATIVE ASPECT There is a tendency to be blindly optimistic and to exaggerate. Can be pompous or reckless at times. Must be careful of gambling and any form of over-indulgence.

SUN AND SATURN

CONJUNCTION A focal point of the chart. Sun-sign influence must not be ignored. A stop-go aspect, which will control impulsive behaviour, adds caution and often common sense, but can inhibit and cause depression and lack of self-confidence.

POSITIVE ASPECT A good combination of positivity from the Sun, blended with Saturn's caution and common sense which will add stability and conventional outlook on life. Few risks will be taken.

NEGATIVE ASPECT A heavy, sometimes depressive influence, causing low self-confidence and inhibition. However, it often acts as a wonderful anchorage in a chart that is extrovert and has planets in a fire sign.

SUN AND URANUS

CONJUNCTION Rebelliousness, eccentricity, and unpredictability – modified if the Sun is in an earth sign. Emotional tension is present. Often considerable originality, but it needs positive expression, perhaps through inventiveness or creativity.

POSITIVE ASPECT Here is personal magnetism and glamour, especially if Venus, which will not be very far away from the Sun, supports this possibility. Unconventional behaviour and outlook will be amusing to others but not too outrageous.

NEGATIVE ASPECT Eccentricity and outrageous behaviour intended to shock is probable, along with perversity and stubbornness. These powerful energies can be controlled and contribute to a positive potential.

SUN AND NEPTUNE

CONJUNCTION Softens the influence of the Sun sign and adds sensitivity. There is often a tendency to unworldliness, with a tender, loving, and caring quality. Should develop creative interests.

POSITIVE ASPECT The fertile imagination will work extremely well. If these individuals are not inhibited by lack of self-confidence, there will be excellent results. Will have a powerful intuition.

NEGATIVE ASPECT A tendency to be deceitful and to take the easy way out of difficult situations. This will unneccessarily complicate life and upset other people. Even prescribed drugs can have a negative effect.

SUN AND PLUTO

CONJUNCTION There is often a power complex. From time to time, these individuals will seek to make drastic and clean breaks with the past – either in their personal lives or in their careers. Sometimes, there are deep-rooted psychological problems, which will quite suddenly be worked on and resolved.

POSITIVE ASPECT There is a loathing of clutter, which will be drastically cleared from time to time. Sudden changes will be made in all spheres of life. These individuals often possess a good business sense.

NEGATIVE ASPECT The inability to unburden oneself of problems will bring about periods of stress and frustration.

SUN AND CHIRON

CONJUNCTION This placing will enhance the qualities of the Sun sign, adding a sense of destiny and a need for achievements to be recognized. A tendency to hold on to psychological problems. Extrovert tendencies are likely to be present – less so if the planets are in the Twelfth House.

POSITIVE ASPECT Not unlike the conjunction, but here there will be fewer and less suppressed psychological problems, while extrovert qualities are far more likely to be present.

NEGATIVE ASPECT There will be inhibition and lack of self-confidence in the ability to develop the full potential, with some lack of motivation to "get going".

THE ASPECTS OF THE MOON

MOON AND MERCURY

CONJUNCTION An intuitive, logical, and quick-thinking mind, with immediate insight into problems – plus a good memory. Frequent changes to the home are often made.

POSITIVE ASPECT The shrewdness of the Moon and the cunningness of Mercury combine, and are well expressed. A clever craftiness and the ability to resolve tricky situations is also present in these individuals. Depending on the Moon sign, here is common sense and decisiveness.

NEGATIVE ASPECT The response to any situation will be extremely sharp, with a tendency to nag and, in particular, to propagate and enjoy gossip. These individuals possess considerable critical acumen.

A tendency to indulge in gossip is a trait of the negative aspect of the Moon and Mercury.

MOON AND VENUS

CONJUNCTION This placing makes the individual sympathetic, kind, caring, and popular. It will increase an instinctive knowledge of the partner's needs.
POSITIVE ASPECT Very similar to the conjunction, with additional sensitivity. Sometimes a tendency to be too laid-back and to use charm to take advantage of others.
NEGATIVE ASPECT Disappointments in love life can be above average because individuals expect too much from their partners. They have a great deal of love to give but can over-burden their partners with it, or with shyness and inhibition.

MOON AND MARS

CONJUNCTION This will increase the emotional level greatly. The response to situations will be immediate. Will take risks if there is danger.
POSITIVE ASPECT Emotional and physical energy works well and needs regular outlet through sports or exercise. Good health and robustness is present. Emotional involvement in the career is necessary. There is willingness to be helpful.
NEGATIVE ASPECT There is a strong tendency to be short-tempered and volatile, and to take premature action. Sometimes this can lead to emotional tension and periods of stress.

MOON AND JUPITER

CONJUNCTION There is kindness, gentleness, and tolerance towards other people. This encourages generosity with time and money. Sometimes there is a degree of pomposity.
POSITIVE ASPECT A heightened imagination is often present, as is generosity, kindness, sympathy, and understanding; identification with people from other cultures. Living abroad is beneficial and much enjoyed.
NEGATIVE ASPECT Here is a tendency to overdramatize situations – and overreact to them. Awareness of these traits is necessary. A liking for rich food often leads to weight gain and bouts of liverishness.

MOON AND SATURN

CONJUNCTION There is a serious, sometimes gloomy outlook on life; here are hard workers who have

Melodrama is a negative aspect of the Moon with Jupiter.

common sense and are practical. They may find it difficult to fully express their feelings.

POSITIVE ASPECT Here is common sense, determination, reliability, and thoroughness, with a conventional outlook on life. Success will come with discipline; patience is also present.

NEGATIVE ASPECT The outlook can become depressive and negative – often due to low self-confidence. The constitution is vulnerable; additional vitamins and "flu jabs" are advisable before winter sets in.

MOON AND URANUS

CONJUNCTION Here is powerful emotional tension which needs positive outlets. There is originality, brilliance, and imaginative thought, along with a magnetic and dynamic personality, but the responses are cool and distant.

POSITIVE ASPECT Emotional forces are usually expressed positively through scientific or creative interests. Perversity is often present, especially in children.

NEGATIVE ASPECT Considerable emotional tension, which will easily build up. Sporting activity is strongly advised in order to counter stress. Self-will is common, and there is plenty of brilliance and originality.

MOON AND NEPTUNE

CONJUNCTION There is increased imagination and sensitivity, and abundant emotion, kindness, generosity, and a caring instinct for others along with a sense of vocation. These individuals will often make sacrifices for others.

POSITIVE ASPECT The qualities of the conjunction are present, but these must be restrained if vagueness and confusion are not to set in. Psychic gifts are present, especially if Neptune is in Scorpio.

NEGATIVE ASPECT Taking the easy way out of difficult situations is usual – with a tendency to lie, motivated by a need not

Consumption of alcohol needs to be kept in check for individuals who have the negative aspect of the Moon and Neptune.

to hurt others. Escapism through recreational drugs and drinking needs conscious controlling.

MOON AND PLUTO

CONJUNCTION Emotions are heightened and expressed with passion and force. This powerful source of energy tends to be released in sudden outbursts; serenity should be aimed for.

POSITIVE ASPECT Emotional scenes and outbursts for good reasons are effective. There is a desire to get rid of clutter – both environmentally and to dispose of psychological hang-ups.

NEGATIVE ASPECT The expression of emotion and feeling is often blocked, and these individuals find it difficult to talk about problems, therefore psychological troubles will be bottled up for long periods.

MOON AND CHIRON

CONJUNCTION This position heightens sensitivity, and there is vulnerability to powerful emotional outpouring. This needs to be treated with tact and sympathy by the partner.

POSITIVE ASPECT Here there is humanitarianism – the emotions will emerge as identification with suffering, and help will be given, either financially or practically. Quite often, there is imaginative creativity.

NEGATIVE ASPECT The emotions need expression, but controlling them will be difficult. Suppressing them completely causes other problems, and can result in unhappiness, especially when these individuals are young.

THE ASPECTS OF MERCURY

MERCURY AND VENUS

The only aspects Mercury and Venus can form are the conjunction, sextile, semi-sextile, and semi-square. The latter two are minor aspects, and will appear only in a more detailed chart.

CONJUNCTION Here is the capacity for mutual understanding between friends and partners. There is often creative ability and a clever use of the hands through craftwork and design.

SEXTILE An influence similar to that of the conjunction. Here, there is friendliness and creative potential. If Mercury is placed in an earth sign, a love of natural materials will follow and inspire. The expression of love and feeling is attractive.

MERCURY AND MARS

CONJUNCTION Quick thinking and decisiveness is adequately present in these individuals, with a need for immediate action to keep well ahead of rivals. Assertiveness and competitiveness are often expressed through sports. Provocative opinions are readily expressed. There is often an aptitude for, and enjoyment of, satire.

POSITIVE ASPECT Much like the qualities of the conjunction, with a strengthened nervous system and the ability to cope with stressful working conditions. Will need and thrive in a demanding career.

NEGATIVE ASPECT There is a risk of tension and stress. Overwork may possibly lead to a nervous breakdown. These individuals tend to make snap decisions and take premature action.

Quick-witted satire is a typical trait when we have the conjunction of Mercury and Mars.

MERCURY AND JUPITER

CONJUNCTION Excellent intellectual potential, which is often expressed through literary ability, a flair for languages, or a mathematical talent. The mind will work well once objectives are decided upon, and a love of challenge and travel is likely.

POSITIVE ASPECT The intellectual potential is very strong and these individuals are optimistic, good-natured, and philosophical. The necessary acceptance of intellectual challenge is exciting.

NEGATIVE ASPECT This is not particularly strenuous. A tendency towards over-optimism, along with exaggeration – but also scepticism – occurs. Ignoring the small print on documents causes problems.

MERCURY AND SATURN

CONJUNCTION Practical thinking and common sense is usual, and a cautious outlook towards life. There is the ability to make and carry out long term plans to achieve ambitions and objectives.

POSITIVE ASPECT This is a useful anchorage, adding much needed practicality to basically extrovert and impulsive individuals. The mind works methodically and cautiously, but lacks natural enthusiasm.

NEGATIVE ASPECT Obsessional tendencies can be present, with a passion for neatness and order. These individuals are very hard on themselves and will adhere to a strict self-inflicted discipline. Depression is likely to occur.

POSITIVE ASPECT Much as the conjunction; equally inspirational but possibly slightly less potent, with an inventive imagination and perhaps scientific flair.

NEGATIVE ASPECT The mind will be bright and original, but there will sometimes be nervous strain and tension. These individuals may think they have special "gifts", and could need therapy.

MERCURY AND PLUTO

CONJUNCTION An ability to think deeply and intuitively is present, and so is the capability to resolve personal problems through self-analysis. These individuals possess a sleuth-like mind and possibly a flair for business.

POSITIVE ASPECT Here is the ability to cope with details – none of which will be ignored. This is a useful aspect, provided the individual does not allow obsessional tendencies to take hold.

NEGATIVE ASPECT Possible inability to talk problems through with intimate friends. This could bring about frustration and stress, and have a negative effect on health, sometimes causing bowel problems.

MERCURY AND CHIRON

CONJUNCTION These individuals have quick and lively minds, with abundant, positively expressed nervous energy. Decisiveness and out of the ordinary reasoning powers are present, but so is inconsistency of thought and opinion.

POSITIVE ASPECT A brilliant and extremely agile mind, with flashes of inspiration and good original ideas. Sometimes duplicity occurs, but so does the ability to wriggle out of it if the deceit is exposed.

NEGATIVE ASPECT Good intellectual potential which will aid achievement, but there is often a conflict between conventional and unconventional outlooks on life, and in the formation and expression of opinions.

The sleuthing capabilities of Sherlock Holmes are within the grasp of those who have the Mercury and Pluto conjunction.

MERCURY AND URANUS

CONJUNCTION This dynamic influence contributes originality and brilliance. While there is often an independent spirit, stubbornness, perversity, and willfulness are likely.

POSITIVE ASPECT Here is a natural talent that is often expressed through an interest in unusual subjects. There will be self-will and sometimes a sense of the dramatic. An independent streak is usually present.

NEGATIVE ASPECT There is the same bright mind as in conjunction, but a considerable vulnerability to nervous stress and tension, which will occur frequently. There can be tactlessness too, and these individuals tend to speak out of turn.

MERCURY AND NEPTUNE

CONJUNCTION The mental attributes of Mercury are combined with the imagination of Neptune. Creative potential can be expressed in different ways – through writing, the fine arts, acting, dancing, skating, or talent for astrology and related disciplines.

THE ASPECTS OF VENUS

VENUS AND MARS

CONJUNCTION Enhanced sexual appeal and sheer enjoyment of sex. The coarsening influence of Mars is countered by Venusian charm and romance. The sign and house placing are important.

POSITIVE ASPECT Similar to the conjunction, but pay special attention to the two signs' elements, as this will colour the sex life: air = additional flirtation and friendship; water and fire = passion and emotion; while earth = bawdiness.

NEGATIVE ASPECT These enliven the love and sex life, adding increased desire. However, these individuals have a tendency to rush into relationships, which can result in disappointment or embarrassment when sudden rejection occurs.

Eroticism and sexual enjoyment are enhanced in the conjunction of Venus, goddess of love, and the warrior, Mars.

VENUS AND JUPITER

CONJUNCTION This configuration bestows charm, warmth, and generosity. It also makes these individuals very affectionate and friendly. It will add a philosophical outlook, and tradition decrees that this is the most beneficial and fortunate of all the aspects.

POSITIVE ASPECT Almost as beneficial as the conjunction, contributing the aforementioned qualities. However, one needs to be cautious about being overgenerous – a tendency that is occasionally present.

NEGATIVE ASPECT These individuals will succumb to dramatic scenes when under stress. Charm can be used to take advantage of others, and a tendency towards over-indulgence is possible, which may lead to weight gain.

VENUS AND SATURN

CONJUNCTION This placing will weaken the expression and joy of love and sex. Shyness will often prevent a relaxed and free response towards sex, which is seriously inhibited by this aspect. Very often there is a sense of disappointment and sadness because of relationship problems.

POSITIVE ASPECT Once emotional security is established, these individuals will prove to be very faithful. Financial hardship is often present, but will be bravely encountered.

NEGATIVE ASPECT Similar to the conjunction, but if there is determination, the inhibition and negative indications will be overcome in time. However, possible setbacks and delays to the formation of a permanent relationship are likely.

VENUS AND URANUS

CONJUNCTION Here is a magnetic power of attraction and a tendency to distance the self from a meaningful commitment. These individuals possess an independent spirit. Excitability and emotional tension will be shown, not only in love and sex life, but also creatively or through an unusual interest.

POSITIVE ASPECT Much the same as the conjunction, with added eccentricity, a desire to shock, and perversity. Sometimes an outrageous image.

NEGATIVE ASPECT Serious stress and nervous tension is usually taken out on the partners, and in relationships generally, making these individuals quite difficult to live with at times.

VENUS AND NEPTUNE

CONJUNCTION Here are the diehard romantics. There is sensitivity and an idealistic attitude which, sadly, can lead to heartbreak and disappointment. A "cloud nine" influence.

POSITIVE ASPECT Very similar to the conjunction, but there is even greater romanticism, along with kindness and sympathy, adding to the enjoyment of the love life. Often creative potential.

NEGATIVE ASPECT It can be difficult for these individuals to relax into the pleasures of love and sex, and there will be a tendency towards restlessness and sometimes discontent. Emotions will overwhelm partners at times.

VENUS AND PLUTO

CONJUNCTION This placing increases passion, with these individuals falling desperately and very deeply in love. The need for sexual fulfilment is high, and a smouldering and sexy image can be stunningly seductive.

POSITIVE ASPECT As with conjunction, with increased powers of sex appeal (especially for those with Pluto in Scorpio). A clever and intuitive financial/business sense.

NEGATIVE ASPECT These aspects cause difficulties in the expression of emotion. There is intensity and passion, but inhibition blocking emotions and a rewarding sex life. Sometimes therapy is required.

VENUS AND CHIRON

CONJUNCTION There is an over-idealized opinion of lovers and a huge yearning for romance. Lovemaking needs to take place in beautiful and seductive surroundings.

POSITIVE ASPECT A tendency to make far too many sacrifices for the partner, so that self-identity is lost. The expression of love is sometimes made through devotion to a study, interest, or hobby which can go on to assume great importance.

NEGATIVE ASPECT The emotional level is very high, and at times these individuals will succumb to hugely dramatic scenes. They need a positive outlet and expression of this powerful force.

A preoccupation with romantic settings is a common trait when Venus and Chiron are in conjunction.

The ability to excel in dangerous occupations is enhanced when Mars and Saturn are in positive aspect.

THE ASPECTS OF MARS

MARS AND JUPITER

CONJUNCTION Here is *the* aspect that makes people "get up and go" – physically or intellectually. There is energy and enthusiasm for challenges (often sporting), along with initiative, decisiveness, and a forthright, uncomplicated attitude.

POSITIVE ASPECT Optimism, enthusiasm, and most of the strong qualities of the conjunction – but with a tendency to express opinions over-assertively.

NEGATIVE ASPECT Restlessness, a tendency to exaggerate and overdo things; but there is physical and intellectual energy, and possibly risk-taking and gambling.

MARS AND SATURN

CONJUNCTION There are periods when these individuals feel confident and assertive, while during others they seriously lack self-confidence. This aspect affects health due to periods of overwork – burn-out and vulnerability to colds and/or depression follows.

POSITIVE ASPECT The ability to cope and work in difficult or even dangerous conditions is present. The will to succeed is there, but also a need to conserve physical energy.

NEGATIVE ASPECT This is a "blow hot, blow cold" influence. Devising and keeping to a regular routine will help to regulate the flow of energy.

MARS AND URANUS

CONJUNCTION Great determination and self-will is combined with obstinacy. Frankness and outspokenness is usual, and it is important that these individuals do not become too fanatical in opinion. A powerful position is often enjoyed.

POSITIVE ASPECT These people are very highly motivated and will burn up abundant nervous energy. Flair for engineering or science is present; also extremely quick reactions and considerable originality.

NEGATIVE ASPECT This is a source of nervous strain and tension, perhaps due to overwork. Migraines can result.

Argumentativeness and perversity usually emerge in these individuals from time to time.

MARS AND NEPTUNE

CONJUNCTION A rich and colourful imagination and fantasy life – both of which are fine if used creatively. Physical energy is low, so exhaustion can occur. Vulnerability to even medical drugs is common for all these aspects.

POSITIVE ASPECT A rich imagination which is usually rewardingly expressed. The emotions are heightened and will find easy and rewarding expression through sex.

NEGATIVE ASPECT This influence brings tension, which is quite often relieved through smoking, drinking, or taking recreational drugs. Good imaginative potential is present, but needs encouragement to be expressed positively.

MARS AND PLUTO

CONJUNCTION Although stubbornness is common, it motivates an energetic determination. There is aggression in this energy which could be countered by karate or other martial arts. A power complex can emerge, especially if the planets are in Scorpio.

Bravery is a hallmark of the Mars and Chiron conjunction.

POSITIVE ASPECT The physical and emotional energy is increased and will always be positively expressed when there is emotional involvement in the career or in some demanding interest or activity.

NEGATIVE ASPECT A tendency to work to breaking point, since the same energy increase is present as with the conjunction. Often, these individuals must overcome serious obstacles in order to succeed.

MARS AND CHIRON

CONJUNCTION Here is a decided warrior instinct expressed through bravery and assertiveness, and perhaps a somewhat devil-may-care attitude. Good-heartedness and caring reactions contrast – but sit happily with – these very different qualities.

POSITIVE ASPECT An excellent influence, with one Chiron specialist discovering that these individuals very often have lucky breaks in life. They are also endowed with an excellent sense of timing.

NEGATIVE ASPECT This placing also adds bravery, with care and understanding being expressed towards weaker people who will also benefit considerably from the individual's Chiron strength and assertiveness.

THE ASPECTS OF JUPITER

JUPITER AND SATURN

CONJUNCTION Here is optimism and caution; a balanced outlook, with enthusiasm but restraint. However, sometimes one planet's influence is stronger than the other, with a negative, restraining effect if Saturn dominates over Jupiter and a more positive, outgoing outlook if Jupiter is the stronger of the two.

POSITIVE ASPECT These aspects are similar to the conjunction at its best. Here, there is breadth of vision combined with caution, and only well-calculated risks will be taken.

NEGATIVE ASPECT These individuals are often pulled in two different directions, so uncertainty is usually present, which often leads to inner discontent. Assess which is the stronger of the two planets.

JUPITER AND URANUS

CONJUNCTION These individuals are fortunate to have this powerful configuration. There is a positive outlook on life, an original mind, and the ability to be extremely forward-looking. The 1983 conjunction in Sagittarius was particularly exciting.

POSITIVE ASPECT There is much good humour, kindness, generosity, and determination. A harmless element of eccentricity can emerge.

NEGATIVE ASPECT Eccentricity can become annoying to others, making these people difficult to get on with, and discontent may be present. The need for independence is strong, so delaying a commitment to a permanent relationship can sometimes occur.

JUPITER AND NEPTUNE

CONJUNCTION Some kind of spirituality is usually present. It often takes the form of a New Age discipline. There is a rich fantasy life, and dreaminess, which if controlled can be expressed positively through imaginative and creative work.

POSITIVE ASPECT Very similar to the conjunction, but with added sympathy, delicacy, and sensitivity, especially if these qualities show in other areas of the chart.

NEGATIVE ASPECT Much the same as above, but a huge tendency to forgetfulness can often cause considerable problems for these individuals.

JUPITER AND PLUTO

CONJUNCTION There is a desire for power, either in big business or perhaps politics. If in education, here is the autocratic head teacher or professor. A near-obsessive need to achieve objectives

A degree of dreaminess is often present with the conjunction of Jupiter and Neptune.

will often lead to stunning success. Ruthlessness may also be present in these individuals.

POSITIVE ASPECT Here is inner strength and determination with a positive and optimistic outlook. Inspiration to make the world a better place leads to philanthropic action.

NEGATIVE ASPECT There is dynamism, but obsessional insistence on achieving what can be fanatical objectives. Care needed in the expression of these traits.

JUPITER AND CHIRON

CONJUNCTION Here are individualists who will want to go their own way, enthusiastically doing their own thing. It is often the case that they find spirituality and inner content in the enlightenment of other cultures.

A playful eccentricity is typical of Jupiter and Chiron in negative aspect.

POSITIVE ASPECT A steady development of potential, and enthusiasm to get on with life. Sporting or literary talent likely.

NEGATIVE ASPECT Social justice is important to these individuals. There is strength of will and good intellectual potential, which will be used assertively. Sometimes they become zany, eccentric professors.

THE ASPECTS OF SATURN

SATURN AND URANUS

CONJUNCTION This configuration is a powerful energy source, which gives potential for determination and hard work, combined with originality. It was operative between December 1986 and December 1989.

POSITIVE ASPECT A blend of conventional behaviour and unconventional traits. If these individuals know how and when to make the most of these contrasts, they will do very well.

NEGATIVE ASPECT The two planets are at loggerheads, therefore these individuals will be stubborn and occasionally bloody-minded. Sometimes, there is tension and stress which can be eased if patience can be developed.

SATURN AND NEPTUNE

CONJUNCTION Many astrologers mistrust the influence of these aspects. Nevertheless, we have always found them to be a controlling, cautious channel for creative and imaginative work, with Neptune softening the harsher side of Saturn.

POSITIVE ASPECT Similar to the qualities of the conjuction, but with added high ideals, sympathy, patience, and understanding.

NEGATIVE ASPECT This will weaken the personality, and often creativity is thwarted by unsupportive authority figures. A tendency to undermine achievement can also be present.

SATURN AND PLUTO

These occurred during the late 1940s in Leo, and again in the early 1980s in Libra. If near the Ascendant, this aspect has a frustrating influence which often causes serious psychological or physical problems that are difficult to resolve.

POSITIVE ASPECT Increased determination and a driving energy force can be present in these individuals. There is also the ability to come to terms with psychological problems or phobias.

NEGATIVE ASPECT Obsessive behavioural problems may occur at times. There is a tendency to say "I can't be bothered", when lack of self-confidence is the real reason.

SATURN AND CHIRON

CONJUNCTION This configuration is extremely rare. It was operative during 1966. The strong influences of Saturn are lightened by the liveliness of Chiron, which adds an optimistic and positive outlook, especially to those who also have the Uranus-Pluto conjunction (*see p280*).

POSITIVE ASPECT This contributes considerable charisma, with these individuals always wanting to have their own way – generally they succeed in getting it too.

NEGATIVE ASPECT Here is a fighting spirit which will be dedicated to humanitarian causes.

ASPECTS OF THE OUTERMOST PLANETS

The aspects of the outermost planets are operative for long periods, so appearing in the birth chart of everyone born when they are "in orb" (*see p265*). Unless Saturn, Uranus, Neptune, or Pluto rule the Sun, Moon, or Ascendant sign, interpretations should not be over-emphasized.

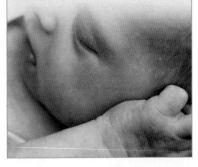

THE ASPECTS OF URANUS

URANUS AND NEPTUNE

CONJUNCTION This configuration occurs only once every 171 years. It was around in 1989 and was still operative as late as 1999. The two planets work well together, bringing the kindness and sympathy of Neptune to the humanitarian qualities of Uranus.
POSITIVE ASPECT Here is the added ability to blend originality and imagination in whatever form shown by the chart, and according to the individual.
NEGATIVE ASPECT A tendency to be very forgetful and somewhat scatterbrained – unless countered by an emphasis on earth signs – increased if either Cancer or Pisces is prominent.

URANUS AND PLUTO

CONJUNCTION This strong generation influence occurs once in 115 years and was operative from Virgo between 1963 and 1966. When placed near the Midheaven, it gives powers of leadership with potent determination and the need to be in an influential position. Sometimes there are quite serious psychological problems, especially if Virgo is the Sun, Moon, or Ascendant sign.

POSITIVE ASPECT A tendency to make drastic, often impulsive changes. Forward planning is advisable, because the disruption can be a source of regret.
NEGATIVE ASPECT A recurrent source of stress and tension. This is especially so if plans are frustrated and a desire for change is impossible to achieve, or there is a tendency to make changes because of restlessness or simply for the sake of doing so.

URANUS AND CHIRON

CONJUNCTION There is no one alive with this conjunction, and there will not be for many years to come.
POSITIVE ASPECT These aspects tend to make individuals tense but energetic, while occasionally they are self-opinionated and stubborn. Restlessness occurs and sometimes there is great difficulty in finding the right niche in life to provide contentment.
NEGATIVE ASPECT A good sense of purpose is present, as is intensity, but build up of stress and tension can mar the progress of a career and may cause personal problems as well.

Powers of leadership are enhanced greatly when the conjunction of Uranus and Pluto occurs near the Midheaven.

THE ASPECTS OF NEPTUNE

NEPTUNE AND PLUTO

CONJUNCTION In the 1880s and 1890s Neptune and Pluto were in the same sign, Gemini (*see box, right*).
SEXTILE This configuration is only really significant if Pisces (Neptune) and/or Scorpio (Pluto) are the Sun, Moon, or Ascendant sign. In such cases, Neptune will soften and sensitize the intensive effects of Pluto, and together they will increase the emotional level.

NEPTUNE AND CHIRON

CONJUNCTION These individuals are highly idealistic and will follow a path of spiritual development; sometimes there is confusion as to whether or not they are actually on the path that is right for them.
POSITIVE ASPECT Here is appreciation of everything that is beautiful and mystical. A tendency to drift off into a dreamlike world can make these individuals lose touch with reality.
NEGATIVE ASPECT Awareness must be developed of an above average negative reaction to all kinds of drugs, otherwise escapism through recreational drugs or drink will take hold when these individuals are under stress.

CONJUNCTION OF NEPTUNE AND PLUTO

English emigrants bound for Australia

There may be no one alive now with this configuration, but our research shows that when these planets were accompanied by a Gemini or Sagittarian Sun, Moon, or Ascendant sign, they gave a surprising spirit of adventure and bravery to these people. Many took off for unknown shores – to Australia and to the U.S.A. – in the knowledge that they would never see home again. Since those times, Neptune has overtaken Pluto in its journey round the Sun, and by the time Neptune entered Virgo in 1928 and Pluto was well into Cancer, they have been keeping a pretty much regular distance apart, which very often creates a sextile aspect – 60° and two signs apart. At the time of writing, Neptune is in Aquarius and will enter Pisces in 2011, while Pluto enters Capricorn in 2008. Therefore, these planets will play cat and mouse for many years to come.

THE ASPECTS OF PLUTO

PLUTO AND CHIRON

CONJUNCTION The sign this conjunction falls in will be considerably energized by this configuration, and will bring some of its characteristics to prominence in these individuals.
POSITIVE ASPECT A tendency to hold extreme opinions needs to be consciously controlled, otherwise unwise actions can be taken, which may ultimately prove detrimental to these individuals.

NEGATIVE ASPECT These will add hints of the darker and more intensive Scorpio characteristics. Sometimes a tendency to plot and scheme is also present.

Voicing strong opinions is a likely consequence of Pluto in positive aspect.

ASPECTS TO THE ASCENDANT

Aspects to the Ascendant are no different from any other aspects, but are less likely to operate if there is any doubt at all about the accuracy of the birth time. If there is doubt, it is as well to rely entirely on the interpretation of the house position of the planet that appears to be in aspect, especially if it falls in either the First House or the Twelfth.

THE SUN

Conjunction The Sun and Ascendant share the same sign. As a result, the characteristics are doubly pronounced.

Positive Sun-sign characteristics will usually blend well with those of the Ascendant.

Negative Opposition: the Sun sign will be the polar of the Ascendant and accentuate relationships. Square: conflict may arise between home life and career.

THE MOON

Conjunction Will respond and react to all situations in the manner of the Ascendant sign.

Positive Harmony will prevail between the Ascendant and Moon sign.

Negative Opposition: good rapport and response will exist with partners. Square: emotional tension may exist at home and in one's career.

MERCURY

Conjunction Quick thinking mind, very changeable; versatile, but restless.

Positive The mind and intellect will work well with Ascendant characteristics.

Negative Opposition: needs friendship in emotional relationships, flirtatiousness. Square: lively, but argumentative at home and work.

VENUS

Conjunction Adds good looks, romantic slant on Ascendant characteristics.

Positive Many love affairs likely.

Negative Opposition: excellent rapport and sympathy with partners. Square: laid-back domestically; often lazy at work.

MARS

Conjunction Energizes Ascendant characteristics; selfishness, a hard worker.

Positive Needs exercise and will enjoy sports. Risk-taking.

Negative Opposition: this placing increases sexual desires and improves performance; individuals can be argumentative. Square: ambitious for career and family life.

JUPITER

Conjunction Optimistic, fun-loving, studious. Will gain weight.

Positive Needs travel and intellectual stimulation.

Negative Opposition: lively attitude towards partners; might expect too much from them. Square: possibly a gambling spirit. Successful; could over-spend

SATURN

Conjunction Inhibits Ascendant characteristics; can weaken constitution.

Positive Practicality and caution added to Ascendant characteristics.

Negative Opposition: permanent relationships often delayed. Older partners are sometimes preferred. Square: restrictions to home life and career.

URANUS

Conjunction Adds dynamic qualities but is often perverse and stubborn. Independent.

Positive A lively intellect; originality, fun. Trendy lifestyle.

Negative Opposition: will delay making permanent relationship due to independent lifestyle. Square: unpredictable at home and work.

NEPTUNE

Conjunction Works well if in Twelfth House. Weakens Ascendant if in the First.

Positive Idealistic, romantic. A bit "off the planet".

Negative Opposition: too romantic. Unrealistic in relationships. Square: confusion occurs. Sometimes deceptive.

PLUTO

Conjunction Striking and intensive good looks.

Positive Will cope well with enforced changes.

Negative Opposition: insistent lover but difficult partner. Square: frustration due to parental control. Will fight for career progress.

CHIRON

Conjunction Will add a lively spiciness to Ascendant characteristics.

Positive Increases energy for sporting activities and creative work.

Negative Opposition: will merge with the partner. Square: originality and keenness shown for family and at work, but stress will build.

Energy for sport will be enhanced by having Chiron in a positive aspect.

ASPECTS TO THE MIDHEAVEN

Any planet making an aspect to the Midheaven will colour the influence of the Midheaven sign. While we may not have the characteristics of the sign, we can identify with them, and they will colour our aspirations and ambitions, and the way in which we are noticed for our achievements. As with the Ascendant, the efficacy of these aspects relies on the accuracy of the birth time. If this is uncertain, rely solely on the house position of the planet involved.

THE SUN

Conjunction The individual is at one with career and objectives. Ambition, success, and often fame according to Sun and Midheaven signs.

Positive A fairly easy passage through career, with steady progress. Usually contentment at, and with, work.

Negative Struggles due to family resistance or limited education.

THE MOON

Conjunction Will be in contact with, or in charge of, a large group of people. Often fame with the general public.

Positive Will react well to career and be considerate of others when promoted.

Negative Emotional tension and stress caused by work pressures.

MERCURY

Conjunction Excellent for media work and selling. A lively attitude.

Positive Steady progress through well-considered changes.

Negative Restlessness and too many changes mar real career progress.

VENUS

Conjunction Laziness spoils progress in spite of a desire to make a lot of money!

Positive A successful career with steady progress.

Negative Needs peaceful workplace, and cannot work in isolation.

MARS

Conjunction A hard, energetic, keen, and ambitious worker. Sometimes ruthless for progress.

Positive Enthusiastic and positive attitude; needs speedy results.

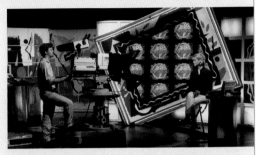

The media often attracts those who have the conjunction of Mercury in the Midheaven.

Negative Prone to overwork and burn-out. Not always an easy colleague.

JUPITER

Conjunction Success through intellectual application and good attitude.

Positive Enthusiasm for career; big ideas will be accepted. Living and working abroad could be an enjoyable option.

Negative A liking for change does not usually get the desired results.

SATURN

Conjunction Heavy responsibility and a lonely top job is usual. Often autocratic; serious attitude towards career.

Positive Ambitious, with steady progress. Very disciplined.

Negative Frustration and setbacks are common; slow progress.

URANUS

Conjunction A liking for power that needs controlling; great originality.

Positive A dynamic attitude with an original approach to career problems.

Negative Discontentment and stress. Often a difficult colleague with radical ideas.

NEPTUNE

Conjunction A somewhat over-idealistic attitude towards ambitions and career.

Positive "Que sera, sera" and a very laid-back attitude. Creative/mystical gifts are advantageous.

Negative Often confused, but talent will blossom if right niche is discovered.

PLUTO

Conjunction A power complex; sometimes joins politics. Ambitious and ruthless.

Positive Will be successful; financial flair likely. Good business sense.

Negative Progress blocked sometimes due to financial problems.

CHIRON

Conjunction A dynamic attitude to career; makes considerable impact.

Positive Sense of drama; will cope with whatever fate has in store.

Negative Above average setbacks, but possesses a good fighting spirit.

"*The soul of the newly-born child is marked for life by the pattern of the stars at the moment it comes into the world*"

Johannes Kepler, 1604

The Returns

This area of astrology concerns the way in which the planets are markers to milestones in our lives. The term "return" refers to the time when a planet, while orbiting the Sun, returns to the precise position it was in on the day of one's birth. It is probably the only area of astrology that can be used without having even the slightest knowledge of astrology.

INTRODUCING THE RETURNS

All planets intermittently return to the position they were in at the time of one's birth. We say "many happy returns" when wishing friends a happy birthday – for a birthday marks the completion of the Earth's journey around the Sun and back to the place it was in one year previously, and indeed when we were born.

Chinese astrology and Western astrology share similarities when it comes to the Jupiter Return, which, like in Chinese astrology, follows a 12-year pattern.

The most interesting return influence is that of Jupiter. It takes 12 years to orbit the Sun – and so every 12 years we get our Jupiter Return. Incidentally, this is one indication where Chinese astrology and Western astrology meet: in Chinese astrology, the year of our sign – the Monkey, the Dog, or whatever – comes round every 12 years and is said to be propitious for us. As will be seen, these indications are very similar to those of the Jupiter Return.

The Saturn Return occurs roughly every 30 years, so we experience our first as we approach 30, the next as 60 looms, and as more of us are living much longer, we experience our third when we are 90 years old.

The influence of Uranus is very powerful. The planet takes 84 years to orbit the Sun. Therefore, we get our quarter Return when we are 21, our very strong half-Uranus Return at around 40 to 42, and our full Uranus Return at 84. Chiron takes some 50 years to come back to the position it was in when we were born.

This astrological clockface illustrates, in a sense, how planets revolve on their orbits and return to former positions at regular intervals – an area of astrology know as "the returns".

SHORT AND LONG RETURNS

Mercury and Venus take 88 and 224.7 days respectively to have their returns, so if you become a keen astrology student, using a full ephemeris you might like to follow the movements of these planets to discover their return influences. The human lifespan is not long enough to experience a Neptune or Pluto Return, since these planets take 146 and 248 years respectively to travel round the Sun and through all the 12 signs of the zodiac.

The Most Influential Returns

Here and on the following pages, we have outlined the major returns that tend to punctuate our lives. These include the 12-yearly Jupiter return and the Saturn returns at the ages of 30 and 60.

JUPITER RETURNS

A Jupiter return is likely only to be really exact for a few days, while Jupiter is in the precise position it was at birth. However, generally speaking, its influence will add a certain amount of colour to a whole year.

The first Jupiter Return occurs as children reach their 12th birthday. This is a good time for parents to consider their child's interests, especially those outside the school curriculum. Examinations taken for music or dance, sporting competitions, or a travelling experience will be particularly rewarding. The young person will do well and should get extra encouragement for his or her efforts at this time.

The year of a Jupiter return usually turns out well: we often end it with rather more money than when it

started. It is not a time to sit around waiting for things to happen – the great thing to remember about Jupiter is to give the planet a push in the direction in which we want it to work for us; then we get good results. At all events, this is not an influence to waste. Being assertive, putting ideas to people who matter, or making long trips are all good ways to use a Jupiter return year. (To discover the years of a Jupiter return simply divide your age by 12.)

URANUS SQUARE TRANSIT

The next milestone occurs at 21, and is the "tense square transit" of Uranus contacting its own place from three signs. Simply put, it means that the planet is 90° from the position it was in at one's birth. The old traditional idea of getting "the key of the door" no longer applies, but this has always been a crucial time as far as the young person's embryonic career is concerned. Many are graduating and going through the experiences of getting their first jobs to kick-start their professional life. Both tension and changes are indicated and usually occur.

FIRST SATURN RETURN

How often have we heard people moaning about the grim fact that they are turning 30? For the most part they are totally unaware that they are in the grips of a very important and serious planetary influence from Saturn. This is certainly a milestone period for them. They will, quite rightly and naturally, reassess their lives and progress so far. Many will move up the ladder by changing jobs and getting a better salary. Some – sadly, but again quite rightly –

University students often graduate or are in their final student year at the time of the Uranus square transit.

may well end a youthful relationship or marriage which is not working any longer. Others will marry for the first time, or will buy their first home, and commit themselves to the long haul of a mortgage, while this is also often the right time for couples to start their families. A keyword for Saturn is responsibility, and additional responsibility is likely to be taken. It must be remembered that while Saturn is a hard task-master what happens under the planet's influence, especially if it relates to the long-term, is usually the right way to go.

A sudden desire to take up vigorous exercise is typical behaviour during the half-Uranus return.

HALF-URANUS RETURN

This crucial transit occurs roughly between the ages of 40 and 42. It relates very powerfully to the mid-life crisis. Under this influence restlessness occurs, and the sudden realization that one is getting old. To counter these feelings drastic action is often taken, with perhaps cosmetic surgery, a change of image, and possibly the indulgence of an invigorating, light-hearted love affair. All this can work extremely well, but sadly, all too often what started out as a fling can go too far and cause a very great deal of hurt and upset to partners and loved ones.

An amorous fling with someone new is a clear sign of a mid-life crisis.

The loss of a youthful figure can result in frantic dieting and exercise. For those who have not exercised for years, serious damage can be done, but again if they pace themselves all should be well. Taking up a new interest, especially if it is something that the individual has wanted to do for years, is an excellent outcome, and even if job and family commitments are heavy, this is to be strongly advised.

This influence needs a lot of controlling, and careful thought is essential before any decisions are made. The tendency to go crazily over the top

and upset others is by no means unlikely, but when this dynamic trend is set to work in a positive way the period can be exciting, invigorating, and positive.

CHIRON RETURN

The 50th birthday has been celebrated in many countries for years and now its popularity is increasing. It has a jolly feel to it. Mostly individuals have been successful in their professions and jobs and may well not be quite as serious or worried as their younger colleagues, who are still treading carefully to get to where they want to be. Provided the 50-year-old is in good health, there will be a feeling that life is more or less under control, families are pretty much grown up, and a

MAIN RETURNS THROUGH A LIFESPAN	
Age	**Return**
12	First Jupiter Return
21	The Uranus Square
30	First Saturn Return
42	The Half Uranus Return
50	The Chiron Return
60	Second Saturn Return
60	Fifth Jupiter Return
84	The Full Uranus Return
90	Third Saturn Return

realization that while retirement will make for a welcome change in lifestyle, it is still a decade away. This, then, is a time when considerable personal achievement is often recognized by individuals, and if they feel a certain smugness and inner satisfaction – they are quite right to do so. This will also be a good time to reward themselves and their partner with a very special holiday.

SECOND SATURN RETURN AND FIFTH JUPITER RETURN

It is at the approach of 60 and for around that 12-month period that we have our Second Saturn Return, and more or less at the same time the Fifth Jupiter Return. This marks one of the most important periods of our lives.

Most people will retire from their careers, or, as one Aries friend of ours put it, re-schedule their lives. This is the right attitude. Those who have no particular interests tend to crumble into old age when they retire. But it is not always easy to start out with something completely different at this age, especially if it involves a lot of effort. Many will, of course, cope well and love the challenge, but for those who find such challenges an uphill struggle, chances are that they will give up. If there has been a long love affair with, for instance, gardening, there is usually no problem; the garden will be totally re-designed and a great deal of newfound free time will be lovingly spent on it. The same goes for any demanding hobby – it can take on a totally different perspective, and for those who are enterprising, very often they graduate from amateur to semi-professional and make extra cash as a result.

Time for a Big Change
Another outcome of this "double whammy" of planetary influences is that a really big change is often considered.

A new hobby can take on greater importance if it is taken up around the time of the Second Saturn Return.

Perhaps a move to a favourite town where many happy holidays have been spent, or the decision that the family house is too big and that there is a need to downsize. Will the pretty retirement seaside town be as attractive in the depths of winter, however? Are there interesting clubs and societies where new friends can be made? Will a lot of the shops and restaurants be closed during the cold winter months? Then it must be remembered, if downsizing, that there are probably many prized possessions that have been collected and treasured over the years. Will there be enough space for them – and for grandchildren when they come to stay?

It is obvious that for everyone about to make important changes in their lives at this age, a great deal of serious discussion and planning must go on before the actual day dawns when going to the office is just not going to happen any more. If the joint influences of Jupiter and Saturn work well, the next phase of life will be rewarding, fun, and thoroughly enjoyable. However, plans must not be rushed for any reason. Nor must any action be taken in a mood of blind optimism.

FULL URANUS RETURN

The long, journey of Uranus round the Sun to eventually return to the position it was in some 84 years previously suggests a milestone year indeed for octogenarians. Here is challenge, and many people we have known have taken on a new lease of life and suddenly made

quite outlandish requests for all kinds of adventurous happenings, from free-fall parachuting to driving a racing car. They often want to do something they have not done before, but sadly their children or grandchildren sometimes try to dissuade them, thinking that what they want will be far too risky or dangerous, and that the ancient one will not be able to cope. Here is good advice: if an octogenarian makes such a request, it can be assumed that Uranus is working at its best for them. They should not be dissuaded. Let them go up in that balloon, or down in a submarine, or whatever. They will have the time of their lives. Do not treat them like some wilful child.

Free-fall parachuting and other wild activities are not unheard of for octogenarians experiencing the full Uranus return.

Remembrance of Things Past

Of course, many of that age will not be in such an adventurous frame of mind; some will love additional mental stimulation. They will, for certain, know a very great deal about their lost generation, what life was like between the Wars or during the Second World War. Even if we have heard their stories before, a great thing to do is to record them talking, and to let them turn out old photographs (making sure they identify everyone in them!) and memorabilia; their memories can often contribute a great deal to our knowledge of the past. If any member of the family is into genealogy, here is a wealth of knowledge about great-grandparents and their contemporaries. We must never miss out on opportunities like this.

Above all, stimulating the interest of these elderly people can be really worthwhile. Many octogenarians have been big achievers, sometimes producing the greatest work of their lives. Verdi wrote *Otello* at that age; two famous dancers, Marie Rambert in England and Martha Graham in the United States, were still choreographing – and there are many other unforgettable achievers whose prime has continued into their 80s – Picasso, Pablo Casals, Segovia, Pierre Monteux, and Winston Churchill.

The composer Verdi wrote *Otello* when he was in his 80s.

THE THIRD SATURN RETURN

This phenomenon is still being researched, but as so many people are now living well into their 90s, the influence is becoming increasingly common. It seems serious in essence, as Saturn tends to put us in a serious frame of mind. So is this something of a down-turn for nonagenarians? Not necessarily – they will make sure that their affairs are in good order and seize the opportunity for good, possibly last, meetings with loved ones. But maybe there will be some who will fall under the wild influence of "Saturnalia" and lay on the biggest birthday bash they have ever given. Britain's late Queen Mother did just this, as did one of our dearest and closest friends; but then he was an energetic Scorpio and she an energetic Leo (who went on to be 100 and have her second Chiron Return), so no surprises there.

Other
AREAS OF
ASTROLOGY

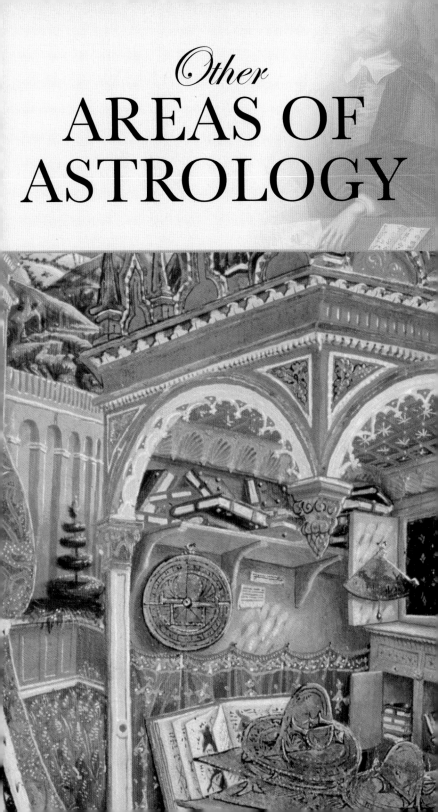

ASTRO*CARTO*GRAPHY

For many centuries there have been associations between certain cities and particular signs of the zodiac. Astro*carto*graphy is a modern approach that looks at the significance of an individual's birth chart when applied to different locations around the world.

The Meaning of Place

Ptolemy (*see p20*) was one of the first astrologers to classify associations between places on Earth and the constellations in the sky. Over the centuries, some places have become significant in astrology. Venice, for example, is regarded as a Libran city, and it is fun to test out whether someone with a Libran Sun sign especially enjoys visiting Venice.

The idea that certain people will strongly identify with certain places has been taken much further in recent years, particularly by the late American astrologer Jim Lewis, who devised a system called Astro*Carto*Graphy.

The system Lewis invented involves the imposition of the four angular positions of the 10 planets of the birth chart onto a map of the world. The "angular positions" are the positions of the Ascendant, Midheaven, Descendant (the degree of the zodiac setting rather than rising), and I.C. (*Imum Coeli*), the point opposite the Midheaven, at the very bottom of the chart.

This arrangement reveals what Lewis called "power zones", which match certain areas of the personality with places that are associated with them.

For instance, a city or a town that falls on the longitudinal equivalent of Venus's Midheaven position in, say, John Smith's birth chart would focus all the qualities associated with his natal Venus (i.e., the planet as seen in his birth chart) as far as the qualities of the Midheaven are concerned. That might affect his career – in Smith's case, maybe his talent for working with people.

A*C*G* CHARTS

There are two ways of approaching relocation astrology – another term for this kind of astrological work. The first involves "manual" calculations and the familiar birth chart; for the second you really need the software that Lewis devised for A*C*G*. This is available from www.astrocartography.co.uk.

This area of astrology can be extremely helpful to anyone in need of advice about a coming move, whether because of a change in working conditions or for any other reason.

Venice is traditionally regarded as a Libran city.

Indeed, the authors found it extremely interesting when considering moving from London to Sydney.

MANUAL CALCULATIONS

Using the traditional, manual way of relocating a chart – that is to say, recalculating a birth chart for a location other than the birthplace – is relatively simple. You use the birth date and time (as drawn, say, for 1 May 1979 in London), but convert the chart to a new location (such as New York). The planets' positions and the aspects between them will be the same as in the original birth chart, but in the chart relocated to New York there will be quite different angles and house

positions. These new house positions and angles will show how well the subject is able to cope with the move, how he or she will react to a foreign city, and how the relocation is likely to affect the personal and working life.

Working with a manually calculated relocation chart, the most important thing to look for is whether a planet falls on an angle of the new chart – you can allow an orb of 5° or 6°. A planet that is right on either the Ascendant or the Midheaven will be expected to work most strongly. However, a planet on the Descendant or I.C. will be almost as strong, and a planet here is likely to reveal quite a lot about reactions to the new location.

READING ASTRO*CARTO*GRAPHY CHARTS

In contrast to the basic natal chart, which represents a map of the sky as seen from Earth, the A*C*G* charts show the planets as seen not against the background of the constellations, but against the background of a flattened map of the Earth. It is not unlike the charts that you see unfolding on-screen in an aeroplane, but instead of showing the path of the aircraft, the A*C*G* chart shows the the path of the Sun, the Moon, and all the other planets as they travel across the map of the Earth. Admittedly, the charts look daunting at first, but are in fact not too difficult to interpret once you have a basic working knowledge of astrology. The A*C*G chart shows many lines. The solid vertical lines show where each planet culminates (on the Midheaven, or M.C.). The dotted vertical lines show the anti-culmination point, or I.C., of each planet. The dramatically curving lines describe the rising and setting of each planet.

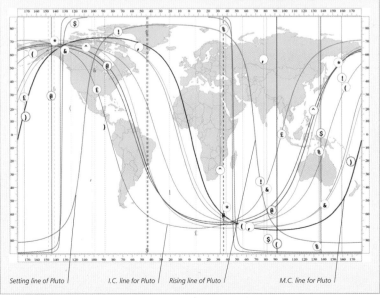

Setting line of Pluto | I.C. line for Pluto | Rising line of Pluto | M.C. line for Pluto

HORARY ASTROLOGY

Horary astrology sets out to address a specific question, the answer to which is arrived at by setting up an astrological chart for the moment when the question is asked. The chart is then interpreted in respect of the question, which is broken down into its significant elements.

Origins and Methodology

Horary astrology has been practised for many centuries. One of the earliest reputable astrologers to use the system was Guido Bonatti, who, in the 13th century, wrote many aphorisms on the subject and published them in his *Liber Astronomicus*. But arguably the most accomplished horary astrologer, and certainly still the best-known, was William Lilly (1602–81), much of whose very considerable fame and

The position of the Moon is a key factor in the process of interpreting horary astrological charts.

income was the result of his apparent success in answering the questions of his clients. His case books are full of charts – over 4,000 of them created between June 1654 and September

William Lilly was the most famous practitioner of horary astrology.

1656 – drawn for the moment when his "querants" (as the questioners were known) anxiously enquired "if my husband would be hanged for stealing 30 bullocks", "if good for my son to go to war, and if returne safely", "if good to take a shoppe", and so on.

When Dennis Prickman enquired as to whether his wife would live, Lilly wrote inside the chart, "She died within a fortnight". Whether he foretold that, we do not know. Other querants enquired after lost dogs and jewellery, disputes with neighbours, and the best time to propose marriage.

This horary chart was plotted for a client called Dennis Prickman; on it Lilly noted that Prickman's wife "died within a fortnight".

TIMING AND PLACING

The time at which the question was asked was regarded as the birth time of the question. The matter asked about (the "quesited") was referred to the house of the horoscope to which it related (the First House concerned with health and wellbeing, the Second with possessions and partners, and so on – see p248). The planet ruling the Ascendant represented the querant.

The rules to be followed when working on horary charts are very complicated. In brief, a great deal of importance is placed on the position of the Moon in the horoscope. Its most recent and potential movements in relation to the other planets were only interpreted as long as it remained in the same sign that it was in when the question was asked. If it made no major aspects to other planets it was said to be "void of course", and the chart could tell one nothing.

From his autobiography, we know that Lilly believed the horoscope he set up for the moment of asking a question acted as a sort of focus for his mind; the relationships between the planets in the chart did not actually tell him what was likely to happen, but concentrated his intuition. Horary astrology was, for him, a method of divination that relied very strongly on a symbolic approach; no question was asked in a vacuum, for it was related to the querant, to the astrologer, and to the world about them. Once one accepts that – and certainly the methodology strikes a chord with Jungian and Eastern philosophy – horary astrology begins to sound far more practical than one might suppose.

ANSWERS

It is also worth pointing out that the "answers" to questions involving future action or events are by no means (and this is true of most other areas of predictive astrology) fatalistic. Astrology offers a choice: if things

---

LILLY, JUNG, & EASTERN PHILOSOPHY

Lilly's attitude was fascinatingly similar to that of the psychologist C. G. Jung (see also pp44–5) in his essay about the way in which the Chinese I Ching, or Book of Changes, is used to survey the future. He pointed out that, though we know, intellectually, that time is an abstract measure, it never actually feels that way. Time seems to have a character of its own, which colours everything that happens to us. When, for example, someone on the radio or TV says a word just as we are reading that same word in a book, it seems as though something significant has happened.

Most people simply dismiss such a happening as meaningless coincidence; but Eastern thinkers take another view – and Jung, too, believed that everything bears the imprint of the moment at which it happens: that since all life has a pattern, anything that happens is related to everything else that happens at the time when the happening occurs.

This Chinese astrological illustration depicts characters that represent four stars: Mercury, Venus, Mars, and Jupiter.

---

seem likely to turn out well, we can relax and let matters take their course. If there seem likely to be difficulties ahead, we can prepare for them. Forewarned is forearmed: we can make the best out of any circumstance.

In some ways, horary astrology is much simpler than natal astrology. Looking at the position and influence of Saturn in a birth chart, for example, one thinks of the way in which it might limit a person, might make them tenacious, persevering, and practical – or, on the other hand, selfish and narrow-minded. Whereas in horary astrology, Saturn might symbolize a physical boundary – a wall, a prison, or the fence at the end of the garden.

Interpreting a Horary Chart

It is impossible in a book of this nature to do more than skim the surface of the technique of interpreting horary charts. It is an area of astrology in which a great deal of practise, experience, and expertise is necessary. Relatively few middle-of-the-road astrologers acquire this; some, like Deborah Houlding in England and Lee Lehman in the US, have concentrated on the subject, and practise and teach it. Here, we can merely show how to begin to interpret a horary chart by giving an example.

This horary chart was drawn up in 1646 by William Lilly, the best-known practitioner of this form of astrology.

PLANET AND SIGN ASSOCIATIONS

Anyone starting to think about horary astrology should first of all look as thoroughly as possible into the significance of the planets and signs. Various emphases on these will indicate the approach to the problem concerned. For instance, we have sketched the meanings of the planets on pp201–45; but in addition to what we have said there about, for instance, Mars, it is important to remember that apart from the suggestions we have made, this planet is also traditionally associated with soldiers and sports-people, those who work with metals (especially iron and steel), with butchers, barbers,

The armed forces and fields of conflict are traditionally associated with Mars.

surgeons, and psychiatrists; the planet is also associated with extremely hot and dry places, with sports-grounds, operating theatres, mines, and heavy industry, as well as (naturally) battlefields.

In a similar way, Sagittarius is associated with mountains and the countryside, the Australian bush and the outback, race-tracks, stables, and sporting venues, with churches and cathedrals, colleges and universities, bookshops and publishing offices. If someone is seeking a lost or stolen object, an emphasis on Sagittarius would suggest that they should look near a fireplace, on a balcony or high up in any room – or perhaps over the Sagittarian fence in next-door's garden!

DIFFICULTIES WITH HORARY CHARTS

It is not easy to give advice from a chart which has a number of contrasting indications. All an astrologer can do is point out that, yes, the job will appeal to her, and she should enjoy it; but that it will be stressful, and that the indications about finance are not very positive.

Here is another example to show that someone consulting an astrologer should no more expect a black-and-white yes-or-no answer to a question than expect a weather forecaster to be accurate all the time. Sometimes, where indications in the chart are extremely clear, there is an excellent chance that advice will clearly suggest a course of action, and lead to the lost kitten or the stolen diamond ring (and horary astrology has sometimes been successfully used in police investigations). In other cases, as in our example, all one can do is hope to clear the mind of the querant, and make a decision easier to reach.

A CASE HISTORY: SAMANTHA

This example concerns a young woman who we'll call Samantha. She has been offered a new job and is now deliberating about whether or not to accept it. If she does so, will she enjoy her new role, will she find it hard work, and will she be successful in it? In horary astrology, the first thing we do is set up a chart for the moment at which Samantha asked the question of the astrologer.

Regiomontanus System In this book, all the example charts we have given use a method of house division called the Equal House system. But in horary astrology the Regiomontanus system is preferred. Regiomontanus tables are available in astrological software or through sites such as www.horary.com.

Samantha's Chart Samantha is represented in the chart by the Ascendant (Sagittarius), its ruling planet (Jupiter), and the Moon – which is in Libra and reflects her feelings of uncertainty. Jupiter is in Gemini in the Sixth House, which will be good for her everyday work. But Mars is on the cusp of the Ninth House, and in Virgo,

which suggests that the work will be stressful and that she will have little time to relax. She should try to find time for relaxation, though, because Jupiter is retrograde – appearing to move backward in the sky – which could represent health problems. This is especially so because Jupiter has an opposition from Pluto, and the Sun and Mercury (though very positively placed in terms of career) are in the *via combusta* (a section of the zodiac between 15° Libra and 16° Scorpio), and planets placed there can have a negative effect on the health.

The Moon's Influence On the other hand, most positively, the Moon is in the Ninth House,

which represents, among other things, long-distance travel – and the job offered to Samantha is that of travel agent!

Further Indications Health is again put in question by the fact that the position of the Sun suggests that Samantha's vitality could be lowered, and Mercury that stress may be a problem. As far as finance goes, Neptune and Uranus are in the Second House, which represents income. Therefore, in order to avoid complications or even some underhandedness, it is important that Samantha is very careful when it comes to such things as checking contracts and properly recording her expenses.

Samantha's Chart

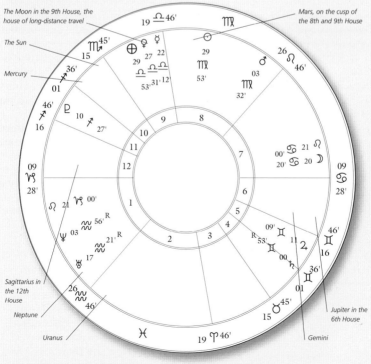

The Moon in the 9th House, the house of long-distance travel

Mars, on the cusp of the 8th and 9th House

The Sun

Mercury

Sagittarius in the 12th House

Neptune

Uranus

Gemini

Jupiter in the 6th House

BEYOND THE SOLAR SYSTEM

Beyond the planets and other astrological bodies in our own solar system are the stars. Traditionally known as the "fixed stars", as they didn't appear to move in independent orbits, they have played a part in astrology for almost two millennia.

An antique planasphere used for studying the heavens.

Wandering Stars and Fixed Stars

Astrologers are often extremely irritated when they see newspaper columns headed "Your Life in the Stars", or "Your Star Sign". Modern natal astrology is so strongly associated with the planets of the solar system that any allusion to "the stars" has sadly become associated with careless journalism, if not charlatanism.

But the stars – the so-called fixed stars, as distinct from the planets, or "wandering stars" as they were called because of their clear

A plotting of the stars in Leo's constellation

Ptolemy was the first to begin to classify the effects of the fixed stars.

movements in the sky – are extremely important in traditional astrology. They have been a useful ingredient since they were first discussed by Ptolemy in the 2nd century CE, and later by Arabian astrologers.

In those earliest discussions, the influences of the fixed stars were associated with those of the planets. In his *Tetrabiblos*, written in c.150BCE, Ptolemy listed them like this: "Of the stars in Leo, the two in the head act in the same way as Saturn and, to a lesser degree, as Mars; the three in the throat, the same as Saturn and, to a less degree, as Mercury; the bright star upon the heart, called Regulus, the same as Mars and Jupiter; those in the hip and the bright star in the tail [Leonis], the same as Saturn and Venus; and those in the thighs, the same as Venus and, to a less degree, Mercury."

So an "evil star", such as Rastaban, might be associated with Saturn; a "benign star", like Nashira, with Venus. Over time, however, stars were gradually assigned their own individual influences.

POSITIONING

The fixed stars are especially important when they are in the Ascendant or near the Sun or Moon in the birth chart; they also have an influence when they are conjuncted, in opposition, or in square aspect with a planet or an important point in the horoscope. If a star is angular – at a specific angle to a planet, especially when it is rising or setting – its influence is particularly strong. The study of *parans* – the angular relationships between planets and fixed stars in a chart – is valuable; a work by Bernadette Brady entitled the *Book of Fixed Stars* (New York, 1998) is probably the best source for this.

There has been some confusion about the allowable orb *(see p265)*. If a relatively small number of stars are used – Lilly's original 50, for instance – a fairly large orb (even as great as 6°) can be allowed for the most important stars, such as Aldebaran, Regulus, and Antares. But if hundreds are used, too large an orb inevitably allows on to the scene several stars that are probably not relevant. It is probably safe in most cases to allow an orb of only 1°. As usual, the closer the orb, the stronger the influence.

PRECESSION

Here, we should consider the more or less vexed question of the precession of the equinoxes. This is the way in which the Earth's pole (and consequently the

first point of Aries) appears to move backwards through the constellations, completing a circle in some 25,920 years – a period known as "the Great Year". A shorter period of 2,160 years – during which the movement is 30°, the equivalent of one zodiac sign – is known as an astrological age. From this term comes the idea of the Age of Aquarius, which was preceded by the Age of Pisces and is to be followed by the Age of Capricorn.

Regulus, one of the most important stars astrologically, is the bright object at the bottom of this picture.

FURTHER STUDY

If you want to do detailed work on the fixed stars in relation to a birth chart, the chart must be fully calculated. If you are simply experimenting, and using a less detailed chart – such as one made by following the instructions in this book – your findings will not be sufficiently accurate.

However, each sign is divided into three 30° sections, each representing 10° and, when consulting our tables, you will see that there are corresponding divisions. The first third (1°–10°) is palely coloured, the middle section (11°–20°) more strongly coloured, and the third section (21°–30°) most strongly coloured. From this, you can estimate the detailed star position. But bear in mind that the orb should not be more than 1°.

Fish are a traditional Christian symbol, and here they have been used decoratively in the architecture of an Early Christian basilica in Greece.

The theory is that each astrological age has its own characteristics, the Piscean Age being identified broadly with Christianity (Christ has often been symbolised as a Fish, and drawings of fish have been found in the earliest Christian tombs); the Age of Aquarius, associated with its ruler Uranus, will have very different characteristics. Given Uranus's traditional association with disruption, sexual excess, and rebellion, the Age of Aquarius is argued by some to have already begun.

The phenomenon of precession has been recognized for centuries – Hipparchus wrote about it in the 2nd century CE, for example. It was only over time, however, that astrologers began to understand the significance of its effect: that the sections of the sky named after the zodiac signs no longer coincided with the positions they were in 2,000 years ago.

Sceptics argue that this makes a nonsense of astrology – that someone born in this age and said to have had the Sun in Gemini at the time of birth, was actually born when it was in Taurus. While it is perfectly true that the Sun may today be placed against the background of the zodiac pattern previous to the one named by astrologers, the fact is that the zodiac names, as understood today, are merely a convenient way of assigning a label to a particular 30° section of the sky; the zodiac figures are only, as they have always been, convenient tags.

THE STARS

William Lilly identified about 50 fixed stars in his writings. They were those that were then most obvious because of their brightness. Among them were Polaris, Betelgeuse, Castor, Pollux, and Regulus; later astrologers identified well over 700. Obviously, with such a great number, they have had to discriminate and, when working with the fixed stars, use only those that make contact with the planets known to the ancient astrologers – that is the Sun and Moon, Mercury, Venus, Mars, Jupiter, and Saturn.

Hipparchus studying the stars

THE MOST IMPORTANT STARS

Any star that closely conjuncts, opposes, squares, or trines a planet in a person's birth chart is potentially significant and so worth consideration. It is the conjunction, though, that will have by far the greatest influence.

Here, we list some of the stars with which William Lilly is known to have worked, together with their positions, the planet or planets with which they are associated, and keywords to suggest their influences.

Caput Algol (26° 10" Taurus) *Saturn, Jupiter*; very negative; "the Evil One" – murder, danger to the neck, strangulation.

Alcyone (0° 58" Gemini) *Moon, Jupiter*; impartial; ambition, difficulties with the opposite sex.

Aldebaran (9°47" Gemini) *Mars*; negative; success, popularity, and honour, but possible chicanery.

Rigel (16°50" Gemini) *Jupiter, Mars*; positive; artistic ability, humour, ingenuity, happiness.

Bellatrix (21°28" Gemini) *Mars, Mercury*; negative; accident-prone, talkative, humiliation.

Alnilam (23°49" Gemini) *Jupiter, Saturn*; positive; short-lived fame, humiliation, irritability.

Al Hecka (24°42" Gemini) *Mars*; positive; honours, authority, self-indulgence, aggression.

Polaris (28°34" Gemini) *Saturn, Venus*; negative; ill health, trouble, loss, spirituality.

Betelgeuse (28°45" Gemini) *Mars, Mercury*; negative; mishaps, danger, aggression.

Sirius (14°05" Cancer) *Jupiter, Mars*; positive; aspiration, self-importance, celebrity, leadership, emotional.

Canopus (14°51" Cancer) *Saturn, Jupiter*; negative; indignity, violent behaviour, devoutness, travel by sea.

Castor (20°51" Cancer) *Saturn, Mars, Venus*; negative; violence, waywardness, sudden celebrity or sudden loss.

Pollux (23°13" Cancer) *Mars, Moon, Uranus*; negative; boldness, destruction, scandal, misfortune, thoughtful, interest in astrology.

Præsæpe (7°12" Leo) *Mars, Moon*; negative; withdrawn, but with good inner drive, possibility of violence. Danger from fire.

Alphard (27°08" Leo) *Saturn, Venus*; negative; sexual hang-ups, possible drug addiction, fear of the sea.

Al Jabhah (27°41" Leo) *Saturn, Mercury*; impartial; intelligence, self-regarding, talent for finance, good judgement.

Regulus (29°53" Leo) *Mars, Jupiter, Uranus*; positive; dignified, gracious, watchful, ambitious, and authoritative, but possible downfall.

Seginus (17°39" Libra) *Mercury, Venus*; positive; good at business and astrology, but untrustworthy and makes bad friends.

Spica (23°50" Libra) *Venus, Mars*; extremely positive; known as "the Fortunate" – brings wealth, respect, and beauty.

Arcturus (24°14" Libra) *Jupiter, Mars*; extremely positive; motivation, recognition, respect, profit from foreign travel, and success in career.

Alphecca (12°16" Scorpio) *Venus, Mercury*; positive; respect, gravity, poetic, but difficulties with sex life and with children.

Zuben Algenubi (15°04" Scorpio) *Saturn, Mars*; negative; suffers pain through others, seeks revenge, has possible involvement with crime, and sexually transmitted diseases.

Alpha Serpentis - 22°04" Scorpio; Saturn, Mars; negative; achievements marred by difficulty; emotional instability; difficulties with relationships.

Antares (9°46" Sagittarius) *Saturn, Venus*; impartial; a strongly adventurous nature brings fame and admiration, yet obstinate and wary, and possible difficulty with sight.

Rastaban (17°58" Sagittarius) *Saturn, Mars*; negative; impetuous and principled,

possible success in literature, sports, the arts, astrology, but beware of short-sighted actions and a criminal tendency.

Vega (15°19" Capricorn) *Venus, Mercury*; positive; said to be "lucky", open-handed and sensible, with possible but transitory success in public life.

Altair (1°47" Aquarius) *Mars, Jupiter*; impartial; reckless, audacious, susceptible to accidents – unexpected notoriety, albeit brief.

Algedi (3°46" Aquarius) *Venus, Mars*; impartial; lucky, promiscuous, generous, overtaken by unexpected events.

Sadalsuud (23°46" Aquarius) *Saturn, Mercury*; positive; a creative thinker with an original mind, possibly psychic, with an interest in astrology; successful in spheres of business.

Fomalhaut (3°52" Pisces) *Venus, Mercury*; positive; an interest in the occult, possibly subject to some addiction; likely to be well-known, and prone to associate with unhelpful companions.

Deneb Adige (5°16" Pisces) *Venus, Mercury*; positive; gifted and resourceful, but perhaps immature; connections with public life, and a fear of dogs.

Markab (23°29" Pisces) *Mars, Venus*; negative; respected by all, eager for possessions, likely to have legal problems, and somewhat accident-prone.

Scheat (29°22" Pisces) *Mars, Mercury*; negative; said to be "unlucky", with a tendency towards melancholy, and possible connection to crime.

How to
DRAW UP
YOUR CHART

DRAWING A BIRTH CHART

By following these simple instructions, you will be able to produce a reasonably accurate birth chart. If you do not know your birth time, you cannot calculate your Ascendant or Midheaven signs. If this is the case, either set your chart for noon on the day you were born and ignore the interpretations for the Ascendant and Midheaven, or put your Sun sign in the white segment of the chart at the "nine o'clock" position. This will set your chart for sunrise on your day of birth.

THE BASIC CHART

Redraw or make photocopies of the basic chart shown below to produce your own charts. The border of the circle is divided into a repeating pattern of three distinct shades – white, medium, and dark. Each block covers 10° of the zodiac circle of 360°, and each repeat of the three shades covers the 30° attributed to each zodiac sign. In astrological jargon these divisions are known as decanates, and for our purpose the white segments represent the first 10° of the sign, the light shaded areas the middle 10°, and the darkest segments the last 10°.

When you come to plotting all the data, note that in some cases, if your birth time is very accurately known, there can be a few variations in the house positions of one or two planets. This is due to the limitations of the calculations for the Ascendant. If you find an interpretation of a planet in a house totally irrelevant to you, read its placing in the previous or the following house instead, as one of these will be far more accurate. There are no problems of this kind with the sign placing of planets.

Before you begin, make sure you are fully conversant with the order of the zodiac signs and the glyphs for signs, planets, and ideally the aspects as well.

The Basic Chart

GOLDEN RULE ONE: As you proceed with your findings, make notes at each stage. List your Ascendant sign (you will know your Sun sign already), the sign and house each planet is in, and what aspect in turn it makes to every other planet. Then start looking up the interpretation pages, and systematically note the main characteristics of each indication in the chart. You will build up a remarkably accurate astrological picture of yourself, and be inspired to go on to study family and friends' birth charts!

PLACING YOUR ASCENDANT LINE

Write down your birth date and time, and the latitude and longitude of your birthplace. Next make quite certain whether or not Daylight Saving Time was in operation. If it was, take one hour off your birth time.

To discover your Ascendant turn to the tables and instruction on pages 344–5. Similarly, to find out your Midheaven sign, turn to pages 346–7 and follow the instructions there. Having carefully noted whether the diagonal time and place line crosses the top, middle, or bottom section of the Ascendant line, you are now in a position to draw the first line on your birth chart.

What you are about to draw is the all important Ascendant/Descendant line, which marks the beginning of your birth chart and represents the horizon at the time and place of your birth. Nine o'clock on the chart is the East, the rising position. Directly opposite it is the West, the setting position. Because the Earth is turning on its axis, the Sun and all the planets rise and set during the course of 24 hours, as do the 12 signs. It is from the horizon line that the 12 houses of the chart begin, and the way in which they are distributed relies on the segment of the sign in which the Ascendant falls.

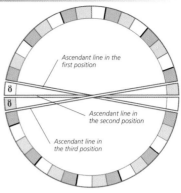

Ascendant line in the first position

Ascendant line in the second position

Ascendant line in the third position

Placing of the Ascendant Line

FIRST POSITION: If the time and place line crosses near the top of the Ascendant line (the beginning of the sign), draw your line in the first position, which denotes the first 10° of your Ascendant.

SECOND POSITION: If the line crosses near the middle of the Ascendant line (the middle of the sign), draw your line at the beginning of the second position, which denotes the middle 10° of the Ascendant.

THIRD POSITION: If the line crosses near to the bottom of the Ascendant line (the end of the sign), draw your line at the beginning of the third position, which denotes the final 10° of the Ascendant.

PLACING THE TWELVE HOUSES

The next stage is to divide up your chart into the 12 houses. As you will see from the diagram these occupy three segments, and start immediately below the Ascendant/Descendant line. Unless your Ascendant falls in the first position, the signs and houses will not entirely match each other. For positions 2 and 3, there will be segments of the next sign covering part of the house. You will also see from the positions of the arrows that the signs rise and set in a clockwise

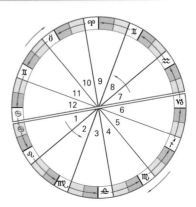

Placing the Twelve Houses

direction, while the houses rotate anti-clockwise. The arrows drawn on the border show where each sign starts and finishes. Now draw in the other 11 signs of the zodiac around the chart as shown in this diagram, and if you find it useful, add the arrows showing where each sign starts and ends. At this point you should now place the Midheaven sign (as shown here).

GOLDEN RULE TWO: Each new sign must begin on a white segment and end on the darkest segment.

Placing of the Midheaven and the Planets

CALCULATING THE POSITIONS OF THE PLANETS

THE SUN To locate the position of the Sun at the time of your birth, turn to pages 308–11 and first find the year of your birth in the top column. Then find the month of your birth – they are numbered 1–12 on the left of the table

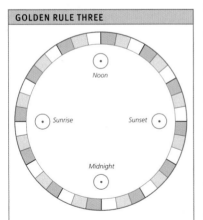

GOLDEN RULE THREE

Noon

Sunrise   *Sunset*

Midnight

This diagram, which shows four positions of the Sun, offers a simple way to check that your chart is accurate. At sunrise, the Sun will be near to the Ascendant, (in which case you will have been born around sunrise, so your Sun and Ascendant signs will be the same). If you were born around noon, the Sun will be at the top of the chart near the Midheaven; if you arrived close to sunset, the Sun will be at the west; and, if you were born around midnight, the Sun is directly opposite the Midheaven. If this isn't working out, try again before going any further.

(1 for January, 2 for February, and so on). The tables indicate the precise date and time at which the Sun enters a given sign. Because the Sun moves at roughly 1° per day, you can then tell which third of the sign is appropriate for the birth date in question: the first 10 days of the sign; the second 10 days; or the final 10 days.

Take an Aries birth date, for example. The Sun enters Aries on 21 March. Therefore, if you were born between 21 and 31 March, plot the Sun in the white segment of Aries; if born between 1 and 10 April place the Sun in the light shaded segment; and if born between 11 and 21 April put the Sun in the darkest shaded segment.

THE MOON The next stage is to discover the position of the Moon at the time of your birth. As the Moon changes signs roughly every two and a half days you have a different process to find out its right sign when you were born. To do this, refer to the guidance on page 315.

THE OTHER PLANETS To locate the positions of the remaining planets, turn to pages 316–43. For each planet, locate the year and month of your birth, just as you did with the Sun tables. However, unlike the Sun tables, the other planetary tables do not indicate a precise time at which a particular planet entered a sign. They do, though, state the date of entry and use tints that correlate to the white, shaded, and dark segments used on our birth charts here. Let's take a birth date of 15 June 1979, for example. On 1 June, Jupiter was in Leo in the white segment, and was still in that segment on the 27th. This means that on the 15 June, Jupiter would be placed in your chart in Leo's white segment, because, at that time it was travelling through the first 10° of that sign.

Your chart should now include all the details on the diagram opposite, with Ascendant, Midheaven, and planets placed in their signs and houses.

PLOTTING THE ASPECTS

Do not be put off from calculating the aspects. Though they can seem forbidding, if you follow these simple rules you'll not go far wrong.

GOLDEN RULE FOUR: For a planet to be in aspect with another they must share the same shading.

♂ **THE CONJUNCTION** This is is formed when two planets fall in the same segment of the same sign.

⚹ △ **THE POSITIVE ASPECTS** The sextile is formed when two planets that share the same shaded segment are two signs, or roughly 60°, apart. The Trine is formed when two planets sharing the same shaded segment are four signs, or roughly 120°, apart. These are joined by a red or fine black line.

□ ☍ **THE NEGATIVE ASPECTS** The square is formed when two planets sharing the same shaded segment are three signs, or roughly 90°, apart. The opposition is formed when two planets sharing the same shaded segment are seven signs, or roughly 180°, apart (directly opposite each other on the chart). They are joined by a black or somewhat thicker line.

⚻ **THE QUINCUNX** This aspect is formed when two planets that share the same shaded segment are five signs, or roughly 150°, apart. On the diagram the black dotted line which joins them, indicates that the quincunx is a minor, but still reasonably important, aspect.

It quite often happens that one planet will make several aspects to a group of other planets in the same chart, so that distinct patterns build up. If a planet receives several aspects from others it is regarded as being of increased importance in the interpretation, and especially so if the planet happens to be the Sun, Moon, or Ascendant Ruler.

Plotting the Aspects

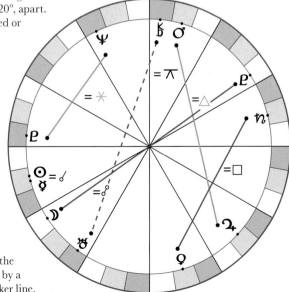

SUN 1931–1950

	1931	1932	1933	1934	1935	1936	1937	1938	1939	1940
1	21 ≈ 0.18	21 ≈ 6.07	20 ≈ 11.53	20 ≈ 17.37	20 ≈ 23.28	20 ≈ 11.01	21 ≈ 0.18	20 ≈ 16.59	20 ≈ 22.51	21 ≈ 4.44
2	19 ♓ 14.40	19 ♓ 20.28	19 ♓ 2.16	19 ♓ 8.02	19 ♓ 13.52	19 ♓ 1.21	19 ♓ 14.40	19 ♓ 7.20	19 ♓ 13.09	19 ♓ 19.04
3	21 ♈ 14.06	20 ♈ 19.54	21 ♈ 1.43	21 ♈ 7.28	21 ♈ 13.18	21 ♈ 0.45	21 ♈ 14.06	21 ♈ 6.43	21 ♈ 12.28	20 ♈ 18.24
4	21 ♉ 1.40	20 ♉ 7.28	20 ♉ 13.18	20 ♉ 19.00	21 ♉ 0.50	20 ♉ 12.19	21 ♉ 1.40	20 ♉ 18.15	20 ♉ 23.55	20 ♉ 5.51
5	22 Ⅱ 1.15	21 Ⅱ 7.07	21 Ⅱ 12.57	21 Ⅱ 18.35	22 Ⅱ 0.25	21 Ⅱ 11.57	22 Ⅱ 1.15	21 Ⅱ 17.5	21 Ⅱ 23.27	21 Ⅱ 5.23
6	22 ♋ 9.28	21 ♋ 15.23	21 ♋ 21.12	22 ♋ 2.48	22 ♋ 8.38	22 ♋ 20.12	22 ♋ 9.28	22 ♋ 2.04	22 ♋ 7.39	21 ♋ 13.36
7	23 ♌ 20.21	23 ♌ 2.18	23 ♌ 8.05	23 ♌ 13.42	23 ♌ 19.33	23 ♌ 7.07	23 ♌ 20.21	23 ♌ 12.57	23 ♌ 18.37	23 ♌ 0.34
8	24 ♍ 3.10	23 ♍ 9.06	23 ♍ 14.52	23 ♍ 20.32	24 ♍ 2.24	23 ♍ 13.58	24 ♍ 3.10	23 ♍ 19.46	24 ♍ 1.31	23 ♍ 7.29
9	24 ♎ 0.23	23 ♎ 6.16	23 ♎ 12.01	23 ♎ 17.45	23 ♎ 23.38	23 ♎ 11.13	24 ♎ 0.23	23 ♎ 17.00	23 ♎ 22.49	23 ♎ 4.46
10	24 ♏ 9.16	23 ♏ 15.04	23 ♏ 20.48	24 ♏ 2.36	24 ♏ 8.29	23 ♏ 20.07	24 ♏ 9.16	24 ♏ 1.54	24 ♏ 7.46	23 ♏ 13.39
11	23 ♐ 6.25	22 ♐ 12.10	22 ♐ 17.53	22 ♐ 23.44	23 ♐ 5.35	22 ♐ 17.17	23 ♐ 6.25	22 ♐ 23.06	23 ♐ 4.59	22 ♐ 10.49
12	22 ♑ 19.30	22 ♑ 1.14	22 ♑ 6.58	22 ♑ 12.49	22 ♑ 18.37	22 ♑ 6.22	22 ♑ 19.30	22 ♑ 12.13	22 ♑ 18.06	21 ♑ 23.55

SUN 1951–1970

	1951	1952	1953	1954	1955	1956	1957	1958	1559	1960
1	20 ≈ 20.52	21 ≈ 2.38	20 ≈ 8.21	20 ≈ 14.11	20 ≈ 20.02	21 ≈ 1.48	20 ≈ 7.39	20 ≈ 13.28	20 ≈ 19.19	21 ≈ 1.10
2	19 ♓ 11.10	19 ♓ 16.57	18 ♓ 22.41	19 ♓ 4.32	19 ♓ 10.19	19 ♓ 16.05	18 ♓ 21.58	19 ♓ 3.48	19 ♓ 9.38	19 ♓ 15.26
3	21 ♈ 10.26	20 ♈ 16.14	20 ♈ 22.01	21 ♈ 3.53	21 ♈ 9.35	20 ♈ 15.20	20 ♈ 21.16	21 ♈ 3.06	21 ♈ 8.55	20 ♈ 14.43
4	20 ♉ 21.48	20 ♉ 3.37	20 ♉ 9.25	20 ♉ 15.20	20 ♉ 20.58	20 ♉ 2.43	20 ♉ 8.41	20 ♉ 14.27	20 ♉ 20.17	20 ♉ 2.06
5	21 Ⅱ 21.15	21 Ⅱ 3.04	21 Ⅱ 8.53	21 Ⅱ 14.47	21 Ⅱ 20.24	21 Ⅱ 2.13	21 Ⅱ 8.10	21 Ⅱ 13.51	21 Ⅱ 19.42	21 Ⅱ 1.34
6	22 ♋ 5.25	21 ♋ 11.13	21 ♋ 17.00	21 ♋ 22.54	22 ♋ 4.31	21 ♋ 10.24	21 ♋ 16.21	21 ♋ 21.57	22 ♋ 3.50	21 ♋ 9.42
7	23 ♌ 16.21	22 ♌ 22.07	23 ♌ 3.52	23 ♌ 9.45	23 ♌ 15.25	22 ♌ 21.20	23 ♌ 3.15	23 ♌ 8.50	23 ♌ 14.45	22 ♌ 20.37
8	23 ♍ 23.16	23 ♍ 5.03	23 ♍ 10.45	23 ♍ 16.36	23 ♍ 22.19	23 ♍ 4.15	23 ♍ 10.08	23 ♍ 15.46	23 ♍ 21.44	23 ♍ 3.34
9	23 ♎ 20.37	23 ♎ 2.24	23 ♎ 8.06	23 ♎ 13.55	23 ♎ 19.41	23 ♎ 1.35	23 ♎ 7.26	23 ♎ 13.09	23 ♎ 19.08	23 ♎ 0.59
10	24 ♏ 5.36	23 ♏ 11.22	23 ♏ 17.06	23 ♏ 22.56	24 ♏ 4.43	23 ♏ 10.34	23 ♏ 16.24	23 ♏ 22.11	24 ♏ 4.11	23 ♏ 10.02
11	23 ♐ 2.51	22 ♐ 8.36	22 ♐ 14.22	22 ♐ 20.14	23 ♐ 2.01	22 ♐ 7.50	22 ♐ 13.39	22 ♐ 19.29	23 ♐ 1.27	22 ♐ 7.18
12	22 ♑ 16.00	21 ♑ 21.43	22 ♑ 3.31	22 ♑ 9.24	22 ♑ 15.11	21 ♑ 20.59	22 ♑ 2.49	22 ♑ 8.40	22 ♑ 14.34	21 ♑ 20.26

1941	1942	1943	1944	1945	1946	1947	1948	1949	1950
20 ♒ 10.34	20 ♒ 16.24	20 ♒ 22.19	21 ♒ 4.07	20 ♒ 9.54	20 ♒ 15.45	20 ♒ 21.32	21 ♒ 3.18	20 ♒ 9.09	20 ♒ 15.00
19 ♓ 0.56	19 ♓ 6.47	19 ♓ 12.40	19 ♓ 18.27	19 ♓ 0.15	19 ♓ 6.09	19 ♓ 11.52	19 ♓ 17.37	18 ♓ 23.27	19 ♓ 5.18
21 ♈ 0.20	21 ♈ 6.11	21 ♈ 12.03	20 ♈ 17.49	20 ♈ 23.37	21 ♈ 5.33	21 ♈ 11.13	20 ♈ 16.57	20 ♈ 22.48	21 ♈ 4.35
20 ♉ 11.50	20 ♉ 17.39	20 ♉ 23.32	20 ♉ 5.18	20 ♉ 11.07	20 ♉ 17.02	20 ♉ 22.39	20 ♉ 4.25	20 ♉ 10.17	20 ♉ 15.59
21 ♊ 11.23	21 ♊ 17.09	21 ♊ 23.03	21 ♊ 4.51	21 ♊ 10.40	21 ♊ 16.34	21 ♊ 22.09	21 ♊ 3.58	21 ♊ 9.51	21 ♊ 15.27
21 ♋ 19.33	22 ♋ 1.16	22 ♋ 7.12	21 ♋ 13.02	21 ♋ 18.52	22 ♋ 0.44	22 ♋ 6.19	21 ♋ 12.11	21 ♋ 18.03	21 ♋ 23.36
23 ♌ 6.26	23 ♌ 12.07	23 ♌ 18.05	22 ♌ 23.56	23 ♌ 5.45	23 ♌ 11.37	23 ♌ 17.14	22 ♌ 23.08	23 ♌ 4.57	23 ♌ 10.30
23 ♍ 13.17	23 ♍ 18.58	24 ♍ 0.55	23 ♍ 6.46	23 ♍ 12.35	23 ♍ 18.26	24 ♍ 0.09	23 ♍ 6.03	23 ♍ 11.48	23 ♍ 17.23
23 ♎ 10.33	23 ♎ 16.16	23 ♎ 22.12	23 ♎ 4.02	23 ♎ 9.50	23 ♎ 15.41	23 ♎ 21.29	23 ♎ 3.22	23 ♎ 9.06	23 ♎ 14.44
23 ♏ 19.27	24 ♏ 1.15	24 ♏ 7.08	23 ♏ 12.56	23 ♏ 18.44	24 ♏ 0.35	24 ♏ 6.26	23 ♏ 12.18	23 ♏ 18.03	23 ♏ 23.45
22 ♐ 16.38	22 ♐ 22.30	23 ♐ 4.22	22 ♐ 10.08	22 ♐ 15.55	22 ♐ 21.46	23 ♐ 3.38	22 ♐ 9.29	22 ♐ 15.16	22 ♐ 21.03
22 ♑ 5.44	22 ♑ 11.40	22 ♑ 17.29	21 ♑ 23.15	22 ♑ 5.04	22 ♑ 10.53	22 ♑ 16.43	21 ♑ 22.33	22 ♑ 4.23	22 ♑ 10.13

1961	1962	1963	1964	1965	1966	1967	1968	1969	1970
20 ♒ 7.01	20 ♒ 12.58	20 ♒ 18.54	21 ♒ 0.41	20 ♒ 6.29	20 ♒ 12.20	20 ♒ 18.08	20 ♒ 23.54	20 ♒ 5.38	20 ♒ 11.24
18 ♓ 21.16	19 ♓ 3.15	19 ♓ 9.09	19 ♓ 14.57	18 ♓ 20.48	19 ♓ 2.38	19 ♓ 8.24	19 ♓ 14.09	18 ♓ 19.55	19 ♓ 1.42
20 ♈ 20.32	21 ♈ 2.30	21 ♈ 8.20	20 ♈ 14.10	20 ♈ 20.05	21 ♈ 1.53	21 ♈ 7.37	20 ♈ 13.22	20 ♈ 19.08	21 ♈ 0.56
20 ♉ 7.55	20 ♉ 13.51	20 ♉ 19.36	20 ♉ 1.27	20 ♉ 7.26	20 ♉ 13.12	20 ♉ 18.55	20 ♉ 0.41	20 ♉ 6.27	20 ♉ 12.15
21 ♊ 7.22	21 ♊ 13.17	21 ♊ 18.58	21 ♊ 0.50	21 ♊ 6.50	21 ♊ 12.32	21 ♊ 18.18	21 ♊ 0.06	21 ♊ 5.50	21 ♊ 11.37
21 ♋ 15.30	21 ♋ 21.24	22 ♋ 3.04	21 ♋ 8.57	21 ♋ 14.56	21 ♋ 20.33	22 ♋ 2.23	21 ♋ 8.13	21 ♋ 13.55	21 ♋ 19.43
23 ♌ 2.24	23 ♌ 8.18	23 ♌ 13.59	22 ♌ 19.53	23 ♌ 1.48	23 ♌ 7.23	23 ♌ 13.16	22 ♌ 19.07	23 ♌ 0.48	23 ♌ 6.37
23 ♍ 9.19	23 ♍ 15.12	23 ♍ 20.58	23 ♍ 2.51	23 ♍ 8.43	23 ♍ 14.18	23 ♍ 20.12	23 ♍ 2.03	23 ♍ 7.43	23 ♍ 13.34
23 ♎ 6.42	23 ♎ 12.35	23 ♎ 18.24	23 ♎ 0.17	23 ♎ 6.06	23 ♎ 11.43	23 ♎ 17.38	22 ♎ 23.26	23 ♎ 5.07	23 ♎ 10.59
23 ♏ 15.47	23 ♏ 21.40	24 ♏ 3.29	23 ♏ 9.21	23 ♏ 15.10	23 ♏ 20.51	24 ♏ 2.44	23 ♏ 8.30	23 ♏ 14.11	23 ♏ 20.04
22 ♐ 13.08	22 ♐ 19.02	23 ♐ 0.49	22 ♐ 6.39	22 ♐ 12.29	22 ♐ 18.14	23 ♐ 0.04	22 ♐ 5.49	22 ♐ 11.31	22 ♐ 17.25
22 ♑ 2.19	22 ♑ 8.15	22 ♑ 14.02	21 ♑ 19.50	22 ♑ 1.40	22 ♑ 7.28	22 ♑ 13.16	22 ♑ 19.00	22 ♑ 0.44	22 ♑ 6.36

SUN 1971–1990

	1971	1972	1973	1974	1975	1976	1977	1978	1979	1980
1	20 ♒ 17.13	20 ♒ 22.59	20 ♒ 4.48	20 ♒ 10.46	20 ♒ 16.36	20 ♒ 22.25	20 ♒ 4.14	20 ♒ 10.04	20 ♒ 16.00	20 ♒ 21.49
2	19 ♓ 7.27	19 ♓ 13.11	18 ♓ 19.01	19 ♓ 0.59	19 ♓ 6.50	19 ♓ 12.40	18 ♓ 18.30	19 ♓ 0.21	19 ♓ 6.13	19 ♓ 12.02
3	21 ♈ 6.38	20 ♈ 12.21	20 ♈ 18.12	21 ♈ 0.07	21 ♈ 5.57	20 ♈ 11.50	20 ♈ 17.42	20 ♈ 23.34	21 ♈ 5.22	20 ♈ 11.10
4	20 ♉ 17.54	19 ♉ 23.37	20 ♉ 5.30	20 ♉ 11.19	20 ♉ 17.07	19 ♉ 23.03	20 ♉ 4.57	20 ♉ 10.50	20 ♉ 16.35	19 ♉ 22.23
5	21 ♊ 17.15	20 ♊ 23.00	21 ♊ 4.54	21 ♊ 10.36	21 ♊ 16.24	20 ♊ 22.21	21 ♊ 4.14	21 ♊ 10.08	21 ♊ 15.54	20 ♊ 21.42
6	22 ♋ 1.20	21 ♋ 7.06	21 ♋ 13.01	21 ♋ 18.38	22 ♋ 0.26	21 ♋ 6.24	21 ♋ 12.14	21 ♋ 18.10	21 ♋ 23.56	21 ♋ 5.47
7	23 ♌ 12.15	22 ♌ 18.03	22 ♌ 23.56	23 ♌ 5.30	23 ♌ 11.22	22 ♌ 17.18	22 ♌ 23.04	23 ♌ 5.00	23 ♌ 10.49	22 ♌ 16.42
8	23 ♍ 19.15	23 ♍ 1.03	23 ♍ 6.54	23 ♍ 12.29	23 ♍ 18.24	23 ♍ 0.18	23 ♍ 6.00	23 ♍ 11.57	23 ♍ 17.47	22 ♍ 23.41
9	23 ♎ 16.45	22 ♎ 22.33	23 ♎ 4.21	23 ♎ 9.58	23 ♎ 15.55	22 ♎ 21.48	23 ♎ 3.29	23 ♎ 9.25	23 ♎ 15.16	22 ♎ 21.09
10	24 ♏ 1.53	23 ♏ 7.41	23 ♏ 13.30	23 ♏ 19.11	24 ♏ 1.06	23 ♏ 6.58	23 ♏ 12.41	23 ♏ 18.37	24 ♏ 0.28	23 ♏ 6.18
11	22 ♐ 23.14	22 ♐ 5.03	22 ♐ 10.54	22 ♐ 16.38	22 ♐ 22.31	22 ♐ 4.22	22 ♐ 10.07	22 ♐ 16.05	22 ♐ 21.54	22 ♐ 3.41
12	22 ♑ 12.24	21 ♑ 18.13	22 ♑ 0.08	22 ♑ 5.56	22 ♑ 11.46	21 ♑ 17.35	21 ♑ 23.23	22 ♑ 5.21	22 ♑ 11.10	21 ♑ 16.56

SUN 1991–2010

	1991	1992	1993	1994	1995	1996	1997	1998	1999	2000
1	20 ♒ 13.47	20 ♒ 19.32	20 ♒ 1.23	20 ♒ 7.07	20 ♒ 13.00	20 ♒ 18.52	20 ♒ 0.43	20 ♒ 6.46	20 ♒ 12.37	20 ♒ 18.23
2	19 ♓ 3.58	19 ♓ 9.43	18 ♓ 15.35	18 ♓ 21.22	19 ♓ 3.11	19 ♓ 9.01	18 ♓ 14.51	18 ♓ 20.55	19 ♓ 2.47	19 ♓ 8.33
3	21 ♈ 3.02	20 ♈ 8.48	20 ♈ 14.41	20 ♈ 20.28	21 ♈ 2.14	20 ♈ 8.03	20 ♈ 13.55	20 ♈ 19.55	21 ♈ 1.46	20 ♈ 7.35
4	20 ♉ 14.08	19 ♉ 19.57	20 ♉ 1.49	20 ♉ 7.36	20 ♉ 13.21	19 ♉ 19.10	20 ♉ 1.03	20 ♉ 6.57	20 ♉ 12.46	19 ♉ 18.40
5	21 ♊ 13.20	20 ♊ 19.12	21 ♊ 1.02	21 ♊ 6.48	21 ♊ 12.34	20 ♊ 18.23	21 ♊ 0.18	21 ♊ 6.05	21 ♊ 11.52	20 ♊ 17.49
6	21 ♋ 21.19	21 ♋ 3.14	21 ♋ 9.00	21 ♋ 14.48	21 ♋ 20.34	21 ♋ 2.24	21 ♋ 8.20	21 ♋ 14.03	21 ♋ 19.49	21 ♋ 1.48
7	23 ♌ 8.11	22 ♌ 14.09	22 ♌ 19.51	23 ♌ 1.41	23 ♌ 7.30	22 ♌ 13.19	22 ♌ 19.15	23 ♌ 0.55	23 ♌ 6.44	22 ♌ 12.43
8	23 ♍ 15.13	22 ♍ 21.10	23 ♍ 2.50	23 ♍ 8.44	23 ♍ 14.35	22 ♍ 20.23	23 ♍ 2.19	23 ♍ 7.59	23 ♍ 13.51	22 ♍ 19.49
9	23 ♎ 12.48	22 ♎ 18.43	23 ♎ 0.22	23 ♎ 6.19	23 ♎ 12.13	22 ♎ 18.00	22 ♎ 23.56	23 ♎ 5.37	23 ♎ 11.32	22 ♎ 17.28
10	23 ♏ 22.05	23 ♏ 3.57	23 ♏ 9.37	23 ♏ 15.36	23 ♏ 21.32	23 ♏ 3.19	23 ♏ 9.15	23 ♏ 14.59	23 ♏ 20.52	23 ♏ 2.47
11	22 ♐ 19.36	22 ♐ 1.26	22 ♐ 7.07	22 ♐ 13.06	22 ♐ 19.01	22 ♐ 0.49	22 ♐ 6.48	22 ♐ 12.34	22 ♐ 18.25	22 ♐ 0.19
12	22 ♑ 8.54	21 ♑ 14.43	21 ♑ 20.26	22 ♑ 2.23	22 ♑ 8.17	21 ♑ 14.06	21 ♑ 20.07	22 ♑ 1.56	22 ♑ 7.44	21 ♑ 13.37

	1981	1982	1983	1984	1985	1986	1987	1988	1989	1990
♒	20 ♒ 3.36	20 ♒ 9.31	20 ♒ 15.17	20 ♒ 21.05	20 ♒ 2.58	20 ♒ 8.46	20 ♒ 14.40	20 ♒ 20.24	20 ♒ 2.07	20 ♒ 8.02
♓	18 ♓ 17.52	18 ♓ 23.47	19 ♓ 5.31	19 ♓ 11.16	18 ♓ 17.07	18 ♓ 22.58	19 ♓ 4.50	19 ♓ 10.35	18 ♓ 16.21	18 ♓ 22.14
♈	20 ♈ 17.03	20 ♈ 22.56	21 ♈ 4.39	20 ♈ 10.24	20 ♈ 16.14	20 ♈ 22.03	21 ♈ 3.52	20 ♈ 9.39	20 ♈ 15.28	20 ♈ 21.19
♉	20 ♉ 4.19	20 ♉ 10.07	21 ♉ 15.50	19 ♉ 21.38	20 ♉ 3.26	20 ♉ 9.12	20 ♉ 14.58	19 ♉ 20.45	20 ♉ 2.39	20 ♉ 8.27
♊	21 ♊ 3.39	21 ♊ 9.23	21 ♊ 15.06	20 ♊ 20.58	21 ♊ 2.43	21 ♊ 8.28	21 ♊ 14.10	20 ♊ 19.57	21 ♊ 1.54	21 ♊ 7.37
♋	21 ♋ 11.45	21 ♋ 17.23	21 ♋ 23.09	21 ♋ 5.02	21 ♋ 10.44	21 ♋ 16.30	21 ♋ 22.11	21 ♋ 3.57	21 ♋ 9.53	21 ♋ 15.33
♌	22 ♌ 22.40	23 ♌ 4.15	23 ♌ 10.04	22 ♌ 15.58	22 ♌ 21.36	23 ♌ 3.24	23 ♌ 9.06	22 ♌ 14.51	22 ♌ 20.45	23 ♌ 2.22
♍	23 ♍ 5.38	23 ♍ 11.15	23 ♍ 17.08	22 ♍ 23.00	23 ♍ 4.36	23 ♍ 10.26	23 ♍ 16.10	22 ♍ 21.54	23 ♍ 3.46	23 ♍ 9.21
♎	23 ♎ 3.05	23 ♎ 8.46	23 ♎ 14.42	22 ♎ 20.33	23 ♎ 2.07	23 ♎ 7.59	23 ♎ 13.45	22 ♎ 19.29	23 ♎ 1.20	23 ♎ 6.56
♏	23 ♏ 12.13	23 ♏ 17.58	23 ♏ 23.54	23 ♏ 5.46	23 ♏ 11.22	23 ♏ 17.14	23 ♏ 23.01	23 ♏ 4.44	23 ♏ 10.35	23 ♏ 16.14
♐	22 ♐ 9.36	22 ♐ 15.23	22 ♐ 21.18	22 ♐ 3.11	22 ♐ 8.51	22 ♐ 14.44	22 ♐ 20.29	22 ♐ 2.12	22 ♐ 8.05	22 ♐ 13.47
♑	21 ♑ 22.51	22 ♑ 4.38	22 ♑ 10.30	21 ♑ 16.23	21 ♑ 22.08	22 ♑ 4.02	22 ♑ 9.46	21 ♑ 15.28	21 ♑ 21.22	22 ♑ 3.07

	2001	2002	2003	2004	2005	2006	2007	2008	2009	2010
♒	20 ♒ 0.16	20 ♒ 6.02	20 ♒ 11.53	20 ♒ 17.42	19 ♒ 23.22	20 ♒ 5.15	20 ♒ 11.01	20 ♒ 16.43	19 ♒ 22.40	20 ♒ 4.28
♓	18 ♓ 14.27	18 ♓ 20.13	19 ♓ 2.00	19 ♓ 7.50	18 ♓ 13.32	18 ♓ 19.26	19 ♓ 1.09	19 ♓ 6.50	18 ♓ 12.46	18 ♓ 18.36
♈	20 ♈ 13.31	20 ♈ 19.16	21 ♈ 1.00	20 ♈ 6.49	20 ♈ 12.33	20 ♈ 18.26	21 ♈ 0.07	20 ♈ 5.48	20 ♈ 11.44	20 ♈ 17.32
♉	20 ♉ 0.36	20 ♉ 6.20	20 ♉ 12.03	19 ♉ 17.5	19 ♉ 23.37	20 ♉ 5.26	20 ♉ 11.07	19 ♉ 16.51	19 ♉ 22.44	20 ♉ 4.30
♊	20 ♊ 23.44	21 ♊ 5.29	21 ♊ 11.12	20 ♊ 16.59	20 ♊ 22.47	21 ♊ 4.32	21 ♊ 10.12	20 ♊ 16.01	20 ♊ 21.51	21 ♊ 3.34
♋	21 ♋ 7.38	21 ♋ 13.24	21 ♋ 19.10	21 ♋ 0.57	21 ♋ 6.46	21 ♋ 12.26	21 ♋ 18.06	20 ♋ 23.59	21 ♋ 5.45	21 ♋ 11.28
♌	22 ♌ 18.26	23 ♌ 0.15	23 ♌ 6.04	22 ♌ 11.50	22 ♌ 17.41	22 ♌ 23.18	23 ♌ 5.00	22 ♌ 10.55	22 ♌ 16.36	22 ♌ 22.21
♍	23 ♍ 1.27	23 ♍ 7.17	23 ♍ 13.08	22 ♍ 18.53	23 ♍ 0.45	23 ♍ 6.23	23 ♍ 12.08	22 ♍ 18.02	22 ♍ 23.39	23 ♍ 5.27
♎	22 ♎ 23.04	23 ♎ 4.55	23 ♎ 10.47	22 ♎ 16.30	22 ♎ 22.23	23 ♎ 4.03	23 ♎ 9.51	22 ♎ 15.44	22 ♎ 21.19	23 ♎ 3.09
♏	23 ♏ 8.26	23 ♏ 14.18	23 ♏ 20.08	23 ♏ 1.49	23 ♏ 7.42	23 ♏ 13.26	23 ♏ 19.15	23 ♏ 1.09	23 ♏ 6.43	23 ♏ 12.35
♐	22 ♐ 6.00	22 ♐ 11.54	22 ♐ 17.43	21 ♐ 23.22	22 ♐ 5.15	22 ♐ 11.02	22 ♐ 16.5	21 ♐ 22.44	22 ♐ 4.23	22 ♐ 10.15
♑	21 ♑ 19.21	22 ♑ 1.14	22 ♑ 7.04	21 ♑ 12.42	21 ♑ 18.35	22 ♑ 0.22	22 ♑ 6.08	21 ♑ 12.04	21 ♑ 17.47	21 ♑ 23.38

MOON 1931–1958

	1931	1932	1933	1934	1935	1936	1937	1938	1939	1940	1941	1942	1943	1944
1	26 ♉.6	5 ♎.1	13 ♓.1	20 ♋.2	0 ♏.2	6 ♓.8	14 ♌.7	20 ♐.8	0 ♈.9	7 ♏.6	14 ♒.4	21 ♊.5	0 ♎.6	7 ♐.3
2	2 ♋.2	9 ♏.8	16 ♈.6	23 ♌.7	3 ♐.9	9 ♉.6	17 ♎.3	24 ♒.3	3 ♊.6	10 ♏.3	18 ♓.9	24 ♌.0	4 ♐.3	11 ♉.0
3	2 ♋.5	10 ♐.6	17 ♈.9	24 ♏.0	3 ♑.2	11 ♊.4	18 ♎.5	24 ♒.6	4 ♊.9	11 ♐.1	18 ♈.2	25 ♌.3	4 ♐.6	12 ♉.8
4	6 ♏.2	14 ♒.3	20 ♊.3	0 ♎.5	6 ♒.9	14 ♌.0	21 ♐.0	0 ♈.2	7 ♌.7	15 ♑.7	22 ♉.7	1 ♏.9	8 ♒.4	15 ♋.3
5	8 ♎.5	16 ♓.4	23 ♋.4	2 ♏.7	9 ♓.2	17 ♍.1	23 ♑.1	3 ♉.4	9 ♎.0	17 ♒.8	24 ♊.8	3 ♍.1	10 ♓.7	18 ♌.4
6	12 ♐.3	19 ♈.9	26 ♌.9	6 ♏.5	12 ♊.0	20 ♎.6	0 ♒.6	6 ♊.2	13 ♏.7	21 ♈.2	0 ♊.3	7 ♐.9	14 ♉.4	21 ♏.9
7	14 ♑.4	22 ♊.0	1 ♎.1	8 ♒.8	15 ♋.1	22 ♏.6	2 ♓.8	9 ♌.5	15 ♐.8	23 ♉.3	2 ♍.6	9 ♒.2	16 ♊.5	24 ♎.9
8	18 ♓.0	25 ♋.5	5 ♏.8	11 ♈.5	18 ♌.7	26 ♑.2	5 ♉.6	12 ♎.2	19 ♒.3	0 ♊.8	6 ♏.3	13 ♓.9	19 ♌.0	0 ♐.5
9	21 ♈.5	1 ♏.1	8 ♐.6	15 ♊.1	22 ♎.1	2 ♒.8	9 ♌.4	15 ♏.8	22 ♓.8	3 ♌.5	9 ♑.1	16 ♉.4	23 ♏.5	3 ♒.2
10	23 ♉.5	4 ♎.4	11 ♒.9	17 ♋.2	24 ♏.2	4 ♈.1	11 ♍.6	18 ♐.9	25 ♈.9	5 ♏.8	12 ♒.3	18 ♊.5	25 ♎.6	6 ♈.4
11	0 ♋.1	7 ♐.2	14 ♈.5	21 ♌.7	0 ♐.8	8 ♉.9	15 ♎.2	21 ♒.3	1 ♊.5	8 ♏.5	15 ♓.9	22 ♌.0	1 ♐.2	9 ♉.2
12	2 ♌.3	10 ♑.4	16 ♉.7	23 ♏.7	3 ♒.0	10 ♋.1	17 ♏.4	24 ♓.4	3 ♋.8	11 ♐.8	18 ♉.0	24 ♏.0	4 ♑.5	11 ♊.5

MOON 1959–1986

	1959	1960	1961	1962	1963	1964	1965	1966	1967	1968	1969	1970	1971	1972
1	3 ♏.5	10 ♒.1	17 ♊.8	24 ♎.8	3 ♓.2	10 ♋.8	18 ♐.5	25 ♈.5	4 ♌.9	11 ♑.5	18 ♊.1	25 ♎.1	5 ♒.7	11 ♋.2
2	6 ♏.2	13 ♓.8	21 ♌.3	0 ♐.4	7 ♉.0	14 ♏.4	21 ♑.9	1 ♊.0	7 ♎.7	14 ♓.1	22 ♋.6	1 ♏.7	8 ♈.5	15 ♌.8
3	7 ♏.6	14 ♈.5	21 ♌.6	1 ♐.7	7 ♉.3	15 ♎.1	22 ♒.2	1 ♊.3	8 ♏.1	16 ♓.8	22 ♋.9	2 ♐.1	8 ♈.8	16 ♏.5
4	10 ♑.3	18 ♊.0	25 ♎.1	4 ♒.3	11 ♋.1	18 ♏.6	25 ♓.7	5 ♌.1	11 ♐.8	19 ♉.3	26 ♍.4	5 ♒.8	12 ♊.5	20 ♍.0
5	13 ♒.6	20 ♋.0	0 ♏.2	6 ♓.6	13 ♌.3	21 ♐.7	0 ♈.9	7 ♍.4	14 ♑.9	21 ♊.4	1 ♎.6	8 ♓.1	14 ♋.6	22 ♐.1
6	16 ♈.1	24 ♌.5	3 ♐.9	10 ♉.4	17 ♏.8	24 ♒.2	4 ♊.6	10 ♏.1	17 ♓.5	25 ♋.9	4 ♐.3	11 ♈.8	18 ♏.1	25 ♑.6
7	18 ♉.2	26 ♍.6	5 ♒.2	12 ♊.7	19 ♎.9	0 ♓.3	6 ♋.9	13 ♐.4	20 ♈.5	0 ♏.0	7 ♑.6	13 ♊.1	20 ♎.2	1 ♒.8
8	22 ♊.7	2 ♏.3	9 ♑.9	16 ♌.3	22 ♐.3	3 ♉.0	10 ♍.7	16 ♓.9	23 ♈.0	3 ♎.7	10 ♏.4	17 ♋.6	24 ♏.6	4 ♈.5
9	25 ♌.2	6 ♑.0	12 ♉.7	19 ♍.8	26 ♑.8	6 ♊.8	13 ♏.4	20 ♓.4	0 ♋.5	7 ♐.5	14 ♉.0	20 ♏.1	0 ♑.2	7 ♊.3
10	0 ♍.3	8 ♒.3	15 ♊.8	21 ♎.8	1 ♓.0	9 ♌.1	15 ♐.5	22 ♈.5	1 ♌.7	9 ♑.8	16 ♊.1	23 ♎.2	2 ♒.4	10 ♋.5
11	4 ♏.0	11 ♈.1	18 ♌.3	25 ♐.4	4 ♈.7	12 ♏.8	19 ♒.0	25 ♊.0	5 ♎.4	13 ♓.5	19 ♋.6	26 ♏.7	6 ♈.1	13 ♏.2
12	6 ♐.3	14 ♉.2	21 ♍.4	0 ♑.5	7 ♊.0	14 ♏.0	21 ♓.0	1 ♋.2	7 ♏.7	15 ♈.6	22 ♉.7	1 ♐.9	8 ♉.4	16 ♍.3

1945	1946	1947	1948	1949	1950	1951	1952	1953	1954	1955	1956	1957	1958
15 ♌.1	22 ♐.2	1 ♈.3	8 ♏.0	15 ♑.8	22 ♉.8	2 ♎.0	8 ♒.7	16 ♋.4	23 ♏.5	2 ♓.7	9 ♌.4	17 ♑.1	23 ♉.2
18 ♍.6	25 ♑.7	4 ♉.0	11 ♎.7	19 ♓.3	26 ♋.4	5 ♏.7	12 ♈.4	19 ♌.9	26 ♑.0	6 ♉.5	12 ♎.1	20 ♒.6	0 ♊.7
19 ♍.9	25 ♒.0	5 ♊.4	13 ♍.5	19 ♓.5	26 ♋.6	5 ♐.1	13 ♉.1	20 ♍.2	0 ♑.3	6 ♉.9	14 ♎.8	21 ♒.9	0 ♋.0
22 ♏.3	2 ♓.6	8 ♌.1	16 ♑.0	23 ♉.0	2 ♏.3	9 ♑.9	17 ♊.7	23 ♎.7	3 ♒.9	9 ♋.6	17 ♐.3	24 ♈.4	3 ♌.6
25 ♐.5	4 ♈.8	11 ♍.4	18 ♒.1	25 ♊.1	5 ♐.5	13 ♈.1	19 ♋.7	26 ♏.8	5 ♓.2	12 ♌.9	20 ♑.4	0 ♉.5	6 ♍.9
1 ♒.0	7 ♉.6	14 ♏.1	22 ♓.5	1 ♋.8	8 ♐.3	15 ♈.8	22 ♍.2	2 ♑.5	9 ♈.0	15 ♎.4	23 ♒.8	2 ♊.2	9 ♍.7
3 ♓.3	10 ♋.9	17 ♐.2	24 ♈.6	4 ♍.0	10 ♑.6	17 ♉.9	25 ♎.3	4 ♒.8	11 ♋.3	18 ♏.5	23 ♉.9	5 ♌.5	12 ♑.0
6 ♉.1	13 ♍.6	20 ♑.7	0 ♊.2	7 ♎.8	14 ♓.2	21 ♋.4	1 ♏.9	8 ♈.5	14 ♌.9	21 ♑.0	2 ♉.6	8 ♍.3	15 ♒.6
10 ♊.8	17 ♏.1	23 ♓.2	4 ♋.9	11 ♐.6	17 ♈.8	24 ♌.8	4 ♑.6	11 ♉.3	18 ♍.4	25 ♒.5	5 ♋.3	12 ♐.0	18 ♈.1
12 ♌.1	19 ♐.2	26 ♈.3	6 ♍.2	13 ♑.8	20 ♉.0	0 ♎.0	7 ♒.9	14 ♋.5	20 ♏.5	0 ♓.7	7 ♌.6	14 ♑.1	21 ♉.2
16 ♍.6	22 ♑.6	2 ♉.9	10 ♎.9	16 ♓.3	23 ♋.3	2 ♏.7	10 ♈.6	17 ♍.0	24 ♑.0	3 ♉.4	11 ♎.3	18 ♒.6	24 ♊.7
18 ♎.7	25 ♒.7	4 ♋.2	12 ♐.2	19 ♈.4	26 ♌.4	5 ♐.9	13 ♉.9	19 ♎.0	26 ♒.1	6 ♊.6	13 ♍.6	20 ♓.7	0 ♋.8

1973	1974	1975	1976	1977	1978	1979	1980	1981	1982	1983	1984	1985	1986
19 ♍.8	26 ♓.8	5 ♌.4	12 ♐.8	20 ♉.5	0 ♏.5	6 ♒.1	13 ♊.6	20 ♍.1	0 ♓.2	6 ♋.8	13 ♐.3	21 ♈.8	0 ♍.0
22 ♑.3	2 ♉.4	9 ♎.2	15 ♒.4	23 ♊.9	3 ♏.2	9 ♓.9	16 ♋.1	24 ♐.6	3 ♈.9	10 ♍.6	17 ♑.8	24 ♊.3	4 ♎.6
23 ♑.5	2 ♉.8	9 ♎.5	17 ♓.2	24 ♋.2	3 ♏.5	10 ♈.1	17 ♌.8	24 ♐.9	4 ♉.3	10 ♍.8	18 ♒.5	25 ♊.5	4 ♎.0
0 ♓.1	6 ♋.5	13 ♐.1	20 ♈.6	0 ♍.7	6 ♑.3	13 ♉.8	21 ♎.3	0 ♒.4	7 ♋.0	14 ♏.5	21 ♉.9	1 ♌.1	8 ♐.8
1 ♈.3	8 ♌.8	15 ♑.3	23 ♉.7	2 ♏.9	9 ♒.6	16 ♊.9	23 ♍.4	3 ♓.6	9 ♋.6	16 ♐.6	24 ♈.1	3 ♍.3	10 ♒.1
5 ♊.0	12 ♎.6	18 ♒.8	26 ♋.3	5 ♏.7	12 ♈.3	19 ♌.4	0 ♑.0	6 ♉.4	13 ♎.0	20 ♒.1	0 ♊.7	7 ♍.1	13 ♓.7
7 ♋.3	14 ♏.8	21 ♓.8	1 ♌.5	8 ♑.0	15 ♉.0	18 ♏.5	2 ♒.2	9 ♊.7	15 ♍.2	22 ♓.2	2 ♋.9	9 ♐.4	16 ♈.8
11 ♍.0	17 ♑.3	24 ♉.3	5 ♎.2	11 ♒.7	18 ♋.0	25 ♏.0	5 ♓.9	12 ♋.4	19 ♐.6	25 ♈.7	6 ♍.7	13 ♒.1	19 ♊.3
14 ♎.7	21 ♒.8	0 ♊.9	8 ♐.0	15 ♈.4	21 ♌.5	1 ♐.6	9 ♉.7	15 ♎.0	22 ♒.1	1 ♊.3	9 ♍.5	16 ♓.7	23 ♋.8
17 ♏.8	23 ♓.9	3 ♋.1	10 ♑.3	17 ♉.5	24 ♏.5	3 ♑.8	11 ♋.0	18 ♍.1	24 ♒.2	4 ♋.5	12 ♐.7	18 ♈.8	25 ♌.9
20 ♑.3	0 ♉.4	6 ♍.8	14 ♒.9	21 ♊.9	0 ♏.1	7 ♓.6	14 ♋.6	21 ♐.6	1 ♈.8	7 ♍.3	15 ♒.3	22 ♊.3	1 ♎.5
22 ♒.3	2 ♊.6	9 ♍.1	16 ♈.0	23 ♌.0	2 ♐.3	9 ♈.8	17 ♍.7	24 ♑.7	3 ♉.0	10 ♎.6	17 ♓.3	24 ♋.4	4 ♏.7

MOON 1987–1998

	1987	1988	1989	1990	1991	1992	1993	1994	1995	1996	1997	1998
1	7 ♑.5	14 ♊.0	21 ♎.4	1 ♒.7	8 ♋.2	14 ♏.7	22 ♈.1	2 ♌.4	8 ♐.9	15 ♉.4	23 ♏.8	2 ♒.1
2	10 ♓.3	17 ♋.5	25 ♏.9	4 ♈.4	11 ♌.9	18 ♑.2	26 ♉.6	5 ♎.1	12 ♒.6	18 ♊.8	26 ♏.3	6 ♓.9
3	11 ♓.5	19 ♌.2	25 ♐.2	5 ♈.7	11 ♏.2	19 ♑.9	26 ♉.9	5 ♎.5	12 ♒.9	20 ♋.5	0 ♏.6	6 ♈.2
4	14 ♉.1	22 ♍.7	1 ♑.8	8 ♉.5	15 ♎.8	23 ♓.3	2 ♋.5	9 ♐.2	16 ♈.5	23 ♏.0	3 ♑.2	9 ♉.9
5	17 ♊.3	24 ♎.8	4 ♒.0	11 ♋.8	17 ♏.9	25 ♈.4	4 ♌.8	11 ♑.5	18 ♉.6	26 ♎.1	5 ♒.5	12 ♋.2
6	20 ♋.7	1 ♐.4	7 ♈.8	14 ♏.4	21 ♑.4	1 ♊.1	8 ♎.6	15 ♓.1	21 ♋.1	2 ♏.7	8 ♈.3	15 ♌.7
7	23 ♌.8	3 ♑.6	10 ♊.1	16 ♎.5	23 ♒.5	4 ♋.3	10 ♏.8	17 ♈.2	24 ♌.2	4 ♑.0	11 ♉.6	18 ♏.8
8	26 ♎.3	6 ♓.4	13 ♋.8	20 ♐.0	0 ♈.0	7 ♏.1	14 ♑.5	20 ♉.6	0 ♍.8	8 ♒.8	14 ♋.2	21 ♏.3
9	2 ♐.0	10 ♉.2	17 ♍.4	23 ♑.4	3 ♉.7	10 ♎.8	17 ♓.0	24 ♋.1	3 ♍.4	11 ♈.5	18 ♌.7	24 ♐.7
10	5 ♑.3	12 ♊.4	19 ♎.5	26 ♒.5	5 ♋.0	13 ♐.0	20 ♈.1	26 ♌.2	6 ♐.7	13 ♉.7	20 ♏.8	0 ♑.9
11	8 ♓.0	16 ♋.9	22 ♏.9	2 ♈.2	9 ♌.8	16 ♑.6	23 ♉.6	2 ♍.8	9 ♒.5	17 ♋.2	24 ♏.3	3 ♓.5
12	10 ♈.3	18 ♍.0	25 ♑.1	4 ♉.4	11 ♎.0	19 ♒.6	25 ♊.7	5 ♏.1	12 ♓.8	19 ♌.3	26 ♐.4	5 ♈.8

MOON 1999–2010

	1999	2000	2001	2002	2003	2004	2005	2006	2007	2008	2009	2010
1	9 ♊.6	16 ♏.0	23 ♓.4	3 ♋.8	9 ♐.3	16 ♈.7	24 ♏.1	3 ♑.5	10 ♊.0	17 ♎.4	25 ♒.8	4 ♋.2
2	12 ♌.3	19 ♐.5	0 ♉.0	6 ♍.6	13 ♒.0	20 ♊.2	0 ♎.7	7 ♓.3	13 ♋.7	20 ♏.8	1 ♈.4	7 ♏.0
3	13 ♌.6	20 ♑.8	0 ♉.3	7 ♍.9	13 ♒.3	21 ♊.8	0 ♏.0	7 ♓.6	14 ♌.0	22 ♐.5	1 ♈.7	8 ♏.2
4	16 ♎.2	24 ♒.6	3 ♋.0	10 ♍.6	17 ♓.9	24 ♌.3	4 ♐.7	11 ♉.3	17 ♏.5	25 ♒.0	4 ♊.4	11 ♍.0
5	19 ♏.3	26 ♓.8	6 ♌.2	12 ♐.8	19 ♉.0	0 ♍.4	6 ♒.0	13 ♊.5	20 ♎.6	0 ♓.1	7 ♋.7	14 ♐.2
6	22 ♐.8	2 ♉.4	9 ♎.0	16 ♒.4	23 ♊.4	3 ♏.1	10 ♓.8	16 ♌.1	23 ♐.1	4 ♈.8	10 ♏.5	17 ♑.7
7	24 ♑.9	5 ♉.7	12 ♏.3	18 ♓.5	25 ♋.6	5 ♐.4	12 ♉.0	19 ♏.1	26 ♑.2	6 ♊.1	13 ♎.7	19 ♒.8
8	0 ♓.5	8 ♌.5	15 ♐.9	22 ♈.9	1 ♏.2	9 ♒.2	16 ♊.6	22 ♎.6	2 ♒.9	9 ♋.9	16 ♐.3	23 ♓.3
9	4 ♉.2	12 ♎.2	18 ♒.4	25 ♊.4	5 ♎.9	12 ♓.9	19 ♌.1	26 ♐.1	5 ♈.6	13 ♏.6	20 ♑.7	26 ♉.8
10	6 ♊.5	14 ♏.4	21 ♓.5	0 ♋.6	7 ♐.2	15 ♉.0	21 ♏.2	1 ♑.3	8 ♊.9	15 ♎.7	22 ♒.8	1 ♋.0
11	10 ♌.3	17 ♐.9	24 ♉.0	4 ♍.2	10 ♒.0	18 ♊.6	25 ♎.7	4 ♓.0	11 ♋.7	19 ♐.2	25 ♈.3	5 ♌.7
12	12 ♍.5	20 ♒.0	0 ♊.1	6 ♎.5	13 ♓.2	20 ♋.6	0 ♏.8	7 ♈.2	13 ♌.9	21 ♑.3	1 ♉.5	7 ♎.0

FINDING THE MOON'S POSITION

The Moon moves fast, travelling through a complete sign of the zodiac every 2.5 days. Our tables – based on noon, GMT – are designed to be used in conjunction with the Lunar and Zodiac paths *(right)*.

STEP ONE
Look to the Moon tables, and locate the year and month in question (such as the year and month of your birth). For each month, you will find a Lunar Cycle Number (LCN) and a Zodiac Path expressed in tenths of a zodiac.

STEP TWO
You now need to find out how far the Moon travelled from the start of the month until the birth date in question, for which you'll need to use the Lunar Cycle Path. Take a piece of paper and place one corner on the month's LCN (given by the table), then mark the edge of the paper at the point where it reaches the birth date (i.e. LCN + birth date).

Note: the tables are set for noon; if you know your birth time to be earlier of later than noon, you can make an approximate allowance for this.

STEP THREE
You now need to apply the distance arrived at in step two to the Zodiac Path. Place the corner of the paper on the Zodiac Path at the degree of sign given by the table. Now read off the position on the path at the point where it matches up to your mark on the paper. This is the sign the Moon was in for the birth date (and time) in question. The shaded sections indicate whether it was the first, second, or third part of the sign – information that can be applied when drawing up a birth chart.

EXAMPLE FOR 6PM ON 15 JUNE 1979

1 The LCN for that month is 19, and the Zodiac Path is .4 of the way through Leo.

2 Put the corner of the paper against 19, and mark it at 34 (19 + 15, since the birth date is the 15th). However, allow for the quarter of a day which passed between noon and 6 pm – so the mark is at 34.25. You have marked off the distance between 19 and 34.25.

3 Using the Zodiac Path Line, put the corner of the paper to the .4 point within Leo, and read off the result against your mark on the paper. The Moon at the birth day and time was in the first third of Pisces (the unshaded part of the sign).

LUNAR CYCLE PATH — ZODIAC PATH

0 1 2 3 4 5 6 7 8 9 10 11 12 13 14 15 16 17 18 19 20 21 22 23 24 25 26 27 28 29 30 31 32 33 34 35 36 37 38 39 40 41 42 43 44 45 46 47 48 49 50 51 52 53 54 55 56 57 58

MERCURY 1931–1942

	1931	1932	1933	1934	1935	1936
1	1 2 10 26 ♑ ♑ ♑ ♑	1 15 22 29 ✗ ♑ ♑ ♑	1 8 15 22 28 ✗ ♑ ♑ ♑ ≈	1 2 8 14 20 26 ✗ ♑ ♑ ♑ ≈ ≈	1 7 13 19 25 ♑ ♑ ≈ ≈ ≈	1 6 13 ♑ ≈ ≈
2	1 4 12 18 25 ♑ ♑ ≈ ≈ ≈	1 5 11 17 23 28 ♑ ≈ ≈ ≈ H H	1 3 9 14 20 25 ≈ ≈ H H H	1 7 13 23 27 H H H H H	1 15 25 H ≈ ≈	1 2 27 ≈ ≈
3	1 3 8 14 19 24 29 ≈ H H ♈ ♈ ♈ ♈	1 5 10 15 22 H H ♈ ♈ ♈ ♈	1 3 26 H ♈ H	1 11 29 H H	1 7 19 27 H H H	1 6 13 20 26 31 ≈ ≈ H H ♈ ♈
4	1 4 12 29 ♈ ♉ ♉ ♉	1 11 ♈ ♈	1 18 27 H ♈ ♈	1 8 15 22 27 H H ♈ ♈ ♈	1 3 9 14 20 25 29 H H ♈ ♈ ♈ ♉ ♉	1 5 10 15 20 25 ♈ ♈ ♈ ♉ ♉ ♉
5	1 27 ♉ ♉	1 7 16 23 29 ♈ ♈ ♉ ♉ ♉	1 4 10 16 21 26 30 ♈ ♉ ♉ ♉ ♊ ♊	1 3 8 12 17 22 27 ♉ ♉ ♉ ♊ ♊ ♊	1 4 9 14 21 30 ♉ ♊ ♊ ♊ ♊ ⊚	1 10 31 ♊ ♊ ♊
6	1 5 11 17 22 27 ♉ ♉ ♊ ♊ ♊ ⊚	1 3 8 12 17 22 27 ♉ ♊ ♊ ♊ ⊚ ⊚	1 4 9 14 20 27 ♊ ♊ ⊚ ⊚ ⊚ ♌	1 8 18 ⊚ ⊚ ⊚	1 21 ⊚ ⊚	1 24 ♊ ♊
7	1 6 11 16 22 29 ⊚ ⊚ ♌ ♌ ♌ ♍	1 2 9 16 28 ⊚ ♌ ♌ ♌ ♌	1 7 26 ♌ ♌	1 9 ⊚ ⊚	1 14 22 28 ⊚ ♌ ♌ ♌	1 3 9 14 19 24 28 ♊ ⊚ ⊚ ♌ ♌ ♌ ♌
8	1 6 ♍ ♍	1 10 24 31 ♍ ♌ ♌ ♌	1 22 28 ♌ ♌	1 2 10 15 20 25 30 ⊚ ♌ ♌ ♌ ♌ ♍ ♍	1 2 7 12 17 22 28 ♌ ♌ ♍ ♍ ♍ ♍ ≏	1 3 8 14 20 28 ♌ ♌ ♍ ♍ ♍ ≏
9	1 7 22 29 ♍ ♍ ♍ ♍	1 9 15 21 26 ♌ ♍ ♍ ♍	1 2 7 13 18 24 30 ♌ ♍ ♍ ♍ ≏ ≏ ≏	1 5 10 17 23 ♍ ≏ ≏ ≏	1 3 10 18 29 ♍ ≏ ♍ ♍	1 6 29 ≏ ≏ ≏
10	1 5 10 16 22 28 ♍ ≏ ≏ ♍ ♍ ♍	1 2 8 14 20 27 ≏ ≏ ♍ ♍ ♍ ♍	1 7 14 21 30 ♍ ♍ ♍ ✗	1 9 ♍ ♍	1 13 22 ♍ ≏	1 21 27 ≏ ≏
11	1 4 10 17 24 ♍ ♍ ✗ ✗ ✗	1 3 11 22 27 ♍ ✗ ✗ ✗ ✗	1 16 25 ✗ ♍	1 3 22 30 ♍ ♍ ✗	1 2 10 17 23 29 ≏ ♍ ♍ ♍ ✗	1 2 9 15 21 29 ≏ ♍ ♍ ✗ ✗
12	1 2 20 ✗ ♑ ✗	1 6 24 ✗ ✗ ✗	1 2 12 19 26 ♍ ♍ ✗ ✗	1 6 13 19 26 ♍ ✗ ✗ ✗ ♑	1 6 12 18 25 31 ✗ ✗ ♑ ♑ ♑ ♑	1 4 10 17 24 ✗ ✗ ♑ ♑ ♑

MERCURY 1943–1954

	1943	1944	1945	1946	1947	1948
1	1 3 13 19 28 ♑ ≈ ≈ ≈ ♑	1 7 16 25 ♑ ♑ ♑ ♑	1 14 22 30 ♑ ♑ ♑	1 2 10 16 23 29 ✗ ✗ ♑ ♑ ♑ ≈	1 3 10 16 22 28 ✗ ♑ ♑ ♑ ≈ ≈	1 2 8 14 20 26 ♑ ♑ ♑ ≈ ≈ ≈
2	1 16 25 ♑ ≈ ≈	1 5 13 20 26 ♑ ≈ ≈ ≈	1 5 12 18 23 ♑ ≈ ≈ ≈ H	1 4 10 16 21 26 ≈ ≈ ≈ H H H	1 2 8 14 21 ≈ ≈ ≈ H H	1 2 20 ≈ H ≈
3	1 5 11 17 23 28 ≈ ≈ H H H ♈	1 3 9 14 19 24 29 ≈ H H ♈ ♈ ♈ ♈	1 6 11 17 23 H ≈ ♈ ♈ ♈	1 4 15 19 H ♈ ♈ ♈	1 6 18 26 H H H ♈	1 18 27 ≈ H ♈
4	1 3 7 12 17 23 ♈ ♈ ♈ ♉ ♉ ♉	1 4 11 ♈ ♉ ♉	1 18 ♈ ♈	1 2 17 28 ♈ H ♈ ♈	1 8 16 23 29 ♈ H ♈ ♈ ♈	1 3 9 15 20 25 30 ♈ ♈ ♈ ♉ ♉ ♉ ♉
5	1 26 ♊ ♉	1 6 25 ♉ ♉ ♉	1 6 17 24 30 ♈ ♉ ♉ ♉ ♉	1 5 12 17 22 27 ♈ ♉ ♉ ♉ ♊ ♊	1 4 9 14 19 23 28 ♈ ♉ ♉ ♉ ♊ ♊ ♊	1 4 9 14 20 28 ♉ ♉ ♉ ♊ ♊ ♊ ⊚
6	1 14 24 ♉ ♊ ♊	1 4 11 17 22 27 ♉ ♉ ♊ ♊ ♊ ⊚	1 4 9 14 19 23 28 ♉ ♊ ♊ ♊ ⊚ ⊚ ⊚	1 5 10 15 21 28 ♊ ♊ ♊ ⊚ ⊚ ♌	1 3 9 17 ♊ ♊ ♊ ⊚	1 29 ⊚ ♊
7	1 6 11 16 21 26 31 ♊ ⊚ ⊚ ♌ ♌ ♌ ♌	1 2 6 11 17 22 29 ⊚ ⊚ ♌ ♌ ♌ ♌ ♍	1 4 10 17 27 ♊ ⊚ ♌ ♌ ♌	1 7 ♍ ♍	1 17 ⊚ ⊚	1 12 22 28 ♊ ⊚ ⊚ ⊚
8	1 5 12 19 27 ♌ ♍ ♍ ♍ ≏	1 6 17 31 ♍ ♍ ♍ ♍	1 17 ♍ ♍	1 2 22 29 ♍ ♍ ♍	1 2 11 17 22 27 ⊚ ♌ ♌ ♌ ♌ ♍	1 3 7 12 17 23 28 ⊚ ♌ ♌ ♌ ♍ ♍ ♍
9	1 25 ≏ ♍	1 12 21 29 ♍ ♍ ♍ ♍	1 10 17 22 28 ♍ ≏ ♍ ♍ ≏	1 4 9 14 20 25 ♍ ≏ ♍ ♍ ♍ ≏	1 6 12 18 25 ♍ ≏ ♍ ♍ ♍	1 4 10 18 27 ♍ ♍ ≏ ♍ ♍
10	1 12 19 25 31 ♍ ≏ ≏ ♍ ♍	1 5 11 17 22 29 ♍ ≏ ≏ ≏ ♍ ♍	1 3 9 15 21 28 ♍ ♍ ♍ ≏ ♍ ♍	1 8 15 22 30 ≏ ♍ ♍ ♍ ✗	1 2 10 21 30 ♍ ≏ ♍ ♍ ♍	1 17 27 31 ♍ ≏ ≏ ≏
11	1 6 12 19 25 ♍ ♍ ♍ ✗ ✗	1 4 10 17 24 ♍ ♍ ✗ ✗	1 4 11 21 ♍ ✗ ✗ ✗	1 21 ♍ ♍	1 8 23 ✗ ♍	1 10 17 23 30 ♍ ♍ ≏ ≏
12	1 8 15 23 ✗ ♑ ♑ ♑	1 2 24 ✗ ♑	1 3 11 24 ✗ ✗ ✗	1 13 21 27 ♍ ✗ ✗	1 8 14 21 27 ♍ ✗ ✗ ♑	1 6 12 19 25 31 ✗ ✗ ♑ ♑ ♑ ♑

Top table — 1937–1942

1937
1	2	10	18		
♑	♒	♑	♑		

| 1 | 5 | 14 | 22 | 28 | |
| ♑ | ♒ | ♒ | ♒ | ♒ | |

| 1 | 7 | 12 | 18 | 23 | 28 |
| ♒ | ♓ | ♓ | ♓ | ♈ | ♈ |

| 1 | 2 | 7 | 13 | 21 | |
| ♈ | ♉ | ♉ | ♉ | | |

| 1 | 12 | | | | |
| ♉ | ♉ | | | | |

| 1 | 5 | 14 | 21 | 26 | |
| ♉ | ♊ | ♊ | ♊ | | |

| 1 | 6 | 10 | 15 | 20 | 26 |
| ♋ | ♋ | ♋ | ♌ | ♌ | ♌ |

| 1 | 8 | 16 | | | |
| ♍ | ♍ | ♍ | | | |

| 1 | 16 | | | | |
| ♍ | ♍ | | | | |

| 1 | 8 | 14 | 20 | 26 | |
| ♍ | ♎ | ♎ | ♏ | | |

| 1 | 7 | 14 | 20 | 27 | |
| ♏ | ♏ | ♐ | ♐ | | |

| 1 | 4 | 12 | 29 | | |
| ♐ | ♑ | ♑ | ♑ | | |

1938
1	7	13	25		
♑	♐	♑	♑		

| 1 | 2 | 9 | 15 | 21 | 27 |
| ♑ | ♒ | ♒ | ♒ | ♒ | ♓ |

| 1 | 5 | 10 | 15 | 20 | 26 |
| ♓ | ♓ | ♓ | ♈ | ♈ | ♈ |

| 1 | 2 | 24 | | | |
| ♈ | ♈ | ♉ | | | |

| 1 | 17 | 26 | | | |
| ♈ | ♉ | ♉ | | | |

| 1 | 2 | 8 | 13 | 18 | 23 | 27 |
| ♉ | ♊ | ♊ | ♊ | ♊ | ♋ | ♋ |

| 1 | 2 | 7 | 13 | 19 | 27 |
| ♋ | ♋ | ♌ | ♌ | ♌ | ♍ |

| 1 | 7 | 22 | | | |
| ♍ | ♍ | ♍ | | | |

| 1 | 7 | 13 | 19 | 25 | 31 |
| ♍ | ♎ | ♎ | ♏ | ♏ | ♏ |

| 1 | 7 | 14 | 22 | | |
| ♏ | ♏ | ♐ | ♐ | | |

| 1 | 16 | | | | |
| ♐ | ♐ | | | | |

| 1 | | | | | |
| ♐ | ♑ | ♑ | | | |

1939
1	4	12	20	26	
♐	♑	♑	♑	♑	

| 1 | 2 | 8 | 14 | 19 | 25 |
| ♑ | ♒ | ♒ | ♒ | ♓ | ♓ |

| 1 | 2 | 7 | 14 | | |
| ♓ | ♈ | ♈ | ♈ | | |

| 1 | 7 | 28 | | | |
| ♈ | ♈ | ♈ | | | |

| 1 | 7 | 15 | 21 | 26 | 31 |
| ♈ | ♈ | ♉ | ♉ | ♉ | ♊ |

| 1 | 5 | 9 | 14 | 19 | 24 | 30 |
| ♊ | ♊ | ♊ | ♋ | ♋ | ♋ | ♌ |

| 1 | 7 | 17 | | | |
| ♌ | ♌ | | | | |

| 1 | 7 | | | | |
| ♌ | ♌ | | | | |

| 1 | 7 | 13 | 18 | 23 | 29 |
| ♌ | ♍ | ♍ | ♍ | ♎ | ♎ |

| 1 | 5 | 11 | 18 | 25 | |
| ♎ | ♎ | ♏ | ♏ | ♏ | |

| 1 | 10 | 25 | | | |
| ♏ | ♏ | ♏ | | | |

| 1 | 3 | 14 | 23 | 30 | |
| ♐ | ♏ | ♐ | ♐ | ♐ | |

1940
1	6	13	19	25	31
♐	♑	♑	♑	♑	♒

| 1 | 6 | 12 | 17 | | |
| ♒ | ♓ | ♓ | ♓ | | |

| 1 | 4 | 8 | 21 | | |
| ♓ | ♓ | ♓ | ♈ | | |

| 1 | 7 | 17 | 25 | | |
| ♈ | ♓ | ♈ | ♈ | | |

| 1 | 7 | 12 | 17 | 22 | 26 | 31 |
| ♈ | ♉ | ♉ | ♉ | ♉ | ♊ | ♊ |

| 1 | 5 | 11 | 17 | 27 | |
| ♊ | ♋ | ♋ | ♋ | ♌ | |

| 1 | 21 | | | | |
| ♌ | ♋ | | | | |

| 1 | 12 | 19 | 24 | 29 | |
| ♋ | ♌ | ♌ | ♌ | ♍ | |

| 1 | 4 | 9 | 14 | 20 | 24 |
| ♌ | ♍ | ♍ | ♎ | ♎ | ♎ |

| 1 | 4 | 11 | 19 | | |
| ♏ | ♏ | ♏ | ♏ | | |

| 1 | 12 | | | | |
| ♏ | ♏ | | | | |

| 1 | 2 | 10 | 16 | 23 | 29 |
| ♏ | ♏ | ♐ | ♐ | ♐ | ♑ |

1941
1	5	11	17	23	29
♑	♑	♑	♒	♒	♒

| 1 | 4 | 11 | 24 | | |
| ♒ | ♓ | ♓ | ♓ | | |

| 1 | 7 | 17 | 29 | | |
| ♓ | ♒ | ♓ | ♓ | | |

| 1 | 6 | 12 | 18 | 24 | 29 |
| ♓ | ♓ | ♈ | ♈ | ♈ | ♉ |

| 1 | 4 | 8 | 13 | 18 | 23 | 30 |
| ♉ | ♉ | ♉ | ♊ | ♊ | ♊ | ♋ |

| 1 | 7 | | | | |
| ♋ | ♋ | | | | |

| 1 | 4 | 23 | 31 | | |
| ♋ | ♋ | ♋ | ♋ | | |

| 1 | 6 | 11 | 16 | 21 | 26 |
| ♋ | ♌ | ♌ | ♌ | ♍ | ♍ |

| 1 | 7 | 13 | 20 | 28 | |
| ♍ | ♎ | ♎ | ♎ | ♏ | |

| 1 | 9 | 21 | 30 | | |
| ♏ | ♏ | ♏ | ♏ | | |

| 1 | 12 | 20 | 27 | | |
| ♏ | ♏ | ♏ | ♏ | | |

| 1 | 3 | 9 | 16 | 22 | 28 |
| ♏ | ♐ | ♐ | ♐ | ♑ | ♑ |

1942
1	4	10	16	23	
♑	♑	♒	♒	♒	

| 1 | 10 | | | | |
| ♒ | | | | | |

| 1 | 9 | 17 | 24 | 30 | |
| ♒ | ♒ | ♓ | ♓ | ♓ | |

| 1 | 5 | 11 | 16 | 21 | 25 | 30 |
| ♓ | ♈ | ♈ | ♈ | ♈ | ♉ | ♉ |

| 1 | 5 | 11 | 20 | | |
| ♉ | ♊ | ♊ | ♊ | | |

| 1 | 15 | | | | |
| ♊ | ♊ | | | | |

| 1 | 3 | 13 | 19 | 24 | 29 |
| ♊ | ♊ | ♋ | ♋ | ♋ | ♌ |

| 1 | 3 | 8 | 13 | 19 | 25 | 31 |
| ♌ | ♌ | ♌ | ♍ | ♍ | ♍ | ♎ |

| 1 | 8 | 17 | | | |
| ♎ | ♎ | | | | |

| 1 | 9 | 31 | | | |
| ♎ | ♎ | | | | |

| 1 | 7 | 13 | 20 | 26 | |
| ♎ | ♏ | ♏ | ♏ | ♏ | |

| 1 | 2 | 9 | 15 | 21 | 28 |
| ♐ | ♐ | ♐ | ♑ | ♑ | ♑ |

Bottom table — 1949–1954

1949
1	6	13	23	26	
♑	♒	♒	♒	♒	

| 1 | 6 | 26 | | | |
| ♒ | ♒ | ♒ | | | |

| 1 | 7 | 14 | 21 | 27 | |
| ♒ | ♒ | ♓ | ♓ | ♈ | |

| 1 | 2 | 7 | 12 | 17 | 21 | 26 |
| ♓ | ♈ | ♈ | ♈ | ♉ | ♉ | ♉ |

| 1 | 2 | 10 | | | |
| ♉ | ♊ | ♊ | | | |

| 1 | 10 | 22 | | | |
| ♊ | ♊ | ♊ | | | |

| 1 | 3 | 10 | 16 | 21 | 25 | 30 |
| ♊ | ♊ | ♋ | ♋ | ♋ | ♌ | ♌ |

| 1 | 4 | 9 | 15 | 22 | 29 |
| ♌ | ♍ | ♍ | ♍ | ♎ | |

| 1 | 6 | | | | |
| ♎ | | | | | |

| 1 | 4 | 22 | 29 | | |
| ♎ | ♎ | ♎ | | | |

| 1 | 4 | 10 | 16 | 22 | 29 |
| ♎ | ♏ | ♏ | ♏ | ♐ | |

| 1 | 5 | 12 | 18 | 25 | |
| ♐ | ♐ | ♑ | ♑ | ♑ | |

1950
1	2	15	24		
♑	♒	♑	♑		

| 1 | 4 | 15 | 23 | | |
| ♑ | ♑ | ♒ | ♒ | | |

| 1 | 2 | 8 | 14 | 19 | 25 | 30 |
| ♒ | ♒ | ♓ | ♓ | ♈ | ♈ | ♈ |

| 1 | 4 | 8 | 14 | 21 | |
| ♈ | ♈ | ♉ | ♉ | ♉ | |

| 1 | 21 | | | | |
| ♉ | ♉ | | | | |

| 1 | 3 | 15 | 22 | 28 | |
| ♉ | ♊ | ♊ | ♊ | ♊ | |

| 1 | 3 | 7 | 12 | 17 | 22 | 27 |
| ♊ | ♋ | ♋ | ♋ | ♌ | ♌ | ♌ |

| 1 | 2 | 9 | 17 | 28 | |
| ♌ | ♍ | ♍ | ♍ | | |

| 1 | 11 | 21 | | | |
| ♍ | ♍ | ♍ | | | |

| 1 | 10 | 16 | 22 | 27 | |
| ♍ | ♎ | ♎ | ♎ | ♏ | |

| 1 | 3 | 9 | 15 | 22 | 28 |
| ♏ | ♏ | ♏ | ♐ | ♐ | ♐ |

| 1 | 5 | 13 | | | |
| ♐ | ♑ | ♑ | | | |

1951
1	2	25			
♑	♑	♑			

| 1 | 3 | 10 | 16 | 23 | |
| ♑ | ♑ | ♒ | ♒ | ♒ | |

| 1 | 6 | 11 | 16 | 22 | 27 |
| ♒ | ♓ | ♓ | ♈ | ♈ | ♈ |

| 1 | 2 | | | | |
| ♈ | ♉ | | | | |

| 1 | 2 | 15 | 27 | | |
| ♉ | ♈ | ♉ | ♉ | | |

| 1 | 9 | 15 | 20 | 24 | 29 |
| ♉ | ♊ | ♊ | ♊ | ♊ | ♋ |

| 1 | 3 | 9 | 14 | 20 | 28 |
| ♋ | ♋ | ♋ | ♌ | ♌ | ♌ |

| 1 | 6 | 28 | | | |
| ♌ | ♍ | ♍ | | | |

| 1 | 21 | 27 | | | |
| ♍ | ♍ | ♍ | | | |

| 1 | 3 | 8 | 14 | 20 | 26 |
| ♍ | ♎ | ♎ | ♏ | ♏ | |

| 1 | 2 | 8 | 15 | 22 | |
| ♏ | ♏ | ♐ | ♐ | | |

| 1 | 2 | 13 | 20 | | |
| ♐ | ♑ | ♐ | | | |

1952
1	4	13	21	28	
♐	♑	♑	♑	♑	

| 1 | 3 | 9 | 15 | 21 | 26 |
| ♑ | ♒ | ♒ | ♓ | ♓ | |

| 1 | 2 | 8 | 14 | 24 | 29 |
| ♓ | ♈ | ♈ | ♈ | ♈ | ♈ |

| 1 | 14 | 25 | | | |
| ♈ | ♈ | | | | |

| 1 | 7 | 15 | 21 | 27 | |
| ♈ | ♈ | ♉ | ♉ | ♉ | |

| 1 | 5 | 10 | 15 | 19 | 25 | 30 |
| ♊ | ♊ | ♊ | ♋ | ♋ | ♋ | ♌ |

| 1 | 7 | 16 | | | |
| ♌ | ♌ | | | | |

| 1 | 13 | | | | |
| ♌ | | | | | |

| 1 | 8 | 13 | 18 | 24 | 29 |
| ♌ | ♍ | ♍ | ♍ | ♎ | ♎ |

| 1 | 5 | 12 | 18 | 25 | |
| ♎ | ♎ | ♏ | ♏ | ♏ | |

| 1 | 10 | 29 | | | |
| ♏ | ♏ | | | | |

| 1 | 23 | 31 | | | |
| ♐ | ♐ | ♐ | | | |

1953
1	7	13	20	26	
♐	♑	♑	♑	♒	

| 1 | 6 | 12 | 17 | 23 | |
| ♒ | ♒ | ♓ | ♓ | ♓ | |

| 1 | 3 | 16 | 30 | | |
| ♓ | ♈ | ♓ | ♓ | | |

| 1 | 3 | 18 | 26 | | |
| ♈ | ♈ | ♈ | ♈ | | |

| 1 | 2 | 8 | 14 | 19 | 23 | 28 |
| ♈ | ♈ | ♉ | ♉ | ♉ | ♊ | ♊ |

| 1 | 6 | 12 | 18 | 26 | |
| ♊ | ♋ | ♋ | ♋ | ♌ | |

| 1 | 29 | | | | |
| ♌ | ♋ | | | | |

| 1 | 12 | 20 | 26 | 31 | |
| ♋ | ♌ | ♌ | ♌ | ♍ | |

| 1 | 5 | 10 | 16 | 22 | 28 |
| ♍ | ♍ | ♍ | ♎ | ♎ | |

| 1 | 5 | 12 | 20 | | |
| ♎ | ♏ | ♏ | ♏ | | |

| 1 | 7 | 16 | | | |
| ♏ | ♏ | ♏ | | | |

| 1 | 3 | 11 | 18 | 24 | 31 |
| ♏ | ♏ | ♐ | ♐ | ♐ | ♑ |

1954
1	6	12	18	24	30
♑	♑	♑	♒	♒	♒

| 1 | 5 | 11 | | | |
| ♒ | ♓ | ♓ | | | |

| 1 | 2 | 29 | | | |
| ♓ | ♓ | | | | |

| 1 | 6 | 13 | 20 | 25 | 30 |
| ♓ | ♈ | ♈ | ♈ | ♈ | ♉ |

| 1 | 5 | 10 | 15 | 19 | 25 | 31 |
| ♉ | ♉ | ♉ | ♊ | ♊ | ♊ | ♋ |

| 1 | 7 | | | | |
| ♋ | ♋ | | | | |

| 1 | 13 | 21 | | | |
| ♋ | ♋ | | | | |

| 1 | 8 | 13 | 18 | 23 | 28 |
| ♋ | ♌ | ♌ | ♍ | ♍ | ♍ |

| 1 | 2 | 8 | 15 | 22 | 29 |
| ♍ | ♍ | ♎ | ♎ | ♎ | ♏ |

| 1 | 9 | 27 | | | |
| ♏ | ♏ | ♏ | | | |

| 1 | 5 | 11 | 21 | 28 | |
| ♏ | ♏ | ♏ | ♏ | | |

| 1 | 4 | 11 | 17 | 24 | 30 |
| ♏ | ♐ | ♐ | ♐ | ♑ | ♑ |

MERCURY 1955–1966

1955
Month	Days	Signs
1	1 5 11 17 23	♑ ♑ ♒ ♒
2	1 16	♒ ♒
3	1 9 18 25	♒ ♒ ♓ ♓
4	1 7 12 17 22 27	♓ ♈ ♈ ♈ ♉ ♉
5	1 2 7 12 20	♉ ♉ ♊ ♊ ♊
6	1	♊
7	1 14 20 26 31	♊ ♋ ♋ ♋ ♌
8	1 5 9 15 20 26	♌ ♌ ♌ ♍ ♍ ♎
9	1 2 9 17	♍ ♎ ♎ ♎
10	1 14	♎
11	1 8 15 21 27	♎ ♏ ♏ ♏ ♐
12	1 4 10 16 23 29	♐ ♐ ♐ ♐ ♑ ♑

1956
Month	Days	Signs
1	1 4 12 25	♑ ♒ ♒ ♒
2	1 3 15 26	♒ ♒ ♓ ♓
3	1 5 11 18 24 29	♒ ♓ ♓ ♈ ♈ ♈
4	1 3 8 13 18 23 30	♈ ♈ ♈ ♉ ♉ ♉ ♊
5	1	♊
6	1 24	♊ ♊
7	1 7 12 17 21 26 31	♊ ♋ ♋ ♋ ♌ ♌ ♌
8	1 6 12 19 27	♌ ♍ ♍ ♍ ♎
9	1 7 20 30	♎ ♎ ♎ ♏
10	1 11 19 25 31	♏ ♎ ♎ ♏ ♏
11	1 6 13 19 25	♏ ♏ ♏ ♐ ♐
12	1 2 8 15 22	♐ ♐ ♑ ♑ ♑

1957
Month	Days	Signs
1	1 11	♑ ♑
2	1 4 13 20 26	♑ ♒ ♒ ♒ ♒
3	1 4 10 16 21 26 31	♒ ♒ ♓ ♓ ♓ ♈ ♈
4	1 5 11	♈ ♉ ♉
5	1 19 20	♉ ♉ ♉
6	1 5 13 19 24 29	♉ ♊ ♊ ♋ ♋ ♋
7	1 3 8 13 18 24 30	♋ ♋ ♋ ♌ ♌ ♌ ♌
8	1 6 16	♌ ♍ ♍
9	1 7 30	♍ ♍ ♍
10	1 6 12 18 24 30	♍ ♎ ♎ ♏ ♏ ♏
11	1 5 12 18 25	♏ ♏ ♐ ♐ ♐
12	1 2 12 20 29	♐ ♑ ♑ ♑ ♑

1958
Month	Days	Signs
1	1 14 23 31	♐ ♑ ♑ ♑
2	1 7 13 19 25	♑ ♒ ♒ ♒ ♒
3	1 2 8 13 18 24	♒ ♒ ♓ ♓ ♈ ♈
4	1 3 11	♈ ♉ ♉
5	1 17 25 31	♈ ♉ ♉ ♉
6	1 6 11 16 20 25 30	♉ ♊ ♊ ♊ ♋ ♋ ♋
7	1 5 11 18 26	♋ ♋ ♌ ♌ ♌
8	1 24	♍ ♍
9	1 11 18 23 29	♌ ♍ ♍ ♍ ♎
10	1 5 10 16 23 29	♎ ♎ ♏ ♏ ♏ ♏
11	1 5 12 21	♏ ♐ ♐ ♐
12	1 8 17 23	♐ ♐ ♐ ♐

1959
Month	Days	Signs
1	1 3 11 18 24 31	♐ ♑ ♑ ♑ ♑ ♒
2	1 6 12 17 22 28	♒ ♒ ♒ ♓ ♓ ♓
3	1 5 13 27	♓ ♈ ♈ ♈
4	1 28	♈ ♈
5	1 6 13 19 24 29	♈ ♉ ♉ ♉ ♉ ♊
6	1 2 7 12 17 22 29	♊ ♊ ♋ ♋ ♋ ♋ ♋
7	1 7	♌ ♌
8	1 9 22 30	♌ ♌ ♌ ♍
9	1 5 10 16 21 27	♌ ♍ ♍ ♍ ♎ ♎
10	1 3 9 16 23 31	♎ ♎ ♏ ♏ ♏ ♐
11	1 25	♐ ♏
12	1 14 22 29	♏ ♐ ♐ ♐

1960
Month	Days	Signs
1	1 4 11 17 23 29	♐ ♑ ♑ ♑ ♒ ♒
2	1 4 9 15 22	♒ ♓ ♓ ♓ ♓
3	1 11	♓ ♓
4	1 8 16 23 29	♓ ♓ ♈ ♈ ♈
5	1 5 10 15 19 24 29	♈ ♉ ♉ ♉ ♊ ♊ ♊
6	1 3 9 17	♊ ♊ ♊ ♊
7	1 6 27 29	♋ ♌ ♌ ♌
8	1 11 17 22 27	♌ ♍ ♍ ♍ ♎
9	1 7 12 18 25	♍ ♍ ♎ ♎ ♎
10	1 2 9 19	♎ ♏ ♏ ♏
11	1 4 12 22	♏ ♏ ♏ ♏
12	1 8 14 21 27	♏ ♐ ♐ ♐ ♑

MERCURY 1967–1978

1967
Month	Days	Signs
1	1 7 14 20 26 31	♑ ♑ ♑ ♑ ♒ ♒
2	1 6 12	♒ ♓ ♓
3	1 7 29	♓ ♓ ♓
4	1 2 7 12 16 21 26	♈ ♉ ♉ ♉ ♊ ♊ ♊
5	1 8 19	♊ ♊ ♊
6	1 4	♋ ♋
7	1 2 9 14 19 24 29	♋ ♋ ♌ ♌ ♌ ♍ ♍
8	1 4 10 16 23 30	♍ ♍ ♎ ♎ ♎ ♏
9	1 9 31	♏ ♏ ♏
10	1 22 29	♏ ♏ ♏
11	1 6 12 18 25 31	♏ ♐ ♐ ♐ ♑ ♑
12	1 6 12 18 25 31	♏ ♐ ♐ ♐ ♐ ♑

1968
Month	Days	Signs
1	1 6 12 18 25	♑ ♑ ♒ ♒ ♒
2	1 2 12 21	♒ ♒ ♒ ♓
3	1 7 18 25	♒ ♒ ♓ ♓
4	1 7 13 18 23 27	♓ ♈ ♈ ♈ ♈ ♉
5	1 2 7 12 19 30	♉ ♉ ♉ ♊ ♊ ♊
6	1 14	♊ ♋
7	1 13 21 26 31	♋ ♋ ♋ ♌ ♌
8	1 5 10 15 20 26	♌ ♌ ♌ ♍ ♍ ♍
9	1 2 9 17 29	♍ ♎ ♎ ♎ ♏
10	1 8 18	♏ ♎ ♎
11	1 8 15 21 28	♎ ♏ ♏ ♏ ♐
12	1 4 10 17 23 29	♐ ♐ ♐ ♑ ♑ ♑

1969
Month	Days	Signs
1	1 5 12 29	♑ ♒ ♒ ♒
2	1 25	♒ ♒
3	1 6 13 19 25 30	♒ ♒ ♓ ♓ ♓ ♈
4	1 5 9 14 19 24	♈ ♈ ♈ ♈ ♉ ♉
5	1 11 25	♉ ♊ ♊
6	1 24	♊ ♊
7	1 2 8 13 18 23 28	♊ ♊ ♋ ♋ ♋ ♌ ♌
8	1 2 7 13 20 27	♌ ♌ ♍ ♍ ♍ ♎
9	1 6 26	♎ ♎ ♎
10	1 7 10 20 27	♎ ♏ ♎ ♎ ♏
11	1 2 8 14 20 27	♎ ♏ ♏ ♏ ♐ ♐
12	1 3 10 16 23	♏ ♐ ♐ ♐ ♐

1970
Month	Days	Signs
1	1 16	♑ ♑
2	1 5 14 21 28	♑ ♑ ♒ ♒ ♒
3	1 6 12 17 22 27	♒ ♒ ♓ ♓ ♈ ♈
4	1 6 12 21	♈ ♈ ♈ ♈
5	1 6	♉ ♉
6	1 5 14 20 25 30	♉ ♉ ♊ ♊ ♊ ♋
7	1 5 10 14 19 25 31	♋ ♋ ♋ ♌ ♌ ♌ ♍
8	1 7 16	♍ ♍ ♍
9	1 12	♍ ♍
10	1 8 14 19 25 31	♍ ♎ ♎ ♏ ♏ ♏
11	1 7 13 20 26	♏ ♏ ♐ ♐ ♐
12	1 3 12 26	♐ ♐ ♐ ♐

1971
Month	Days	Signs
1	1 3 14 24	♑ ♐ ♑ ♑
2	1 8 14 21 26	♑ ♒ ♒ ♒ ♓
3	1 4 9 14 19 25	♓ ♓ ♓ ♈ ♈ ♈
4	1 2 19	♈ ♈ ♈
5	1 17 26	♈ ♉ ♉
6	1 2 7 12 17 22 26	♉ ♉ ♊ ♊ ♊ ♋ ♋
7	1 6 12 19 27	♋ ♋ ♋ ♌ ♌
8	1 9 16 30	♍ ♍ ♍ ♌
9	1 11 19 25 30	♌ ♍ ♍ ♎ ♎
10	1 6 12 18 24 31	♎ ♎ ♏ ♏ ♏ ♏
11	1 6 13 21	♏ ♏ ♐ ♐
12	1 13	♐ ♐

1972
Month	Days	Signs
1	1 4 12 19 26	♐ ♐ ♑ ♑ ♑
2	1 7 13 19 24 29	♑ ♒ ♒ ♒ ♓ ♓
3	1 6 12	♓ ♈ ♈
4	1 2 27	♈ ♈ ♈
5	1 6 13 19 24 29	♈ ♉ ♉ ♉ ♊ ♊
6	1 3 7 12 17 23 29	♊ ♊ ♋ ♋ ♋ ♌ ♌
7	1 6 17	♋ ♌ ♌
8	1 2 30	♌ ♌ ♌
9	1 5 11 16 22 27	♌ ♍ ♍ ♎ ♎ ♎
10	1 3 9 16 23 31	♎ ♎ ♏ ♏ ♏ ♐
11	1 10 21 29	♐ ♐ ♐ ♐
12	1 13 22 29	♏ ♐ ♐ ♐

1961

| 1 3 9 15 21 27 |
| ♑ ♑ ♑ ♒ ♒ ♒ |
| 1 2 25 |
| ♒ ♓ ♓ |
| 1 18 28 |
| ♓ ♓ |
| 1 4 10 16 22 27 |
| ♓ ♓ ♈ ♈ ♈ ♉ |
| 1 6 11 16 22 29 |
| ♉ ♉ ♊ ♊ ♊ ♋ |
| 1 11 18 |
| ♋ ♋ ♋ |
| 1 23 30 |
| ♋ ♋ ♋ |
| 1 4 9 14 19 24 30 |
| ♋ ♌ ♌ ♌ ♍ ♍ ♍ ♎ |
| 1 5 12 19 28 |
| ♍ ♎ ♎ ♎ ♏ |
| 1 22 |
| ♏ ♎ |
| 1 11 18 25 |
| ♎ ♏ ♏ ♏ |
| 1 7 14 20 26 |
| ♐ ♐ ♐ ♑ ♑ |

1962

| 1 8 14 22 |
| ♑ ♒ ♒ ♒ |
| 1 2 11 25 |
| ♒ ♒ ♒ ♒ |
| 1 8 15 22 28 |
| ♒ ♓ ♓ ♓ ♓ |
| 1 3 8 13 18 23 28 |
| ♓ ♈ ♈ ♈ ♈ ♉ ♉ ♉ |
| 1 3 10 23 30 |
| ♉ ♊ ♊ ♊ ♊ |
| 1 |
| ♊ |
| 1 4 11 17 22 27 |
| ♊ ♋ ♋ ♋ ♋ ♌ |
| 1 6 11 17 23 30 |
| ♌ ♌ ♍ ♍ ♍ ♎ |
| 1 7 18 30 |
| ♎ ♎ ♎ |
| 1 9 22 30 |
| ♎ ♎ ♎ |
| 1 5 11 17 24 30 |
| ♎ ♏ ♏ ♏ ♐ ♐ |
| 1 6 13 19 26 |
| ♐ ♐ ♑ ♑ ♑ |

1963

| 1 2 20 |
| ♑ ♑ |
| 1 15 24 |
| ♒ ♒ |
| 1 3 9 15 21 26 31 |
| ♒ ♓ ♓ ♈ ♈ ♈ ♈ |
| 1 5 10 15 21 |
| ♈ ♈ ♉ ♉ ♉ |
| 1 3 11 |
| ♉ ♊ ♊ |
| 1 15 23 29 |
| ♊ ♊ ♊ ♊ |
| 1 4 9 14 18 24 29 |
| ♋ ♋ ♋ ♌ ♌ ♌ ♌ |
| 1 3 10 17 27 |
| ♌ ♍ ♍ ♍ ♎ |
| 1 17 |
| ♎ |
| 1 11 17 23 29 |
| ♏ ♏ ♎ ♎ ♏ |
| 1 4 10 16 23 30 |
| ♏ ♏ ♏ ♐ ♐ ♐ |
| 1 6 13 23 29 |
| ♐ ♑ ♑ ♑ ♑ |

1964

| 1 7 26 |
| ♑ ♑ ♑ |
| 1 3 11 18 24 |
| ♑ ♑ ♒ ♒ ♒ |
| 1 7 12 17 22 27 |
| ♒ ♓ ♓ ♈ ♈ ♈ |
| 1 2 12 23 |
| ♈ ♉ ♉ ♉ |
| 1 26 |
| ♉ ♉ |
| 1 |
| ♉ |
| 1 4 9 14 21 27 |
| ♉ ♊ ♊ ♊ ♋ ♋ |
| 1 5 |
| ♋ ♋ |
| 1 2 21 27 |
| ♋ ♍ ♍ ♍ |
| 1 11 17 23 29 |
| ♍ ♎ ♎ ♎ ♏ |
| 1 2 8 15 22 |
| ♏ ♏ ♏ ♏ ♏ |
| 1 17 25 |
| ♐ ♐ ♐ |

1965

| 1 3 13 21 28 |
| ♐ ♐ ♑ ♑ ♑ |
| 1 3 10 16 21 27 |
| ♑ ♒ ♒ ♒ ♓ ♓ |
| 1 4 9 15 22 |
| ♓ ♈ ♈ ♈ ♈ |
| 1 7 |
| ♈ ♈ |
| 1 7 16 22 28 |
| ♈ ♈ ♉ ♉ ♉ |
| 1 2 7 12 16 21 26 |
| ♉ ♊ ♊ ♊ ♊ ♋ ♋ |
| 1 2 8 16 31 |
| ♌ ♌ ♌ ♌ ♍ |
| 1 3 19 |
| ♍ ♌ ♌ |
| 1 9 14 20 25 |
| ♌ ♍ ♍ ♍ ♎ |
| 1 7 13 19 26 |
| ♎ ♎ ♏ ♏ ♏ |
| 1 2 10 |
| ♏ ♏ |
| 1 4 24 |
| ♐ ♐ ♐ |

1966

| 1 8 14 21 27 |
| ♑ ♑ ♑ ♒ |
| 1 2 8 13 19 24 |
| ♒ ♒ ♒ ♓ ♓ ♓ |
| 1 3 22 |
| ♓ ♈ |
| 1 18 27 |
| ♓ ♈ ♈ |
| 1 4 10 15 20 25 29 |
| ♈ ♈ ♉ ♉ ♉ ♊ ♊ |
| 1 3 8 13 19 27 |
| ♊ ♊ ♋ ♋ ♋ ♌ |
| 1 9 21 |
| ♌ ♌ |
| 1 21 27 |
| ♌ ♌ ♌ |
| 1 7 12 17 23 29 |
| ♍ ♍ ♍ ♎ ♎ |
| 1 6 13 21 30 |
| ♎ ♏ ♏ ♏ ♐ |
| 1 13 21 |
| ♐ ♐ |
| 1 3 12 19 25 |
| ♏ ♏ ♐ ♐ |

1973

| 1 5 11 18 24 30 |
| ♐ ♑ ♑ ♑ ♒ ♒ |
| 1 4 10 15 22 |
| ♒ ♒ ♓ ♓ ♓ |
| 1 17 |
| ♓ ♓ |
| 1 7 17 24 30 |
| ♓ ♈ ♈ ♈ ♈ |
| 1 6 11 16 21 25 30 |
| ♈ ♉ ♉ ♉ ♊ ♊ ♊ |
| 1 4 10 17 27 |
| ♊ ♋ ♋ ♋ ♌ |
| 1 16 |
| ♌ ♋ |
| 1 12 18 24 29 |
| ♋ ♌ ♌ ♌ ♍ |
| 1 3 8 14 20 26 |
| ♍ ♎ ♎ ♎ ♏ ♏ |
| 1 3 10 19 |
| ♎ ♏ ♏ ♏ |
| 1 9 |
| ♏ ♏ |
| 1 2 9 16 22 29 |
| ♏ ♏ ♐ ♐ ♐ ♑ |

1974

| 1 4 10 16 22 28 |
| ♒ ♑ ♑ ♑ ♒ ♒ |
| 1 3 11 21 |
| ♒ ♓ ♓ ♓ |
| 1 3 18 28 |
| ♓ ♒ ♓ ♓ |
| 1 5 12 18 23 28 |
| ♓ ♈ ♈ ♈ ♈ ♉ |
| 1 3 8 12 17 23 29 |
| ♉ ♉ ♉ ♊ ♊ ♊ ♋ |
| 1 8 29 |
| ♋ ♋ ♋ |
| 1 23 31 |
| ♋ ♋ ♋ |
| 1 5 11 15 20 26 31 |
| ♋ ♌ ♌ ♌ ♍ ♍ ♍ |
| 1 6 13 20 28 |
| ♍ ♎ ♎ ♎ ♏ |
| 1 11 17 27 |
| ♏ ♏ ♏ ♏ |
| 1 12 19 26 |
| ♎ ♏ ♏ ♏ |
| 1 2 9 15 21 28 |
| ♏ ♐ ♐ ♐ ♑ ♑ |

1975

| 1 3 9 15 22 |
| ♑ ♑ ♒ ♒ ♒ |
| 1 7 20 22 |
| ♒ ♒ ♒ ♒ |
| 1 8 16 23 30 |
| ♒ ♓ ♓ ♓ ♈ |
| 1 5 10 15 20 24 29 |
| ♓ ♈ ♈ ♈ ♉ ♉ ♉ |
| 1 4 11 20 |
| ♈ ♉ ♊ ♊ |
| 1 9 |
| ♊ ♊ |
| 1 4 12 18 24 28 |
| ♊ ♊ ♊ ♋ ♋ ♌ |
| 1 2 7 12 18 24 31 |
| ♌ ♋ ♌ ♍ ♍ ♍ ♎ |
| 1 7 17 |
| ♎ ♎ ♎ |
| 1 7 |
| ♎ ♎ |
| 1 6 15 22 31 |
| ♎ ♏ ♏ ♏ ♐ |
| 1 8 14 21 27 |
| ♏ ♐ ♐ ♐ ♑ |

1976

| 1 3 25 |
| ♑ ♑ ♑ |
| 1 16 25 |
| ♒ ♒ |
| 1 3 10 16 21 27 |
| ♒ ♓ ♓ ♈ ♈ ♈ |
| 1 6 10 15 21 30 |
| ♈ ♉ ♉ ♉ ♉ ♊ |
| 1 20 |
| ♊ ♉ |
| 1 14 23 29 |
| ♊ ♊ ♊ ♊ |
| 1 5 9 14 19 24 29 |
| ♊ ♋ ♋ ♋ ♌ ♌ ♌ |
| 1 4 10 17 26 |
| ♍ ♍ ♍ ♎ ♎ |
| 1 21 |
| ♎ ♏ |
| 1 11 17 23 29 |
| ♏ ♎ ♎ ♎ ♏ |
| 1 4 10 17 23 30 |
| ♏ ♏ ♏ ♐ ♐ ♐ |
| 1 6 13 22 |
| ♐ ♑ ♑ ♑ |

1977

| 1 3 11 24 |
| ♐ ♑ ♑ ♑ ♑ |
| 1 3 11 18 24 |
| ♑ ♑ ♒ ♒ ♒ |
| 1 2 8 13 18 23 29 |
| ♒ ♓ ♓ ♈ ♈ ♈ ♈ |
| 1 3 11 |
| ♈ ♉ ♉ |
| 1 26 |
| ♉ ♉ |
| 1 4 11 17 22 26 |
| ♉ ♊ ♊ ♊ ♋ ♋ |
| 1 6 10 16 22 28 |
| ♋ ♌ ♌ ♌ ♌ ♍ |
| 1 8 21 29 |
| ♍ ♍ ♍ ♍ |
| 1 4 10 16 22 28 |
| ♍ ♎ ♎ ♎ ♏ ♏ |
| 1 3 10 16 23 |
| ♎ ♏ ♏ ♏ ♐ |
| 1 21 |
| ♐ ♐ |

1978

| 1 14 22 29 |
| ♐ ♑ ♑ ♑ |
| 1 5 11 17 23 28 |
| ♑ ♒ ♒ ♒ ♓ ♓ |
| 1 5 11 16 23 |
| ♓ ♈ ♈ ♈ ♈ |
| 1 14 |
| ♈ ♈ |
| 1 7 16 23 29 |
| ♈ ♈ ♉ ♉ ♉ |
| 1 4 8 13 18 22 27 |
| ♉ ♊ ♊ ♊ ♋ ♋ ♋ |
| 1 3 9 17 27 |
| ♋ ♌ ♌ ♌ ♍ |
| 1 13 |
| ♍ ♍ |
| 1 10 16 21 27 |
| ♍ ♍ ♍ ♍ ♎ |
| 1 2 8 14 21 27 |
| ♎ ♎ ♎ ♏ ♏ ♏ |
| 1 3 11 21 30 |
| ♏ ♐ ♐ ♐ ♐ |
| 1 8 24 |
| ♐ ♐ |

MERCURY 1979–1990

(Zodiac signs: ♈ Aries, ♉ Taurus, ♊ Gemini, ♋ Cancer, ♌ Leo, ♍ Virgo, ♎ Libra, ♏ Scorpio, ♐ Sagittarius, ♑ Capricorn, ♒ Aquarius, ♓ Pisces. Each cell lists the day of the month followed by the sign Mercury occupies.)

Month	1979	1980	1981	1982	1983	1984
1	1♐ 2♑ 9♑ 16♑ 22♑ 29♒	1♐ 2♑ 9♑ 15♑ 21♒ 27♒	1♑ 7♑ 13♒ 19♒ 25♒	1♑ 6♒ 12♒	1♑ 2♒ 12♒ 21♓	1♑ 25♑
2	1♒ 4♒ 9♒ 15♓ 20♓ 26♓	1♒ 2♒ 7♒ 13♓ 22♓	1♓ 16♒	1♒ 3♒ 26♒	1♓ 5♒ 14♒ 22♒	1♑ 2♒ 9♒ 16♒ 22♒ 28♓
3	1♓ 4♈ 28♓	1♓ 13♈ 27♈	1♒ 4♓ 18♓ 26♈	1♒ 7♒ 14♓ 20♓ 26♓	1♒ 7♓ 13♓ 19♈ 24♈ 29♈	1♓ 4♈ 10♈ 15♈ 20♈ 25♈
4	1♓ 18♈ 27♈	1♈ 7♈ 15♈ 21♈ 27♈	1♈ 2♈ 8♈ 14♉ 19♉ 24♉ 29♊	1♓ 6♈ 11♈ 16♈ 21♉ 26♉	1♈ 3♈ 8♈ 13♉ 21♉	1♈ 25♈
5	1♈ 5♈ 11♉ 16♉ 22♉ 26♊ 31♊	1♈ 2♉ 7♉ 12♉ 17♊ 21♊ 26♊	1♊ 4♊ 8♊ 14♋ 20♋ 29♋	1♉ 2♊ 10♊	1♉ 15♉	1♈ 16♉ 26♉
6	1♊ 4♊ 9♋ 14♋ 20♋ 27♌	1♊ 8♋ 17♋	1♋ 23♋	1♊ 4♊ 23♊	1♉ 2♉ 9♊ 15♊ 21♋ 27♋	1♉ 2♉ 8♊ 13♊ 18♊ 22♋ 27♋
7	1♌ 7♌ 29♌	1♋ 11♋	1♋ 13♋ 22♋ 28♋	1♊ 9♋ 15♋ 20♋ 24♋ 29♌	1♋ 8♋ 16♌ 29♍	1♋ 6♌ 23♌
8	1♌ 22♌ 28♌	1♋ 2♋ 9♌ 15♌ 20♌ 25♍ 30♍	1♋ 2♋ 7♌ 11♌ 17♌ 22♍ 28♍	1♌ 3♌ 9♍ 14♍ 21♍ 28♎	1♍ 6♍	1♌ 19♌ 25♌
9	1♌ 3♍ 8♍ 13♎ 19♎ 25♎	1♍ 4♍ 10♎ 16♎ 23♎ 30♏	1♍ 3♍ 10♎ 18♎ 27♏	1♎ 6♎	1♍ 6♎ 18♎	1♌ 19♍ 25♍
10	1♎ 7♏ 14♏ 22♏ 30♐	1♏ 8♏	1♏ 14♏ 23♎	1♎ 21♎ 28♎	1♎ 2♎ 9♏ 15♏ 21♏ 27♐	1♍ 6♎ 12♎ 18♎ 24♏ 31♏
11	1♏ 18♏ 28♏	1♏ 4♏ 22♏ 29♏	1♎ 10♏ 16♏ 23♏ 29♐	1♎ 3♏ 9♏ 15♏ 22♐ 28♐	1♐ 2♐ 8♐ 14♐ 21♑ 28♑	1♏ 7♏ 13♏ 21♐
12	1♏ 2♏ 13♐ 20♐ 27♐	1♏ 6♐ 12♐ 19♐ 25♑ 31♑	1♐ 5♐ 12♐ 18♑ 24♑ 30♑	1♐ 4♐ 11♑ 17♑ 24♑	1♑ 4♑ 12♐ 31♐	1♐ 2♐ 8♑ 17♑

MERCURY 1991–2002

Month	1991	1992	1993	1994	1995	1996
1	1♐ 14♑ 23♑ 30♑	1♐ 3♑ 10♑ 17♑ 24♑ 30♒	1♐ 3♑ 9♑ 15♑ 21♒ 27♒	1♑ 2♑ 8♑ 14♒ 20♒ 26♒	1♑ 7♒ 13♒ 22♒ 30♒	1♑ 2♑ 17♒ 27♒
2	1♑ 6♒ 12♒ 18♒ 24♓	1♒ 5♒ 11♒ 16♓ 22♓ 27♓	1♒ 2♒ 8♓ 13♓ 21♓	1♒ 22♒	1♒ 8♒ 26♒	1♒ 3♒ 15♒ 23♓
3	1♓ 2♓ 7♈ 12♈ 17♈ 23♈	1♓ 4♈ 13♈ 22♈	1♓ 8♓	1♒ 19♓ 27♓	1♒ 7♒ 15♓ 22♓ 28♓	1♒ 7♓ 13♓ 19♈ 24♈ 29♈
4	1♈ 21♈	1♈ 4♓ 15♈ 27♈	1♓ 7♓ 16♈ 22♈ 28♈	1♓ 3♈ 10♈ 15♈ 21♈ 26♉	1♓ 3♈ 10♈	1♈ 3♈ 8♉ 13♉ 20♉
5	1♈ 6♉ 17♉ 24♊ 31♊	1♈ 5♉ 11♉ 17♉ 22♊ 27♊ 31♊	1♈ 4♉ 9♉ 14♉ 18♊ 23♊ 28♊	1♉ 5♉ 10♊ 15♊ 21♊ 29♋	1♈ 3♉ 10♉	1♉ 25♉ 31♊
6	1♊ 5♊ 10♋ 15♋ 19♋ 24♋ 29♌	1♊ 5♋ 10♋ 15♋ 21♋ 27♋	1♊ 2♋ 8♋ 17♋	1♋	1♉ 15♊ 20♊	1♊ 14♋ 21♋ 27♋
7	1♋ 4♌ 10♌ 17♌ 27♍	1♋ 6♋	1♋ 19♋	1♋ 3♊ 11♊ 23♋ 29♋	1♊ 4♋ 11♋ 16♋ 21♌ 26♌ 31♌	1♋ 2♋ 7♌ 12♌ 16♌ 21♍ 27♍
8	1♍ 20♍	1♋ 4♋ 21♌ 29♌	1♋ 10♌ 16♌ 21♌ 26♍ 31♍	1♋ 3♌ 8♌ 13♌ 18♍ 23♍ 29♎	1♌ 5♌ 10♍ 16♍ 22♍ 29♎	1♍ 2♍ 8♎ 16♎ 26♎
9	1♌ 11♍ 17♍ 23♎ 28♎	1♌ 3♍ 9♍ 14♍ 19♎ 25♎	1♍ 6♍ 11♎ 18♎ 24♎	1♎ 4♎ 11♏ 18♏ 27♏	1♎ 6♎ 21♎ 24♎	1♎ 12♎ 23♎ 30♏
10	1♎ 4♎ 10♏ 16♏ 22♏ 29♐	1♎ 7♏ 14♏ 21♏ 30♐	1♎ 9♏ 19♏	1♏ 19♎	1♎ 6♎ 22♏ 29♏	1♏ 9♎ 15♎ 21♎ 27♏
11	1♏ 4♏ 12♏ 21♏	1♐ 22♏	1♏ 9♏ 22♏ 30♐	1♎ 11♏ 17♏ 24♏ 30♐	1♏ 4♏ 10♏ 17♐ 23♐ 29♐	1♏ 2♏ 8♏ 15♐ 21♐ 28♐
12	1♏ 6♐ 14♐ 24♐	1♏ 12♐ 20♐ 27♑	1♏ 7♐ 14♐ 20♐ 27♑	1♐ 7♐ 13♑ 19♑ 26♑	1♐ 6♐ 12♑ 19♑ 25♑	1♐ 5♑ 12♑

1985–1990

	1985	1986	1987	1988	1989	1990
Jan	1 3 12 19 26 — ♐ ♐ ♑ ♑	1 6 12 19 25 31 — ♐ ♑ ♑ ♑ ♒ ♒	1 5 12 18 23 29 — ♑ ♑ ♑ ♒ ♒ ♒	1 4 10 16 23 — ♑ ♑ ♒ ♒	1 3 11 21 29 — ♑ ♑ ♒ ♒ ♒	1 8 18 22 — ♑ ♑ ♑ ♑
Feb	1 7 13 19 24 — ♒ ♒ ♓ ♓	1 6 11 17 23 — ♒ ♒ ♓ ♓ ♓	1 4 11 26 — ♒ ♓ ♓ ♓	1 13 — ♒ ♒	1 15 24 — ♒ ♒ ♒	1 4 12 19 26 — ♑ ♑ ♒ ♒ ♒
Mar	1 2 7 13 — ♓ ♓ ♈ ♈	1 3 12 24 — ♓ ♓ ♈ ♈	1 12 14 29 — ♓ ♓ ♈	1 8 16 24 30 — ♒ ♒ ♓ ♓ ♈	1 4 11 17 23 28 — ♒ ♒ ♓ ♓ ♓ ♈	1 4 9 15 20 25 30 — ♒ ♓ ♓ ♈ ♈ ♈ ♈
Apr	1 8 26 — ♈ ♈ ♈	1 6 18 25 — ♓ ♓ ♈ ♈	1 6 13 19 25 30 — ♈ ♈ ♈ ♈ ♈ ♉	1 5 10 15 20 25 30 — ♈ ♈ ♈ ♈ ♉ ♉ ♊	1 2 7 12 17 22 30 — ♈ ♈ ♈ ♉ ♉ ♉ ♊	1 4 11 — ♈ ♉ ♉
May	1 7 14 20 26 31 — ♈ ♈ ♉ ♉ ♊ ♊	1 2 8 13 18 22 27 — ♈ ♈ ♉ ♉ ♊ ♊ ♊	1 4 9 14 19 24 30 — ♉ ♉ ♉ ♊ ♊ ♊ ♋	1 5 11 19 — ♊ ♊ ♋ ♋	1 29 — ♊ ♉	1 9 25 — ♉ ♉ ♉
Jun	1 5 9 14 19 24 30 — ♊ ♊ ♊ ♋ ♋ ♋ ♌	1 6 11 18 27 — ♊ ♋ ♋ ♋	1 8 — ♋ ♋	1 18 — ♊ ♊	1 12 24 30 — ♉ ♊ ♊ ♊	1 5 12 18 23 28 — ♉ ♉ ♊ ♊ ♊ ♋
Jul	1 7 16 — ♌ ♌ ♌	1 24 — ♌ ♌	1 7 23 — ♋ ♋	1 2 12 19 24 29 — ♊ ♊ ♋ ♋ ♋ ♌	1 6 11 16 20 25 30 — ♊ ♋ ♋ ♋ ♌ ♌ ♌	1 2 7 12 17 23 29 — ♋ ♋ ♋ ♌ ♌ ♌ ♍
Aug	1 9 31 — ♌ ♌ ♌	1 12 19 25 30 — ♋ ♌ ♌ ♍	1 7 12 17 22 27 — ♋ ♌ ♌ ♌ ♍ ♍	1 3 8 13 18 24 31 — ♌ ♌ ♍ ♍ ♍ ♎	1 5 11 18 26 — ♌ ♍ ♍ ♍ ♎	1 6 16 — ♍ ♍ ♍
Sep	1 7 12 18 23 29 — ♌ ♍ ♍ ♍ ♎ ♎	1 4 10 15 21 27 — ♍ ♍ ♎ ♎ ♎	1 2 8 14 21 29 — ♍ ♍ ♎ ♎ ♎ ♏	1 7 16 — ♎ ♎	1 8 15 27 — ♎ ♎ ♍ ♏	1 3 15 20 30 — ♍ ♍ ♍ ♍
Oct	1 5 11 17 24 — ♎ ♎ ♏ ♏	1 4 11 20 — ♎ ♏ ♏	1 9 24 — ♎ ♏	1 10 31 — ♎ ♎	1 11 19 25 31 — ♍ ♎ ♎ ♎ ♏	1 6 11 17 23 29 — ♍ ♎ ♎ ♎ ♏ ♏
Nov	1 10 26 — ♏ ♏	1 14 — ♏ ♏	1 12 20 27 — ♎ ♏ ♏ ♏	1 7 13 19 25 — ♎ ♏ ♏ ♏	1 6 12 18 25 — ♏ ♏ ♏ ♐	1 5 11 18 25 — ♏ ♏ ♐ ♐ ♐
Dec	1 5 12 23 30 — ♐ ♏ ♐ ♐	1 2 10 17 23 30 — ♏ ♏ ♐ ♐ ♐ ♑	1 4 10 16 23 29 — ♐ ♐ ♐ ♐ ♐ ♑	1 2 8 14 21 27 — ♐ ♐ ♐ ♑ ♑	1 8 14 22 — ♐ ♑ ♑ ♑	1 2 26 — ♐ ♑ ♐

1997–2002

	1997	1998	1999	2000	2001	2002
Jan	1 3 24 — ♑ ♑ ♑	1 3 13 20 27 — ♐ ♐ ♑ ♑ ♑	1 7 14 20 26 — ♐ ♐ ♑ ♑ ♒	1 7 13 19 25 31 — ♑ ♑ ♑ ♒ ♒ ♒	1 5 11 17 23 — ♑ ♑ ♒ ♒ ♒	1 4 11 26 — ♑ ♒ ♒ ♒
Feb	1 2 9 16 22 28 — ♑ ♑ ♒ ♒ ♒ ♓	1 3 9 15 20 26 — ♑ ♒ ♒ ♒ ♓ ♓	1 7 13 18 24 — ♒ ♒ ♓ ♓ ♓	1 5 12 — ♒ ♓ ♓	1 7 17 — ♓ ♒ ♒	1 4 14 25 — ♒ ♑ ♒ ♒
Mar	1 6 11 16 21 26 — ♓ ♓ ♓ ♈ ♈ ♈	1 3 8 14 23 — ♓ ♈ ♈ ♈	1 3 18 — ♓ ♈ ♓	1 3 28 — ♓ ♓ ♓	1 8 17 25 31 — ♒ ♒ ♓ ♓ ♈	1 5 12 18 24 30 — ♒ ♒ ♓ ♓ ♈ ♈
Apr	1 2 — ♈ ♉	1 2 18 23 — ♈ ♈ ♈	1 18 26 — ♓ ♈ ♈	1 6 13 19 25 30 — ♈ ♈ ♈ ♈ ♈ ♉	1 6 12 17 22 27 — ♓ ♈ ♈ ♈ ♈ ♉	1 4 9 13 18 24 30 — ♈ ♈ ♉ ♉ ♉ ♊
May	1 5 12 26 — ♉ ♈ ♉ ♉	1 7 15 22 27 — ♈ ♉ ♉ ♉	1 3 9 14 19 24 28 — ♈ ♈ ♉ ♉ ♊ ♊ ♊	1 5 10 14 19 24 30 — ♉ ♉ ♊ ♊ ♊ ♋	1 6 12 19 — ♈ ♉ ♉ ♊	1 — ♊
Jun	1 3 9 14 19 24 28 — ♉ ♉ ♊ ♊ ♊ ♋	1 6 11 15 20 25 — ♉ ♊ ♊ ♊ ♋ ♋	1 2 7 12 19 27 — ♊ ♊ ♋ ♋ ♋ ♌	1 7 — ♋ ♋	1 — ♊	1 24 — ♊ ♊
Jul	1 3 8 14 20 27 — ♋ ♋ ♌ ♌ ♍	1 8 16 — ♋ ♌ ♌	1 — ♌	1 — ♋	1 13 20 25 30 — ♊ ♋ ♋ ♋ ♌	1 2 7 13 17 22 27 — ♊ ♊ ♋ ♋ ♋ ♌ ♌
Aug	1 5 30 — ♍ ♏ ♏	1 15 — ♌ ♌	1 11 21 26 — ♋ ♌ ♌ ♌	1 7 13 17 22 28 — ♋ ♌ ♌ ♌ ♍ ♍	1 4 9 14 20 26 — ♋ ♌ ♌ ♍ ♍ ♍	1 6 12 19 27 — ♋ ♌ ♌ ♍ ♍
Sep	1 20 27 — ♏ ♏ ♏	1 8 14 19 24 30 — ♌ ♍ ♍ ♍ ♎ ♎	1 6 11 17 22 29 — ♍ ♍ ♍ ♎ ♎ ♎	1 2 8 14 21 29 — ♍ ♍ ♍ ♎ ♎ ♎	1 8 17 — ♍ ♍	1 6 22 — ♎ ♎ ♎
Oct	1 2 8 14 20 26 — ♏ ♎ ♎ ♎ ♏ ♏	1 6 12 19 25 — ♎ ♎ ♎ ♏ ♏	1 5 12 20 31 — ♎ ♎ ♏ ♏ ♏	1 8 28 — ♍ ♎ ♎	1 15 — ♎	1 2 11 20 26 — ♎ ♍ ♎ ♎ ♎
Nov	1 8 15 22 — ♏ ♐ ♐ ♐	1 2 10 — ♎ ♏ ♏	1 10 18 — ♏ ♏ ♏	1 7 9 20 27 — ♏ ♎ ♏ ♏ ♏	1 8 14 20 27 — ♎ ♏ ♏ ♏ ♏	1 7 13 19 26 — ♏ ♏ ♏ ♐ ♐
Dec	1 14 22 — ♑ ♐ ♐	1 23 31 — ♐ ♐ ♐	1 3 11 18 25 31 — ♏ ♏ ♐ ♐ ♐ ♑	1 4 10 17 23 29 — ♏ ♐ ♐ ♐ ♑ ♑	1 3 9 16 22 28 — ♐ ♐ ♐ ♑ ♑ ♑	1 2 9 15 23 — ♐ ♑ ♑ ♑ ♑

MERCURY 2003–2010

Month	2003	2004	2005	2006
1	1 ♑, 13 ♑	1 ♐, 14 ♑, 24 ♑, 31 ♑	1 ♐, 2 ♐, 10 ♑, 17 ♑, 24 ♑, 30 ♒	1 ♐, 4 ♑, 10 ♑, 17 ♑, 23 ♒, 29 ♒
2	1 ♑, 5 ♑, 13 ♒, 20 ♒, 27 ♒	1 ♑, 7 ♒, 14 ♒, 20 ♒, 26 ♓	1 ♒, 5 ♒, 11 ♒, 17 ♓, 22 ♓, 27 ♓	1 ♒, 3 ♒, 9 ♓, 15 ♓, 21 ♓
3	1 ♒, 5 ♓, 11 ♓, 16 ♓, 22 ♈, 26 ♈, 31 ♈	1 ♓, 2 ♓, 7 ♓, 12 ♓, 18 ♈, 23 ♈	1 ♓, 5 ♈, 12 ♈, 29 ♈	1 ♓, 14 ♓
4	1 ♈, 6 ♉, 12 ♉, 23 ♉, 30 ♉	1 ♉, 13 ♈	1 ♈, 27 ♈	1 ♓, 8 ♓, 17 ♈, 24 ♈, 30 ♈
5	1 ♉	1 ♈, 16 ♉, 24 ♉, 31 ♉	1 ♈, 6 ♈, 12 ♉, 18 ♉, 24 ♉, 28 ♊	1 ♈, 5 ♉, 10 ♉, 15 ♉, 20 ♊, 24 ♊, 29 ♊
6	1 ♉, 5 ♉, 13 ♊, 19 ♊, 25 ♊, 29 ♊	1 ♉, 6 ♊, 11 ♊, 15 ♊, 20 ♋, 24 ♋, 29 ♋	1 ♊, 2 ♊, 7 ♊, 11 ♋, 16 ♋, 22 ♋, 28 ♌	1 ♊, 3 ♋, 9 ♋, 17 ♋, 29 ♌
7	1 ♋, 4 ♋, 9 ♋, 14 ♋, 19 ♋, 24 ♌, 31 ♍	1 ♋, 5 ♋, 10 ♋, 17 ♌, 26 ♍	1 ♌, 6 ♌, 20 ♌, 26 ♌	1 ♋, 11 ♌
8	1 ♍, 7 ♍, 16 ♍	1 ♍, 25 ♌	1 ♌, 11 ♌, 21 ♌, 30 ♌	1 ♋, 11 ♌, 18 ♌, 23 ♌, 28 ♍
9	1 ♍, 9 ♍	1 ♌, 10 ♍, 17 ♍, 23 ♍, 29 ♎	1 ♌, 5 ♍, 10 ♍, 15 ♍, 21 ♎, 26 ♎	1 ♍, 2 ♍, 7 ♍, 13 ♎, 19 ♎, 25 ♎
10	1 ♍, 7 ♎, 13 ♎, 19 ♎, 24 ♏, 31 ♏	1 ♎, 4 ♎, 10 ♎, 16 ♏, 22 ♏, 29 ♏	1 ♎, 2 ♎, 9 ♏, 15 ♏, 23 ♏, 30 ♐	1 ♎, 2 ♏, 10 ♏, 19 ♏
11	1 ♏, 6 ♏, 12 ♐, 19 ♐, 26 ♐	1 ♏, 5 ♐, 12 ♐, 20 ♐	1 ♐, 11 ♐, 18 ♐, 26 ♐	1 ♏, 6 ♏, 15 ♐, 21 ♐
12	1 ♐, 3 ♑, 12 ♑, 23 ♑, 31 ♐	1 ♐, 9 ♐	1 ♏, 13 ♐, 21 ♐, 28 ♐	1 ♏, 8 ♐, 15 ♐, 21 ♐, 28 ♑

VENUS 1931–1946

Month	1931	1932	1933	1934	1935	1936	1937	1938
1	1 ♏, 4 ♐, 17 ♐, 28 ♐	1 ♒, 3 ♒, 11 ♒, 19 ♓, 27 ♓	1 ♐, 6 ♑, 14 ♑, 22 ♑, 30 ♒	1 ♒	1 ♐, 9 ♐, 17 ♑, 25 ♑	1 ♏, 4 ♐, 12 ♐, 20 ♐, 29 ♑	1 ♒, 6 ♒, 15 ♓, 24 ♓	1 ♑, 8 ♑, 16 ♒, 23 ♒, 31 ♓
2	1 ♐, 7 ♑, 16 ♑, 25 ♑	1 ♓, 4 ♈, 13 ♈, 21 ♈	1 ♒, 7 ♒, 15 ♓, 23 ♓	1 ♒, 16 ♒	1 ♑, 2 ♒, 10 ♒, 18 ♓, 26 ♓	1 ♑, 6 ♒, 14 ♒, 22 ♒	1 ♓, 2 ♈, 12 ♈, 24 ♈	1 ♓, 8 ♓, 16 ♈, 24 ♈
3	1 ♑, 6 ♒, 15 ♒, 23 ♒	1 ♈, 9 ♉, 18 ♉, 27 ♉	1 ♓, 3 ♈, 12 ♈, 20 ♈, 28 ♉	1 ♒, 8 ♓, 25 ♓	1 ♓, 6 ♈, 14 ♈, 22 ♈, 31 ♉	1 ♒, 9 ♓, 18 ♓, 26 ♓	1 ♈, 10 ♉	1 ♉, 4 ♉, 12 ♉, 20 ♊, 28 ♊
4	1 ♓, 9 ♓, 18 ♓, 26 ♈	1 ♉, 5 ♊, 15 ♊, 25 ♊	1 ♉, 5 ♉, 13 ♊, 21 ♊, 29 ♊	1 ♈, 6 ♈, 17 ♈	1 ♉, 8 ♉, 16 ♊, 25 ♊	1 ♈, 3 ♈, 11 ♈, 19 ♉, 27 ♉	1 ♉, 14 ♉	1 ♊, 6 ♊, 14 ♋, 22 ♋, 30 ♋
5	1 ♈, 4 ♈, 13 ♉, 21 ♉	1 ♊, 6 ♊, 21 ♋	1 ♉, 7 ♉, 15 ♊, 23 ♊, 31 ♋	1 ♈, 5 ♉, 15 ♉, 23 ♊, 31 ♊	1 ♊, 3 ♋, 12 ♋, 21 ♋, 30 ♌	1 ♉, 5 ♊, 14 ♊, 22 ♊, 30 ♋	1 ♉, 4 ♉, 15 ♉, 22 ♊	1 ♋, 8 ♋, 16 ♋
6	1 ♉, 7 ♊, 15 ♊, 23 ♊	1 ♋, 25 ♊	1 ♋, 9 ♌, 17 ♌, 25 ♌	1 ♊, 2 ♋, 11 ♋, 20 ♋, 28 ♌	1 ♌, 8 ♌, 17 ♍	1 ♋, 7 ♋, 15 ♋, 23 ♋	1 ♊, 4 ♊, 17 ♊, 28 ♊	1 ♋, 6 ♋, 14 ♌, 23 ♌
7	1 ♊, 10 ♋, 18 ♋, 26 ♋	1 ♊, 13 ♊, 29 ♊	1 ♍, 3 ♍, 11 ♍, 19 ♎, 28 ♎	1 ♌, 7 ♌, 15 ♍, 24 ♍	1 ♍, 8 ♍, 20 ♍	1 ♋, 10 ♌, 18 ♌, 26 ♌	1 ♊, 7 ♊, 17 ♊	1 ♌, 6 ♌, 13 ♌, 21 ♍
8	1 ♋, 3 ♌, 11 ♌, 19 ♌, 27 ♍	1 ♊, 17 ♋, 29 ♋	1 ♎, 5 ♎, 13 ♏, 22 ♏, 30 ♏	1 ♍, 3 ♍, 11 ♍, 19 ♎, 27 ♎	1 ♍, 17 ♍	1 ♌, 4 ♌, 13 ♍, 21 ♍, 29 ♍	1 ♊, 8 ♊, 17 ♋, 25 ♋	1 ♍, 7 ♍, 18 ♎, 29 ♎
9	1 ♍, 5 ♍, 13 ♍, 21 ♎, 31 ♎	1 ♋, 9 ♋, 19 ♋, 28 ♌	1 ♏, 4 ♎, 11 ♎, 20 ♎, 29 ♎	1 ♎, 5 ♏, 13 ♏, 21 ♏, 29 ♏	1 ♍, 14 ♍, 29 ♎	1 ♍, 4 ♎, 11 ♎, 19 ♎, 27 ♏	1 ♋, 8 ♌, 16 ♌, 25 ♌	1 ♎, 4 ♎, 11 ♎, 19 ♏
10	1 ♎, 7 ♎, 15 ♏, 23 ♏, 31 ♏	1 ♌, 7 ♍, 16 ♍, 25 ♍	1 ♏, 3 ♏, 11 ♐, 20 ♐, 28 ♐	1 ♏, 4 ♏, 14 ♏, 22 ♐, 30 ♐	1 ♎, 5 ♎, 13 ♏, 21 ♏, 29 ♏	1 ♏, 7 ♏, 15 ♏, 23 ♐, 31 ♐	1 ♌, 3 ♍, 12 ♍, 20 ♎, 28 ♎	1 ♏, 14 ♏
11	1 ♏, 8 ♐, 16 ♐, 24 ♐	1 ♍, 2 ♎, 11 ♎, 19 ♎, 27 ♏	1 ♐, 7 ♑, 16 ♑, 24 ♑	1 ♐, 6 ♐, 14 ♑, 22 ♑, 30 ♑	1 ♏, 4 ♎, 14 ♎, 22 ♏	1 ♐, 9 ♐, 17 ♑, 25 ♑	1 ♎, 5 ♏, 13 ♏, 21 ♏, 29 ♏	1 ♏, 16 ♏
12	1 ♐, 2 ♑, 10 ♑, 18 ♒, 26 ♒	1 ♏, 5 ♏, 13 ♐, 21 ♐, 29 ♐	1 ♑, 6 ♑, 17 ♑	1 ♑, 8 ♈, 16 ♈, 24 ♈	1 ♏, 9 ♏, 17 ♐, 26 ♐	1 ♑, 3 ♒, 12 ♒, 20 ♒, 29 ♓	1 ♏, 7 ♏, 15 ♐, 23 ♐, 31 ♑	1 ♏, 6 ♏, 15 ♏

2007–2010

2007						2008						2009						2010					
1	3	9	15	21	27	1	2	8	15	22		1	21					1	8	25			
♑	♑	♑	♒	♒	♒		♑	♑	♒	♒	♒		♒	♑					♑	♑	♑		
1	2	13	16	27		1	4	14	25			1	15	23				1	3	10	17	24	
♒	♓	♒	♒	♒		♒	♒	♒	♒			♑	♒	♒				♑	♑	♒	♒	♒	
1	18	28				1	7	15	22	28		1	2	9	15	21	26	31	1	2	7	13	18	23	28
♓	♓	♓				♒	♒	♓	♓	♓		♒	♒	♓	♓	♓	♈	♈	♒	♓	♓	♓	♈	♈	♈
1	4	11	17	22	27	1	3	8	13	18	23	27	1	5	10	15	21	1	3	11	26		
♓	♓	♈	♈	♈	♉	♓	♈	♈	♈	♉	♉	♉	♈	♈	♉	♉	♉	♈	♉	♉	♉		
1	2	7	11	16	22	29	1	3	9	20		1	14					1	26				
♉	♉	♉	♊	♊	♊	♋	♉	♊	♊	♊		♊	♉					♉	♉				
1	9	23				1	2					1	14	22	29			1	4	10	16	21	25	30
♋	♋	♋				♊	♊					♉	♊	♊	♊			♉	♊	♊	♊	♊	♊	♋
1	23	30				1	3	11	17	22	26	31	1	4	9	13	18	23	28	1	5	11	15	21	28
♋	♋	♋				♊	♊	♋	♋	♋	♌	♌	♊	♋	♋	♋	♌	♌	♌	♋	♋	♌	♌	♌	♍
1	5	10	15	20	25	30	1	5	10	16	22	29	1	3	9	17	26	1	5				
♋	♌	♌	♍	♍	♍	♌	♌	♍	♍	♎		♌	♍	♍	♍	♎		♍	♍				
1	6	12	19	28		1	6	17				1	18					1	4	21	28		
♍	♎	♎	♍			♎	♎	♎				♎	♍					♍	♍	♍	♍		
1	24					1	11	21	29			1	10	17	23	28		1	4	9	15	21	27
♍	♎					♎	♎	♎	♍			♍	♎	♎	♎	♍	♍	♍	♎	♎	♎	♍	♍
1	11	19	25			1	5	11	17	23	30	1	3	10	16	22	29	1	2	9	16	23	
♎	♍	♍	♍			♎	♍	♍	♍	♍	♍	♍	♍	♍	♍	♐	♐	♍	♍	♐	♐	♐	
1	2	8	14	21	27	1	6	12	19	25		1	6	13	22	31		1	19	28			
♍	♐	♐	♐	♑	♑	♐	♐	♐	♑	♑		♐	♑	♑	♑	♑		♑	♐	♐			

1939–1946

1939				1940				1941				1942			1943			1944				1945			1946			
1	5	17	28	1	2	10	19	27	1	6	14	22	30	1	5	21	1	8	16	24	1	3	12	20	28	1	6	15	24	1	7	15	23	31
♏	♐	♐	♐	♒	♒	♒	♓	♓	♐	♐	♑	♑	♑	♒	♒	♒	♏	♐	♐	♐	♑	♒	♒	♒	♒	♏	♐	♐	♐	♑	♒	♓	♓	♓	♑	♑	♑	♑	♒	♒
1	6	16	25	1	4	12	21	29	1	7	15	23	1	8	1	9	17	26	1	5	14	22	1	2	13	24	1	8	16	24
♐	♑	♑	♑	♓	♓	♈	♈	♈	♒	♒	♒		♒	♒		♓	♓	♓	♈	♑	♑	♑	♒	♒	♒	♓	♈	♈	♈	♒	♒	♓	♈
1	6	14	23	31	1	9	17	26	1	3	11	19	27	1	11	26	1	6	14	22	30	1	9	17	25	1	11	1	4	12	20	28
♑	♒	♒	♓	♈	♈	♉	♉	♉	♒	♓	♓	♓	♈	♒	♒	♒	♈	♈	♈	♉	♈	♒	♒	♒	♒	♈	♉	♒	♒	♒	♓	♈	♈	♈	♈
1	9	17	26	1	5	15	25	1	4	12	20	28	1	7	17	27	1	7	16	24	1	2	11	19	27	1	8	25	1	5	13	21	29
♓	♓	♓	♈	♈	♉	♊	♊	♈	♈	♈	♉	♉	♒	♓	♓	♈	♉	♉	♊	♈	♈	♈	♈	♈	♈	♈	♉	♈	♈	♉	♉	♉	♊
1	4	12	21	29	1	7	23	1	6	15	23	31	1	6	15	23	1	3	11	20	29	1	9	19	1	19	1	8	16	24
♈	♈	♈	♉	♊	♉	♊	♋	♊	♊	♉	♉	♉	♉	♊	♊	♊	♊	♉	♉	♊	♊	♉	♊	♊	♈	♈	♊	♊	♊	♋
1	6	14	23	1	18	1	8	16	24	1	2	11	19	28	1	8	17	1	7	15	23	1	5	17	28	1	10	18	27
♉	♉	♊	♊	♋	♋	♊	♋	♋	♋	♈	♉	♉	♉	♊	♋	♋	♋	♊	♊	♊	♊	♈	♉	♉	♉	♋	♋	♌	♌
1	9	17	25	1	6	1	3	11	19	27	1	6	15	23	1	8	21	1	9	17	25	1	8	17	26	1	5	14	23	31
♊	♋	♋	♋	♋	♊	♋	♌	♌	♌	♍	♊	♊	♊	♋	♌	♍	♍	♋	♋	♋	♋	♉	♊	♊	♊	♋	♌	♌	♍	♍
1	3	11	19	27	1	17	29	1	4	13	21	29	1	7	25	1	10	21	1	2	11	19	27	1	4	13	22	31	1	9	19	28
♋	♌	♌	♍	♋	♋	♉	♉	♍	♍	♍	♎	♌	♋	♋	♊	♌	♌	♍	♍	♍	♍	♌	♍	♍	♍	♊	♋	♋	♌	♎	♎	♊	♌	♎	♎
1	4	12	20	28	1	9	19	28	1	7	15	24	1	2	11	19	27	1	10	1	4	12	20	28	1	8	16	25	1	7	18	30
♌	♍	♎	♎	♍	♎	♎	♌	♌	♌	♍	♍	♎	♌	♍	♍	♍	♍	♍	♌		♍	♎	♎	♎	♌	♍	♍	♍	♌	♌	♍	♍
1	6	14	22	30	1	7	16	24	1	2	11	20	28	1	5	13	21	29	1	16	30	1	6	15	23	31	1	3	11	19	27	1	16
♎	♎	♏	♏	♏	♏	♌	♍	♍	♍	♍	♐	♐	♍	♎	♎	♎	♏	♎	♏	♏	♏	♍	♍	♍	♐	♏	♎	♎	♎	♎	♐	♏
1	7	15	23	1	2	10	18	27	1	6	16	25	1	6	14	22	30	1	10	20	29	1	8	16	25	1	4	12	20	28	1	8	26
♏	♐	♐	♐	♏	♎	♎	♎	♏	♑	♑	♑	♏	♏	♏	♏	♐	♎	♎	♎	♎	♐	♐	♑	♑	♎	♏	♏	♏	♐	♏	♏	♎	♏
1	9	17	25	1	5	13	21	29	1	6	18	1	8	16	23	31	1	8	17	26	1	3	11	20	28	1	6	14	22	30	1	21
♑	♑	♑	♒	♏	♏	♏	♐	♐	♐	♏	♒	♐	♑	♑	♑	♏	♏	♏	♏	♑	♑	♑	♒	♒	♏	♐	♐	♑	♏	♏

VENUS 1947–1962

	1947	1948	1949	1950	1951	1952	1953	1954
1	1 6 17 28 ♏ ♐ ♐ ♐	1 2 10 18 26 ♒ ♒ ♒ ♓ ♓	1 5 13 21 29 ♐ ♐ ♑ ♑ ♒	1 ♒	1 8 16 24 ♑ ♒ ♒ ♒	1 3 11 19 28 ♏ ♐ ♐ ♐ ♑	1 5 14 24 ♒ ♒ ♓ ♓	1 6 14 22 30 ♑ ♑ ♑ ♒ ♒
2	1 6 15 24 ♐ ♑ ♑ ♑	1 3 12 20 29 ♓ ♈ ♈ ♈ ♉	1 6 14 22 ♒ ♓ ♓ ♈	1 2 ♒ ♒	1 9 17 25 ♒ ♓ ♓ ♈	1 5 13 21 29 ♑ ♒ ♒ ♒ ♓	1 2 13 25 ♈ ♈ ♉ ♉	1 7 15 23 ♒ ♓ ♓ ♈
3	1 5 14 22 31 ♑ ♒ ♒ ♒ ♓	1 8 17 26 ♈ ♉ ♉ ♉	1 2 10 18 26 ♓ ♈ ♈ ♈ ♓	1 13 26 ♓ ♈ ♈	1 5 13 21 30 ♈ ♈ ♈ ♈ ♓	1 8 17 25 ♓ ♈ ♈ ♈	1 15 31 ♈ ♉ ♉	1 3 11 19 27 ♓ ♈ ♈ ♈ ♈
4	1 8 17 25 ♓ ♓ ♓ ♈	1 5 14 25 ♉ ♊ ♊ ♊	1 4 12 20 28 ♈ ♈ ♈ ♉	1 7 17 26 ♈ ♈ ♈ ♉	1 7 15 24 ♓ ♈ ♈ ♈	1 2 10 18 26 ♈ ♉ ♉ ♉	1 18 ♉ ♊	1 4 13 21 29 ♈ ♉ ♉ ♉ ♈
5	1 3 12 20 28 ♈ ♈ ♈ ♉ ♊	1 7 26 ♉ ♊ ♊	1 6 14 22 30 ♉ ♊ ♊ ♊	1 6 15 24 ♉ ♊ ♊ ♊	1 2 11 20 29 ♓ ♈ ♈ ♈	1 4 13 21 29 ♈ ♉ ♉ ♉ ♊	1 4 13 21 29 ♊ ♊ ♊ ♊ ♋	1 7 15 24 ♊ ♊ ♊ ♋
6	1 6 14 22 30 ♉ ♉ ♊ ♊ ♊	1 11 29 ♉ ♉ ♊	1 7 16 24 ♊ ♋ ♋ ♋	1 2 10 19 27 ♊ ♉ ♉ ♉ ♊	1 7 17 27 ♈ ♉ ♉ ♉	1 6 14 22 30 ♊ ♊ ♋ ♋ ♋	1 5 17 28 ♋ ♋ ♋ ♊	1 5 13 22 31 ♋ ♋ ♋ ♊ ♋
7	1 9 17 25 ♊ ♋ ♋ ♋	1 ♊	1 2 10 18 27 ♋ ♌ ♌ ♌ ♍	1 6 14 23 31 ♊ ♊ ♋ ♋ ♋	1 8 21 ♉ ♊ ♊	1 9 17 25 ♋ ♋ ♌ ♌	1 7 17 26 ♊ ♊ ♊ ♊	1 9 18 28 ♋ ♌ ♌ ♌
8	1 2 10 18 26 ♋ ♌ ♌ ♌ ♍	1 3 18 29 ♍ ♍ ♍ ♎ ♎	1 4 12 21 29 ♍ ♎ ♎ ♎ ♏	1 8 17 25 ♋ ♌ ♌ ♌	1 ♊	1 2 10 18 26 ♌ ♌ ♍ ♍ ♍	1 4 13 22 30 ♊ ♊ ♊ ♊	1 9 18 28 ♍ ♍ ♎ ♎
9	1 3 11 20 28 ♍ ♍ ♍ ♎	1 9 18 28 ♎ ♏ ♏ ♏	1 6 15 23 ♎ ♏ ♏ ♏	1 2 10 18 26 ♌ ♌ ♍ ♍ ♍	1 4 ♊ ♋	1 3 11 20 28 ♍ ♍ ♍ ♎	1 8 16 24 ♊ ♋ ♋ ♋	1 7 18 ♎ ♏ ♏
10	1 6 14 22 30 ♎ ♎ ♏ ♏ ♏	1 7 15 24 ♏ ♐ ♐ ♐	1 2 10 19 28 ♏ ♐ ♐ ♐ ♐	1 4 12 20 28 ♍ ♍ ♍ ♎ ♎	1 17 30 ♋ ♋ ♊	1 6 14 22 30 ♎ ♏ ♏ ♏ ♎	1 2 11 19 27 ♋ ♌ ♌ ♌ ♍	1 24 27 ♏ ♏
11	1 7 15 23 ♏ ♐ ♐	1 10 18 26 ♐ ♑ ♑ ♑	1 6 16 26 ♐ ♑ ♑ ♑	1 5 13 21 29 ♎ ♏ ♏ ♏	1 10 20 29 ♊ ♊ ♎ ♎	1 2 11 19 28 ♏ ♎ ♎ ♏ ♏	1 6 14 22 30 ♍ ♏ ♏ ♏ ♏	1 19 ♏
12	1 9 17 25 ♑ ♑ ♑ ♒	1 4 12 20 28 ♏ ♏ ♏ ♐ ♐	1 6 19 ♒ ≈ ♒	1 7 15 23 31 ♐ ♐ ♑ ♑ ♑	1 8 17 25 ♎ ♏ ♏ ♏	1 5 13 21 29 ♐ ♐ ♒ ♒ ♒	1 23 ♐ ♏	1 4 26 ♑ ♏ ♏

VENUS 1963–1978

	1963	1964	1965	1966	1967	1968	1969	1970
1	1 7 18 27 ♏ ♐ ♐ ♐	1 9 17 25 ♒ ♒ ♓ ♓	1 4 12 20 28 ♐ ♐ ♑ ♑ ♒	1 19 ♒	1 7 15 23 31 ♑ ♒ ♒ ♒ ♓	1 2 10 19 27 ♏ ♐ ♐ ♐ ♑	1 5 14 23 ♒ ♒ ♓ ♓	1 5 13 21 29 ♑ ♑ ♑ ♒ ♒
2	1 6 15 24 ♐ ♑ ♑ ♑	1 3 11 19 28 ♓ ♈ ♈ ♈ ♈	1 5 13 21 ♒ ≈ ♒	1 7 25 ♒ ♓ ♒	1 8 16 24 ♒ ♓ ♓ ♈	1 4 12 20 28 ♑ ♒ ♒ ♒ ♓	1 2 13 27 ♈ ♈ ♉ ♉	1 6 14 22 ♒ ♓ ♓
3	1 4 13 22 30 ♑ ♒ ♒ ♒ ♓	1 8 16 26 ♈ ♉ ♉ ♉	1 9 17 25 ♓ ♈ ♈ ♈	1 15 27 ♈ ♈ ♈	1 4 12 20 29 ♓ ♈ ♈ ♈ ♈	1 7 16 24 ♓ ♈ ♈ ♈	1 ♈	1 2 10 18 26 ♓ ♈ ♈ ♈ ♈
4	1 7 16 24 ♓ ♓ ♓ ♈	1 4 14 25 ♉ ♊ ♊ ♊	1 2 11 19 27 ♈ ♈ ♈ ♉ ♉	1 7 17 26 ♈ ♈ ♈ ♉	1 6 14 23 ♈ ♉ ♉ ♉	1 9 17 25 ♉ ♊ ♊ ♊	1 6 ♈ ♈	1 3 12 20 28 ♈ ♉ ♉ ♉ ♈
5	1 2 11 19 27 ♈ ♈ ♈ ♉ ♊	1 9 ♉ ♊	1 5 13 23 ♉ ♊ ♊ ♊	1 5 13 22 30 ♉ ♊ ♊ ♊ ♊	1 2 10 19 28 ♓ ♈ ♈ ♈	1 2 10 19 28 ♈ ♉ ♉ ♉ ♊	1 24 ♊ ♊	1 6 14 23 31 ♊ ♊ ♊ ♊ ♋
6	1 5 13 21 29 ♉ ♉ ♊ ♊ ♊	1 18 ♉ ♉	1 6 15 23 ♊ ♋ ♋ ♋	1 9 18 26 ♊ ♉ ♉ ♉	1 7 17 27 ♈ ♉ ♉ ♉	1 5 13 21 29 ♊ ♊ ♋ ♋ ♋	1 6 17 27 ♋ ♋ ♋ ♉	1 8 17 25 ♋ ♋ ♋ ♊
7	1 7 16 24 ♊ ♋ ♋ ♋	1 ♊	1 9 17 26 ♋ ♌ ♌ ♌	1 5 13 22 30 ♊ ♊ ♋ ♋ ♋	1 9 24 ♋ ♌ ♌	1 7 16 24 ♋ ♋ ♌ ♌	1 7 16 25 ♉ ♊ ♊ ♊	1 4 13 21 30 ♋ ♌ ♌ ♌ ♍
8	1 9 17 25 ♌ ♌ ♌ ♍	1 5 18 29 ♍ ♍ ♍ ♎	1 3 10 20 28 ♍ ♍ ♎ ♎ ♎	1 9 17 25 ♋ ♌ ♌ ♌	1 23 ♌ ♌	1 9 17 25 ♌ ♍ ♍ ♍	1 3 12 21 29 ♊ ♋ ♋ ♋ ♌	1 7 19 ♍ ♍ ♎
9	1 2 10 18 26 ♍ ♍ ♍ ♎ ♎	1 8 18 27 ♎ ♏ ♏ ♏	1 5 14 22 ♎ ♏ ♏	1 9 17 25 ♌ ♌ ♍ ♍	1 9 ♌ ♍	1 2 10 19 27 ♍ ♎ ♎ ♎ ♏	1 5 13 21 29 ♌ ♌ ♍ ♍ ♍	1 3 ♎ ♏
10	1 4 12 21 29 ♎ ♎ ♏ ♏ ♏	1 6 14 23 31 ♏ ♍ ♍ ♍ ♐	1 10 19 28 ♏ ♐ ♐ ♐	1 3 11 19 27 ♍ ♎ ♎ ♎ ♏	1 2 18 30 ♍ ♎ ♎ ♏	1 5 13 21 29 ♏ ♎ ♎ ♏ ♏	1 9 18 26 ♍ ♍ ♍ ♏ ♎	1 6 28 ♏ ♏
11	1 6 14 22 30 ♏ ♐ ♐ ♐ ♑	1 9 17 25 ♎ ♎ ♎ ♏	1 6 15 23 ♐ ♐ ♑ ♑	1 4 12 20 28 ♏ ♏ ♏ ♐ ♐	1 10 19 28 ♎ ♎ ♎ ♎	1 7 15 23 ♏ ♏ ♏ ♐	1 3 11 19 27 ♐ ♐ ♐ ♏ ♏	1 6 28 ♏ ♏ ♏
12	1 8 16 24 ♑ ♑ ♑ ♒	1 3 11 19 27 ♏ ♏ ♏ ♐ ♐	1 7 22 ♒ ≈ ♒	1 6 14 22 30 ♐ ♐ ♑ ♑ ♑	1 7 16 25 ♎ ♏ ♏ ♏	1 2 10 18 27 ♐ ♐ ♒ ♒ ♒	1 5 13 21 28 ♐ ♐ ♐ ♐ ♑	1 4 26 ♏ ♏ ♏

Venus Tables — 1955–1962

1955
- 1 ♏ · 6 ♐ · 17 ♐ · 28 ♐
- 1 ♐ · 6 ♑ · 15 ♑ · 24 ♑
- 1 ♑ · 5 ♒ · 13 ♒ · 22 ♒ · 30 ♓
- 1 ♓ · 8 ♓ · 16 ♓ · 25 ♓
- 1 ♈ · 3 ♈ · 11 ♈ · 20 ♉ · 28 ♉
- 1 ♉ · 5 ♉ · 13 ♊ · 22 ♊ · 30 ♋
- 1 ♊ · 8 ♊ · 16 ♊ · 24 ♊
- 1 ♋ · 10 ♋ · 18 ♋ · 26 ♍
- 1 ♌ · 3 ♌ · 11 ♌ · 19 ♍ · 27 ♍
- 1 ♎ · 5 ♎ · 13 ♏ · 21 ♏ · 29 ♏
- 1 ♏ · 6 ♐ · 14 ♐ · 22 ♑ · 30 ♑
- 1 ♑ · 8 ♑ · 16 ♑ · 24 ♒

1956
- 1 ♒ · 9 ♒ · 18 ♓ · 26 ♓
- 1 ♓ · 3 ♈ · 11 ♈ · 20 ♈ · 28 ♈
- 1 ♈ · 8 ♉ · 17 ♉ · 26 ♉
- 1 ♉ · 4 ♉ · 14 ♊ · 25 ♊
- 1 ♊ · 8 ♊
- 1 ♋ · 24 ♋
- 1 ♋ · 8 ♋ · 16 ♋ · 24 ♋
- 1 ♌ · 4 ♌ · 18 ♌ · 29 ♌
- 1 ♍ · 8 ♍ · 18 ♍ · 27 ♎
- 1 ♎ · 6 ♎ · 15 ♏ · 23 ♏
- 1 ♏ · 9 ♐ · 17 ♐ · 26 ♐
- 1 ♏ · 4 ♏ · 12 ♐ · 20 ♐ · 28 ♐

1957
- 1 ♑ · 5 ♒ · 13 ♒ · 21 ♓ · 29 ♓
- 1 ♓ · 6 ♈ · 14 ♈ · 22 ♈
- 1 ♈ · 8 ♉ · 17 ♉ · 26 ♉
- 1 ♉ · 3 ♊ · 11 ♊ · 19 ♋ · 27 ♋
- 1 ♋ · 5 ♋ · 13 ♊ · 22 ♊ · 30 ♊
- 1 ♊ · 7 ♊ · 15 ♋ · 23 ♋
- 1 ♋ · 10 ♋ · 18 ♌ · 26 ♌
- 1 ♌ · 3 ♌ · 12 ♍ · 20 ♍ · 28 ♎
- 1 ♎ · 6 ♎ · 14 ♏ · 23 ♏
- 1 ♏ · 10 ♐ · 19 ♐ · 28 ♐
- 1 ♏ · 6 ♏ · 15 ♐ · 26 ♐
- 1 ♑ · 8 ♑ · 26 ♒

1958
- 1 ♒ · 26 ♒
- 1 ♒
- 1 ♓ · 14 ♈ · 27 ♈
- 1 ♈ · 7 ♉ · 17 ♉ · 26 ♉
- 1 ♊ · 5 ♊ · 14 ♋ · 22 ♋ · 31 ♋
- 1 ♋ · 8 ♋ · 16 ♌ · 24 ♌
- 1 ♌ · 3 ♌ · 12 ♍ · 20 ♍ · 28 ♎
- 1 ♎ · 10 ♎ · 18 ♏ · 26 ♏
- 1 ♏ · 10 ♐ · 18 ♐ · 26 ♐
- 1 ♐ · 4 ♑ · 12 ♑ · 19 ♑ · 27 ♒
- 1 ♒ · 6 ♒ · 14 ♓ · 22 ♓ · 30 ♓
- 1 ♈ · 8 ♈ · 16 ♈ · 25 ♈

1959
- 1 ♑ · 7 ♑ · 15 ♒ · 23 ♒ · 31 ♒
- 1 ♒ · 8 ♓ · 16 ♓ · 24 ♓
- 1 ♈ · 5 ♈ · 13 ♉ · 21 ♉ · 29 ♉
- 1 ♊ · 7 ♊ · 17 ♋ · 26 ♋
- 1 ♋ · 2 ♋ · 11 ♋ · 20 ♊ · 29 ♊
- 1 ♊ · 7 ♊ · 17 ♊ · 27 ♋
- 1 ♋ · 9 ♋ · 23 ♌
- 1 ♌ · 29 ♌
- 1 ♍ · 20 ♍ · 25 ♎
- 1 ♎ · 18 ♏ · 30 ♏
- 1 ♐ · 5 ♐ · 13 ♑ · 21 ♑ · 29 ♑
- 1 ♐ · 6 ♐ · 14 ♐ · 22 ♑ · 30 ♑

1960
- 1 ♑ · 2 ♑ · 11 ♒ · 19 ♒ · 27 ♓
- 1 ♓ · 4 ♈ · 13 ♈ · 21 ♈ · 29 ♈
- 1 ♈ · 8 ♉ · 16 ♉ · 24 ♉
- 1 ♉ · 6 ♊ · 15 ♊ · 23 ♊
- 1 ♊ · 2 ♋ · 11 ♋ · 20 ♋ · 29 ♋
- 1 ♋ · 7 ♋ · 17 ♋ · 27 ♌
- 1 ♌ · 9 ♌ · 18 ♍ · 26 ♍
- 1 ♍ · 3 ♍ · 11 ♎ · 19 ♎ · 27 ♎
- 1 ♎ · 5 ♎ · 14 ♏ · 22 ♏ · 30 ♏
- 1 ♏ · 7 ♐ · 15 ♐ · 24 ♐
- 1 ♐ · 5 ♑ · 14 ♑ · 22 ♒ · 30 ♒
- 1 ♒ · 10 ♒ · 19 ♓ · 27 ♓

1961
- 1 ♒ · 5 ♓ · 14 ♓ · 23 ♓
- 1 ♈ · 2 ♈ · 13 ♈ · 25 ♈
- 1 ♈ · 8 ♉ · 16 ♉ · 24 ♉
- 1 ♊ · 9 ♊ · 18 ♋ · 26 ♋
- 1 ♋ · 4 ♋ · 12 ♋ · 20 ♋ · 28 ♌
- 1 ♌ · 6 ♌ · 17 ♍ · 27 ♍
- 1 ♍ · 7 ♎ · 16 ♎ · 25 ♎
- 1 ♎ · 3 ♏ · 11 ♏ · 19 ♏ · 27 ♐
- 1 ♐ · 7 ♐ · 15 ♐ · 24 ♑
- 1 ♑ · 3 ♑ · 11 ♒ · 19 ♒ · 27 ♒
- 1 ♓ · 2 ♓ · 10 ♓ · 18 ♈ · 26 ♈
- 1 ♈ · 2 ♈ · 10 ♉ · 19 ♉ · 27 ♊

1962
- 1 ♐ · 6 ♑ · 14 ♑ · 22 ♒ · 30 ♒
- 1 ♒ · 7 ♓ · 15 ♓ · 23 ♓
- 1 ♈ · 3 ♈ · 11 ♈ · 19 ♈ · 27 ♈
- 1 ♈ · 4 ♉ · 12 ♉ · 20 ♉ · 28 ♊
- 1 ♊ · 7 ♋ · 15 ♋ · 23 ♋ · 31 ♋
- 1 ♋ · 9 ♋ · 17 ♌ · 26 ♌
- 1 ♌ · 4 ♌ · 13 ♍ · 21 ♍ · 31 ♍
- 1 ♍ · 9 ♎ · 18 ♎ · 28 ♎
- 1 ♎ · 7 ♏ · 18 ♏
- 1 ♐ · 13 ♐
- 1 ♐ · 2 ♐
- 1 ♐ · 25 ♑

Venus Tables — 1971–1978

1971
- 1 ♏ · 7 ♐ · 18 ♐ · 27 ♐
- 1 ♐ · 6 ♑ · 15 ♑ · 23 ♑
- 1 ♑ · 4 ♒ · 13 ♒ · 21 ♓ · 30 ♓
- 1 ♈ · 7 ♈ · 15 ♈ · 24 ♉
- 1 ♉ · 2 ♉ · 10 ♊ · 19 ♊ · 27 ♊
- 1 ♋ · 4 ♋ · 12 ♋ · 21 ♋ · 29 ♋
- 1 ♌ · 7 ♌ · 15 ♌ · 23 ♍ · 31 ♍
- 1 ♍ · 9 ♎ · 17 ♎ · 25 ♎
- 1 ♎ · 2 ♏ · 10 ♏ · 18 ♏ · 26 ♏
- 1 ♐ · 4 ♐ · 12 ♐ · 20 ♐ · 28 ♑
- 1 ♑ · 5 ♑ · 13 ♒ · 21 ♒ · 29 ♒
- 1 ♓ · 7 ♓ · 15 ♓ · 23 ♈ · 31 ♈

1972
- 1 ♒ · 8 ♒ · 17 ♓ · 25 ♓
- 1 ♓ · 2 ♈ · 10 ♈ · 19 ♈ · 27 ♈
- 1 ♈ · 5 ♉ · 13 ♉ · 21 ♉
- 1 ♉ · 4 ♉ · 14 ♊ · 26 ♊
- 1 ♊ · 11 ♊
- 1 ♋ · 12 ♋ · 30 ♋
- 1 ♋ · 19 ♋
- 1 ♋ · 6 ♌ · 18 ♌ · 29 ♌
- 1 ♍ · 8 ♍ · 17 ♎ · 27 ♎
- 1 ♎ · 5 ♏ · 14 ♏ · 23 ♏ · 31 ♐
- 1 ♐ · 8 ♐ · 16 ♐ · 25 ♑
- 1 ♑ · 3 ♑ · 11 ♒ · 19 ♒ · 27 ♒

1973
- 1 ♒ · 4 ♓ · 12 ♓ · 20 ♓ · 28 ♈
- 1 ♈ · 5 ♈ · 13 ♈ · 21 ♉
- 1 ♉ · 9 ♉ · 17 ♊ · 25 ♊
- 1 ♊ · 2 ♊ · 10 ♋ · 18 ♋ · 26 ♋
- 1 ♋ · 4 ♌ · 12 ♌ · 20 ♌ · 29 ♌
- 1 ♍ · 6 ♍ · 14 ♍ · 22 ♎ · 30 ♎
- 1 ♎ · 9 ♏ · 17 ♏ · 25 ♏
- 1 ♏ · 2 ♐ · 11 ♐ · 19 ♐ · 27 ♐
- 1 ♑ · 5 ♑ · 13 ♑ · 22 ♒
- 1 ♒ · 9 ♒ · 18 ♓ · 27 ♓
- 1 ♈ · 6 ♈ · 15 ♈ · 26 ♉
- 1 ♉ · 8 ♉ · 26 ♊

1974
- 1 ♐ · 11 ♐ · 30 ♑
- 1 ♑
- 1 ♑ · 16 ♒ · 27 ♒
- 1 ♓ · 7 ♓ · 16 ♈ · 26 ♈
- 1 ♈ · 5 ♉ · 14 ♉ · 23 ♉ · 31 ♊
- 1 ♊ · 9 ♊ · 17 ♋ · 26 ♋
- 1 ♋ · 4 ♌ · 13 ♌ · 21 ♌ · 29 ♌
- 1 ♍ · 7 ♍ · 15 ♎ · 23 ♎ · 31 ♎
- 1 ♏ · 8 ♏ · 17 ♏ · 25 ♏
- 1 ♐ · 3 ♐ · 11 ♐ · 19 ♐ · 27 ♐
- 1 ♑ · 4 ♑ · 12 ♑ · 19 ♒ · 27 ♒
- 1 ♒ · 5 ♓ · 13 ♓ · 21 ♓ · 29 ♈

1975
- 1 ♑ · 6 ♒ · 14 ♒ · 22 ♓ · 30 ♓
- 1 ♓ · 7 ♈ · 15 ♈ · 23 ♈
- 1 ♈ · 4 ♉ · 12 ♉ · 20 ♉ · 28 ♊
- 1 ♊ · 6 ♋ · 14 ♋ · 22 ♋
- 1 ♋ · 5 ♌ · 14 ♌ · 23 ♌ · 31 ♌
- 1 ♍ · 6 ♍ · 16 ♍ · 27 ♍
- 1 ♍ · 9 ♍ · 27 ♍
- 1 ♍ · 16 ♍
- 1 ♌ · 3 ♌
- 1 ♌ · 4 ♌ · 19 ♍ · 30 ♍
- 1 ♎ · 10 ♎ · 19 ♏ · 28 ♏
- 1 ♐ · 7 ♐ · 16 ♐ · 24 ♑

1976
- 1 ♑ · 2 ♒ · 10 ♒ · 18 ♓ · 26 ♓
- 1 ♓ · 3 ♈ · 12 ♈ · 20 ♈ · 28 ♈
- 1 ♈ · 7 ♉ · 15 ♉ · 23 ♉ · 31 ♊
- 1 ♊ · 8 ♊ · 16 ♋ · 25 ♋
- 1 ♋ · 3 ♋ · 11 ♌ · 19 ♌ · 27 ♌
- 1 ♍ · 4 ♍ · 12 ♍ · 21 ♍ · 29 ♎
- 1 ♎ · 7 ♎ · 15 ♏ · 23 ♏ · 31 ♏
- 1 ♐ · 8 ♐ · 16 ♐ · 25 ♑
- 1 ♑ · 10 ♑ · 18 ♒ · 26 ♒
- 1 ♒ · 4 ♓ · 13 ♓ · 21 ♈ · 29 ♈
- 1 ♈ · 6 ♉ · 14 ♉ · 23 ♉
- 1 ♊ · 10 ♊ · 18 ♊ · 27 ♋

1977
- 1 ♎ · 5 ♎ · 14 ♏ · 23 ♏
- 1 ♏ · 2 ♏ · 14 ♏ · 28 ♐
- 1 ♐ · 31 ♑
- 1 ♑ · 18 ♒
- 1 ♒ · 7 ♓ · 25 ♓
- 1 ♈ · 6 ♈ · 17 ♈ · 27 ♉
- 1 ♉ · 7 ♉ · 16 ♊ · 25 ♊
- 1 ♋ · 3 ♋ · 12 ♋ · 20 ♋ · 29 ♌
- 1 ♌ · 6 ♌ · 14 ♍ · 23 ♍
- 1 ♎ · 9 ♎ · 17 ♏ · 25 ♏
- 1 ♏ · 2 ♏ · 10 ♐ · 18 ♐ · 26 ♐
- 1 ♑ · 4 ♑ · 12 ♑ · 20 ♒ · 28 ♒

1978
- 1 ♒ · 5 ♓ · 13 ♓ · 21 ♓ · 29 ♒
- 1 ♒ · 6 ♓ · 14 ♓ · 22 ♓
- 1 ♈ · 2 ♈ · 10 ♈ · 18 ♉ · 26 ♉
- 1 ♉ · 3 ♉ · 11 ♊ · 19 ♊ · 27 ♊
- 1 ♋ · 6 ♋ · 14 ♋ · 22 ♋ · 30 ♌
- 1 ♌ · 8 ♌ · 16 ♍ · 25 ♍
- 1 ♍ · 3 ♍ · 12 ♎ · 21 ♎ · 30 ♎
- 1 ♏ · 8 ♏ · 18 ♏ · 28 ♏
- 1 ♐ · 7 ♐ · 19 ♐
- 1 ♐ · 6 ♐ · 30 ♑
- 1 ♑ · 17 ♑
- 1 ♒ · 11 ♒ · 27 ♒

VENUS 1979–1994

	1979	1980	1981	1982	1983	1984	1985	1986
1	1 7 18 27 ♏ ♐ ♐	1 8 16 24 ♒ ♒ ♓ ♓	1 3 11 19 27 ♐ ♐ ♑ ♑ ♒	1 23 ♑	1 6 14 22 30 ♑ ♒ ♒ ♓	1 9 18 26 ♐ ♐ ♐ ♑	1 4 13 23 ♒ ♓ ♓ ♓	1 4 12 20 28 ♑ ♑ ♑ ♒ ♒
2	1 5 14 23 ♐ ♑ ♑ ♒	1 2 10 18 27 ♓ ♈ ♈ ♈	1 4 12 20 28 ♒ ♓ ♓ ♈	1 ♒	1 7 15 23 ♓ ♓ ♈ ♈	1 3 11 19 27 ♑ ♒ ♒ ♓ ♈	1 2 14 ♈ ♈	1 5 13 21 ♒ ♓ ♓
3	1 4 12 21 29 ♑ ♒ ♒ ♓ ♓	1 7 16 25 ♈ ♉ ♉ ♉	1 8 16 24 ♈ ♈ ♉	1 2 16 27 ♓ ♈ ♈	1 3 11 19 28 ♈ ♈ ♉ ♉	1 6 15 23 31 ♒ ♓ ♈ ♈ ♈	1 3 24 ♈ ♈	1 9 17 25 ♈ ♈ ♈
4	1 7 15 23 ♓ ♓ ♓ ♈	1 4 14 26 ♉ ♊ ♊ ♊	1 9 18 26 ♈ ♉ ♉	1 7 16 25 ♈ ♉ ♉	1 5 13 22 ♉ ♉ ♊	1 8 16 24 ♈ ♈ ♈ ♈	1 11 ♈ ♈	1 2 10 19 27 ♈ ♉ ♉ ♉ ♊
5	1 10 18 26 ♈ ♈ ♉ ♉	1 13 ♊ ♋	1 4 12 20 28 ♉ ♉ ♊ ♊ ♊	1 5 13 22 31 ♊ ♋ ♋ ♋ ♋	1 9 18 28 ♊ ♋ ♋ ♋	1 2 10 18 27 ♉ ♉ ♉ ♊ ♊	1 10 26 ♈ ♈	1 5 13 22 30 ♉ ♉ ♊ ♊
6	1 4 12 20 28 ♉ ♉ ♊ ♊	1 5 23 ♋ ♊	1 5 13 22 30 ♊ ♋ ♋ ♋	1 8 17 26 ♋ ♋ ♋ ♋	1 6 16 27 ♋ ♋ ♋	1 4 12 20 28 ♊ ♋ ♋ ♋	1 6 17 27 ♈ ♉ ♉	1 7 16 24 ♋ ♋ ♋
7	1 6 15 23 31 ♊ ♋ ♋ ♋ ♌	1 22 ♊ ♊	1 8 16 25 ♋ ♌ ♌	1 4 12 21 29 ♋ ♌ ♌ ♌	1 10 ♋ ♋	1 6 14 23 31 ♋ ♌ ♌ ♌	1 6 16 25 ♉ ♉ ♊ ♊	1 3 12 21 30 ♋ ♌ ♌ ♌
8	1 8 16 24 ♌ ♌ ♌ ♍	1 7 18 29 ♊ ♋ ♋ ♋	1 2 10 19 27 ♍ ♍ ♍ ♎	1 6 14 23 31 ♌ ♌ ♌ ♌	1 27 ♌	1 8 16 24 ♌ ♌ ♍	1 2 11 20 28 ♊ ♋ ♋ ♋	1 8 17 28 ♌ ♍ ♍
9	1 9 17 25 ♍ ♍ ♎ ♎	1 8 17 26 ♋ ♌ ♌ ♌	1 4 13 22 30 ♎ ♎ ♏ ♏	1 8 16 24 ♍ ♍ ♍	1 ♌	1 9 18 26 ♍ ♍ ♎	1 6 14 22 30 ♋ ♌ ♌ ♍	1 7 20 ♍ ♍
10	1 3 11 19 27 ♎ ♎ ♏ ♏ ♐	1 5 14 22 30 ♌ ♍ ♍ ♍	1 9 18 27 ♏ ♏ ♐	1 2 10 18 26 ♎ ♎ ♎ ♎	1 6 19 30 ♍ ♎ ♎	1 4 12 20 28 ♎ ♎ ♏ ♏	1 8 17 25 ♍ ♎ ♎	1 11 20 ♎ ♎
11	1 4 13 21 29 ♏ ♐ ♐ ♑ ♑	1 8 16 24 ♍ ♎ ♎ ♎	1 6 15 26 ♐ ♑ ♑	1 3 11 19 27 ♏ ♏ ♐ ♐	1 9 19 29 ♏ ♐ ♐	1 6 14 22 ♏ ♏ ♐	1 2 10 18 26 ♎ ♏ ♏ ♏	1 10 ♏ ♏
12	1 7 15 23 31 ♑ ♑ ♒ ♒	1 2 10 18 26 ♎ ♏ ♏ ♏	1 9 ♑		1 5 13 21 29 ♐ ♑ ♑ ♒	1 7 15 24 ♐ ♑ ♑	1 9 18 26 ♏ ♏ ♐	1 4 11 19 27 ♏ ♐ ♐ ♐	1 13 27 ♏ ♏ ♏

VENUS 1995–2010

	1995	1996	1997	1998	1999	2000	2001	2002
1	1 8 17 27 ♏ ♐ ♐	1 7 15 23 ♒ ♒ ♓ ♓	1 2 10 18 26 ♐ ♐ ♑ ♑ ♒	1 10 28 ♑	1 5 13 21 29 ♑ ♒ ♒ ♓	1 8 17 25 ♐ ♐ ♐ ♑	1 4 13 23 ♒ ♓ ♓ ♓	1 3 11 19 27 ♑ ♑ ♑ ♒ ♒
2	1 5 14 22 ♐ ♑ ♑ ♒	1 9 18 26 ♓ ♈ ♈ ♈	1 3 11 19 27 ♒ ♓ ♓ ♈	1 15 ♒	1 6 14 22 ♓ ♓ ♈	1 2 10 18 26 ♑ ♒ ♒ ♓	1 3 16 ♈ ♈	1 4 12 20 28 ♒ ♓ ♓ ♈
3	1 3 11 20 28 ♑ ♒ ♒ ♓ ♈	1 6 15 25 ♈ ♉ ♉ ♉	1 7 15 23 31 ♈ ♈ ♈ ♉	1 5 17 27 ♓ ♈ ♈	1 2 10 18 27 ♈ ♈ ♉ ♉	1 5 13 22 30 ♒ ♓ ♈ ♈ ♈	1 29 ♈ ♈	1 8 16 24 ♈ ♈ ♈
4	1 6 14 22 30 ♓ ♓ ♈ ♈ ♈	1 4 15 28 ♉ ♊ ♊ ♊	1 8 16 24 ♉ ♉ ♊	1 6 16 25 ♈ ♈ ♉ ♉	1 6 16 25 ♉ ♉ ♊	1 4 13 21 30 ♉ ♉ ♊ ♊ ♊	1 7 15 23 ♈ ♈ ♈	1 ♈	1 9 18 26 ♈ ♉ ♉
5	1 9 17 25 ♈ ♈ ♉ ♉	1 ♊	1 3 11 19 27 ♊ ♋ ♋ ♋	1 4 13 21 30 ♉ ♉ ♊ ♊	1 9 18 27 ♊ ♋ ♋ ♋	1 9 18 ♊ ♋	1 13 26 ♈ ♈	1 4 12 21 29 ♉ ♉ ♊ ♊
6	1 2 11 19 27 ♉ ♉ ♊ ♊ ♊	1 11 ♊	1 4 12 21 29 ♋ ♋ ♋ ♋	1 8 16 25 ♋ ♋ ♋	1 6 16 28 ♋ ♋ ♋	1 3 11 19 27 ♊ ♋ ♋ ♋	1 6 17 26 ♈ ♉ ♉	1 6 15 23 ♊ ♋ ♋
7	1 5 13 22 30 ♊ ♊ ♋ ♋ ♋	1 25 ♊	1 7 15 24 ♋ ♌ ♌	1 3 11 20 28 ♋ ♌ ♌ ♌	1 13 ♋	1 5 13 21 30 ♋ ♌ ♌ ♌	1 6 15 24 ♉ ♊ ♊	1 2 11 20 29 ♋ ♌ ♍ ♍
8	1 7 15 23 31 ♌ ♌ ♌ ♍ ♍	1 7 18 29 ♊ ♋ ♋ ♋	1 9 18 26 ♌ ♌ ♎	1 5 13 22 30 ♌ ♌ ♌ ♌	1 16 ♋	1 7 15 23 31 ♌ ♌ ♎ ♎	1 2 10 19 27 ♊ ♋ ♋ ♋	1 7 17 28 ♌ ♍ ♍
9	1 8 16 24 ♍ ♍ ♎ ♎	1 7 16 25 ♋ ♌ ♌ ♌	1 4 12 21 29 ♎ ♎ ♏ ♏	1 7 15 23 ♍ ♍ ♍	1 3 19 ♌ ♌	1 8 16 25 ♍ ♍ ♎	1 5 13 21 29 ♋ ♌ ♌ ♍	1 8 23 ♍ ♍
10	1 2 10 18 26 ♎ ♎ ♏ ♏ ♐	1 4 13 21 30 ♌ ♍ ♍ ♍	1 8 17 27 ♏ ♏ ♐	1 9 17 25 ♎ ♎ ♎	1 8 20 30 ♍ ♎ ♎	1 3 11 19 28 ♎ ♎ ♏ ♏	1 7 15 24 ♍ ♎ ♎	1 28 ♎
11	1 3 11 20 28 ♏ ♐ ♐ ♑	1 7 15 23 ♍ ♎ ♎ ♏	1 5 16 27 ♐ ♑ ♑	1 2 10 18 26 ♏ ♏ ♐ ♐	1 9 18 27 ♏ ♐ ♐	1 5 13 21 30 ♏ ♐ ♐ ♑	1 9 17 25 ♏ ♏ ♐	1 ♏
12	1 6 14 22 30 ♑ ♑ ♒ ♒	1 9 17 25 ♏ ♏ ♐	1 12 ♑ ♒		1 4 12 20 28 ♐ ♑ ♑ ♒	1 6 14 23 31 ♐ ♑ ♑ ♒	1 8 17 26 ♏ ♐ ♐	1 2 10 18 26 ♐ ♐ ♑ ♑	1 16 28 ♏ ♏ ♏

1987	1988	1989	1990	1991	1992	1993	1994
1♍ 7♐ 18♐ 27♐	1♒ 7♒ 16♓ 24♓	1♐ 3♐ 11♑ 19♑ 27♑	1♒ 17♑	1♑ 5♒ 13♒ 21♒ 29♓	1♐ 9♐ 17♐ 25♑	1♒ 4♓ 13♓ 23♓	1♑ 4♑ 12♑ 20♒ 28♒
1♐ 5♑ 14♑ 23♑	1♓ 10♈ 18♈ 27♈	1♑ 4♒ 12♒ 20♒ 28♓	1♑	1♓ 6♓ 14♓ 22♈	1♑ 2♑ 11♑ 19♒ 27♒	1♓ 3♈ 15♈	1♒ 5♒ 13♓ 21♓
1♑ 3♒ 12♒ 20♒ 29♓	1♈ 6♉ 15♉ 25♉	1♓ 8♓ 16♓ 24♈	1♑ 4♒ 17♒ 27♒	1♈ 3♈ 11♈ 19♉ 27♉	1♒ 6♒ 14♓ 22♓ 30♓	1♈ 10♈ 12♈	1♓ 9♈ 17♈ 25♈
1♓ 6♓ 14♓ 23♈	1♉ 4♊ 14♊ 27♊	1♈ 9♈ 17♉ 25♉	1♒ 6♓ 16♓ 25♓	1♉ 5♉ 13♊ 22♊ 30♊	1♓ 7♈ 15♈ 24♈	1♈ 4♈	1♈ 2♉ 10♉ 18♉ 26♊
1♈ 9♈ 17♉ 26♉	1♊ 18♋ 27♊	1♉ 3♉ 11♊ 19♊ 28♊	1♓ 4♈ 13♈ 22♈ 30♉	1♊ 9♋ 18♋ 27♋	1♈ 2♉ 10♉ 18♉ 26♊	1♈ 12♈ 26♈	1♊ 4♊ 13♊ 21♋ 29♋
1♉ 3♉ 11♊ 19♊ 28♊	1♊ 17♊	1♊ 5♋ 13♋ 21♋ 29♌	1♉ 8♉ 17♉ 25♊	1♋ 6♌ 16♌ 28♌	1♊ 3♊ 11♊ 19♋ 28♋	1♈ 6♉ 17♉ 27♉	1♋ 7♋ 15♌ 24♌
1♊ 6♋ 14♋ 22♋ 30♌	1♊ 24♊	1♌ 8♌ 16♌ 24♍	1♊ 3♊ 12♊ 20♋ 28♋	1♌ 11♍	1♋ 6♋ 14♌ 22♌ 30♌	1♉ 6♊ 15♊ 24♊	1♌ 3♌ 11♍ 20♍ 29♍
1♌ 7♌ 16♌ 24♍	1♊ 7♋ 18♋ 29♋	1♍ 10♍ 18♎ 27♎	1♋ 6♋ 14♌ 22♌ 30♌	1♍ 22♌	1♌ 7♍ 15♍ 24♍	1♊ 2♋ 11♋ 19♋ 28♌	1♍ 8♎ 17♎ 28♎
1♍ 9♍ 17♎ 25♎	1♋ 7♌ 17♌ 26♌	1♎ 4♎ 13♏ 21♏ 30♏	1♌ 7♍ 15♍ 23♍	1♌	1♎ 9♎ 17♎ 25♏	1♌ 5♌ 13♌ 22♍ 30♍	1♎ 8♏ 21♏
1♎ 3♎ 11♏ 19♏ 27♏	1♌ 5♍ 13♍ 22♍ 30♎	1♏ 9♐ 18♐ 27♐	1♍ 2♎ 10♎ 18♎ 26♏	1♌ 7♍ 20♍ 30♍	1♏ 3♏ 12♏ 20♐ 28♐	1♍ 8♍ 16♎ 24♎	1♏
1♏ 4♐ 12♐ 20♐ 28♑	1♎ 7♎ 15♎ 24♏	1♐ 5♑ 16♑ 27♑	1♏ 2♏ 10♏ 18♐ 26♐	1♍ 9♎ 19♎ 28♎	1♐ 5♐ 14♑ 22♑ 30♑	1♎ 9♏ 17♏ 25♏	1♏ 3♏
1♑ 6♑ 14♑ 22♒ 30♒	1♏ 2♏ 10♏ 18♐ 26♐	1♑ 10♒	1♐ 4♐ 12♑ 20♑ 28♑	1♎ 6♏ 15♏ 23♏	1♑ 9♒ 17♒ 26♒	1♏ 3♐ 11♐ 19♐ 27♑	1♏ 15♏ 28♏

2003	2004	2005	2006	2007	2008	2009	2010
1♏ 8♐ 17♐ 27♐	1♒ 7♒ 15♓ 23♓ 31♓	1♐ 2♐ 10♑ 18♑ 26♑	1♒ 2♑ 20♑	1♑ 4♒ 12♒ 20♒ 28♓	1♐ 8♐ 16♐ 24♑	1♒ 4♓ 13♓ 23♓	1♑ 3♑ 11♑ 19♒ 27♒
1♐ 5♑ 13♑ 22♑	1♓ 9♈ 17♈ 26♈	1♑ 3♒ 11♒ 19♒ 27♓	1♑ 18♑	1♓ 5♓ 13♓ 21♈	1♑ 10♑ 18♒ 26♒	1♓ 3♈ 17♈	1♒ 4♒ 12♓ 19♓ 27♓
1♑ 3♒ 11♒ 19♒ 28♓	1♈ 6♉ 15♉ 24♉	1♓ 7♓ 15♓ 23♈ 31♈	1♑ 5♒ 17♒ 27♒	1♈ 10♈ 18♉ 26♉	1♒ 5♒ 13♓ 21♓ 29♓	1♈ 23♈	1♓ 8♈ 16♈ 24♈
1♓ 5♓ 13♓ 22♈ 30♈	1♉ 4♊ 15♊ 29♊	1♈ 8♈ 16♉ 24♉	1♒ 6♓ 15♓ 25♓	1♉ 4♉ 12♊ 21♊ 29♊	1♓ 6♈ 14♈ 22♈	1♈ 12♓ 24♈	1♉ 9♉ 17♉ 25♊
1♈ 8♈ 16♉ 25♉	1♊	1♉ 2♉ 10♊ 18♊ 26♊	1♓ 3♈ 12♈ 21♈ 30♉	1♊ 8♋ 17♋ 27♋	1♉ 9♉ 17♉ 25♊	1♈ 14♈ 27♈	1♊ 3♊ 12♊ 20♋ 28♋
1♉ 2♉ 10♊ 18♊ 27♊	1♊ 5♊ 26♊	1♊ 4♋ 12♋ 20♋ 28♌	1♉ 7♉ 16♉ 24♊	1♋ 6♌ 16♌ 28♌	1♊ 2♊ 10♊ 18♋ 27♋	1♈ 6♉ 16♉ 26♉	1♋ 6♋ 14♌ 23♌
1♊ 5♋ 13♋ 21♋ 29♌	1♊ 4♊ 26♊	1♌ 6♌ 15♌ 23♍ 31♍	1♊ 2♊ 11♊ 19♋ 27♋	1♌ 15♍	1♋ 5♋ 13♌ 21♌ 29♌	1♉ 5♊ 14♊ 23♊	1♌ 2♌ 10♍ 19♍ 29♍
1♌ 6♌ 14♌ 22♍ 31♍	1♊ 7♋ 18♋ 28♋	1♍ 9♍ 17♎ 26♎	1♋ 5♋ 13♌ 21♌ 29♌	1♍ 9♌ 27♌	1♌ 6♍ 14♍ 22♍ 31♎	1♊ 10♋ 18♋ 27♌	1♍ 7♎ 17♎ 28♎
1♍ 8♍ 16♎ 24♎	1♋ 7♌ 16♌ 25♌	1♎ 3♎ 12♏ 20♏ 29♏	1♌ 6♍ 14♍ 22♍ 30♎	1♌ 23♌	1♎ 8♎ 16♎ 24♏	1♌ 4♌ 12♌ 21♍ 29♍	1♎ 9♏ 25♏
1♎ 2♎ 10♏ 18♏ 26♏	1♌ 4♍ 12♍ 21♍ 29♎	1♏ 8♐ 17♐ 27♐	1♎ 8♎ 16♎ 24♏	1♌ 8♍ 20♍ 30♍	1♏ 2♏ 11♏ 19♐ 27♐	1♍ 7♍ 15♎ 23♎ 31♎	1♏ 21♏
1♏ 3♐ 11♐ 19♐ 27♑	1♎ 6♎ 14♎ 23♏	1♐ 5♑ 16♑ 28♑	1♏ 9♏ 17♐ 25♐	1♍ 9♎ 18♎ 27♎	1♐ 4♐ 13♑ 21♑ 29♑	1♎ 8♏ 16♏ 24♏	1♏ 8♎ 30♏
1♑ 5♑ 13♑ 21♒ 29♒	1♏ 9♏ 17♐ 25♐	1♑ 16♒	1♐ 3♐ 11♑ 19♑ 27♑	1♎ 6♏ 14♏ 22♏ 31♐	1♑ 8♒ 17♒ 25♒	1♏ 2♐ 10♐ 18♐ 26♑	1♏ 17♏ 28♏

MARS 1931–1950

	1931	1932	1933	1934	1935	1936	1937	1938	1939	1940
1	1 20 / ♌ ♌	1 5 18 31 / ♑ ♑ ♒ ♒	1 14 28 / ♏ ♏ ♏	1 10 23 / ♒ ♒ ♒	1 2 29 / ♎ ♎	1 2 15 27 / ♒ ♒ ♓ ♓	1 6 25 / ♏ ♏	1 4 17 31 / ♓ ♓ ♓ ♈	1 13 29 / ♏ ♏ ♐	1 4 19 / ♓ ♈ ♈
2	1 17 / ♌	1 12 25 / ♒ ♒ ♓	1 / ♏	1 4 17 / ♒ ♓ ♓	1 / ♎	1 9 22 / ♓ ♈ ♈	1 15 / ♏ ♏	1 13 27 / ♈ ♈ ♈	1 15 / ♐	1 2 17 / ♈ ♈ ♉
3	1 30 / ♋ ♌	1 9 21 / ♓ ♓ ♓	1 4 / ♏ ♏	1 2 14 27 / ♓ ♓ ♈ ♈	1 27 / ♎ ♎	1 6 19 / ♈ ♈ ♉	1 13 / ♏ ♐	1 12 26 / ♉ ♉ ♊	1 4 21 / ♐ ♐ ♑	1 3 18 / ♉ ♉ ♉
4	1 30 / ♌ ♌	1 3 16 29 / ♓ ♈ ♈ ♈	1 / ♏	1 9 23 / ♈ ♈ ♉	1 23 / ♎	1 2 16 29 / ♈ ♉ ♉ ♉	1 / ♐	1 9 24 / ♉ ♊ ♊	1 9 29 / ♐ ♑ ♑	1 2 17 / ♉ ♊ ♊
5	1 22 / ♌ ♌	1 12 26 / ♈ ♉ ♉	1 25 / ♏ ♏	1 6 20 / ♉ ♉ ♊	1 / ♎	1 13 28 / ♉ ♊ ♊	1 15 / ♐ ♏	1 8 23 / ♊ ♊ ♋	1 25 / ♑ ♒	1 2 18 / ♊ ♊ ♊
6	1 11 29 / ♌ ♍ ♍	1 8 22 / ♉ ♊ ♊	1 17 / ♏ ♏	1 3 17 / ♊ ♊ ♋	1 13 / ♎ ♎	1 11 26 / ♊ ♋ ♋	1 19 / ♏ ♏	1 7 22 / ♋ ♋ ♌	1 / ♒	1 2 18 / ♋ ♋ ♋
7	1 16 / ♍ ♍	1 7 21 / ♊ ♊ ♊	1 7 25 / ♏ ♎ ♎	1 16 31 / ♊ ♋ ♋	1 10 30 / ♎ ♏ ♏	1 11 26 / ♋ ♋ ♌	1 6 / ♏ ♏	1 7 23 / ♋ ♌ ♌	1 22 / ♒ ♓	1 3 19 / ♋ ♌ ♌
8	1 2 18 / ♍ ♎ ♎	1 5 20 / ♊ ♋ ♋	1 10 26 / ♎ ♎ ♏	1 15 31 / ♋ ♋ ♌	1 16 / ♏ ♏	1 10 26 / ♋ ♌ ♌	1 9 29 / ♏ ♐ ♐	1 7 23 / ♌ ♌ ♌	1 / ♓	1 4 20 / ♌ ♌ ♍
9	1 2 17 / ♎ ♎ ♏	1 5 21 / ♋ ♋ ♋	1 11 25 / ♏ ♏ ♏	1 15 / ♌ ♌	1 17 / ♏	1 11 27 / ♌ ♌ ♍	1 15 30 / ♐ ♐ ♑	1 8 24 / ♍ ♍ ♍	1 24 / ♓	1 4 20 / ♍ ♍ ♍
10	1 2 16 31 / ♏ ♏ ♏ ♐	1 8 26 / ♋ ♌ ♌	1 9 23 / ♏ ♐ ♐	1 2 18 / ♌ ♌ ♍	1 15 29 / ♏ ♐ ♐	1 13 29 / ♍ ♍ ♍	1 15 29 / ♑ ♑ ♑	1 9 25 / ♍ ♎ ♎	1 16 / ♒ ♒	1 6 21 / ♍ ♎ ♎
11	1 13 27 / ♐ ♐ ♐	1 14 / ♌ ♍	1 6 19 / ♐ ♐ ♑	1 4 22 / ♍ ♍ ♎	1 11 24 / ♐ ♑ ♑	1 15 / ♍ ♍	1 12 25 / ♑ ♒ ♒	1 10 26 / ♎ ♎ ♏	1 3 20 / ♒ ♓ ♓	1 5 21 / ♎ ♎ ♎
12	1 10 23 / ♐ ♑ ♑	1 6 / ♍ ♍	1 2 15 28 / ♑ ♑ ♑ ♒	1 11 / ♏ ♎	1 7 20 / ♑ ♒ ♒	1 2 19 / ♎ ♎ ♎	1 9 22 / ♒ ♒ ♓	1 12 28 / ♏ ♏ ♏	1 5 20 / ♓ ♈ ♈	1 6 21 / ♏ ♏ ♏

MARS 1951–1970

	1951	1952	1953	1954	1955	1956	1957	1958	1959	1960
1	1 10 23 / ♒ ♒ ♓	1 20 / ♎ ♏	1 13 26 / ♓ ♓ ♓	1 6 23 / ♏ ♏ ♏	1 15 29 / ♓ ♈ ♈	1 14 29 / ♏ ♐ ♐	1 12 29 / ♐ ♐ ♑	1 6 21 / ♑ ♑ ♑	1 14 / ♏ ♏	1 14 28 / ♐ ♑ ♑
2	1 4 17 / ♓ ♓ ♓	1 13 / ♏ ♏	1 8 21 / ♓ ♈ ♈	1 10 28 / ♏ ♐ ♐	1 12 26 / ♈ ♈ ♉	1 14 29 / ♐ ♐ ♑	1 14 / ♑	1 4 18 / ♑ ♒ ♒	1 11 / ♏ ♐	1 10 23 / ♑ ♑ ♒
3	1 2 15 28 / ♓ ♈ ♈ ♈	1 / ♏	1 7 20 / ♈ ♈ ♉	1 20 / ♐	1 13 27 / ♉ ♉ ♉	1 15 30 / ♑ ♑ ♑	1 2 18 / ♑ ♑ ♒	1 4 17 31 / ♒ ♒ ♒ ♓	1 4 23 / ♐ ♑ ♑	1 7 20 / ♒ ♒ ♒
4	1 10 24 / ♈ ♉ ♉	1 / ♏	1 3 17 / ♉ ♉ ♊	1 13 / ♐	1 11 26 / ♉ ♊ ♊	1 15 / ♑	1 3 19 / ♒ ♒ ♒	1 14 27 / ♒ ♒ ♓	1 10 28 / ♑ ♒ ♒	1 2 15 28 / ♒ ♓ ♓ ♓
5	1 8 22 / ♉ ♉ ♊	1 3 / ♏ ♏	1 16 30 / ♊ ♊ ♊	1 / ♑	1 / ♊	1 11 26 / ♒ ♓ ♓	1 17 / ♒ ♒	1 5 21 / ♓ ♈ ♈	1 15 / ♋ ♋	1 11 24 / ♓ ♈ ♈
6	1 5 19 / ♊ ♊ ♊	1 / ♏	1 14 29 / ♊ ♋ ♋	1 / ♑	1 10 26 / ♊ ♋ ♋	1 3 23 / ♒ ♓ ♓	1 6 22 / ♒ ♓ ♓	1 7 21 / ♈ ♈ ♉	1 18 / ♌ ♌	1 7 20 / ♈ ♈ ♉
7	1 4 19 / ♊ ♋ ♋	1 20 / ♏ ♏	1 14 30 / ♋ ♋ ♌	1 3 / ♑ ♐	1 11 27 / ♋ ♌ ♌	1 18 / ♒	1 7 23 / ♓ ♈ ♈	1 6 21 / ♈ ♈ ♉	1 4 20 / ♌ ♌ ♍	1 4 8 / ♉ ♉ ♉
8	1 3 18 / ♋ ♋ ♌	1 10 28 / ♏ ♏ ♐	1 14 30 / ♌ ♌ ♍	1 25 / ♐	1 12 27 / ♌ ♌ ♍	1 / ♓	1 8 24 / ♈ ♉ ♉	1 7 26 / ♉ ♉ ♉	1 6 21 / ♍ ♍ ♍	1 2 18 / ♉ ♊ ♊
9	1 3 19 / ♌ ♌ ♍	1 13 28 / ♐ ♐ ♑	1 15 / ♍ ♍	1 17 / ♍	1 12 28 / ♍ ♍ ♎	1 4 / ♈	1 9 24 / ♉ ♊ ♊	1 21 / ♉ ♉	1 6 21 / ♍ ♎ ♎	1 3 21 / ♊ ♊ ♋
10	1 5 21 / ♌ ♍ ♍	1 12 26 / ♐ ♑ ♑	1 17 / ♍	1 5 22 / ♎ ♎ ♎	1 13 29 / ♎ ♎ ♏	1 / ♈	1 10 25 / ♊ ♋ ♋	1 29 / ♉ ♊	1 6 21 / ♎ ♎ ♏	1 13 / ♋ ♋
11	1 7 24 / ♍ ♍ ♎	1 9 22 / ♑ ♑ ♒	1 2 18 / ♍ ♎ ♎	1 6 20 / ♎ ♏ ♏	1 14 29 / ♏ ♏ ♏	1 14 / ♈ ♈	1 9 24 / ♋ ♋ ♌	1 28 / ♊ ♊	1 5 20 / ♏ ♏ ♏	1 / ♋
12	1 12 31 / ♎ ♎ ♎	1 5 18 31 / ♒ ♒ ♒ ♓	1 4 20 / ♎ ♎ ♏	1 4 18 / ♏ ♏ ♏	1 14 30 / ♏ ♏ ♏	1 6 25 / ♈ ♈ ♈	1 9 23 / ♌ ♌ ♍	1 / ♊	1 4 18 / ♏ ♐ ♐	1 27 / ♋ ♋

1941–1950

	1941	1942	1943	1944	1945	1946	1947	1948	1949	1950
	1 5 20 ♏♐♐	1 12 31 ♈♉♉	1 13 27 ♐♐♑	1 ♊	1 6 19 ♐♑♑	1 22 ♋♋	1 13 25 ♑♑♒	1 ♏	1 5 17 30 ♑♒♒♒	1 30 ♎♎
	1 3 18 ♐♑	1 18 ♉♉	1 10 23 ♑♑♑	1 10 ♊♊	1 14 27 ♑♒♒	1 ♋	1 7 20 ♒♒♒	1 12 ♍♌	1 12 24 ♒♓♓	1 25 ♎♎
	1 5 19 ♑♑♒	1 7 24 ♉♊♊	1 9 22 ♑♒♒	1 7 28 ♊♋♋	1 12 25 ♒♒♓	1 28 ♌♌	1 5 17 30 ♒♓♓♈	1 12 ♌♌	1 9 22 ♓♈♈	1 28 ♎♏
	1 2 17 ♒♒♒	1 10 26 ♊♊♋	1 4 17 ♒♒♓	1 17 ♋♋	1 7 20 ♓♓♈	1 23 ♌♌	1 ♒	1 12 25 ♍♈♈	1 4 17 30 ♈♈♉♉	1 ♏
	1 2 16 31 ♒♒♓♓	1 13 29 ♋♋♋	1 14 27 ♓♓♈	1 5 23 ♋♋♌	1 3 16 29 ♓♈♈♈	1 14 ♌♍	1 8 21 ♈♈♉	1 19 ♍♏	1 14 27 ♉♉♉	1 ♏
	1 16 ♓♓	1 14 30 ♋♌♌	1 10 24 ♈♈♈	1 9 26 ♌♌♌	1 11 25 ♈♉♉	1 2 20 ♍♍♎	1 4 17 ♉♉♉	1 10 29 ♏♏♏	1 10 24 ♉♊♊	1 12 ♏♎
	1 2 21 ♓♈♈	1 16 ♌♌	1 8 23 ♈♉♉	1 12 28 ♌♍♍	1 9 23 ♉♉♊	1 8 24 ♎♏♏	1 15 30 ♊♊♊	1 17 ♏♏	1 9 23 ♊♊♋	1 5 24 ♎♎♎
	1 14 ♈	1 17 ♍♍	1 7 24 ♉♉♊	1 13 29 ♍♍♎	1 7 23 ♊♊♊	1 10 25 ♏♏♏	1 14 29 ♋♋♋	1 3 19 ♎♎♏	1 7 23 ♋♋♋	1 11 27 ♎♏♏
	1 30 ♈♈	1 2 17 ♍♍♎	1 12 ♊♊	1 13 29 ♎♎♎	1 8 26 ♊♋♋	1 10 25 ♏♏	1 14 ♋♋	1 4 19 ♎♏♏	1 7 23 ♋♌♌	1 11 26 ♏♏♐
	1 ♈	1 3 18 ♎♎♎	1 10 ♊♊	1 14 28 ♎♏♏	1 16 ♋♋	1 9 24 ♏♏♏	1 19 ♎♎	1 3 17 31 ♏♏♐♐	1 10 27 ♏♏♏	1 10 24 ♏♏♐
	1 ♈	1 2 17 ♎♏♏	1 15 ♊♊	1 12 26 ♏♏♐	1 12 ♋♌	1 7 21 ♏♐♐	1 8 ♏♐	1 14 27 ♐♐♑	1 14 ♏♏	1 6 19 ♐♐♑
	1 21 ♈♈	1 16 30 ♏♐♐	1 13 ♊♊	1 10 23 ♐♐♐	1 27 ♌♌	1 4 17 31 ♑♑♑♒	1 ♐	1 10 23 ♑♑♑	1 4 26 ♏♑♑	1 3 15 28 ♑♑♒♒

1961–1970

	1961	1962	1963	1964	1965	1966	1967	1968	1969	1970
	1 ♋	1 7 20 ♑♑♑	1 22 ♌♌	1 13 26 ♑♒♒	1 ♏	1 5 18 30 ♒♒♒♓	1 14 ♎♎	1 9 22 ♒♓♓	1 17 ♏♏	1 11 25 ♓♓♈
	1 5 7 ♋♋♋	1 2 15 28 ♒♒♒♒	1 18 ♌♌	1 8 20 ♒♓♓	1 ♏	1 12 25 ♓♓♈	1 13 ♎♏	1 4 17 ♈♈♈	1 5 25 ♏♏♐	1 7 21 ♈♈♈
	1 23 ♋♋	1 12 25 ♒♓♓	1 ♌	1 4 17 29 ♓♓♈♈	1 6 ♏♏	1 10 22 ♈♈♈	1 31 ♎♏	1 15 28 ♈♈♉	1 22 ♐♐	1 7 21 ♈♉♉
	1 16 ♋♋	1 7 20 ♓♓♈	1 15 ♌♌	1 11 24 ♈♈♈	1 6 ♏	1 5 18 ♈♈♈	1 29 ♎♎	1 11 25 ♉♉♉	1 ♐	1 4 19 ♉♉♊
	1 6 25 ♋♌♌	1 3 16 29 ♈♈♈♉	1 13 ♌♌	1 8 21 ♈♉♉	1 5 ♏	1 15 29 ♏♏♎	1 ♎	1 9 23 ♉♊♊	1 ♐	1 3 18 ♊♊♊
	1 12 29 ♌♌♍	1 11 25 ♉♉♉	1 3 22 ♍♍♎	1 4 17 ♉♉♊	1 7 29 ♏♏♎	1 12 26 ♉♊♊	1 25 ♎♎	1 6 21 ♊♊♊	1 ♐	1 2 17 ♊♋♋
	1 16 ♍♍	1 9 24 ♉♊♊	1 10 27 ♍♍♎	1 2 16 31 ♊♊♊♋	1 18 ♏♏	1 11 26 ♊♋♋	1 20 ♎♏	1 6 21 ♊♊♊	1 ♐	1 3 18 ♊♋♋
	1 17 ♍♎	1 7 22 ♊♊♋	1 12 28 ♎♎♎	1 15 30 ♋♋♋	1 4 21 ♐♎♎	1 10 26 ♋♋♌	1 8 25 ♐♏♏	1 6 21 ♊♊♊	1 14 ♐♐	1 3 19 ♊♋♋
	1 2 17 ♎♎♎	1 7 24 ♋♋♋	1 12 27 ♎♏♏	1 15 ♋♋	1 5 20 ♐♏♏	1 10 26 ♌♌♌	1 10 25 ♏♏♐	1 6 22 ♊♋♋	1 4 21 ♐♑♑	1 3 19 ♋♍♍
	1 2 16 31 ♏♏♏♐	1 12 ♋♋	1 12 26 ♏♏♐	1 2 19 ♋♋♌	1 4 18 ♐♐♑	1 13 30 ♌♍♍	1 9 23 ♐♐♑	1 8 24 ♋♋♌	1 7 22 ♑♑♑	1 5 20 ♍♍♎
	1 14 28 ♏♐♐	1 27 ♌♌	1 9 22 ♐♐♑	1 6 26 ♐♏♏	1 14 27 ♐♑♑	1 16 ♍♍	1 6 19 ♌♍♍	1 9 26 ♌♎♎	1 5 19 ♑♒♒	1 5 21 ♎♎♎
	1 11 25 ♐♐♑	1 ♌	1 5 18 31 ♐♑♑♑	1 20 ♐♐	1 10 23 ♑♑♒	1 4 23 ♍♎♎	1 2 15 28 ♒♒♒♒	1 13 30 ♎♎♏	1 2 16 29 ♒♓♓♈	1 7 22 ♎♏♏

MARS 1971–1990

	1971	1972	1973	1974	1975	1976	1977	1978	1979	1980
1	1 7 23 ♏ ♏ ♐	1 11 26 ♈ ♈ ♈	1 14 29 ♐ ♐ ♐	1 19 ♉ ♉	1 8 22 ♐ ♐ ♑	1 ♊	1 14 27 ♑ ♑ ♑	1 26 ♌ ♋	1 8 21 ♑ ♑ ♒	1 ♏
2	1 8 24 ♐ ♐ ♐	1 11 26 ♈ ♉ ♉	1 12 27 ♐ ♑ ♑	1 9 27 ♉ ♉ ♊	1 4 18 ♑ ♑ ♑	1 21 ♊ ♊	1 9 22 ♑ ♒ ♒	1 ♋	1 2 15 28 ♒ ♒ ♓ ♈	1 14 ♍ ♍
3	1 12 29 ♐ ♑ ♑	1 12 27 ♉ ♉ ♊	1 13 27 ♑ ♒ ♒	1 17 ♊ ♊	1 3 16 30 ♑ ♒ ♒	1 19 ♊ ♋	1 7 20 ♒ ♒ ♒	1 ♋	1 13 25 ♓ ♓ ♈	1 12 ♍ ♌
4	1 15 ♑ ♑	1 12 27 ♊ ♊ ♊	1 10 24 ♒ ♒ ♒	1 3 20 ♊ ♊ ♋	1 12 25 ♒ ♓ ♓	1 9 28 ♋ ♋ ♋	1 2 15 28 ♓ ♓ ♈ ♈	1 11 ♋ ♌	1 7 20 ♓ ♈ ♈	1 ♌
5	1 4 25 ♑ ♒ ♒	1 13 28 ♊ ♋ ♋	1 8 22 ♒ ♓ ♓	1 7 24 ♋ ♋ ♋	1 8 21 ♓ ♈ ♈	1 16 ♋ ♌	1 11 24 ♈ ♈ ♈	1 6 26 ♌ ♌ ♌	1 3 16 30 ♈ ♈ ♉ ♉	1 4 ♌ ♍
6	1 23 ♒ ♒	1 13 29 ♋ ♋ ♌	1 6 21 ♓ ♓ ♈	1 9 25 ♋ ♋ ♌	1 4 17 ♈ ♈ ♈	1 3 20 ♌ ♌ ♌	1 8 ♈ ♉ ♉	1 14 ♌ ♍	1 12 26 ♉ ♉ ♊	1 22 ♍ ♍
7	1 29 ♒ ♒	1 14 30 ♋ ♌ ♌	1 7 24 ♈ ♈ ♉	1 12 28 ♌ ♌ ♍	1 15 30 ♈ ♉ ♉	1 7 23 ♌ ♍ ♍	1 3 18 ♉ ♉ ♊	1 2 19 ♍ ♍ ♍	1 10 25 ♊ ♊ ♊	1 11 28 ♍ ♎ ♎
8	1 ♒	1 15 31 ♌ ♍ ♍	1 13 ♈ ♉	1 12 28 ♍ ♍ ♍	1 15 ♉ ♊	1 8 24 ♍ ♍ ♎	1 16 ♊ ♊	1 4 20 ♍ ♎ ♎	1 9 24 ♊ ♋ ♋	1 14 29 ♎ ♎ ♏
9	1 ♒	1 15 ♍ ♍	1 ♉	1 13 28 ♍ ♎ ♎	1 20 ♊ ♊	1 9 24 ♎ ♎ ♎	1 18 ♊ ♊	1 5 20 ♎ ♎ ♏	1 9 25 ♋ ♋ ♌	1 13 28 ♏ ♏ ♏
10	1 16 ♒ ♒	1 16 ♎ ♎	1 30 ♉ ♈	1 13 28 ♎ ♎ ♏	1 17 ♊ ♋	1 9 23 ♎ ♏ ♏	1 6 27 ♎ ♏ ♏	1 5 19 ♏ ♏ ♐	1 12 30 ♌ ♌ ♌	1 12 26 ♏ ♐ ♐
11	1 7 24 ♒ ♒ ♓	1 16 ♎ ♏	1 ♈	1 12 27 ♏ ♏ ♏	1 26 ♋ ♋	1 7 21 ♏ ♏ ♐	1 27 ♐ ♐	1 2 16 29 ♏ ♐ ♐ ♐	1 20 ♌ ♌	1 9 22 ♐ ♐ ♐
12	1 11 27 ♓ ♓ ♈	1 16 31 ♏ ♐ ♐	1 24 ♈ ♉	1 11 25 ♐ ♐ ♐	1 24 ♊ ♊	1 5 19 ♐ ♐ ♐	1 28 ♐ ♐	1 13 26 ♐ ♑ ♑	1 16 ♌ ♌	1 5 18 31 ♐ ♑ ♑ ♒

MARS 1991–2010

	1991	1992	1993	1994	1995	1996	1997	1998	1999	2000
1	1 21 ♉ ♊	1 9 23 ♐ ♑ ♑	1 2 ♋ ♋	1 2 15 28 ♑ ♑ ♒ ♒	1 23 ♒ ♌	1 8 21 ♑ ♒ ♒	1 3 ♏ ♏	1 13 25 ♒ ♒ ♓	1 4 26 ♎ ♏	1 4 17 30 ♒ ♓ ♓ ♈
2	1 20 ♊ ♊	1 5 18 ♑ ♑ ♒	1 ♋	1 10 23 ♒ ♒ ♒	1 20 ♌ ♌	1 3 15 28 ♒ ♒ ♓ ♓	1 9 ♏ ♏	1 7 20 ♓ ♓ ♓	1 27 ♏ ♏	1 12 25 ♓ ♈ ♈
3	1 14 ♊ ♊	1 2 15 28 ♒ ♒ ♒ ♓	1 2 ♋ ♋	1 7 20 ♒ ♓ ♓	1 ♌	1 12 25 ♓ ♓ ♈	1 9 ♏ ♏	1 5 18 31 ♈ ♈ ♈	1 ♏	1 10 23 ♈ ♈ ♉
4	1 3 21 ♊ ♋ ♋	1 10 23 ♓ ♓ ♓	1 5 28 ♋ ♋ ♌	1 2 15 28 ♓ ♈ ♈ ♉	1 30 ♌ ♌	1 7 20 ♈ ♈ ♈	1 5 ♏ ♏	1 13 27 ♈ ♉ ♉	1 6 ♏ ♏	1 6 20 ♈ ♉ ♉
5	1 9 27 ♋ ♋ ♌	1 6 19 ♓ ♈ ♈	1 18 ♌ ♌	1 11 24 ♉ ♉ ♊	1 26 ♌ ♌	1 3 16 30 ♈ ♉ ♉	1 22 ♉ ♉	1 10 24 ♉ ♊ ♊	1 6 ♏ ♏	1 4 18 ♉ ♉ ♊
6	1 12 29 ♌ ♌ ♌	1 15 28 ♈ ♉ ♉	1 6 23 ♌ ♌ ♍	1 6 20 ♉ ♊ ♊	1 15 ♍ ♍	1 13 27 ♉ ♊ ♊	1 19 ♊ ♊	1 7 22 ♊ ♊ ♊	1 ♏	1 2 17 ♊ ♊ ♋
7	1 16 ♌ ♍	1 12 27 ♉ ♉ ♊	1 10 27 ♍ ♍ ♍	1 4 18 ♊ ♊ ♊	1 4 21 ♊ ♊ ♋	1 11 26 ♊ ♊ ♋	1 10 29 ♊ ♋ ♋	1 6 21 ♋ ♋ ♋	1 5 29 ♋ ♋ ♋	1 2 17 ♋ ♋ ♋
8	1 17 ♍ ♍	1 11 26 ♊ ♊ ♊	1 12 28 ♍ ♎ ♎	1 2 17 ♊ ♊ ♋	1 7 23 ♋ ♋ ♋	1 10 25 ♋ ♋ ♌	1 14 30 ♋ ♌ ♌	1 5 21 ♌ ♌ ♌	1 3 18 ♋ ♌ ♌	1 17 ♋ ♋
9	1 17 ♎ ♎	1 12 ♋ ♋	1 12 27 ♎ ♎ ♎	1 18 ♋ ♋	1 7 22 ♋ ♌ ♌	1 10 26 ♌ ♌ ♌	1 14 29 ♌ ♍ ♍	1 5 21 ♌ ♌ ♍	1 3 18 ♌ ♍ ♍	1 17 ♌ ♌
10	1 2 17 31 ♎ ♎ ♏ ♏	1 23 ♋ ♋	1 12 26 ♎ ♏ ♏	1 5 23 ♌ ♌ ♌	1 7 21 ♌ ♍ ♍	1 13 30 ♍ ♍ ♍	1 13 27 ♍ ♎ ♎	1 8 24 ♍ ♎ ♎	1 3 17 31 ♍ ♎ ♎	1 3 19 ♍ ♍ ♍
11	1 15 29 ♏ ♏ ♐	1 ♋	1 9 23 ♏ ♏ ♐	1 13 ♌ ♌	1 4 17 ♍ ♍ ♍	1 18 ♍ ♍	1 9 22 ♍ ♎ ♎	1 10 27 ♎ ♎ ♏	1 13 26 ♎ ♏ ♏	1 4 20 ♍ ♎ ♎
12	1 13 27 ♐ ♐ ♐	1 ♋	1 7 20 ♐ ♐ ♑	1 12 ♌ ♌	1 14 27 ♍ ♍ ♍	1 9 ♏ ♏	1 5 18 31 ♏ ♏ ♐	1 16 ♏ ♏	1 9 22 ♎ ♎ ♎	1 7 24 ♎ ♏ ♏

Mars Tables 1981–1990

1981	1982	1983	1984	1985	1986	1987	1988	1989	1990

Mars Tables 2001–2010

2001	2002	2003	2004	2005	2006	2007	2008	2009	2010

JUPITER 1931–1970

	1931	1932	1933	1934	1935	1936	1937	1938	1939	1940	1941	1942	1943	1944	1945	1946	1947	1948	1949	1950
1	1 ♋	1 20 ♌ ♌	1 ♍	1 ♎	1 22 ♏ ♏	1 ♐	1 15 ♑ ♑	1 ♒	1 ♓	1 ♈	1 ♉	1 ♊	1 13 ♋ ♋	1 ♌	1 ♎	1 ♏	1 25 ♐	1 ♑	1 16 ♒ ♒	1 ♓
2	1 ♋	1 ♌	1 24 ♍ ♎	1 26 ♎	1 ♏	1 15 ♐	1 ♑	1 14 ♒	1 21 ♓	1 21 ♈	1 ♉	1 ♊	1 28 ♋	1 ♌ ♌	1 ♎	1 ♏	1 ♐	1 ♑	1 13 ♒	1 27 ♓
3	1 ♋	1 ♌	1 ♍	1 26 ♎	1 27 ♏	1 ♐	1 4 ♑	1 17 ♒	1 27 ♓	1 ♈	1 ♉	1 ♊	1 ♋	1 ♌	1 ♎	1 ♏	1 ♐	1 ♑	1 ♒ ♒	1 ♓
4	1 ♋	1 ♌	1 ♍	1 ♎	1 27 ♏	1 ♐	1 ♑	1 4 ♒	1 14 ♓	1 24 ♈	1 ♉	1 ♊ ♊	1 ♋	1 ♌	1 3 ♎	1 ♏	1 ♐	1 ♑	1 13 ♒	1 15 ♓
5	1 31 ♋ ♋	1 ♌	1 ♍	1 ♎	1 ♏	1 ♐	1 14 ♑	1 12 ♒	1 16 ♓	1 27 ♈ ♉	1 ♉	1 ♊	1 9 ♋	1 28 ♌	1 ♎	1 3 ♏	1 ♐	1 ♑	1 ♒	1 ♓
6	1 ♋	1 22 ♌ ♍	1 ♍	1 ♎	1 7 ♏	1 ♐ ♐	1 ♑	1 ♒	1 ♓	1 ♈	1 ♉	1 ♊ ♋	1 10 ♋	1 ♌	1 25 ♎	1 6 ♏ ♏	1 ♐	1 28 ♑	1 ♒	1 ♓
7	1 17 ♋	1 ♌	1 21 ♍ ♍	1 ♎	1 ♏	1 ♐	1 30 ♑	1 ♒	1 5 ♓	1 10 ♈	1 25 ♉	1 ♊	1 26 ♋	1 ♌ ♍	1 27 ♎	1 ♏	1 23 ♐	1 ♑	1 ♒	1 ♓
8	1 ♌	1 ♌ ♍	1 11 ♍	1 ♎	1 21 ♏	1 ♐	1 4 ♑	1 ♒	1 ♓	1 ♈	1 ♉	1 ♊	1 15 ♋	1 ♌	1 25 ♎	1 ♏ ♏	1 25 ♐	1 ♑	1 ♒	1 ♓
9	1 ♌	1 27 ♍ ♍	1 10 ♎	1 ♎	1 20 ♏	1 ♐	1 ♑	1 ♒	1 ♓	1 ♈	1 10 ♉	1 14 ♊	1 ♋	1 11 ♌ ♍	1 ♎	1 ♏	1 25 ♐	1 9 ♑	1 ♒	1 15 ♓
10	1 29 ♌	1 ♍	1 27 ♎	1 11 ♎	1 ♏	1 13 ♐	1 24 ♑	1 ♒	1 30 ♓	1 ♈	1 ♉	1 ♊	1 4 ♋	1 30 ♌ ♍	1 11 ♎	1 ♏	1 24 ♐	1 ♑	1 ♒	1 ♓
11	1 ♌	1 22 ♍ ♍	1 ♎	1 26 ♎	1 9 ♏	1 ♐	1 ♑	1 ♒	1 ♓	1 ♈	1 8 ♉	1 9 ♊	1 ♋	1 ♌	1 30 ♎	1 11 ♏	1 ♐	1 15 ♑	1 ♒	1 ♓
12	1 ♌	1 ♍	1 23 ♎	1 24 ♎	1 2 ♏	1 20 ♐	1 30 ♑	1 21 ♒	1 ♓	1 ♈	1 ♉	1 ♊	1 ♋	1 ♌	1 ♎	1 30 ♏	1 9 ♐	1 30 ♑	1 2 ♒ ♓	1 ♓

JUPITER 1971–2010

	1971	1972	1973	1974	1975	1976	1977	1978	1979	1980	1981	1982	1983	1984	1985	1986	1987	1988	1989	1990
1	1 14 ♏	1 ♐	1 10 ♐	1 26 ♒ ♒	1 ♓	1 ♈	1 ♉	1 ♊	1 8 ♌	1 9 ♍ ♎	1 ♎	1 20 ♏	1 9 ♐	1 15 ♐	1 ♑ ♑	1 ♒ ♒	1 ♓ ♈	1 ♈	1 ♉	1 ♋
2	1 ♐	1 7 ♐ ♑	1 23 ♒ ♒	1 ♓	1 4 ♈ ♈	1 6 ♉	1 ♉	1 ♊	1 ♌	1 9 ♍	1 10 ♎	1 ♏	1 7 ♐	1 21 ♑	1 ♒ ♒	1 ♓	1 ♈	1 ♉	1 ♊	1 ♋
3	1 ♐	1 ♑	1 ♒	1 8 ♓ ♓	1 19 ♈	1 26 ♉ ♉	1 ♉	1 ♊	1 ♌	1 11 ♍ ♎	1 3 ♎	1 16 ♏	1 27 ♐	1 ♑	1 3 ♒	1 9 ♓	1 11 ♈	1 ♉	1 ♊	1 ♋
4	1 ♐	1 ♑	1 24 ♒ ♒	1 24 ♓	1 30 ♈ ♈	1 ♉	1 4 ♊	1 12 ♋	1 20 ♌	1 ♍	1 22 ♎	1 ♏	1 ♐	1 5 ♑	1 13 ♒	1 22 ♓	1 ♈	1 ♉	1 ♊	1 18 ♋
5	1 ♐	1 ♑	1 ♒	1 ♓	1 8 ♈	1 20 ♉	1 ♊	1 ♋	1 ♌	1 ♍	1 ♎	1 ♏	1 14 ♐	1 31 ♑ ♑	1 28 ♒	1 ♓	1 3 ♈	1 16 ♉	1 ♊	1 ♋
6	1 5 ♏ ♐	1 ♑	1 ♒	1 ♓	1 20 ♈	1 21 ♉	1 5 ♊	1 27 ♋	1 ♌	1 ♍	1 ♎	1 ♏	1 ♐	1 14 ♑	1 ♒	1 ♓	1 ♈	1 22 ♉	1 31 ♊	1 4 ♋
7	1 ♏	1 25 ♑	1 8 ♒	1 ♓	1 ♈	1 2 ♉	1 20 ♊	1 24 ♋	1 ♌	1 ♍	1 ♎	1 ♏	1 ♐	1 ♑	1 ♒	1 ♓	1 ♈	1 ♉	1 ♊	1 ♋
8	1 ♏	1 ♐	1 ♒	1 ♓	1 23 ♈	1 21 ♉	1 ♊	1 13 ♋	1 ♌	1 23 ♍	1 ♎	1 ♏	1 ♐	1 21 ♑	1 25 ♒	1 ♓	1 ♈	1 ♉	1 ♋	1 18 ♌
9	1 12 ♏	1 26 ♐	1 ♒	1 29 ♓	1 ♈	1 ♉	1 5 ♊	1 29 ♋	1 10 ♌	1 ♍	1 11 ♎	1 ♏	1 ♐	1 ♑	1 ♒	1 ♓	1 ♈	1 ♉	1 6 ♊	1 12 ♋
10	1 ♏	1 ♐	1 ♒	1 ♓	1 11 ♈	1 ♉	1 17 ♊	1 ♋	1 ♌	1 27 ♍	1 11 ♎	1 ♏	1 20 ♐	1 ♑	1 ♒	1 ♓	1 ♈	1 ♉	1 21 ♊	1 ♋
11	1 7 ♏	1 27 ♐	1 ♒	1 ♓	1 ♈	1 ♉	1 ♊	1 ♋	1 ♌	1 ♍	1 27 ♎	1 10 ♏	1 ♐	1 8 ♑	1 15 ♒	1 ♓	1 ♈	1 ♉	1 21 ♊	1 ♋
12	1 22 ♏	1 ♐	1 10 ♒	1 8 ♓	1 ♈	1 ♉	1 31 ♊	1 ♋	1 14 ♌	1 ♍	1 26 ♎	1 6 ♏	1 26 ♐	1 ♑	1 4 ♒	1 27 ♓	1 ♈	1 ♉	1 ♊	1 ♌

1951–1970

1951	1952	1953	1954	1955	1956	1957	1958	1959	1960	1961	1962	1963	1964	1965	1966	1967	1968	1969	1970
1 27	1 30	1	1	1	1	1 18	1	1 14	1	1 7	1 26	1	1 6	1	1	1	1 16	1	1
♓	♓	♈	♉	♊	♋	♌ ♌	♎	♎ ♏	♏	♐	♐	♑ ♒	♒	♓ ♓	♈	♉	♊	♌ ♋ ♍	♎	♏
1	1	1	1	1	1	1	1 20	1	1 11	1	1	1 11	1 22	1 29	1	1	1	1 27	1
♓	♈	♉	♊	♋	♋	♌	♎ ♏	♏	♏ ♐	♐	♑	♒ ♒	♓ ♈	♈ ♉	♊	♋	♍ ♌	♎	♏
1 10	1 18	1 25	1 31	1 8	25	1	1	1 21	1	1 2	1 15	1 26	1	1	1	1	1	1 31	1
♓ ♓	♈	♉ ♉	♊ ♊	♋ ♋	♌	♌	♏	♏ ♐	♐	♑ ♒	♒ ♓	♓ ♈	♈	♉	♊	♋	♍	♎ ♏ ♏	♏
1 22	1 29	1	1	1	1	1	1	1 25	1	1	1 4	1 12	1 23	1	1	1	1	1	1 30
♓ ♈	♈	♉	♊	♋	♋	♌	♏	♐ ♐	♑	♒	♓ ♈	♈ ♉	♉ ♊	♊	♋	♌	♎	♏ ♎	♏ ♎
1	1	1 10	1 24	1	1	1	1	1	1	1	1 21	1 19	1 24	1	1 6	1 23	1	1	1
♈	♉	♉ ♊	♊ ♋	♋	♌	♌	♏	♐	♑	♒	♓ ♓	♈ ♈	♉ ♉ ♊	♊	♋ ♋	♌ ♌	♍	♎	♏
1 13	1 12	1 22	1	1 13	1	1	1	1	1 10	1	1	1	1 5	1 22	1	1 16	1	1	1
♈ ♈	♉ ♉	♊ ♊	♋	♋	♌	♌	♏	♐	♑ ♐	♒	♓	♈	♉	♉ ♊ ♊	♋ ♋	♌ ♍ ♍	♎	♏	♏
1	1	1	1 8	1 30	1 8	1	1	1	1	1	1	1	1 12	1 20	1	1 14	1	1 16	1
♈	♉	♊	♋ ♋	♋ ♌	♌	♍ ♌ ♍	♏	♐	♑	♒	♓	♈	♉ ♉ ♊ ♊	♊ ♋	♌	♍ ♍	♎	♏ ♏	♏
1	1 16	1 9	1 23	1	1 26	1 7	1	1	1	1 12	1 14	1	1	1 6	1 29	1 10	1	1 16
♈	♉ ♉	♊ ♊	♋ ♋	♌	♍ ♍ ♍	♍ ♎	♏	♏	♐	♑ ♒	♒ ♓ ♓	♈	♉	♊ ♋ ♋	♌ ♍ ♍	♎ ♎	♏	♏
1 27	1	1	1	1 15	1	1 26	1 7	1	1	1	1	1	1 21	1 28	1	1 26	1 10	1
♈ ♈	♉	♊	♋	♌ ♌	♍	♎	♎ ♎ ♏	♏	♐	♑	♒	♓	♉	♉ ♋ ♋	♌	♍ ♍ ♎	♎ ♏	♏
1	1 4	1	1	1	1 12	1	1 26	1 6	1 26	1	1	1	1	1	1 19	1	1 26	1 10
♈	♉ ♉	♊	♋	♌	♍ ♍	♎	♏ ♏	♏ ♐ ♐	♐ ♑	♒	♓	♈	♉	♊	♋ ♍ ♍	♎	♎ ♎ ♏	♏ ♏
1	1	1	1	1 17	1	1 12	1	1 23	1	1 4	1	1 19	1 21	1 17	1	1 16	1	1 25
♈	♉	♊	♋	♌ ♍	♍	♎ ♎	♏	♐ ♐	♑	♒ ♒	♓	♈ ♉ ♉	♉ ♊ ♊	♋	♍	♎ ♎	♏ ♏	♏
1	1	1 24	1	1	1 13	1	1 12	1	1 14	1 30	1	1 22	1	1	1	1	1 17	1
♈	♉	♊ ♊	♋	♍	♍	♎ ♎	♏ ♏	♐	♑ ♑ ♒ ♒	♒ ♓	♓	♉	♊	♋	♍	♎	♏ ♏

1991–2010

1991	1992	1993	1994	1995	1996	1997	1998	1999	2000	2001	2002	2003	2004	2005	2006	2007	2008	2009	2010
1 18	1	1	1	1 3	1 30	1 3	1 22	1	1	1	1	1 6	1	1	1	1 10	1	1 6	1 18
♌ ♌	♍	♎	♏ ♏	♐ ♐	♑	♑ ♒ ♒	♒	♓	♈	♊	♋ ♋	♌	♍	♎	♏	♐ ♐	♑	♒ ♒	♓
1	1 27	1	1	1 20	1	1 4	1 13	1 15	1	1 28	1	1	1	1	1	1	1 17	1
♌	♍ ♍ ♏	♎	♏	♐	♑ ♑ ♒	♒ ♓ ♓	♈ ♈	♉	♊	♋	♌ ♌ ♍	♎	♏	♐	♑	♒ ♒	♓
1	1	1 29	1	1	1 7	1 18	1 28	1	1	1	1	1	1	1 31	1	1 2
♌	♍	♎ ♎ ♏	♏	♐	♑	♒ ♒ ♓ ♓ ♈ ♈	♉	♊	♋	♌	♍	♎	♏	♐ ♐	♑ ♒ ♒	♓ ♓
1	1	1	1 29	1	1	1	1	1 5	1 14	1 25	1	1 8	1	1	1	1 6	1 13
♌	♍	♎ ♎ ♏	♏	♐	♑	♒	♓	♈	♉ ♉ ♊ ♊	♋ ♋ ♌	♍ ♍ ♎	♎	♏	♐	♑	♒ ♒ ♓ ♓
1	1	1	1	1 5	1 3	1 9	1 17	1 30	1	1 10	1	1 9	1	1	1	1	1
♌	♍	♎	♏	♐	♒ ♒ ♓ ♓ ♈ ♈ ♉ ♉	♊ ♊	♋ ♋ ♌	♍ ♍ ♎	♏	♐	♑	♒
1 7	1	1	1	1 6	1	1	1	1 28	1 30	1	1 17	1	1	1 10	1	1 19	1	1 6
♌ ♌ ♍	♎	♏	♐	♑	♒	♈ ♈ ♉ ♉ ♊ ♊	♋ ♋ ♌	♍	♎	♏ ♏	♐ ♐ ♑	♒ ♒	♈
1 28	1 3	1	1	1 27	1 16	1	1	1 13	1	1 11	1	1 2	1 31	1
♌ ♌ ♍ ♍ ♎	♏	♐	♑ ♑ ♒ ♒ ♓	♉	♊	♊ ♋ ♋	♌ ♌ ♎ ♎ ♏	♐ ♐	♒	♈
1	1 25	1 3	1	1	1	1	1 2	1 27	1 8	1 2	1 14	1	1 31	1
♌	♍ ♍ ♎ ♎	♏	♐	♑	♈	♉	♊	♋	♌ ♍ ♍ ♎	♏ ♏ ♐ ♐	♒ ♒ ♈
1 12	1	1 25	1 2	1 28	1	1	1 2	1 19	1 25	1 9	1	1	1 9
♌ ♍ ♍	♎ ♎ ♏ ♏ ♐	♑	♒	♈	♉	♊ ♊ ♋	♌ ♌ ♍	♎ ♎ ♏	♐	♒	♈ ♓
1	1 11	1	1 25	1 11	1	1 11	1 23	1 27	1	1 15	1	1 26	1 9	1
♏	♏ ♎ ♎ ♏ ♏	♐	♑ ♑ ♒	♓ ♓ ♈ ♈ ♉ ♉ ♊ ♊	♋	♌ ♍ ♍	♎ ♎ ♏ ♏	♐	♒	♓
1 5	1	1 10	1	1 20	1	1	1	1	1	1	1 13	1	1 24	1 3	1 20	1 24	1
♏ ♏ ♎	♎ ♎ ♏ ♏	♐ ♐	♑ ♑ ♒	♓	♈	♉	♊	♋	♌	♎ ♎ ♏	♏ ♐ ♐ ♑ ♑ ♒ ♒
1	1 3	1	1 9	1	1 9	1 21	1 17	1	1	1	1	1	1 13	1	1 19	1	1
♏	♎ ♎ ♏	♏ ♐	♐ ♑	♑ ♑ ♒ ♒ ♓ ♓ ♈ ♈	♉	♊	♋	♌	♍	♎ ♏ ♏ ♐	♐ ♑ ♑ ♒	♓

SATURN 1931–2010

1931	1932	1933	1934	1935	1936	1937	1938	1939	1940
JAN 1 ♑	JAN 1 ♑	JAN 1 ♒	JAN 1 ♒	JAN 1 ♒	JAN 1 ♓	JAN 1 ♓	JAN 1 ♓	JAN 1 ♈	JAN 1 ♈
FEB 27 ♑	FEB 24 ♒	FEB 21 ♒	FEB 18 ♒	FEB 15 ♓	FEB 9 ♓	JAN 31 ♓	JAN 14 ♈	APR 4 ♈	MAR 20 ♉
JUL 13 ♑	AUG 13 ♑	SEP 26 ♒		JUN 5 ♓	MAY 8 ♓	APR 25 ♈	APR 15 ♈	JUL 6 ♉	JUN 10 ♉
NOV 27 ♑	NOV 20 ♒	NOV 2 ♒		JUL 8 ♓	SEP 1 ♓	OCT 18 ♓		SEP 22 ♈	NOV 20 ♉

1951	1952	1953	1954	1955	1956	1957	1958	1959	1960
JAN 1 ♎	JAN 1 ♎	JAN 1 ♎	JAN 1 ♏	JAN 1 ♏	JAN 1 ♏	JAN 1 ♐	JAN 1 ♐	JAN 1 ♐	JAN 1 ♑
MAR 8 ♍	APR 23 ♎	OCT 23 ♏	OCT 19 ♏	JAN 23 ♏	JAN 13 ♐	JAN 8 ♐	JAN 6 ♐	JAN 6 ♑	JAN 6 ♑
AUG 14 ♎	JUL 28 ♎			APR 9 ♏	MAY 14 ♏	JUN 16 ♐	JUL 21 ♐		
NOV 6 ♎	OCT 28 ♎			OCT 15 ♏	OCT 11 ♐	OCT 6 ♐	SEP 27 ♐		

1971	1972	1973	1974	1975	1976	1977	1978	1979	1980
JAN 1 ♉	JAN 1 ♊	JAN 1 ♊	JAN 1 ♋	JAN 1 ♋	JAN 1 ♌	JAN 1 ♌	JAN 1 ♍	JAN 1 ♍	JAN 1 ♍
MAR 30 ♉	JAN 10 ♉	MAY 14 ♊	JAN 8 ♊	JUN 26 ♋	JAN 15 ♋	APR 4 ♌	JAN 5 ♌	MAR 9 ♍	SEP 21 ♎
JUN 19 ♊	FEB 22 ♊	AUG 2 ♋	APR 19 ♋	SEP 17 ♌	JUN 5 ♌	APR 19 ♌	JUL 27 ♍	JUL 9 ♍	
	JUN 1 ♊		JUL 13 ♋		AUG 26 ♌	AUG 10 ♌	OCT 17 ♍	OCT 3 ♍	
	SEP 7 ♊					NOV 17 ♍			
	OCT 28 ♊								

1991	1992	1993	1994	1995	1996	1997	1998	1999	2000
JAN 1 ♑	JAN 1 ♒	JAN 1 ♒	JAN 1 ♒	JAN 1 ♓	JAN 1 ♓	JAN 1 ♈	JAN 1 ♈	JAN 1 ♈	JAN 1 ♉
FEB 7 ♒	FEB 5 ♒	FEB 2 ♒	JAN 29 ♓	JAN 22 ♓	JAN 9 ♓	MAR 29 ♈	MAR 18 ♈	MAR 1 ♉	MAY 7 ♉
		MAY 21 ♓	APR 29 ♓	APR 18 ♓	APR 7 ♈	JUL 12 ♈	JUN 9 ♉	MAY 23 ♉	AUG 10 ♊
		JUN 30 ♒	AUG 20 ♓	OCT 2 ♓		AUG 22 ♈	OCT 26 ♈		OCT 16 ♉

1941		1942		1943		1944		1945		1946		1947		1948		1949		1950	
JAN 1	♉	JAN 1	♉	JAN 1	♊	JAN 1	♊	JAN 1	♋	JAN 1	♋	JAN 1	♌	JAN 1	♌	JAN 1	♍	JAN 1	♍
FEB 27	♉	MAY 9	♊	APR 20	♊	FEB 2	♊	JUN 2	♋	JAN 30	♋	JUL 18	♌	JAN 31	♌	APR 3	♌	AUG 25	♍
MAY 24	♉	AUG 2	♊	JUL 9	♊	MAR 10	♊	AUG 21	♋	MAY 8	♋	OCT 10	♌	JUN 29	♌	MAY 30	♍	NOV 21	♎
		NOV 20	♊			JUN 20	♋			AUG 3	♌			SEP 19	♍	SEP 6	♍		
						SEP 24	♋												
						NOV 22	♋												

1961		1962		1963		1964		1965		1966		1967		1968		1969		1970	
JAN 1	♑	JAN 1	♑	JAN 1	♒	JAN 1	♒	JAN 1	♓	JAN 1	♓	JAN 1	♓	JAN 1	♈	JAN 1	♈	JAN 1	♉
JAN 5	♑	JAN 4	♒	JAN 2	♒	MAR 24	♓	MAR 18	♓	MAR 12	♓	MAR 4	♈	FEB 20	♈	JAN 29	♈	APR 16	♉
		APR 10	♒	APR 1	♒	SEP 17	♒					MAY 31	♈	MAY 13	♈	APR 30	♉	JUL 11	♉
		JUL 4	♒	AUG 10	♒	DEC 16	♓					SEP 20	♈	NOV 13	♈			NOV 1	♉
				DEC 28	♒														

1981		1982		1983		1984		1985		1986		1987		1988		1989		1990	
JAN 1	♎	JAN 1	♎	JAN 1	♏	JAN 1	♏	JAN 1	♏	JAN 1	♐	JAN 1	♐	JAN 1	♐	JAN 1	♑	JAN 1	♑
SEP 13	♎	MAR 26	♎	MAY 7	♎	JUN 24	♏	NOV 17	♐	NOV 16	♐	FEB 22	♐	FEB 14	♑	FEB 10	♑	FEB 8	♑
DEC 11	♎	SEP 4	♎	AUG 24	♏	AUG 1	♏					MAY 9	♐	JUN 10	♐	JUL 11	♑	AUG 13	♑
		NOV 29	♏	NOV 23	♏	NOV 19	♏					NOV 15	♐	NOV 12	♑	NOV 9	♑	NOV 2	♑

2001		2002		2003		2004		2005		2006		2007		2008		2009		2010	
JAN 1	♉	JAN 1	♊	JAN 1	♊	JAN 1	♋	JAN 1	♋	JAN 1	♌	JAN 1	♌	JAN 1	♍	JAN 1	♍	JAN 1	♎
APR 21	♊	MAR 27	♊	JUN 4	♋	MAY 13	♋	JUL 17	♌	JUN 29	♌	MAR 4	♌	AUG 20	♍	FEB 16	♍	APR 8	♏
JUL 10	♊	JUN 21	♊	AUG 25	♋	AUG 2	♋	OCT 15	♌	SEP 18	♌	JUN 5	♌	NOV 17	♍	AUG 7	♍	JUL 22	♎
DEC 22	♊			DEC 29	♋			DEC 31	♌			SEP 3	♍			OCT 30	♎	OCT 19	♎

URANUS 1931–2010

1931		1932		1933		1934		1935		1936		1937		1938		1939		1940	
JAN	1 ♈	JAN	1 ♈	JAN	1 ♈	JAN	1 ♈	JAN	1 ♈	JAN	1 ♉	JAN	1 ♉	JAN	1 ♉	JAN	1 ♉	JAN	1 ♉
		APR	21 ♈	FEB	3 ♈	JUN	7 ♉	MAR	28 ♉			MAY	8 ♉	FEB	13 ♉	JUN	18 ♉	APR	7 ♉
		NOV	22 ♈			OCT	10 ♈					DEC	23 ♉			NOV	12 ♉		

1951		1952		1953		1954		1955		1956		1957		1958		1959		1960	
JAN	1 ♋	JAN	1 ♋	JAN	1 ♋	JAN	1 ♋	JAN	1 ♋	JAN	1 ♌	JAN	1 ♌	JAN	1 ♌	JAN	1 ♌	JAN	1 ♌
JUL	8 ♋	MAR	3 ♋	AUG	1 ♋	FEB	7 ♋	AUG	25 ♌	JAN	28 ♋	SEP	16 ♌	JAN	21 ♌	OCT	9 ♌	JAN	17 ♌
		APR	2 ♋			MAY	15 ♋					JUN	10 ♌			JUL	3 ♌			JUL	22 ♌

1971		1972		1973		1974		1975		1976		1977		1978		1979		1980	
JAN	1 ♎	JAN	1 ♎	JAN	1 ♎	JAN	1 ♎	JAN	1 ♏	JAN	1 ♏	JAN	1 ♏	JAN	1 ♏	JAN	1 ♏	JAN	1 ♏
MAY	12 ♎	NOV	2 ♎	MAY	6 ♎	NOV	21 ♏	MAY	2 ♎	DEC	13 ♏	APR	25 ♏			JAN	8 ♏		
JUL	24 ♎			AUG	16 ♎			SEP	8 ♏			SEP	30 ♏			APR	15 ♏		
																OCT	24 ♏		

1991		1992		1993		1994		1995		1996		1997		1998		1999		2000	
JAN	1 ♑	JAN	1 ♑	JAN	1 ♑	JAN	1 ♑	JAN	1 ♑	JAN	1 ♑	JAN	1 ♒	JAN	1 ♒	JAN	1 ♒	JAN	1 ♒
JAN	6 ♑			FEB	10 ♑			APR	2 ♒	JAN	12 ♒			FEB	20 ♒			APR	10 ♒
AUG	30 ♑			JUL	18 ♑			JUN	9 ♑					AUG	23 ♒			JUL	11 ♒
OCT	9 ♑			DEC	3 ♑									DEC	12 ♒				

1941	1942	1943	1944	1945	1946	1947	1948	1949	1950
JAN 1 ♉	JAN 1 ♉	JAN 1 ♊	JAN 1 ♊	JAN 1 ♊	JAN 1 ♊	JAN 1 ♊	JAN 1 ♊	JAN 1 ♊	JAN 1 ♋
AUG 8 ♊	MAY 15 ♊		JUN 18 ♊	APR 3 ♊	JUL 23 ♊	MAY 11 ♊	AUG 31 ♋	JUN 10 ♋	
OCT 5 ♉			DEC 31 ♊		DEC 7 ♊		NOV 13 ♊		

1961	1962	1963	1964	1965	1966	1967	1968	1969	1970
JAN 1 ♌	JAN 1 ♍	JAN 1 ♍	JAN 1 ♍	JAN 1 ♍	JAN 1 ♍	JAN 1 ♍	JAN 1 ♍	JAN 1 ♎	JAN 1 ♎
NOV 2 ♍	JAN 10 ♌	DEC 4 ♍	AUG 27 ♍		SEP 13 ♍		SEP 29 ♎	MAY 21 ♍	OCT 16 ♎
	AUG 10 ♍	DEC 28 ♍						JUN 24 ♎	

1981	1982	1983	1984	1985	1986	1987	1988	1989	1990
JAN 1 ♏	JAN 1 ♐	JAN 1 ♐	JAN 1 ♐	JAN 1 ♐	JAN 1 ♐	JAN 1 ♐	JAN 1 ♐	JAN 1 ♑	JAN 1 ♑
FEB 17 ♐		DEC 13 ♐	JUL 15 ♐		JAN 10 ♑		FEB 15 ♑		
MAR 21 ♏			SEP 20 ♐		JUN 21 ♐		MAY 27 ♐		
NOV 17 ♐					OCT 30 ♐		DEC 3 ♑		

2001	2002	2003	2004	2005	2006	2007	2008	2009	2010
JAN 1 ♒	JAN 1 ♒	JAN 1 ♒	JAN 1 ♓	JAN 1 ♓	JAN 1 ♓	JAN 1 ♓	JAN 1 ♓	JAN 1 ♓	JAN 1 ♓
JAN 26 ♒		MAR 11 ♓		MAY 2 ♓	FEB 17 ♓		APR 2 ♓	JAN 22 ♓	MAY 28 ♈
		SEP 15 ♒		JUL 30 ♓			SEP 30 ♓		AUG 14 ♓
		DEC 30 ♓							

NEPTUNE 1931–2010

1931		1932		1933		1934		1935		1936		1937		1938		1939		1940	
JAN	1 ♏	JAN	1 ♏	JAN	1 ♏	JAN	1 ♏	JAN	1 ♏	JAN	1 ♏	JAN	1 ♏	JAN	1 ♏	JAN	1 ♏	JAN	1 ♏
		NOV	17 ♏	JAN	8 ♏	APR	12 ♏					OCT	19 ♏	MAR	3 ♏				
				SEP	5 ♏	JUN	29 ♏							AUG	21 ♏				

1951		1952		1953		1954		1955		1956		1957		1958		1959		1960	
JAN	1 ♎	JAN	1 ♎	JAN	1 ♎	JAN	1 ♎	JAN	1 ♎	JAN	1 ♏	JAN	1 ♏	JAN	1 ♏	JAN	1 ♏	JAN	1 ♏
NOV	2 ♎	APR	23 ♎					DEC	25 ♏	MAR	12 ♎	JUN	16 ♎					DEC	3 ♏
		SEP	3 ♎							OCT	19 ♏	AUG	6 ♏						

1971		1972		1973		1974		1975		1976		1977		1978		1979		1980	
JAN	1 ♐	JAN	1 ♐	JAN	1 ♐	JAN	1 ♐	JAN	1 ♐	JAN	1 ♐	JAN	1 ♐	JAN	1 ♐	JAN	1 ♐	JAN	1 ♐
						DEC	20 ♐	JUN	17 ♐							FEB	9 ♐	AUG	13 ♐
						OCT	22 ♐									MAY	6 ♐	SEP	20 ♐
																DEC	7 ♐		

1991		1992		1993		1994		1995		1996		1997		1998		1999		2000	
JAN	1 ♑	JAN	1 ♑	JAN	1 ♑	JAN	1 ♑	JAN	1 ♑	JAN	1 ♑	JAN	1 ♑	JAN	1 ♑	JAN	1 ♒	JAN	1 ♒
				FEB	15 ♑									JAN	29 ♒				
				JUL	3 ♑									AUG	23 ♑				
				DEC	19 ♑									NOV	28 ♒				

1941		1942		1943		1944		1945		1946		1947		1948		1949		1950	
JAN 1	♏	JAN 1	♏	JAN 1	♎	JAN 1	♎	JAN 1	♎	JAN 1	♎	JAN 1	♎	JAN 1	♎	JAN 1	♎	JAN 1	♎
		OCT 4	♎	APR 17	♏					NOV 19	♎	MAR 10	♎						
				AUG 3	♎							SEP 20	♎						

1961		1962		1963		1964		1965		1966		1967		1968		1969		1970	
JAN 1	♏	JAN 1	♏	JAN 1	♏	JAN 1	♏	JAN 1	♏	JAN 1	♏	JAN 1	♏	JAN 1	♏	JAN 1	♏	JAN 1	♏
APR 29	♏							FEB 15	♏	JUN 13	♏							JAN 5	♐
OCT 6	♏							FEB 25	♏	SEP 18	♏							MAY 3	♏
								NOV 19	♏									NOV 7	♐

1981		1982		1983		1984		1985		1986		1987		1988		1989		1990	
JAN 1	♐	JAN 1	♐	JAN 1	♐	JAN 1	♐	JAN 1	♑	JAN 1	♑	JAN 1	♑	JAN 1	♑	JAN 1	♑	JAN 1	♑
						JAN 19	♑							MAR 16	♑	JAN 3	♑		
						JUN 23	♐							MAY 9	♑	AUG 13	♑		
						NOV 22	♑									OCT 29	♑		

2001		2002		2003		2004		2005		2006		2007		2008		2009		2010	
JAN 1	≈	JAN 1	≈	JAN 1	≈	JAN 1	≈	JAN 1	≈	JAN 1	≈	JAN 1	≈	JAN 1	≈	JAN 1	≈	JAN 1	≈
		MAR 13	≈	JAN 13	≈							FEB 22	≈						
		JUL 17	≈									SEP 7	≈						
												DEC 23	≈						

PLUTO 1931–2010

1931		1932		1933		1934		1935		1936		1937		1938		1939		1940	
JAN 1	♋	JAN 1	♋	JAN 1	♋	JAN 1	♋	JAN 1	♋	JAN 1	♋	JAN 1	♋	JAN 1	♋	JAN 1	♌	JAN 1	♌
JAN 2	♋	MAR 19	♋									OCT 8	♌	AUG 4	♌	FEB 8	♋		
JUN 28	♋	APR 18	♋									NOV 25	♋			JUN 14	♌		

1951		1952		1953		1954		1955		1956		1957		1958		1959		1960	
JAN 1	♌	JAN 1	♌	JAN 1	♌	JAN 1	♌	JAN 1	♌	JAN 1	♌	JAN 1	♍	JAN 1	♍	JAN 1	♍	JAN 1	♍
AUG 29	♌	FEB 24	♌									OCT 20	♍	JAN 15	♌	APR 12	♌		
		JUL 5	♌									AUG 19	♍	JUN 11	♍				

1971		1972		1973		1974		1975		1976		1977		1978		1979		1980	
JAN 1	♍	JAN 1	♎	JAN 1	♎	JAN 1	♎	JAN 1	♎	JAN 1	♎	JAN 1	♎	JAN 1	♎	JAN 1	♎	JAN 1	♎
OCT 5	♎	APR 17	♍					OCT 26	♎	APR 12	♎					NOV 4	♎	APR 24	♎
		JUL 30	♎							AUG 22	♎							AUG 30	♎

1991		1992		1993		1994		1995		1996		1997		1998		1999		2000	
JAN 1	♏	JAN 1	♏	JAN 1	♏	JAN 1	♏	JAN 1	♏	JAN 1	♐	JAN 1	♐	JAN 1	♐	JAN 1	♐	JAN 1	♐
JAN 17	♏							JAN 17	♐							JAN 31	♐		
MAR 31	♏							APR 21	♏							APR 26	♐		
NOV 6	♏							NOV 11	♐							NOV 24	♐		

1941		1942		1943		1944		1945		1946		1947		1948		1949		1950	
JAN	1 ♌	JAN	1 ♌	JAN	1 ♌	JAN	1 ♌	JAN	1 ♌	JAN	1 ♌	JAN	1 ♌	JAN	1 ♌	JAN	1 ♌	JAN	1 ♌
						OCT	8 ♌	AUG	7 ♌	MAR	1 ♌								
						DEC	16 ♌			JUN	13 ♌								

1961		1962		1963		1964		1965		1966		1967		1968		1969		1970	
JAN	1 ♍	JAN	1 ♍	JAN	1 ♍	JAN	1 ♍	JAN	1 ♍	JAN	1 ♍	JAN	1 ♍	JAN	1 ♍	JAN	1 ♍	JAN	1 ♍
NOV	20 ♍	JAN	4 ♍	APR	8 ♍							NOV	4 ♍	FEB	13 ♍				
		SEP	7 ♍	JUL	4 ♍									SEP	2 ♍				

1981		1982		1983		1984		1985		1986		1987		1988		1989		1990	
JAN	1 ♎	JAN	1 ♎	JAN	1 ♎	JAN	1 ♏	JAN	1 ♏	JAN	1 ♏	JAN	1 ♏	JAN	1 ♏	JAN	1 ♏	JAN	1 ♏
				NOV	6 ♏	MAY	19 ♎					NOV	5 ♏	JUN	20 ♏				
						AUG	28 ♏							AUG	18 ♏				

2001		2002		2003		2004		2005		2006		2007		2008		2009		2010	
JAN	1 ♐	JAN	1 ♐	JAN	1 ♐	JAN	1 ♐	JAN	1 ♐	JAN	1 ♐	JAN	1 ♐	JAN	1 ♐	JAN	1 ♑	JAN	1 ♑
				DEC	19 ♐	JUL	19 ♐							JAN	26 ♑				
				OCT	11 ♐									JUN	14 ♐				
														NOV	27 ♑				

CHIRON 1931–2010

1931	1932	1933	1934	1935	1936	1937	1938	1939	1940
JAN 1 ♉	JAN 1 ♉	JAN 1 ♉	JAN 1 ♉	JAN 1 ♊	JAN 1 ♊	JAN 1 ♊	JAN 1 ♊	JAN 1 ♋	JAN 1 ♋
MAY 30 ♉	MAR 20 ♉	JUN 7 ♊	MAR 24 ♊	MAY 29 ♊	JUL 15 ♊	APR 25 ♊	MA 29 ♋	JUN 16 ♋	JUN 22 ♋
DEC 7 ♉		DEC 22 ♉			DEC 22 ♊	AUG 28 ♋	OCT 12 ♋	OCT 23 ♋	SEP 30 ♌
						NOV 23 ♊	OCT 29 ♋	NOV 10 ♋	DEC 27 ♋

1951	1952	1953	1954	1955	1956	1957	1958	1959	1960
JAN 1 ♐	JAN 1 ♑	JAN 1 ♑	JAN 1 ♑	JAN 1 ♑	JAN 1 ♒	JAN 1 ♒	JAN 1 ♒	JAN 1 ♒	JAN 1 ♒
FEB 9 ♑	FEB 20 ♑	MAR 20 ♑		JAN 28 ♒	MAR 22 ♒	JAN 7 ♒	MAR 14 ♒	JAN 5 ♒	MAR 27 ♓
JUN 19 ♐	JUN 24 ♑	JUN 8 ♑			JUL 15 ♒		AUG 16 ♒		AUG 19 ♒
NOV 9 ♑	NOV 23 ♑	DEC 21 ♑							

1971	1972	1973	1974	1975	1976	1977	1978	1979	1980
JAN 1 ♈	JAN 1 ♈	JAN 1 ♈	JAN 1 ♈	JAN 1 ♈	JAN 1 ♈	JAN 1 ♈	JAN 1 ♉	JAN 1 ♉	JAN 1 ♉
APR 4 ♈	JAN 28 ♈	JUN 8 ♈	APR 5 ♈	JAN 11 ♈	MA 28 ♉	MAR 29 ♉		MA 10 ♉	MAR 1 ♉
NOV 13 ♈		SEP 9 ♈	DEC 22 ♈		OCT 14 ♈			DEC 8 ♉	

1991	1992	1993	1994	1995	1996	1997	1998	1999	2000
JAN 1 ♋	JAN 1 ♌	JAN 1 ♌	JAN 1 ♍	JAN 1 ♍	JAN 1 ♎	JAN 1 ♏	JAN 1 ♏	JAN 1 ♏	JAN 1 ♐
JUL 22 ♌	JUL 9 ♌	FEB 15 ♌	AUG 4 ♍	MA 15 ♍	APR 16 ♎	APR 5 ♎	OCT 21 ♏	JAN 7 ♐	DEC 10 ♐
	OCT 2 ♌	JUN 14 ♌	OCT 16 ♍	MA 22 ♍	JUL 23 ♎	SEP 3 ♏		JUN 1 ♏	
		SEP 4 ♍		SEP 10 ♎	OCT 11 ♎	NOV 17 ♏		SEP 22 ♐	
				NOV 21 ♎	DEC 29 ♏			DEC 19 ♐	

1941		1942		1943		1944		1945		1946		1947		1948		1949		1950	
JAN 1	♋	JAN 1	♌	JAN 1	♌	JAN 1	♏	JAN 1	♎	JAN 1	♎	JAN 1	♏	JAN 1	♏	JAN 1	♐	JAN 1	♐
JUN 17	♌	FEB 21	♌	JUL 27	♍	APR 11	♍	MAR 24	♏	MAR 15	♎	OCT 10	♏	JUN 4	♏	NOV 14	♐	FEB 14	♐
SEP 12	♌	MA 25	♌	OCT 10	♍	JUN 3	♍	JUL 23	♎	AUG 30	♎	DEC 24	♏	AUG 31	♏			MA 21	♐
		AUG 22	♌					SEP 4	♍	OCT 7	♎	NOV 10	♏			NOV 29	♐			NOV 6	♐
								NOV 18	♎	DEC 30	♎								

1961		1962		1963		1964		1965		1966		1967		1968		1969		1970	
JAN 1	♒	JAN 1	♓	JAN 1	♓	JAN 1	♓	JAN 1	♓	JAN 1	♓	JAN 1	♓	JAN 1	♓	JAN 1	♓	JAN 1	♈
JAN 21	♓	MA 1	♓	FEB 22	♓			APR 6	♓	FEB 6	♓			APR 1	♈	JAN 30	♈	JUN 14	♈
		JUL 29	♓					SEP 18	♓					OCT 19	♓			AUG 12	♈

1981		1982		1983		1984		1985		1986		1987		1988		1989		1990	
JAN 1	♉	JAN 1	♉	JAN 1	♉	JAN 1	♉	JAN 1	♊	JAN 1	♊	JAN 1	♊	JAN 1	♊	JAN 1	♋	JAN 1	♋
JUN 8	♉	APR 3	♉	JUN 22	♊	APR 11	♊	JUN 14	♊	JAN 11	♊	MA 19	♊	JUN 21	♋	JUL 13	♋	JUL 23	♋
NOV 20	♉			NOV 30	♉					MAR 23	♊								
										AUG 11	♊								
										NOV 17	♊								

2001		2002		2003		2004		2005		2006		2007		2008		2009		2010	
JAN 1	♐	JAN 1	♑	JAN 1	♑	JAN 1	♑	JAN 1	♑	JAN 1	♒	JAN 1	♒	JAN 1	♒	JAN 1	♒	JAN 1	♒
DEC 12	♑	DEC 25	♑			JAN 17	♑	FEB 22	♒			JAN 29	♒	APR 9	♒	JAN 25	♒	APR 20	♓
								AUG 1	♑					JUL 13	♒			JUL 20	♒
								DEC 6	♒										

ASCENDANT TABLES

To discover your Ascendant you have to first
find out the latitude of your place of birth.
Look at the tables below and refer to the one
closest to the location of your birth. Find your
date and time of birth in the appropriate
columns. Draw a line between these two points.
The glyph to the right on this diagonal line
reveals your Ascendant. Take particular notice
whether it crosses near the top (the beginning
of the sign), the middle area, or towards the
bottom of the line (the end of the sign).

**The ancient Greek astronomer
Hipparchus** observes the
night sky through an early
scientific instrument.

KEY TO GLYPHS FOR THE PLANETS

☉	Sun	♃	Jupiter
☽	Moon	♄	Saturn
☿	Mercury	♅	Uranus
♀	Venus	♆	Neptune
♂	Mars	♇	Pluto

KEY TO GLYPHS FOR THE SIGNS OF THE ZODIAC

♈	Aries	♎	Libra
♉	Taurus	♏	Scorpio
♊	Gemini	♐	Sagittarius
♋	Cancer	♑	Capricorn
♌	Leo	♒	Aquarius
♍	Virgo	♓	Pisces

LONDON 51° 32'N

DATE   ASCENDANT   TIME

Cities listed:
- CALGARY (CANADA) 51° 2'N
- ANTWERP (BELGIUM) 51° 13'N
- LEIPZIG (GERMANY) 51° 20'N
- CARDIFF (WALES) 51° 28'N
- WARSAW (POLAND) 52° 13'N
- AMSTERDAM (NETHERLANDS) 52° 23'N
- BIRMINGHAM (ENGLAND) 52° 30'N
- BERLIN (GERMANY) 52° 32'N

PARIS 48° 50'N

DATE   ASCENDANT   TIME

Cities listed:
- BUDAPEST (HUNGARY) 47° 29'N
- SEATTLE (U.S.A.) 47° 45'N
- MUNICH (GERMANY) 48° 8'N
- VIENNA (AUSTRIA) 48° 12'N
- STUTTGART (GERMANY) 48° 46'N
- VANCOUVER (CANADA) 49° 14'N
- WINNIPEG (CANADA) 49° 55'N
- KIEV (UKRAINE) 50° 24'N

TORONTO 43° 40'N

DATE   ASCENDANT   TIME

Cities listed:
- MILWAUKEE (U.S.A.) 43° 9'N
- VLADIVOSTOK (RUSSIA) 43° 9'N
- BILBAO (SPAIN) 43° 16'N
- MARSEILLE (FRANCE) 43° 18'N
- TOULOUSE (FRANCE) 43° 37'N
- BUCHAREST (ROMANIA) 44° 27'N
- HALIFAX (CANADA) 44° 45'N
- BELGRADE (SERBIA) 44° 50'N

ROME 41° 54'N

DATE   ASCENDANT   TIME

Cities listed:
- TASHKENT (UZBEKISTAN) 41° 7'N
- PORTO (PORTUGAL) 41° 8'N
- BARCELONA (SPAIN) 41° 21'N
- ZARAGOZA (SPAIN) 41° 39'N
- CHICAGO (U.S.A.) 41° 50'N
- SHENYANG (CHINA) 41° 50'N
- BOSTON (U.S.A.) 42° 18'N
- DUBROVNIK (CROATIA) 42° 39'N

NEW YORK 40° 45'N

DATE   ASCENDANT   TIME

Cities listed:
- VALENCIA (SPAIN) 39° 27'N
- RENO (U.S.A.) 39° 32'N
- BEIJING (CHINA) 39° 49'N
- DENVER (U.S.A.) 39° 50'N
- ANKARA (TURKEY) 39° 58'N
- BAKU (AZERBAIJAN) 40° 27'N
- MADRID (SPAIN) 40° 27'N
- PITTSBURG (U.S.A.) 40° 30'N
- SALT LAKE CITY (U.S.A.) 40° 45'N

SAN FRANCISCO 37° 47'N

DATE	ASCENDANT	TIME

Norfolk (U.S.A.) 36° 52'N
Dodge City (U.S.A.) 37° 42'N
Athens (Greece) 37° 59'N
St. Louis (U.S.A.) 38° 04'N
Lisbon (Portugal) 38° 43'N
Washington, D.C. (U.S.A.) 38° 58'N

TOKYO 35° 41'N

DATE	ASCENDANT	TIME

Los Angeles (U.S.A.) 34° 0'N
Pasadena (U.S.A.) 34° 5'N
Kyoto (Japan) 35° 0'N
Chattanooga (U.S.A.) 35° 2'N
Albuquerque (U.S.A.) 35° 5'N
Memphis (U.S.A.) 35° 7'N
Oklahoma City (U.S.A.) 35° 25'N
Tangier (Morocco) 35° 50'N

NEW ORLEANS 29° 57'N

DATE	ASCENDANT	TIME

New Delhi (India) 28° 42'N
Houston (U.S.A.) 29° 45'N
New Orleans (U.S.A.) 29° 57'N
Cairo (Egypt) 30° 1'N
Jacksonville (U.S.A.) 30° 15'N
Shanghai (China) 31° 15'N
Marrakech (Morocco) 31° 40'N
Nanjing (China) 32° 3'N

MEXICO CITY 19° 26'N

DATE	ASCENDANT	TIME

Puebla (Mexico) 19° 0'N
Santiago de Cuba (Cuba) 20° 1'N
Guadalajara (Mexico) 20° 40'N
Haiphong (Vietnam) 20° 55'N
Honolulu (Hawaii) 21° 19'N
Mecca (Saudi Arabia) 21° 30'N
Macao (China) 22° 11'N
Hong Kong 22° 16'N

MUMBAI 18° 55'N

DATE	ASCENDANT	TIME

Chennai (India) 13° 8'N
Bangkok 13° 45'N
Dakar 14° 34'N
Guatemala City 14° 40'N
Asmara (Eritrea) 15° 19'N
Khartoum 15° 31'N
Kingston (Jamaica) 18° 0'N
San Juan (Puerto Rico) 18° 28'N
Port-au-Prince (Haiti) 18° 33'N

RIO DE JANEIRO 22° 54'S

DATE	ASCENDANT	TIME

Port Louis (Mauritius) 20° 09'S
Bulawayo (Zimbabwe) 20° 10'S
Concepcion (Paraguay) 20° 30'S
Rockhampton (Australia) 23° 32'S
Alice Springs (Australia) 23° 36'S
Sao Paulo (Brazil) 23° 40'S
Antofagasta (Chile) 23° 50'S
Santos (Brazil) 23° 56'S

JOHANNESBURG 26° 10'S

DATE	ASCENDANT	TIME

Asuncion (Paraguay) 25° 25'S
Pretoria (South Africa) 25° 44'S
Mafikeng (South Africa) 25° 50'S
Maputo (Mozambique) 25° 58'S
Bethanien (Namibia) 26° 29'S
Tucuman (Argentina) 26° 50'S
Brisbane (Australia) 27° 25'S
Corrientes (Argentina) 27° 28'S

SYDNEY 33° 52'S

DATE	ASCENDANT	TIME

Cordoba (Argentina) 31° 22'S
Perth (Australia) 31° 57'S
Fremantle (Australia) 32° 3'S
Valparaiso (Chile) 33° 5'S
Santiago (Chile) 33° 24'S
Cape Town (South Africa) 33° 59'S
Buenos Aries (Argentina) 34° 40'S
Adelaide (Australia) 34° 55'S

WELLINGTON, N.Z. 41° 18'S

DATE	ASCENDANT	TIME

Canberra (Australia) 35° 15'S
Auckland (New Zealand) 36° 52'S
Melbourne (Australia) 37° 40'S
Bahia Blanca (Argentina) 38° 35'S
Valdivia (Chile) 39° 50'S
Launceston (Tasmania) 41° 25'S
Christchurch (New Zealand) 43° 33'S
Dunedin (New Zealand) 45° 51'S

MIDHEAVEN TABLES

To discover your Midheaven sign you have to follow an almost identical process to that for discerning your Ascendant. However, instead of finding out the latitude of your place of birth, for the Midheaven you need to note the longitude. Then, from the tables below, select the one closest to your place of birth. Following the same procedure as for finding the Ascendant, locate your date and time of birth in the appropriate columns and draw a line between these two points. The glyph to the right on this diagonal line reveals your Midheaven. Again, take particular notice whether it crosses the top, middle, or towards the bottom of the line.

KEY TO GLYPHS FOR THE PLANETS

☉	Sun	♃	Jupiter
☽	Moon	♄	Saturn
☿	Mercury	♅	Uranus
♀	Venus	♆	Neptune
♂	Mars	♇	Pluto

KEY TO GLYPHS FOR THE SIGNS OF THE ZODIAC

♈	Aries	♎	Libra
♉	Taurus	♏	Scorpio
♊	Gemini	♐	Sagittarius
♋	Cancer	♑	Capricorn
♌	Leo	♒	Aquarius
♍	Virgo	♓	Pisces

LONDON 0° 0'E

Places listed:
- Le Havre (France) 0° 7'E
- Accra (Ghana) 0° 14'W
- Valencia (Spain) 0° 22'W
- Alicante (Spain) 0° 30'W
- Bordeaux (France) 0° 35'W
- Lome (Togo) 1° 14'W
- Nantes (France) 1° 33'W
- Cherbourg (France) 1° 37'W

PARIS 2° 20'E

Places listed:
- Boulogne (France) 1° 37'E
- Orleans (France) 1° 55'E
- Barcelona (Spain) 2° 9'E
- Amiens (France) 2° 20'E
- Arras (France) 2° 47'E
- Ostend (Belgium) 2° 55'E
- Bruges (Belgium) 3° 13'E
- Lagos (Nigeria) 3° 30'E

FRANKFURT 8° 41'E

Places listed:
- Koln (Germany) 6° 58'E
- Bonn (Germany) 7° 5'E
- Basel (Switzerland) 7° 5'E
- Kano (Nigeria) 8° 31'E
- Zurich (Switzerland) 8° 43'E
- Ajaccio (France) 8° 43'E
- Stuttgart (Germany) 9° 11'E
- Milan (Italy) 9° 12'E

CAPE TOWN 18° 25'E

Places listed:
- Vienna (Austria) 16° 23'E
- Bari (Italy) 16° 53'E
- Poznan (Poland) 16° 55'E
- Brindisi (Italy) 17° 56'E
- Stockholm (Sweden) 18° 3'E
- Simon's Town (South Africa) 18° 26'E
- Sarajevo (Bosnia and Herzegovina) 18° 30'E
- Tromso (Norway) 19° 0'E

HONG KONG 114° 10'E

Places listed:
- Sarawak (Malaysia) 113° 15'E
- Macau (China) 113° 30'E
- Hankou (China) 114° 17'E
- Brunei (Borneo) 115° 0'E
- Bali (Indonesia) 115° 19'E
- Fremantle (Australia) 115° 45'E
- Perth (Australia) 115° 50'E
- Tianjin (China) 117° 12'E

TOKYO 139° 45'E

DATE	ASCENDANT	TIME

			KYOTO (JAPAN) 135° 45'E
			ADELAIDE (AUSTRALIA) 138° 35'E
			YOKOHAMA (JAPAN) 139° 38'E
			AKITA (JAPAN) 140° 7'E
			GEELONG (AUSTRALIA) 144° 21'E
			MELBOURNE (AUSTRALIA) 145° 0'E
			LAUNCESTON (TASMANIA) 147° 9'E

am / pm

SYDNEY 151° 10'E

DATE	ASCENDANT	TIME

			CANBERRA (AUSTRALIA) 149° 10'E
			WOLLONGONG (AUSTRALIA) 150° 53'E
			NEWCASTLE (AUSTRALIA) 151° 45'E
			RABAUL (BRITISH NEW GUINEA) 152° 12'E
			MARYBOROUGH (AUSTRALIA) 152° 42'E
			BRISBANE (AUSTRALIA) 153° 2'E
			LISMORE (AUSTRALIA) 153° 16'E

am / pm

WELLINGTON, N.E. 174° 47'E

DATE	ASCENDANT	TIME

			NOUMEA (NEW CALEDONIA) 166° 28'E
			NORFOLK ISLAND (SOUTH PACIFIC) 167° 56'E
			VANUATU (PACIFIC ISLANDS) 168° 0'E
			MARSHALL ISLANDS (PACIFIC ISLANDS) 170° 0'E
			DUNEDIN (NEW ZEALAND) 170° 32'E
			CHRISTCHURCH (NEW ZEALAND) 172° 59'E
			BLENHEIM (NEW ZEALAND) 173M:59'E
			AUCKLAND 174° 45'E

am / pm

RIO DE JANEIRO 43° 09'W

DATE	ASCENDANT	TIME

			RECIFE (BRAZIL) 34° 53'W
			SALVADOR (BRAZIL) 38° 31'W
			FORTALEZA (BRAZIL) 38° 31'W
			VITORIA (BRAZIL) 40° 20'W
			BELO HORIZONTE (BRAZIL) 43° 54'W
			SANTOS (BRAZIL) 46° 18'W
			SAO PAULO (BRAZIL) 46° 40'W
			BELEM (BRAZIL) 48° 29'W

am / pm

NEW YORK 73° 57'E

DATE	ASCENDANT	TIME

			LA PAZ (BOLIVIA) 68° 0'W
			VALPARAISO (CHILE) 71° 38'W
			CUZCO (PERU) 71° 57'W
			STATE OF CONNECTICUT (U.S.A.) 73° 0'W
			CONCEPCION (CHILE) 73° 5'W
			JERSEY CITY (U.S.A.) 74° 2'W
			PHILADELPHIA (U.S.A.) 75° 11'W
			BALTIMORE (U.S.A.) 76° 37'W

am / pm

OTTAWA 75° 42'W

DATE	ASCENDANT	TIME

			MONTREAL (CANADA) 73° 34'W
			BOGOTA (COLOMBIA) 74° 5'W
			KINGSTON (JAMAICA) 76° 48'W
			WASHINGTON, D.C. (U.S.A.) 77° 0'W
			LIMA (PERU) 77° 3'W
			NASSAU (BAHAMAS) 77° 20'W
			RICHMOND (U.S.A.) 77° 26'W

am / pm

MEXICO CITY 99° 09'W

DATE	ASCENDANT	TIME

			KANSAS CITY (U.S.A.) 94° 38'W
			HOUSTON (U.S.A.) 95° 23'W
			DALLAS (U.S.A.) 96° 48'W
			OKLAHOMA CITY (U.S.A.) 97° 31'W
			TAMPICO (MEXICO) 97° 51'W
			SAN ANTONIO (U.S.A.) 98° 29'W
			MONTERREY (MEXICO) 100° 18'W
			DENVER (U.S.A.) 104° 59'W

am / pm

SAN FRANCISCO 122°26'W

DATE	ASCENDANT	TIME

			CALGARY (CANADA) 144° 4'W
			SAN DIEGO (U.S.A.) 117° 10'W
			LONG BEACH (U.S.A.) 118° 11'W
			LOS ANGELES (U.S.A.) 118° 15'W
			RENO (U.S.A.) 119° 48'W
			SEATTLE (U.S.A.) 122° 20'W
			PORTLAND (U.S.A.) 122° 41'W
			VANCOUVER (CANADA) 123° 7'W

am / pm

HONOLULU 157° 52'W

DATE	ASCENDANT	TIME

			TAHITI 149° 30'W
			ANCHORAGE (ALASKA) 150° 0'W
			BARROW (ALASKA) 156° 24'W
			CHRISTMAS ISLANDS 157° 20'W
			COOK ISLANDS 158° 8'W
			FANNING ISLAND (PACIFIC ISLANDS) 159° 40'W
			JARVIS ISLAND (PACIFIC ISLANDS) 160° 2'W
			PALMYRA ISLAND (HAWAII) 162° 6'W

am / pm

Date labels (all panels): DEC, JAN, FEB, MAR, APR, MAY, JUN, JUL, AUG, SEP, OCT, NOV, DEC

GLOSSARY

air signs *see* triplicities

Ascendant (or Rising sign) The degree of the zodiac rising over the eastern horizon at any given moment. Each degree takes about four minutes to rise.

aspects One planet is in aspect to another when there is a specific number of degrees between them, counted around the circle of the zodiac. The major aspects used by astrologers are the *conjunction* (0°), the *sextile* (when two planets are 60° apart), *square* (90°); the *trine* (120°); the *opposition* (180°); the minor aspects are the *semi-sextile* (30°), the *semi-square* (45°), the *quincunx* (150°) and the *sesquiquadrate* or *sesquare* (135°).

astrological age *see* Great Year

birth chart A map of the sky showing the planets in the precise position they occupied at the moment of birth. The traditional word for the birth chart is horoscope. A horoscope can be drawn for any location and moment in time – in horary astrology, for example, it is drawn for the moment a particular question is asked.

birth time The precise time of birth. The time of the first cry or the moment of cutting the umbilical cord have traditionally been used.

cardinal signs *see* quadruplicities

celestial sphere An imaginary sphere around the Earth onto which are positioned all the visible planets and stars of the heavens. Though essentially imaginary, it is a useful device for visualizing the stars and planets vis-à-vis each other and in relation to locations on Earth.

conjunction A conjunction takes place between two planets when they occupy the same degree of the zodiac. *See also* orb.

cusp The line that divides one astrological sign or house from its neighbour. It is extremely rare to be born "on the cusp"; almost everyone is born with the Sun in one sign or another, if only by a single degree. If one is born with the Sun 1° in Aries, there will not be any effect from Pisces simply because the Sun has just left that sign. More nonsense is talked about being "born on the cusp" than any other area of astrology.

decans Each sign occupies a 30° slice of the zodiac and is itself divided into three sections, called decans, of 10° each.

ecliptic The imaginary path of the Sun around the Earth.

element *see* triplicities

ephemeris Annual ephemerides are published to show the movements of the planets with astronomical accuracy; these are now available on the Internet.

feminine signs Taurus, Cancer, Virgo, Scorpio, Capricorn and Pisces are traditionally known as feminine signs, the others being masculine. Feminine signs are regarded as negative, masculine as positive.

fixed signs *see* quadruplicities

generation influence Those planets which spend many years in the same sign influence whole generations of people.

Great Year The Earth, while revolving, wobbles rather like a top running down, and the pole moves backwards through the zodiac, passing through a sign in about 2,500 years – this is known as an astrological age. The period during which the pole completes a full circle is known as the Great Year and lasts for about 25,868 years.

horary astrology When a particular question is asked, an astrologer suggests an answer based on the horoscope for the moment at which the question was posed.

horoscope *see* birth chart

houses The birth chart or horoscope is divided into 12 sections, distinct from the sections of the zodiac signs, each of which represents different aspects of human life.

Immum Cœli (I.C.) The meridian point, opposite the M.C.

inferior planets Mercury and Venus, placed between the Earth and Sun, are known as inferior, or inner, planets; those further from the Sun are called superior, or outer, planets. The terms relate only to position, and not to the astrological nature of the planets concerned.

inner planets *see* inferior planets

Medium Cœli (M.C.) – the meridian of an astrological chart.

meridien An imaginary line in the sky arcing north to south and passing through the zenith, or point in the sky directly above an observer.

Midheaven Another name for the M.C.

mutable signs *see* quadruplicities

negative signs *see* feminine signs

opposition *see* aspects

orb Astrologers allow an orb – a specific number of degrees – within which an aspect between two planets will operate, if it is not exact. The degree allowed depends on the strength of the aspect.

outer planets *see* inferior planets

planets For convenience, astrologers refer to the Sun and Moon as planets (knowing perfectly well that the Sun is a star, and the Moon merely Earth's satellite). These – along with Mercury, Venus, Mars, Jupiter, Saturn, Chiron, Uranus, Neptune, and Pluto – are used by astrologers, who estimate the effect they have on affairs on Earth, and the human race in particular.

polar sign The polar sign is the one positioned on the directly opposite side of the zodiac to the sign under discussion. For example, Libra is the polar sign of Aries, and vice versa. There is a special relationship between such signs.

positive signs *see* feminine signs

prediction Many, perhaps most, astrologers avoid the word prediction, preferring forecast or progression – events are not predicted with complete accuracy, but suggested, much in the manner of a weather forecast.

quadruplicities The zodiac signs have traditionally been divided into three groups (cardinal, fixed and mutable) of four signs, known as the quadruplicities. The cardinal signs are Aries, Cancer, Libra, and Capricorn; the fixed signs are Taurus, Leo, Scorpio, and Aquarius; and the mutable signs Gemini, Virgo, Sagittarius, and Pisces. The signs of a particular group are said to share certain quadruplicities, or qualities.

qualities *see* quadruplicities

quincunx *see* aspects

retrograde motion As seen from Earth, a planet sometimes looks as though it is moving backwards in its course (due to their relative orbits); the planet is then said to be retrograde.

returns When a planet returns to the precise position in the sky in which it stood at the time of a birth, the individual is said to be celebrating its return. Astrologers also take into consideration

timescales known as half-returns. These periods – at which times of change tend to occur – are: the Jupiter return, every 12 years; the Saturn return, at 29+ years; the Uranus half-return, at 40+; the Chiron return, at 50+; the second Saturn return, at 60; the full Uranus return, at 84; and the third Saturn return at 90.

Rising sign *see* Ascendant

rulership, or **ruling planets** Each sign is traditionally said to be ruled by a particular planet, and a sign's influence can be affected by this. There has been much discussion about the theory of rulerships, and in particular how the modern planets have been assigned. It is perhaps not such a particularly important feature of astrological theory, however.

semi-square *see* aspects

sesquiquadrate *see* aspects

semi-sextile *see* aspects

sextile *see* aspects

solar chart A chart drawn up with the Sun on the cusp of the first house – i.e. at sunrise; this is done when a birth time is unknown. It is also used by Sun-sign astrologers.

stars Some modern astrologers are increasingly studying the effect fixed stars may have when they fall within the zodiac. In general, though, the stars have no importance in popular astrology, and their effect remains questionable.

stellium A group of planets gathered in the same area of the sky; a multiple conjunction.

square *see* aspects

Sun sign astrology Popular newspaper and magazine astrologers make predictions for the day, month, or year ahead on the basis of solar charts set up for specific Sun signs. The result is good fun, but it would be a mistake to make any decision based upon it.

superior planets *see* inferior planets

triplicity Signs are traditionally assigned to the four elements – fire, earth, air, and water – and are thus placed in four groups of three. The fire signs are Aries, Leo, Sagittarius; earth signs are Taurus, Virgo, Capricorn; air signs are Gemini, Libra, Aquarius; and water signs Cancer, Scorpio, Pisces.

INDEX

ACKNOWLEDGEMENTS

Picture credits

Dorling Kindersley would like to thank the following for their kind permission to reproduce their photographs:

Picture Key: a-above; b-below/bottom; c-centre; l-left; r-right; t-top

Chapter Top Bar Images:
Introduction – **Alamy**, *History* – **Corbis**: Stapleton collection, *The Twelve Signs of the Zodiac* – **Alamy**: Martin Vickery, **Alamy**: Mary Evans Picture Library, *The Planets* – **NASA**: Courtesy JPL/ Voyager 1, *Other Areas of Astrology, How to Draw Your Chart* – **Mary Evans Picture Library.**

1. Alamy: INSADCO Photography, **2–3. Alamy:** Image State, **4. AKG Images, 5. DK Images:** Judith Miller / Sloan's, **6–7. Alamy:** Visual Arts Library (London), **8–9. AKG Images:** (t), (b), **10. DK Images:** Courtesy of The National Maritime Museum, London, **11. AKG Images:** Eric Lessing, **12. Alamy:** V&A Images, **12. AKG Images:** Eric Lessing, **14–15. Corbis:** Enzo & Paolo Ragazzini, **15. Corbis:** Dave G. Houser, (t), **16. Alamy:** Visual Arts Library (London) (c), **16. Corbis:** Gianni Dagli Orti (b) **18. Corbis:** Bettmann (c) **19. Getty:** Time Life Pictures (c) **20. Corbis:** Avaldo de Lucas (b) **21. Corbis:** Enzo & Paolo Ragazzini (c), **Getty Images** (b), **22. Alamy:** Mary Evans Picture Library (b), **24. Alamy:** Mary Evans Picture Library (b) **26. Alamy:** Adam Eastland (b), **Alamy:** (c) **27. Alamy:** Visual Arts Library (London) (c) **28. Alamy:** Visual Arts Library (London) (c) **29. AKG Images:** (t), **Alamy:** The Print Collector (b), **30. Alamy:** The Print Collector (c), **Getty:** Time Life Pictures (c), **31. DK Images:** Agostini Editore Picture Library (b), **32. Alamy:** Visual Arts Library (London) (b), **Science Photo Library:** Jean-Loup Charmet (c), **34-35. Getty:** The Map House of London, **36. Science Photo Library:** Crawford Library/ Royal Observatory, Edinburgh (c), **36–37. DK Images:** Agostini Editore Picture Library (c), **37. Getty Images** (c), **38. Getty Images** (c), **39. Getty Images** (t) **40. AKG Images:** British Library (c), **40. Alamy:** Justin Kasel (b), **41. AKG Images:** Electra (b), **42. AKG Images:** Laurent Lecat (c), **43. NASA:** Courtesy JPL/ Voyager 2 (t), **44. Corbis:** Hulton-Deutsch Collection (b), (t), **Corbis:** Bettmann (c), (t), **45. AKG Images:** (c), (t), **46. Getty Images:** (b), **Corbis:** Swim Ink 2, LLC (c), **47. Corbis:** Bettmann (c), **Getty:** Time Life Pictures (b), **48–49. Alamy:** Visual Arts Library (London) **49. Alamy:** Martyn Vickery (t), **50. Corbis:** Bettmann, **51. Alamy:** Martyn Vickery, **52. Corbis:** Christie's Images (c), **Alamy:** The Print Collector (b), **53. Science Photo Library:** Dr. Jeremy Burgess (c), **54. AKG Images:** British Library (b), **55. AKG Images:** Eric Lessing, **56. AKG Images:** (c), **57. Corbis:** Bettmann (b), **58. Corbis:** Christoph Wilhelm/ Veer (c), **AKG Images:** (b), **59. AKG Images:** (b), **61. Corbis:** Mike Watson Images (c), **AKG Images:** British Library (b), **62. Corbis:** Lake County Museum (c), **63. Alamy:** Image State (b), **64. Alamy:** Stock Image (b), **66. AKG Images:** British Library (b), **67. AKG:** Eric Lessing (c), **68. Alamy:** Brand X Pictures (b), **69. AKG Images:** (c), **70. AKG Images:** (b), **71. Corbis:** Brooklyn Productions (b), **72. AKG Images:** (b), **73. DK Images:** Rough Guides/Alex Robinson (c), **AKG Images:** (b), **75. Corbis:** Image Source (b), **76. Alamy:** Comstock Images (b), **Corbis:** Hurewitz Creative (c), **78. AKG Images:** British Library (b), **79. AKG Images:** Eric Lesing (c), **80. Alamy:** Images 100 (b), **82. DK Images:** Rough Guides (c), **84. Alamy:** Chad Ehlers (b), **88. Alamy:** Plain Picture GmbH & Co. KG (b), **90. AKG Images:** British Library (b), **91. AKG Images:** Eric Lessing (c), **92. Corbis:** Bettman (b), **93. DK Images:** Angus Beare (c),

94. Corbis: Barry Lewis (c), **100. Corbis:** Stockbyte (c), **Corbis:** Sean Justice (b), **102. AKG Images:** British Library (b), **103. AKG Images:** Eric Lessing (c), **105. DK Images:** Agostini Editore Picture Library (b), **106. Corbis:** Gideon Mendel (c), **110. DK Images:** Agostini Editore Picture Library (b) **111. Alamy:** Dynamic Graphics Group/IT Stock Free (c), **112. DK Images:** Agostini Editore Picture Library (b), **114. AKG Images:** British Library (b), **115. AKG Images:** Eric Lessing (c), **119. Corbis:** Brooke Fasani (b), **121. Corbis:** Senthil Kumar (b), **123. Corbis:** John Henley (b), **126. AKG Images:** British Library (b), **127. AKG Images:** Eric Lessing (c), **129. Corbis:** Lake County Museum (b), **136. Corbis:** Flint (b), **138. AKG Images:** British Library (b), **139. AKG Images:** Eric Lessing (c), **140. Corbis:** Sunset Boulevard (b), **147. Corbis:** Kevin Dodge (c) **150. AKG Images:** British Library (b), **151. AKG Images:** Eric Lessing (c), **154. Corbis:** Michael S Yamashita (b), **158. Corbis:** Stapleton Collection (c), **162. AKG Images:** British Library (b), **163. AKG Images:** Eric Lessing (c), **164. AKG Images:** Polygram/Album (b), **166. Alamy:** Transtock.Inc (c), **166. Corbis:** Tom & Dee Ann McCarthy (b), **167. Alamy:** Photos 12 (c), **168. Alamy:** Pictorial Press Ltd (b), **174. AKG Images:** British Library (b), **175. AKG Images:** Eric Lessing (c), **178. Corbis:** Historical Picture Archive (c), **180. Corbis:** Bettmann (b), **182. Corbis:** William Taufic (c), **184. Corbis:** Jim Reed (b), **186. AKG Images:** British Library (b), **187. AKG Images:** Eric Lessing (c), **192. Corbis:** Chad Ehlers (b), **194. Alamy:** INTERFOTO Pressebildagentur (c), **196. Corbis:** Simon Marcus (b), **Alamy:** Pictorial Press (c), **198–199. Science Photo Library:** Detlev Van Ravensswaay, **199. Corbis:** Stockbyte (t), **200. Corbis:** Denis Scott, **202. Corbis:** Stapleton Collection (b), **203. Alamy:** Photo Bliss (c), **208. AKG:** British Library (b), **215. Corbis:** Roy Morsch (c), **217. Corbis:** Sonja Pacho/ zefa (b), **219. Corbis:** Dylan Ellis (b), **220. NASA:** Courtesy JPL/ Voyager 1 (b), **223. DK Images:** Agostini Editore Picture Library (b), **228. Corbis:** Steve Prezant (b), **232. Corbis:** Andrew Holbrooke (b), **234. NASA:** Courtesy JPL/ Voyager 1 (t), (b), **235. Corbis:** (c), **237. Corbis:** Andrew Brooke, **238. Corbis:** Bettmann (b), **240. DK Images:** Agostini Editore Picture Library (b), **241. Alamy:** Paul Debios, **242. Corbis:** Peter Finger (b), **245. AKG Images:** (b), **249. Alamy:** Visual Arts Library (London) (c), **252. Science Photo Library:** Detlev Van Ravensswaay (b), **264. Corbis:** Stapleton Collection (b), **265. Science Photo Library:** Jean-Loup Charmet (c), **266. Science Photo Library:** Jerry Lodriguss (b), **269. Corbis:** Hulton Deutsch Collection (b), **270. AKG:** Cameraphoto (b), **272. Mary Evans Picture Library:** (b), **274. AKG Images:** Eric Lessing (b), **278. Corbis:** Simon Marus (b), **Corbis:** Bettmann (b), **279. Alamy:** Roger Tamblyn (c), **280. Corbis:** DLILLC (b), **281. Corbis:** Hulton Deutsch Collection (b), **284. Getty Images:** Richard Utinich (b), **285. Alamy:** Directphoto.org (c), **287. Corbis:** Stapleton Collection (b), **289. Corbis:** Chuck Bryan/epa (t), Stefano Bianchetti (b), **290–91. Corbis:** Gianni Dagli Orti, **291. Mary Evans Picture Library:** (t), **294. Alamy:** Chris Luneski (b), **Mary Evans Picture Library:** (c), **295. Science Photo Library** Jean-Loup Charmet, **296. Corbis:** Mike Watson Images (b), **298. Corbis:** Stapleton Collection (b), **DK Images:** Courtesy of the National Maritime Museum, London **299. Corbis:** Roger Ressmeyer, **300. Alamy:** Aliki Sapountzi/ aliki image library (c), North Wind Picture Archives (c), **302–03. Corbis:** Fine Art Photographic Library, **303. Mary Evans Picture Library:** (t)

All other images © Dorling Kindersley
For further information see: www.dkimages.com